Society

LIVING WITH CHANGE

Society

LIVING WITH CHANGE

Geoff Irvine
Sir Wilfrid Laurier High School
Carleton Board of Education

Richard Deering
Cairine Wilson High School
Carleton Board of Education

Dennis Gerrard
Dr. Norman Bethune Collegiate
Scarborough Board of Education

Paul Sheahan
Brother André Catholic High School
York Region Roman Catholic
Separate School Board

Addison-Wesley Publishers Limited
Don Mills, Ontario • Reading, Massachusetts
Menlo Park, California • Wokingham, England • Amsterdam
Sydney • Singapore • Tokyo • Madrid • Bogotá
Santiago • San Juan

Acknowledgements

The authors wish to acknowledge the contributions and support of the following individuals, without whom this book could not have been written: their wives, **Anne**, **Penelope**, and **Hilary**; their children, **Jenessa**, **Jonathan**, **Kate**, **Michael**, and **Karen**; their editor at **Addison-Wesley**, **Jennifer Mix**; and the *Society: Challenge and Change* students of **Sir Wilfrid Laurier High School**, **Carleton Board of Education**, whose comments and suggestions truly helped bring a student-centred textbook to life.

Photography credits are on page 394.

Care has been taken to determine and locate ownership of copyright material used in this text. In the case of any errors or omissions, the publisher will be pleased to make suitable acknowledgements in future editions.

Sponsoring Editor: Jennifer Mix
Editorial: Sarah Swartz and Jane McNulty,
     The Editorial Centre
     Craig Doyle, Lisa Guthro
Design: Peter Maher
Photo Research: Sandra Lafortune
Illustrations: Graham Pilsworth
Technical Illustrations: Pronk and Associates
Typesetting: Golda D. Wiseman
Cover photograph: © Don Landwehrle/
     The Image Bank Canada

Canadian Cataloguing in Publication Data

Main entry under title:
Society: living with change
Includes index.
ISBN 0-201-11538-7
1. Sociology. 2. Anthropology. 3. Psychology.
I. Irvine, Geoff.
HM66.S63 1988   301   C88-093624-X

ISBN 0-201-11538-7

Printed and bound in Canada

B   C   D   E - BP - 92 91 90 89 88

Preface

Society: Living With Change will assist you in exploring the ways in which the social sciences can help explain the behaviour of individuals and groups... and some of the challenges you and your society must face in the wake of rapid technological and social change.

What do we mean by the term "social sciences"? These are the sciences which relate to *people*, their lives and natures: *sociology, anthropology, psychology, psychiatry, criminology*, and *penology*. As you investigate the role of the social sciences, you will examine how individuals see themselves and others, how people relate in social settings, and how they deal with social change. You will become a more aware, active participant in shaping your life and the society around you.

The word *active* appropriately sums up how *you* will be responding to the challenges in this book. You will be practising active thinking skills as you process and communicate information effectively, in a variety of ways. The learning experience of *Society: Living With Change* will actively involve you in acquiring knowledge, sharing it with others, and using it as the basis of creative problem-solving and decision-making now and in the future.

To successfully live with change, individuals and society as a whole must deal with controversial issues head-on — issues that may be troubling, even profoundly disturbing — issues which often present questions that are not easily answered. Ignoring such challenges does not make them go away. Thus you will be examining critically articles that present various points of view — views you may not agree with, ones the authors of this book may not necessarily embrace. It is not the intent of this book to support or defend any particular point of view, but rather to provide ample opportunities to assess various opinions so that you may draw your own conclusions and make your own value judgments.

Above all, this book is designed to *interact* with you, the student. It is not one of those texts which are merely handy sources of authoritative information, with a few questions added to help students review what they have read. While such an approach is important, it can leave you with the impression that the text alone is the final word on the subject — that it can answer all the questions. *Society: Living With Change*, on the other hand, provides you with much more: an exciting "workbench" on which to explore and master your own understanding of the forces that shape your life and your society. The following "Features of This Book" section briefly outlines the process by which you will investigate challenge and change in society.

Features of this book

Chapter Introductions

Each chapter is introduced through a variety of activities: experiments, self-tests, and puzzling situations which challenge students to become involved in the concepts to be explored.

From Ideas to Action

Each section within a chapter is followed by questions and individual and group activities that help students assess their mastery of new concepts by moving their learning beyond the textbook and into the real world.

Skills

Throughout the book, special "Skills" sections provide practical, relevant exercises (note taking, paragraph writing, essay writing, interpreting tables, and so on) that teach, illustrate, and provide practice in research, communication, and social-inquiry skills. Closely allied to the content of the text, these exercises move from simpler skills at the beginning of the book to more complex skills in later chapters.

Issues and Problems

These sections present current news articles and other sources that allow a more in-depth analysis of contemporary issues. Follow-up questions and activities encourage students to respond critically to these issues and problems.

FYI (For Your Interest)

Throughout the text, case histories, stories, facts, and human-interest items provide students with additional, thought-provoking information relating to chapter topics.

What Have You Learned?

This end-of-chapter review provides a brief, point-form summary of the main topics and skills covered.

To Help You Study

The main words, facts, and ideas of each chapter are reviewed in a self-directed chart to aid in student recall.

Projects, Activities and Explorations

Near the end of each chapter, students are challenged to generate collages, surveys, reports, field studies, poems, essays, debates, and presentations designed to deepen and personalize learning.

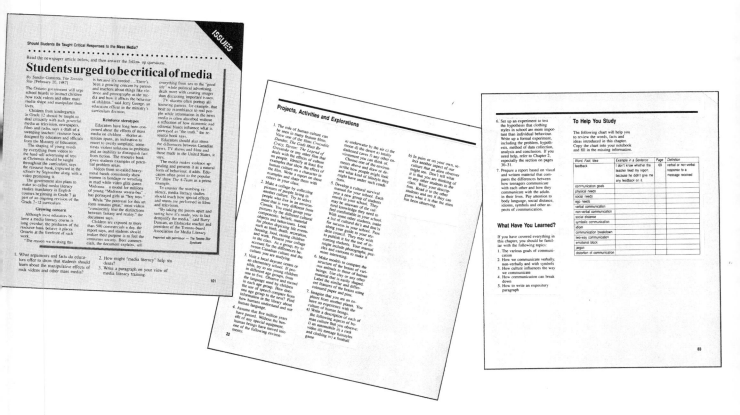

Contents

17 Social Change   338

18 The Future   362

Society

LIVING WITH CHANGE

The Uniqueness of Human Beings

1

2

3

4

Are You Unique?

Take a moment to look at the students in your classroom before you do the following activity.

1. Make a two-column chart in your notebook with the headings "Ways I am Different" and "Ways I am the Same."

2. List all the ways that you are different from the other students. Pay attention not only to how you look, but also to other things you know about yourself and the other students.

3. Now, list all the ways that you are similar to them.

As a class or in a group, compare your charts and discuss the following questions:

1. In what ways are people different from each other?

2. In what ways are people similar to each other?

3. Why do these similarities and differences exist?

4. Are people generally more similar to or more different from each other?

Are Humans Unique?

After you examine the pictures on these pages, try the following activities.

1. Draw three columns in your notebook. Write the following categories in your notebook as column heads: "Human Beings Only," "Human Beings and Other Animals," and "Other Animals Only."

2. Under each column head, list the number of each picture which fits into that category. You may want to shift the pictures from one category to another until you are satisfied with the results.

3. List the various ways that the pictures within one category are similar to each other. Be prepared to explain your categories and why they suit these pictures.

As a class or as a group, discuss the following questions.

1. Which pictures did you put in each category? Why?

2. Did other students or groups put the pictures in different categories? If so, why?

3. How is this exercise comparing human beings to other animals similar to the one in which you compared yourself to other students?

4. Are human beings animals, or are they something different? What examples or evidence would support your view?

5

6

7

8

3

The Question of Uniqueness

The activities on pages 2–3 were meant to make you think about your own uniqueness as a human being. **Unique** means "one of its kind" or "existing as the only one." You have probably discovered that even though you share many characteristics with other human beings, you are, nevertheless, different. While human beings are similar to many animals, they are unique in the animal kingdom.

A good example of your uniqueness as a human being is the fact that you are taking this course. No other animal would take a course designed to examine its own species. This makes you very different from the neighbourhood dog or a chimpanzee.

We are the most adaptable animal on earth. We can live in almost any environment. We have even found ways of taking our environment with us so that we can live in space and under water. Unlike any other creature, we can make the environment adapt to *us* by altering it. We can argue whether this ability is good or bad for us, but we cannot deny that it makes us unique.

This chapter will start you on a journey of self-discovery. It will challenge you to redefine what you call human. It may raise as many questions as it will answer. This book, your teacher and your experiences in this course will give you some important insights into what it means to be human.

Changing Views of Human Uniqueness

From ancient times until today, people have wondered about the uniqueness of human beings. It is a question that has been debated in classrooms, lecture halls, churches and laboratories — anywhere there is an inquiring mind. Over the centuries, our views have changed; in centuries to come there may be other changes as people debate human uniqueness.

The Traditional View

For many years, people of many religions have believed that human beings are unique because they have a soul and can distinguish between good and evil. The soul is believed to be distinct from the body and, unlike the body, cannot be observed or measured. (A long time ago, some people thought that the soul was hidden in the heart, while others thought it was located in the head.) Until the nineteenth century, most people believed our moral and spiritual characteristics made it impossible to compare us with other animals.

Man as an animal: A nineteenth century caricature of Charles Darwin

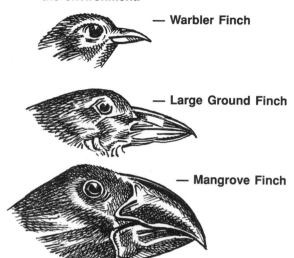

The beaks of these finches demonstrated to Darwin the principle of *adaptation* to the environment.

— Warbler Finch

— Large Ground Finch

— Mangrove Finch

Darwin's Theories

The first important challenge to the view that human beings were totally different and unrelated to other animals came from Charles Darwin. In his work *The Origin of Species,* published in 1859, he described the way in which he felt animal species had developed. He argued that an animal species did not simply appear in its present form at some point in history. His theory was that all species changed gradually, in order to accommodate themselves to the environments in which they lived. These changes occurred slowly but continuously from generation to generation, through a process called **evolution**.

According to Darwin, nature is a rough neighbourhood. Only animals born with special characteristics are likely to survive. These special characteristics are passed on from parents to offspring. Thus, successful changes, or **adaptations**, are constantly being added to the next generation of a species.

Animals that do not possess the characteristics to adapt do not survive long enough to reproduce and, in time, their kind die out. In other words, they are "selected out" by the forces of nature. Eventually, only the more successful species are left. In this way, species gradually change. In time a species might evolve into another form that looks quite unlike its ancestors and is better adapted to its environment. According to Darwin, all animals are part of this process of **natural selection**.

Early humans hunting

5

Darwin's theory of natural selection was accepted by the scientific community as being relevant to human beings, even though he carefully avoided any mention of human beings in his original book. He knew that many people would be disturbed by the idea that human beings might be descended from common ancestors that we share with apes. In fact, organized religions of that time fought very hard against Darwin's ideas. They worried that the Bible and its story of creation were threatened. Some religious groups argued that Darwin's theories threatened the belief in the existence of a divine being.

Today's Views

In Darwin's day, many people felt the need to choose between their religious faith and science. Today, many people have reconciled both views. For example, some religious authorities have suggested that people were created in the image of a divine being; that evolution was the chosen method of creating this form. Other religious groups maintain their belief that the story of creation in the Bible is true in every detail, and is not subject to interpretation or change.

The view that human beings gradually evolved from early apes is now widely accepted. Discoveries of bones from early human beings show that slow but definite changes actually did take place. Exactly how, when and why these changes occurred is still hotly debated. But most people agree that we are the most adaptable animal on earth.

Anthropologist Richard Leakey holding a skull he believes to be 2.5 million years old — the oldest complete skull of a creature of our own family Homo.

From Ideas to Action

1. Explain how each of the following examples illustrates the idea of natural selection.

   a) The Sherpas are a mountain tribe that live in the Himalayan Mountains, where the air is low in oxygen. Mountain climbers who have lived near sea level all their lives gasp for breath at high levels, whereas their Sherpa guides calmly hoist extremely heavy packs up steep trails. This is because, after centuries of living at such high altitudes, the respiratory and blood circulation systems of the Sherpas have adapted to provide their bodies with sufficient oxygen from the thin supply.

   b) People living close to the equator are affected by the sun's strong rays. Long periods of exposure can result in serious skin damage and some forms of skin cancer. People who have lived in these areas for a long time have developed a dark pigment. The sun's rays do not penetrate and damage their skin.

2. The idea that certain characteristics can be passed from one generation to another is fascinating. Do a study of your own family. Trace the following characteristics through your brothers and sisters, your parents and other family members, as far back as you can:

   a) hair colour b) eye colour c) body build (thin, average, athletic) d) adult height e) hair texture (straight, curly, wiry) f) other characteristics

3. a) Invite a guest scientist or a biology teacher to your class to discuss the subject of natural selection and genetics.

   b) Invite a religious leader to your class to talk about what makes humans unique.

4. Develop a "family tree" for human beings. Modern human beings have the following family ancestors:

   a) *Australopithecus africanus*
   b) *Homo habilis* c) *Homo erectus*
   d) *Homo sapiens*

   Research these early forms of human beings. Find out about when they came into being and/or disappeared, their physical features and statistics, and important differences from earlier forms.

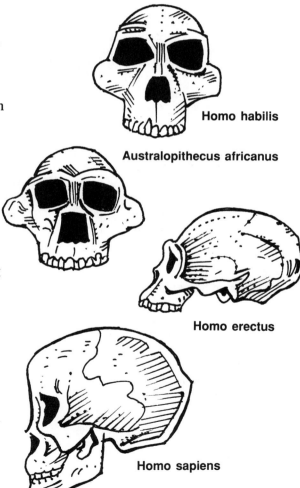

Homo habilis

Australopithecus africanus

Homo erectus

Homo sapiens

SKILLS

Effective Reading and Note-Taking — Level 1

This exercise will teach you to read carefully and then make notes to help you understand and remember more effectively.

The secret to effective note-taking is to identify the main, or most general, idea of an assigned reading and to recognize important supporting statements. **Supporting statements** are explanations, arguments, facts or examples that prove or reinforce the main idea.

Finding the Main Idea of an Assigned Reading

A quick reading of the headings, subheadings, and opening and closing paragraphs of the text should give you the main idea. Look at these items in the reading entitled "Changing Views of Human Uniqueness" on pages 4–6. Which of the statements below best describes the main idea of this reading? Which are the supporting statements?

a) Traditionally, human beings have been considered unique because they have a soul.

b) Darwin's theory suggested that human beings were nothing but successful monkeys and therefore not unique at all.

c) From ancient times until today, people have wondered about what has made human beings unique.

d) Today, the view that human beings evolved from early apes is widely accepted.

Finding the Main Idea in a Section of a Reading

A **section** is a part of a reading usually divided from other sections by a heading. Usually the heading, first sentences and last few sentences of a section in a text will tell you the main idea of the section. See how this works by reading "The Traditional View" on page 5. Indicate which of the following statements is the main idea of this section.

a) Some people believe that the human soul is distinct from the body.

b) Early views of our uniqueness focused on the idea that human beings, unlike animals, had a soul.

c) Unlike the body, the soul cannot be observed or measured.

d) The soul was thought to be hidden in the heart or the head.

Figure 1 at right demonstrates how the reading "Changing Views of Human Uniqueness" is constructed. This reading is made up of three sections: The Traditional View, Darwin's Theories and Today's View. Each section contains a main idea and a number of supporting statements that prove or reinforce the main idea, as the discussion moves from the general to the specific.

Making Notes From Your Reading

1. First, read the entire assigned reading, "Changing Views of Human Uniqueness," looking at headings, opening and closing paragraphs, etc. In your notebook, copy Chart 1 at right and finish filling in the supporting statements for the whole reading.

2. Now reread the first section, "The Traditional View." Chart 2 at right has been partially filled in for this section. Add to your chart any supporting statements that have not been included. This number may vary from section to section.

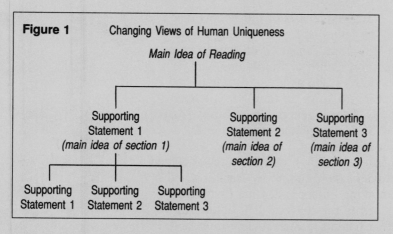

Figure 1   Changing Views of Human Uniqueness

Main Idea of Reading

Supporting Statement 1 *(main idea of section 1)*

Supporting Statement 2 *(main idea of section 2)*

Supporting Statement 3 *(main idea of section 3)*

Supporting Statement 1

Supporting Statement 2

Supporting Statement 3

Chart 1

Title of Reading: *Changing Views of Human Uniqueness*

Main Idea
From ancient times until to-day, people have wondered about what makes people unique.

Supporting Statements
a. Traditionally human be-ings have been considered unique because they have a soul.
b. Darwin's theory suggested that human beings were nothing but successful mon-keys and therefore not unique at all.
c. _____

Chart 2

Title of Section: *The Traditional View*

Main Idea
Early views of our unique-ness focussed on the idea that human beings, unlike animals, have a soul.

Supporting Statements
a. Some people believe that the human soul is distinct from the body.
b. Unlike the body, the soul cannot be observed or measured.
c. _____

3. Do a similar chart for the *second section* of the reading, "Darwin's Theories."

4. Do the same for the last section of the reading.

Human Culture

Is Robert Human?

Boy Found Among Monkeys

KAMPALA (Reuters) – A small boy with the behaviour of a monkey has been found in Uganda where he lived wild in the jungle near the site of bru-tal massacres that took place during the country's civil war.

The boy, whose age is estimated between five and seven years, shuns humans and moves by jumping from place to place like a monkey with his hands clenched ... When he is still he squats on his rump. He eats grass and anything he can find.

Retreating Ugandan government troops found him living with mon-keys last September. He is now at the Nagura orphanage in Kampala where nurses have named him Robert ...

He is about two feet, six inches tall and weighs 22 pounds. He cannot speak and just grunts and squeals .... When Robert was brought to Nagura he cried all the time and tried to hide his face ....

He ate everything and still does – grass, clothes, blankets and sheets, even stones. He looks miserable all the time. No one has ever seen a smile on his face. He is not interested in his surroundings at all.

Calgary Herald, July 3, 1986, p. B4

In a group or as a class, discuss the fol-lowing questions:

1. In what ways is Robert a human be-ing?

2. In what ways does Robert not seem human?

9

3. How do you decide whether or not Robert is a human being? Discuss whether being born into the human species makes one human. What more might be needed?

Innate and Learned Behaviour

Consider the following list of behaviours that both human beings and animals practise. Determine whether each behaviour is **innate** (inborn, inherited at birth) or whether it must be learned. Do this for human beings and then for other animals, such as a fox, a Canada goose and a Pacific salmon.
a) building a shelter b) caring for a baby
c) travelling long distances d) providing food e) getting a mate f) settling fights

In a group or as a class, discuss the following questions:

1. How do human beings and other animals compare in terms of learned and innate behaviour? How would you account for this?
2. Now reconsider the original question of whether Robert can be considered human.
3. What conclusions could you draw about the central differences between humans and other animals?

Creators of Culture

One thing that makes us unique in the animal kingdom is that we form very complicated cultures. **Culture** is made by human beings; it does not exist naturally. It is the huge body of knowledge, skills and attitudes that we learn throughout our lives. We learn it in order to be accepted and to survive in human society.

Culture consists of our beliefs (such as the idea that loyalty among friends is important), material objects (such as portable radios and buildings) and behaviours (such as going to school and getting to work on time). It is learned by each new generation and then passed on by language and example to the next set of offspring. It is not genetically inherited. Children may learn the accepted ways of their culture by watching and imitating others. They are first introduced to the rules of their culture by their parents. Later, society influences their beliefs and behaviours.

Culture began as a way of adapting to the environment. This is why cultures vary widely throughout the world. For example, East Indians have developed clothing from light cloth that shields them from the sun and still keeps them cool. In Yellowknife, a fur or down-filled parka is more likely to be worn. Both types of clothing are cultural inventions that are appropriate to the environment.

The Importance of Culture

Culture is important for two reasons. First, it allows us to take part in human society. Second, culture has given us power over our environment. Thus, culture is the reason that humans have become the most successful animal on this planet in a relatively short time.

In order to function in our society, we must learn certain skills, knowledge and behaviour. Most animal behaviour is inborn or innate. A mother bear may have to show her cub how to put its natural hunting behaviour to best use. However, simply by being born a bear, the cub possesses the instinct to hunt. The same is not true of human beings. We seem to have very few truly innate behaviours. Babies will instinctively suck at birth

and seem to be instinctively afraid of heights. However, most of what we call normal human behaviour must be learned.

Culture has given us the ability to develop technology. We draw on the experiences and inventions stored in our culture by countless people over many centuries. The result is that in less than 25 years, a human can learn the knowledge and skills that have taken our species more than a million years to discover. We can constantly build on the inventions and knowledge of the generations that came before us.

Culture has taught us behaviour that helps us adapt to our environment. For example, while few animals can live successfully in a desert, people today need not struggle to come up with ways of surviving in such a harsh place. We can use our cultural knowledge to turn a desert into good farmland. But we also use our knowledge to damage the environment we live in. Polluted air and water, barren land and lakes dead from acid rain are as much cultural products as language, churches and microwave ovens.

From Ideas to Action

1. Identify a belief, a material object and a behaviour that is associated with each of the following aspects of North American culture:
   a) school b) dating c) marriage
   d) friendship e) preparing food
   f) working at a job

2. View a movie or a video presentation of cultures in other countries that are very different from your own. As you watch, list examples of characteristics common to all human cultures, such as beliefs, material objects and behaviours.

Can Animals Create a Culture?

Look at the picture below.

"So what?" you are probably asking in response to this picture. Usually, monkeys are afraid of water and instinctively avoid it. Other monkey groups living in the same area as the ones in the picture will not go near water. Have the monkeys in this picture *learned* this behaviour?

Another example of unusual behaviour is a troop of apes in Japan that wash their food before eating it. Although monkeys will brush off their food, normally they will not wash it. Luckily, scientists have observed how this troop of monkeys picked up the behaviour of food-washing. It began in 1952, when potatoes were left on a Japanese beach. One young female monkey wandered down to the waterfront and cleaned off her potato in the water. She showed this behaviour to her mother, who then demonstrated it to each of her new babies. In addition, the young female that had invented the behaviour showed it to her playmates. They too began washing their food frequently, even if it wasn't dirty. By 1962, every monkey in the troop, except for a few very old ones, was washing its food.

According to our definition of culture, do these animals have culture, however simple? If so, how does it differ from human culture?

Developing Focus Questions – Level 1

What Is a Focus Question?

Before we begin to investigate a problem, we need to develop suitable questions for our inquiry. Social scientists call this a **focus.** It is a question or series of questions that limits, defines or directs the investigation into a problem or issue. For example, for the problem of whether animals can create a culture, a good focus question might be:

Do monkeys create cultural behaviours that help them adapt to their environment and that are passed on to future generations?

Notice how the focus question helps define or limit the problem.

Answering the focus question requires several steps. In this case, the focus question directs you to:

1. Examine monkeys as an example of non-human animals.

2. Look at their creation of cultural behaviours only.

3. See if these behaviours relate to environmental adaptation.

4. See if these behaviours are passed on to future generations.

Creating Your Own Focus Questions

Read about the issue of human warfare at right and do the following activities:

1. Clearly state the problem to be investigated.

2. Create several questions to help you investigate the issue.

3. Discuss each question. Select the best questions and explain why they are the best.

4. Now list the rules for creating effective focus questions.

Human Warfare — Innate or Learned?

We are the only species on this planet that murders its own kind in an organized way. People who have studied violent human behaviour have different opinions as to why this is so. Here are just a few.

In *African Genesis,* Robert Ardrey argues that human beings behave like other animals when we are threatened or desire something. As individuals we act aggressively, on instinct, to attack or kill enemies. When we are in groups, we display the same behaviour, which is then called warfare.

Konrad Lorenz, in his book *On Aggression,* says that the problem with people is that we have no instinctive ways of limiting our inborn desire to kill each other. Other animals rarely get into fights that lead to the death of one of the opponents. In the animal kingdom, at a critical point in the battle, one of the fighters recognizes that it is weaker. Instinctively, this animal will do something to show its retreat (for example, putting its tail between its legs or rolling over to expose its throat). The meanings of these behaviours are instinctively understood by the other animal. At this point the fight is over. Perhaps the human problem is that people do not have the instinctive urges or behaviours for breaking off fights – and so we kill.

Richard Leakey in *People of the Lake* argues that we are by nature both aggressive and co-operative. We co-operate to achieve goals that the group decides are worthwhile. When people discovered how to grow crops, they settled down and tended farms. They then claimed ownership of land and tools. If a neighbour's crop succeeded, the temptation was strong to take the neighbour's fields. Unfortunately, people quickly learned that warfare was a very profitable way of behaving. Warfare was invented by our culture.

The Uniqueness of Human Communication

Communicating Without Words

Tell another student about each of the following — without using words:

a) how to brush your teeth properly
b) how you feel about another person in your class
c) the job you would really like to have some day
d) your most embarrassing moment
e) what you like about your favourite musical group

Now as a group or as a class, discuss the following questions.

1. What kinds of things are fairly easy to express without words? Why?
2. What kinds of things are difficult to express without words? Why?
3. How successful were you in expressing yourself during this exercise? How would you explain this?
4. Would animal sounds such as barking or hooting be enough to enable you to communicate these things? Why or why not?

Human Culture Demands a Complex Language

Without language, it would be impossible to teach, or even to talk about, your culture. Our language allows us to talk about the past, present and future in a very complex way. It allows us to communicate about things that are not physically present, such as memories and emotions. No other animal can do this. Unlike the hoot or screech of an animal, our language has a rich variety of meanings.

Our unique way of communicating through spoken language and our culture cannot be separated. The world of animals requires simple forms of communication. The complex world of human beings demands the use of complex language. As human invention and understanding have grown, so has our need for a language which helps us to express our expanding knowledge and to pass it on to the next generation.

Can Animals Use Human Language?

Human babies are born with the ability to learn language quickly and easily. If parents encourage language use, it takes only three to four years for the average child with proper hearing to develop from cooing to speaking in adult-style sentences.

Animals can't speak as we do, since they lack our human larynx (voice box). More than that, they are not genetically programmed as we are to learn language. However, two American psychologists immersed a chimp named Washoe in American Sign Language. Washoe lived in their home and was raised as a deaf human child would be. Washoe now has a vocabulary of over 200 signs, can combine signs to form new meanings and has even taught her son to use ASL. This is a remarkable achievement for a chimp, but Washoe still can't compare with a normal human two-year-old's language abilities.

From Ideas to Action

1. Let's test the idea that human culture might lead to the development of complex language. Each of the items in the list below are inventions of human culture. No other animal makes or does these things. List as many words as you can that would be needed to talk about each of the following cultural inventions:
   a) the making and use of fire b) a carved hand axe c) clothing, d) burial of the dead e) farming f) building a city g) a government

2. a) In the early stages of life, a person cannot use language to communicate. How does a baby express each of the following:
   i) happiness or contentment ii) hunger iii) desire for an object that is out of reach iv) fear or insecurity
   b) How do other animals communicate the same messages?
   c) How does the ability to express these messages change when people learn to use language?

3. Research and report on the efforts of scientists to understand the methods that other animals use to communicate. You might want to look at some of the following: whales, dolphins, apes, bees. How do these methods of animal communication compare with human language?

Using Symbols

All animals communicate. But there is something that you do when you communicate that no other animal can do. You use symbols.

A **symbol** is an object, a word, an action or a sound that has been created to represent something else. Its meaning is agreed upon by a group of people and must be learned by others who use it. A symbol also has a rich set of personal meanings that can lead to a variety of behaviours, emotions and beliefs.

A good example of a symbol is the Canadian national flag. It is an object that represents Canada. We have also created and agreed on a set of sounds (f-l-a-g) to represent the object. Clearly, we are not born understanding the meaning of the Canadian flag; we must learn its meaning. The flag also has a rich set of personal meanings for the people that use it. For some people, the flag raises feelings of national pride and identity. For others, it may be a source of anger, if they disagree strongly with the national government.

National flags also lead to a variety of actions that are unique to people. For example, Canadians might purposely buy goods that have our flag on the label. Others might protest the government's actions by burning the flag. Some people have even been willing to lay down their lives to protect all that they believe the flag symbolizes.

Developing an Organizer — Level 1

What Is an Organizer?

After you have decided on a focus question to guide your inquiry into an issue, you need to organize your research in an effective way. This will ensure that you have considered all the important sides of an issue. An **organizer** is a chart that will help you visualize your focus.

Organizer for a Comparison Problem

Problem: Do other animals create a human-like culture?
Focus: Do monkeys create cultural beliefs, objects or behaviours that help them adapt to their environment and that are passed on to future generations?

Do Animals Use Symbols?

To our knowledge, when animals communicate, they do not use symbols the same way people do. Instead, they more frequently use **signs**, which are indicators that something exists or is happening. For example, when a chimpanzee spots food, it announces this fact with a series of hooting sounds. Honey bees do a complex dance when they return to the hive to tell the other bees of the location of flowers.

It may be that there are symbols for animals, but the meaning behind them does not seem to be learned or agreed upon. Rather, hoots and direction dances are innate behaviours.

With a symbolic language we can weave a rich culture. We can tell stories and express our feelings to each other. We can share ideas and understandings. It is our unique ability to create symbols and to use them that makes us very unusual animals.

Categories of Comparison	Monkeys	Human Beings
Cultural Beliefs	– no evidence	– religion (belief in God) – morality (honesty)
Cultural Objects	– some monkeys make tools (special sticks to catch insects)	– buildings – paintings – everything we have invented or created
Cultural Behaviours	– some evidence that monkeys teach each other new behaviour	– language – wedding ceremonies – school attendance
Passed on to Next Generation	– some evidence that behaviour is passed on (food washing) – no passing on of objects	– obvious teaching of beliefs, behaviours and passing on of objects

Creating Your Own Organizer

Use the material on the reading "Human Warfare – Innate or Learned?" on page 13 to develop a simple organizer for further research.

1. State the problem and the focus for this issue.
2. Note that you may have to add categories of comparison as you extend your research on the topic.
3. How did you decide on the various categories of comparison?
4. Trade your organizer with that of another student and evaluate each other's work.
5. What are some of the rules for creating effective organizers?

A honey bee's dance communicates both distance and direction to a food source.

From Ideas to Action

1. For each of the following give a sign and a symbol: a) happiness b) anger c) ownership d) fear e) danger
2. Name some symbols that we use to indicate the following: a) high status or power b) low status c) ownership d) a strong feeling of affection or attraction for another person
3. The chart below asks you to explore other symbols in our society. In your notebooks, reproduce the chart and fill in the sections for each symbol. Let your imagination and experience help you here.

	Symbol	Word	Meaning	Resulting Behaviour, Emotion, Belief
1.		love		
2.	$			
3.		power		
4.	⊙⊙⊙⊙⊙			

Human Biological Uniqueness

Do Human Beings Have Special Abilities?

Examine the following list of abilities and put each of them into one of three categories: "Human Beings Only," "Human Beings and Other Animals," and "Other Animals Only."

a) the ability to stand upright and walk on two legs
b) the ability to move faster than 50 km/h without mechanical aids
c) the ability to communicate using sounds
d) the ability to grasp objects between an opposing thumb and finger
e) the ability to use tools to gather food
f) the ability to solve mathematical problems
g) the ability to lift objects five times one's body weight
h) the ability to communicate by reading and writing symbols
i) the ability to jump ten times the body length
j) the ability to think creatively to make new objects or designs
k) the ability to see patterns and shapes
l) the ability to detect objects in the dark or underwater
m) the ability to swim in or under water
n) the ability to make plans for the future

In a group or as a class, discuss the following questions:

1. Which abilities were most difficult to categorize. Why?

2. Which parts of the human body are associated with those abilities you thought were uniquely human?

3. Do human beings have superior abilities or merely different abilities?

You have been born with a body that is unique in the animal kingdom. Unlike your cultural inheritance, which can vary widely, your biological inheritance is very similar to that of all human beings. All human beings are born with a similar brain. Like every other person, you can walk upright and do very fine work with your hands. In fact, the unique combination of these physical features enables humans to invent and to learn a culture.

The Amazing Human Brain

From the series of diagrams, you can see that human beings have all the brain sections that other animals have — and then some. As a result, we are very much like other animals and at the same time very different.

The parts of our brains that are similar to those of other animals control our automatic responses. Breathing, heart rate, ability to hear and see, basic emotions, and urges such as fear, aggression and sex are controlled by these areas of the brain. When you are terrified, you will automatically scream, fight or run away. These actions and abilities are "prewired" or innate and require no learning.

The unique part of the human brain is the **cerebral cortex**, the huge, wrinkled outer surface of our brain. This large portion of the human brain has no definite role at birth. This means that, unlike the brain of most other animals, the human brain has a large section that enables human beings to learn new ideas, skills and activities.

The cerebral cortex contains millions of nerve cells. They can store thousands of pieces of information and recall a single fact or a total memory in a split second. They are the location of both logical and creative thought.

The Importance of a Cerebral Cortex

It is likely that without a large cerebral cortex, humans would never be able to discuss, create or even remember our complex way of life. In short, culture depends on the existence of the unique human cerebral cortex.

Without the cerebral cortex, people could not make or use a language that has symbols. This part of the brain enables us to discuss our culture. Talking with a friend about a concert or a movie would be impossible without your cortex. It also gives us the ability to communicate culture to the next generation. Teaching someone to fix a car or to use a computer would be hard without the benefit of words and symbols. These are all the products of your cerebral cortex.

The cerebral cortex is also important to culture because it is the part of the brain that solves problems. In the cerebral cortex, old memories are compared to new experiences to look for solutions. If this fails, the cortex can look at the situation and combine the information it has in some new way. A new idea or invention can then be added to our culture. In this way, the cerebral cortex permits us to constantly expand the knowledge and skills of our culture.

Finally, the cerebral cortex is vital to human culture because of its vast ability to store information. To function in our society we need to know millions of things. We also have to learn countless

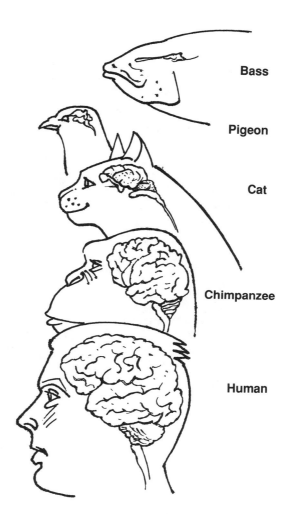

Bass

Pigeon

Cat

Chimpanzee

Human

tasks and skills. Once these things have been learned, we must be able to recall them when we need to. Without the memory that the cerebral cortex gives us, this would be impossible.

Walking Upright and Skillful Hands

As a human being, you have the ability to stand upright and to walk on two legs all the time. This is called **bipedalism** (bi = two, pedal = foot). It might not seem like much, but no other animal can do it. Some apes do stand up and walk on two legs for short distances. However, they cannot do this for long.

Bipedalism is important to the rapid growth of culture because it frees the hands. Unlike apes' hands, our hands are not busy trying to get from one place to another. Instead, we can use the capabilities of our hands to change things in our environment.

Like many apes, we have an **opposable thumb** which can easily touch our other fingers. You can demonstrate this by touching the tip of your thumb to your first finger to make an "O." This opposable thumb makes the hand capable of very fine and delicate work. We can make carefully crafted tools and other forms of technology. We can also create works of art or do brain surgery.

Together, bipedalism and our opposable thumbs have allowed the rapid development of technology. With the free use of our hands, we can easily make the inventions that our brains imagine.

Without these talents, many of the objects that are part of our culture would never have been created or would have been developed at a much slower pace. They might even have remained locked forever in the minds of their original inventors.

Human Adaptability

Many animal species have unique, highly developed physical skills. These abilities enable them to do things which no other animal can do quite as well. These skills are usually vital to the survival of the animal in its environment.

Although the human race is a very successful species, we have fewer special physical skills than many other animals. For example, some birds have developed much keener eyesight than ours. The family dog can hear sounds and can smell odors that we cannot. Furthermore, there are many animals that can run faster and can easily beat us in a fight. Why, then, have we done so well, when we seem to be able to do so little?

We are successful *because* we are not a very specialized creature. Many animals do only one or two things exceptionally well. In fact, their whole survival may depend on a single skill. By contrast, human beings can do a long list of things reasonably well. In the long run, this non-specialization has been one of the reasons for our survival and success. Combined with our amazing brain, it has made us the most adaptable species on earth.

From Ideas to Action

1. Explain how each of the following activities depends on the combination of a human brain, bipedalism and free hands capable of grasping:
   a) making machines b) planting a garden c) fighting with a sword d) playing hockey e) fixing a car

2. Let's look at animal specialists. Research the non-human record holders for each of the following:
   a) fastest species in water b) fastest species on land c) best eyesight — during the day, during the night d) strongest e) most sensitive hearing f) other specialty areas in which you are interested

3. For each of the areas of specialty above, list some human inventions that have allowed us to break the records of other animal specialists.

4. "The human brain is the only real specialty that human beings have or need." Discuss the truth of this statement with a group of students.

Projects, Activities and Explorations

1. The role of human culture can be seen in many feature films. View one of the films *Crocodile Dundee, The Gods Must Be Crazy, Tarzan: The Legend of Greystoke* or any other film that deals with the effects of culture on people. Identify at least five examples that show the effect of human culture on a character in the film. Write a report on these examples and share them with others in your class.

2. Make a collage by collecting pictures of people living in another culture. Try to select people who live in an environment that is very different from Canada. You could group your pictures by the different cultural components: beliefs, material objects and behaviours. Look for photos depicting life events such as birth, death, recreation, housing, food, raising children and work. Present your collage to the class. As a group, try to account for the differences between Canadian culture and the culture you are studying.

3. Visit a local daycare centre or an elementary school. If possible, try to see young children in different age groups, from one to five. Observe and record the language used by children in each age group. How does the use of speech compare from one age group to the next? Find information in the library about how humans understand and use human language.

4. Assume that five million years have passed. Without the benefit of any special equipment, human beings have moved into one of the following environments:

a) underwater b) the air c) the moon d) the desert e) totally darkened caves f) any other environment you can think of.

   Choose one of the environments above and draw or describe how people might look and what kind of lifestyle they might have under such conditions.

5. Develop a cultural survival manual for your school. Each year a new group of students enrols in your school. They may be unaware of the cultural knowledge they need to feel comfortable in your school. With some other students, make a list of cultural do's and don'ts for success in your school. Pass along your guide to your student council. They may wish to publish it for the use of incoming students. Your manual might include photographs, puzzles and cartoons to make it more interesting.

6. Make models to compare the structure of the brains of various animals to those of human beings. Use clay or any other material that is easily shaped. Label the similar and different features of the brains using coloured paper and pins.

7. Imagine that you are an explorer from another planet. You have no experience with the culture of human beings.
a) Write a description of each of the following aspects of human culture that you observe: i) an automobile ii) a rock video iii) teenage hairstyles and clothing iv) a football game

b) In pairs or on your own, select another aspect of our culture that an alien observer might see. Don't tell what it is that you are thinking of to any other students in the class. Write your description. Read it to the other students and see if they can guess what it is that the alien has been observing.

What Have You Learned?

If you have covered everything in this chapter, you should be familiar with the following topics:

1. How views of human uniqueness have changed

2. How species change as a result of natural selection

3. The characteristics of human culture

4. Why human cultures make us unique as a species

5. The relationship between our unique form of language and our unique cultures

6. The importance of symbols as a unique feature of human language

7. The biological uniqueness of human beings

8. The importance of the cerebral cortex

9. How to make effective notes and how to develop focus questions and organizers

To Help You Study

The following chart will help you to review the words, facts and ideas that were introduced in this chapter. Copy the chart into your notebook and fill in the missing information.

Word, Fact, Idea	Example in a Sentence	Page	Definition
innate	Breathing is an innate behaviour in human beings.	10	inborn, inherited at birth
unique			
evolution			
adaptations			
natural selection			
culture			
symbol			
sign			
cerebral cortex			
bipedalism			
opposable thumb			

Social Science and Human Behaviour

1

What Do You See?

What are the people in each of these pictures doing? If possible, discuss your answers with another student. Compare your views with the rest of the class.

How Do You Interpret What You See?

Did your classmates agree on what they saw? Probably not. Each person's personal **interpretation** (judgement, viewpoint) of what he or she sees is different. This is why it is always difficult to know the truth about human behaviour. How can we study human behaviour in a more scientific way so that we can be more accurate about what we see or experience? What sources of knowledge can we use and which of these are reliable? These are some of the main questions to be answered in this chapter.

2

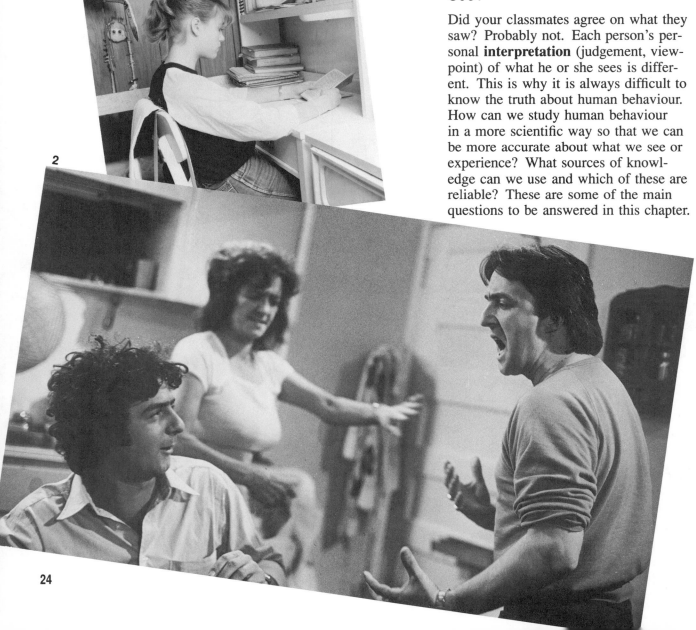

3

4

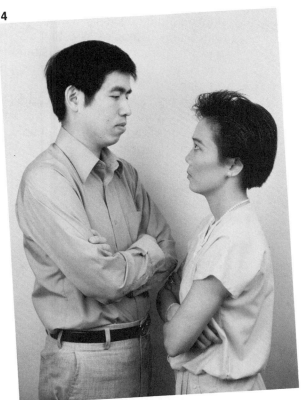

Unscientific
Sources of
Knowledge

Most of us go through life confident that
we have a fairly good understanding of
human nature. For example, when we
try to understand the behaviour of our
friends, we usually have some explanation for their actions. We can explain
or even anticipate their behaviour because we have stored information in our
memories about the way human beings
behave. This "common sense" knowledge about human nature comes to us
from many sources, such as:
- personal experience
- proverbs, myths and stereotypes
- popular books, magazines, TV and
  radio

Personal Experience

Probably the most common source of
our knowledge about human behaviour
is our own personal experience. We are
with people every day of our lives. The
experiences we have with them gradually form our picture of how people
generally act in certain situations. When
we come across similar situations, we
predict how people will behave or we
explain what they are doing, using past
experience as a guide.

There are several problems with using personal experience as a guide in
understanding other people. We are influenced by our experiences and often
accept them as truths or laws of human behaviour. We tend to apply these
"laws" of human nature to similar situ-

ations and ignore the many exceptions to our laws. Our past experiences may give us some understanding, but rarely a complete understanding, of others.

Also, we are often unaware of our own biases. A **bias** is a personal opinion, formed in advance, about an event, person or thing. Bias is one reason why people interpret the same facts differently. It also causes people to select different facts and to ignore others. This makes finding the truth about any person or human activity very difficult.

A person's biases have been shaped by his or her **frame of reference**, which is all the personal experiences gained from culture, family, religion, friends and interests. For example, you may be biased in favour of your new science class this year because you have always found science an interesting subject. Your friend may have a bias against the same class because he or she has almost failed science every year.

Proverbs, Myths and Stereotypes

Proverbs are short, well-known sayings about human behaviour. For example, we often say, "Two heads are better than one." What we mean is that a group is often more effective at a task than an individual. Most people accept that this is generally true. There is another proverb that states, "Too many cooks spoil the broth." This second piece of wisdom contradicts the first.

For each proverb, there is often another proverb equally wise but obviously contradictory. We generally apply the proverb that seems to best fit the situation and we ignore the other sayings.

Myths are commonly accepted beliefs or ideas that have no factual basis and have not been proved. For example, students who are not athletic have been calling school athletes "dumb jocks" for years. This myth assumes that all athletes are unintelligent. In fact, research shows that some of the best athletes are also among the best students. This kind of myth — one that encourages us to prejudge individuals by the group to which they belong — is called a **stereotype**. A stereotype is an oversimplified mental picture shared by many people in a group.

Both myths and proverbs lead us to ignore contradictory information. This keeps our view of the world simple, but often, also, inaccurate.

Frame of reference

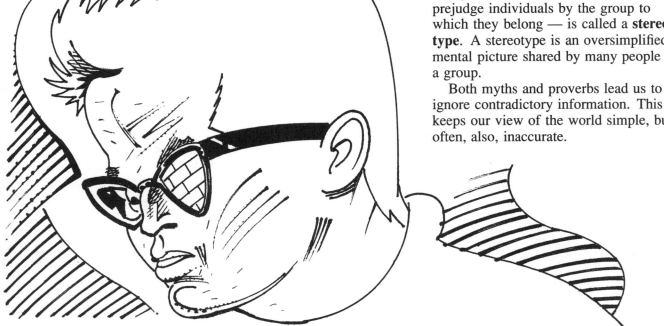

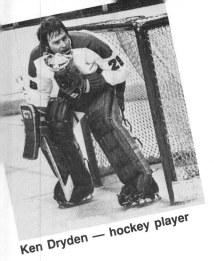

Ken Dryden — hockey player

Ken Dryden — lawyer

Abbie Hoffman — runner

Abbie Hoffman — Director of Sport Canada

Believing in a stereotype can lead us to misjudge human abilities and potential.

Popular Books, Magazines, TV and Radio

Books, magazines, newspapers, TV and radio may seem like reliable sources of information. But they also have weaknesses. These vehicles of information are designed to make money, and sometimes a particular viewpoint or exaggeration sells better than the whole truth. These sources are only as reliable as the people who write and produce them. Sometimes they suffer from the biases of people who select or interpret information in a particular way. Also, the people producing these sources are not always experts in a field. They may be limited in the amount of time or space they can devote to a topic.

All of these factors may mean that the end product may not be complete or reliable. Although these sources are useful, they are not always accurate and we must be aware of their limitations.

From Ideas to Action

1. a) Explain the proverbs below. As a class, add more proverbs to the list.
   - Practice makes perfect.
   - Out of sight, out of mind.
   - Misfortunes make us wise.
   - Once bitten, twice shy.
   - Absence makes the heart grow fonder.
   - You can lead a horse to water, but you can't make it drink.

   b) Can you think of other proverbs that contradict the ones above?

   c) To what extent are each of the proverbs true?

2. Here are three common myths:
   a) Punk rockers are not interested in serious issues.
   b) Blondes have more fun.
   c) Teenagers are irresponsible.

   As a group, guess how they might have developed. Once you have discussed them, think of other myths and determine their origins.

3. List three important experiences in your life. Write a paragraph explaining how these experiences have affected the way you see yourself or others. You may wish to do this exercise in the form of a drawing or a poem.

4. Watch a favourite television program, or read a magazine or newspaper article that discusses human behaviour. Describe how you think this source of information might be incomplete, biased or unreliable.

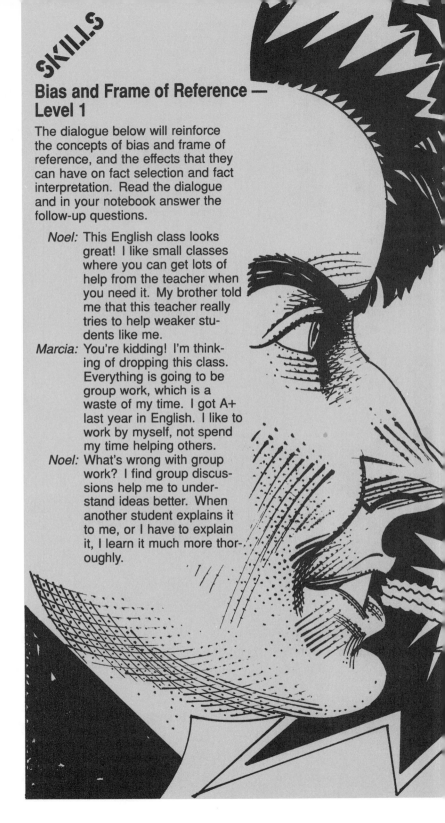

SKILLS

Bias and Frame of Reference — Level 1

The dialogue below will reinforce the concepts of bias and frame of reference, and the effects that they can have on fact selection and fact interpretation. Read the dialogue and in your notebook answer the follow-up questions.

Noel: This English class looks great! I like small classes where you can get lots of help from the teacher when you need it. My brother told me that this teacher really tries to help weaker students like me.

Marcia: You're kidding! I'm thinking of dropping this class. Everything is going to be group work, which is a waste of my time. I got A+ last year in English. I like to work by myself, not spend my time helping others.

Noel: What's wrong with group work? I find group discussions help me to understand ideas better. When another student explains it to me, or I have to explain it, I learn it much more thoroughly.

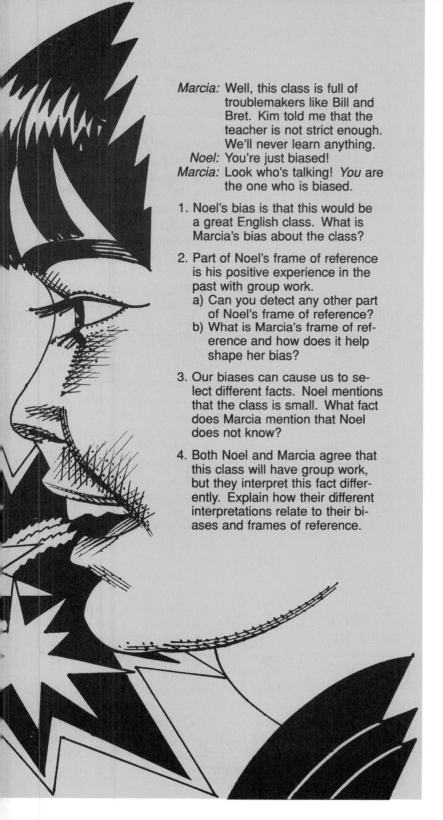

Marcia: Well, this class is full of troublemakers like Bill and Bret. Kim told me that the teacher is not strict enough. We'll never learn anything.

Noel: You're just biased!

Marcia: Look who's talking! *You* are the one who is biased.

1. Noel's bias is that this would be a great English class. What is Marcia's bias about the class?

2. Part of Noel's frame of reference is his positive experience in the past with group work.
   a) Can you detect any other part of Noel's frame of reference?
   b) What is Marcia's frame of reference and how does it help shape her bias?

3. Our biases can cause us to select different facts. Noel mentions that the class is small. What fact does Marcia mention that Noel does not know?

4. Both Noel and Marcia agree that this class will have group work, but they interpret this fact differently. Explain how their different interpretations relate to their biases and frames of reference.

The Scientific Method: Some General Characteristics

By now you may doubt whether anything you ever thought about human behaviour is accurate. However, take heart! Social scientists have methods of solving problems and getting answers to questions about human behaviour.

Social scientists are people who study human behaviour. Psychologists, sociologists and anthropologists are all social scientists. They believe that our behaviour can be measured in a scientific way, just as chemists or biologists measure the physical world. The methods they use are similar to those used in other sciences.

The **scientific method** that social scientists use is a system for thinking about problems and finding solutions in a logical and reliable manner. The key steps in this method are:

1. Define the problem to be examined.
2. State a hypothesis (possible explanation).
3. Gather and observe the information.
4. Interpret and analyse the observations.
5. State a conclusion.

The social scientist follows these procedures carefully to ensure that the results of the study are precise. The results may then be published for other scientists to read and consider. Occasionally, the results are not replicable; that is, another scientist hasn't been able to obtain the same results after following the same methods. In this case, it's back to the drawing board until everyone can agree on the results.

Let's apply these steps to a specific problem of human behaviour.

Define the problem
The social scientist starts by asking a question. In an incident in New York City, a young woman was attacked and killed. An inquiry showed that 36 people heard her screams, but no one helped her. Only one person called the police, long after the attack started. Social scientists examined the question: How do people decide what to do in an emergency?

State a hypothesis
Social scientists begin by listing **hypotheses** (possible explanations) for the question being studied. For example, bystanders may not help in an emergency because they fear for their lives. They may assume that someone else will act. Or they may be uncertain if their help is needed. To find out the importance of each of these explanations, the scientist must test the truth of each hypothesis.

In this case, we will look at the hypothesis: People determine what their behaviour should be by the reactions of others in the group.

Gather and observe information
One way social scientists gather information to prove or disprove their hypotheses is to use experiments. Other methods of gathering information are case studies, surveys and questionnaires.

There are two basic types of experiments: the laboratory experiment and the field experiment. In a laboratory experiment, the scientist can control the experimental situation. Controls are used in science to make sure that the results of an experiment are not made invalid by other factors. In a field experiment, people do not know that they are part of an experiment. Therefore, having controls over the experimental situation is more difficult.

Here is an example of a laboratory experiment set up by a social scientist to test the validity of our hypothesis. Two groups of subjects (participants) were selected. The first was the **control group**. Each subject in the control group was seated alone in a waiting room and asked to fill out a series of questionnaires. Within seconds, a foul-smelling smoke billowed into the room through an air vent. The smoke clouded vision and made breathing difficult. Each subject's reaction to what appeared to be an emergency situation was recorded.

The second group was the **experimental group**. In this group, each subject was seated in the waiting room alone, but was later joined by two other "subjects." These two were actors, but the first subject did not know this. As the smoke filled the room, the two actors looked at each other, shrugged and continued working on their questionnaires. The reactions of each real subject in the experimental group were recorded.

The controls in this experiment were that the control group had no contact with other people, while the experimental group clearly saw the reactions of the two actors to the smoke.

The recorded results of an experiment are called **observations**. In this case, the observations showed that 75 per cent of the people in the control group checked out the cause of the smoke within two minutes, and left the waiting room within four minutes. The subjects in the experimental group stayed in the room as long as the actors chose to stay. Ninety per cent of the experimental group did not report the smoke to anyone.

Interpret and analyse the observations

The next stage of the scientific method is to analyse the observations recorded. Patterns in the results are located, interpreted and explained. For example, in the experiment described above, the observations were interpreted as showing that people will ignore their instincts to act in an obvious emergency, as long as others act as though no emergency exists. Since 90 per cent of the subjects made their decision based on the actions of others, the hypothesis was considered proved.

Suppose, however, that the actors' behaviour made no difference to the experimental group. If the subjects in the experimental group got up and investigated the smoke, just as the control group did, it would mean that the original hypothesis was wrong. A second hypothesis would then be tested.

The same experiment can be rerun with all the same conditions except for one factor. For example, the "actors" might be replaced by friends of the subjects. These friends could be advised to ignore the smoke, just as the previous actors had been. If the subjects react differently this time, we know that the one factor is the cause of the change of behaviour: the fact that the subjects knew their companions. These factors are called variables. In an experiment we can change the variables, one by one, to arrive at observations that prove the hypothesis.

State a conclusion

The last step in the scientific method is to present a **conclusion**. This is a statement that sums up the observations and the analysis of the results, and relates these to the question being examined. In this experiment, the conclusion was that people base their decision to act or not to act in an emergency situation depending on how others in the group are behaving.

Laboratory Experiments and Field Experiments

In a laboratory experiment, the social scientist can control the conditions that result in the behaviour of the subjects involved. But there is sometimes a problem when the subjects are aware that they are being tested in an experiment. They may feel nervous and therefore change their normal behaviour, or they may work unusually hard at a task. The careful scientist tries to anticipate factors that might affect the validity of the experiment. If the factors cannot be eliminated, some attempt is at least made to measure their effect.

The field experiment is an attempt to measure behaviour without these problems, because the subjects are not aware that they are part of an experiment. A field experiment to test helping behaviour, for instance, might involve measuring the number of motorists who offer assistance to someone whose car has

These observations of an experiment are being made through a two-way mirror.

broken down. In this experiment, a car, with its hood up and several people apparently helping the owner, is beside the highway. About 1.5 km down the road, another car is stopped, with the hood up, but no one assisting. The experiment would measure how many people stop to aid the second motorist after seeing a helping model.

The problem with this field experiment is that there is no way to measure why cars *don't* stop. Passing drivers may not notice the "helping" example. Some may be in a hurry. Some may feel that they do not have the mechanical skills to offer assistance. There are no ways to find out the reasons some motorists do not stop.

The task of the social scientist is to select the kind of test that best measures the behaviour they are interested in, and to be aware of the general limitations of experiments.

From Ideas to Action

1. Make a chart like the one below to organize your notes on lab experiments and field experiments.

	Lab Experiment	Field Experiment
Examples		
Advantages		
Problems		

2. For each of the following questions, decide whether a field experiment or a lab experiment is preferable. Explain your choice.
   a) Why do people cheat?
   b) Are signs and posters an effective way to change peoples' behaviour?
   c) Does "letting off steam" reduce the chances of physical violence?
   d) When do brothers and sisters show open affection for each other?

3. Identify which part of an experiment is being referred to in each of the following sentences. These parts include: the problem, the hypothesis, the method used to gather information, analysis of the observations and the conclusion.
   a) Do students perform better if they are offered rewards?
   b) The students who volunteered to be subjects in the study were given standard intelligence tests, especially in mathematics ability. Only those who scored between 100 and 110 were selected. Those who passed this screening process were given a test to determine how hard they worked on any assigned task. Only those showing an average amount of willingness to work hard on a task were selected.
   c) Students will do better at tasks if they know that they are going to get a reward for their efforts.

d) The scores of the two groups of students were recorded.

e) The students were divided into two groups. The first group was given a series of mathematics problems. The number of correct answers and the total number of questions completed were then recorded. The second group was given the same math problems, but was told that money would be awarded for each correct answer.

f) Tests given before the experiment ensured that no one participating in the experiment had either very poor or superior mathematics skills. Also, care was taken to make sure that the subjects did not talk to each other before or after the experiment.

g) Charts and graphs were drawn to compare the performance of the two groups of students. Scientists doing the experiment noted patterns in the performance of students in both groups. It was noted that the students who were rewarded had an average correct score of 72 per cent and completed an average of 31 questions. The group that was not rewarded had an average correct score of 61 per cent and completed an average of 27 questions. Since the only difference between these two groups was the offer of a reward, it would seem that the reward itself was the reason for the different performance levels seen in the experiment.

h) It would seem that rewards play an important role in the performance of tasks.

4. Are there any improvements that could be made to the experiment described in question 3? If so, what changes would you make? Discuss why these changes would make it a better experiment.

5. For each of the following problems, write a short paragraph explaining how you would scientifically discover which of the possible causes listed is the real cause.
   a) You are having trouble getting dates. You have narrowed the possible causes to:
      • You are too forceful on the phone.
      • Your style of dress is "out-of-step" with that of most other students.
      • You are not involved enough in activities where you can meet people of the opposite sex.
   b) Your boss seems displeased with your work. You have narrowed the possible causes to:
      • You are late twice a week for work.
      • Your hair is too long.
      • You are not friendly with difficult customers.

6. Select a problem from your own life, the cause of which you are curious to discover, and do the following:
   a) List all the possible causes of the problem.
   b) Check off the most likely causes.
   c) Write out a plan describing how you might test these selected causes, one at a time.
   d) For each cause that you are investigating, write a few sentences describing what you would do if your research proved that this was the main cause of your problem.
   e) If possible, carry out the investigation that you have planned.

Other Means of Collecting Information

The Case Study

Social scientists use other methods to gather information about human behaviour. The **case study** is a very detailed investigation of one individual or event. The inquiry may involve parents, brothers and sisters, friends and any other individuals who can contribute information about past behaviour. By gathering information about the person's early life, schooling, friends, activities and thoughts, the social scientist can begin to understand an individual's behaviour.

Although case studies can tell us a great deal about individual behaviour, they are not intended to give a total picture of human behaviour. A great many cases must be studied before a pattern can be seen. This is very expensive, since the researcher must spend so much time with each person. For this reason, case studies are not used when the goal is to test a hypothesis that can be applied to many people.

The validity of case studies also depends on the amount and reliability of the information gathered. The people interviewed may not reveal useful information. Sometimes they have forgotten events, or do not want to talk about them. Also, their selection of details will be influenced by their opinions and biases. Details can be cross-checked or further researched, but getting a complete and factual account, not influenced by opinions or feelings, is always a challenge.

The Survey

When you think of surveys, perhaps you imagine the person in front of the department store who wants to ask you a few questions. A **survey** is an attempt to find out opinions, characteristics or behaviours of people by looking at a representative group of individuals. This representative group is called a **sample**. The sample must be large enough to give a clear picture of the "average" viewpoint on an issue or a problem.

The scientist conducting the survey decides on the sample before beginning the test. Will it be a **random sample**, in which perhaps every twentieth person on the street is stopped for questioning? Or will the sample be a **matched sample**, in which the people in the group are chosen because they have one or more characteristics in common? If, for exam-

ple, you want to find out the attitudes of daughters towards caring for an elderly parent, you would survey a matched sample, only daughters with elderly parents. Most surveys, however, are random, and the people selected have little or nothing in common.

The Questionnaire

Surveys may be conducted by an interview in person, by telephone or by written questionnaires. Whichever method, the scientist has to think carefully about which questions to ask.

It is not easy to design a good questionnaire. Each question has to be carefully and clearly worded. The question should not hint at an expected answer. For example, replace the question "Did you get good marks on your exams?" with "What was the average of your exam marks?" The designer of the questionnaire has to think about the level of response that is required. Will a "yes/no" answer give enough information, or should the response be graded to allow for indifferent, strongly positive or strongly negative feelings?

It is usual to pre-test surveys on a small group of people. The results are then analysed to see if the questions are clear. Usually the members of the sample group are interviewed to see if each question meant the same thing to them as it did to the person who wrote it. Some questions may have to be removed, others altered and some added. At this point, the survey is ready to be used.

A Survey

Problem: Does part-time work during the school year affect students' marks? This statement is the problem you are investigating.

Hypothesis: Part-time work does not affect school marks, provided that the hours of work do not exceed 30 hours per week.

Method of gathering information: A survey of high school students.

The following questionnaire was designed to gather information. First, pre-test this questionnaire on a sample group of at least six students.

Sample Survey

Check the appropriate answer.

1. Age: a) 14 ___ b) 15 ___ c) 16 ___
         d) 17 ___ e) 18+ ___

2. Sex: a) F ___   b) M ___

3. Do you have a part-time job or jobs?

   a) Yes ___   b) No ___

4. If you answered yes to 3, state the average number of hours that you work per week:

   a) 1–10 ___ b) 11–20 ___ c) 21–30 ___
   d) 31–40 ___

5. What was the average of your marks on your most recent report card?

   a) Below 65% ___ b) Above 65% ___

On the basis of interviews with the students, change the questionnaire, if necessary, to get the information you need. Some questions might need to be reworded. Decide whether you need a matched sample or a random sample. Add questions if needed.

To interpret the data, first collect the answers. You need to make a chart that helps you to see all the information at a glance. This is called a **tabulation chart**. The following format may be useful:

Subject Number	Question 1	2	3	4	5
1	b	a	a	e	a
2					

Now analyse your findings. What patterns, if any, do you see in the chart? A pattern is obvious when a large number of people answer a question in the same way. For example, you might notice that most students do not work more than ten hours a week. A pattern can also be a recurring relationship between the answers given for two or more questions. For example, you might find that people who worked 20 hours or more had low marks. Do any patterns support the hypothesis? Or are the patterns so unclear that you must reject the hypothesis?

State your conclusions in a paragraph. Explain what you think the survey has shown.

The Value of Surveys

One of the great advantages of surveys is that they can provide the views of a large number of people easily and cheaply. Political parties and advertisers, for example, depend on surveys to discover public reaction to policies and trends.

The drawbacks to surveys as a means of studying human behaviour are that they can only measure peoples' views, feelings and personal opinions. They cannot tell us *why* people behave as they do.

Another problem is that there is no way of judging if the person taking part in the survey is giving enough thought to the questions. Many surveys are long, and often people give inaccurate or incomplete answers to complex questions. One way to ensure satisfactory results is to design a questionnaire that works well. Your survey is only as good as the questionnaire you are using.

A telephone bank at Decima Research Limited, a company that conducts public opinion surveys by phone.

From Ideas to Action

1. In your notebooks, fill in the chart below to organize your notes.

	Case Study	Survey
Method		
Advantages/Uses		
Disadvantages/Limitations		

2. Decide which scientific method you would use to investigate the human behaviours listed below. Choose a lab experiment, field experiment, case study or survey. Explain your choice.
   a) Why was John Lennon murdered?
   b) Are billboards an effective way to change peoples' behaviour?
   c) Does the threat of a nuclear holocaust influence student attitudes toward their futures?
   d) What makes a movie successful?

Bias and the Scientific Method

How do social scientists deal with the problem of bias? All people have biases and particular viewpoints because of their own life experiences. Social scientists have to undergo extensive training to make them aware of their own biases and their own frames of reference. They must try to be objective (neutral; not influenced by personal opinions or feelings).

Suppose, for example, that a researcher was brought up in a family that stressed the importance of strong religious beliefs. This frame of reference could make the scientist intolerant of the beliefs of someone who follows another religion, or no religion at all. The scientist may view religious beliefs in other cultures as "superstitions." To overcome this kind of bias, the researcher has to be aware of his or her frame of reference, and deliberately work towards a balanced viewpoint.

Scientists also insist on systematic experimental procedures based on accurate and **standardized measurement**. This means that everyone agrees to measure the observations in the same way. Suppose a scientist says 30 per cent of the subjects acted in a certain way. Other scientists automatically understand how this number was calculated and what "per cent" means. This standardization will enable them to check the results using precisely the same method or methods as the first investigator's.

Fact, Opinion and Argument — Level 1

Social scientists value facts and factual arguments, which they use to support their theories. Knowing the difference between facts, arguments and opinions is important. The following exercise will help you to distinguish between these three things.

Facts

Exact, specific things that have happened, that can be investigated and that have been proved again and again.

Examples

- Earth is further from the sun than Venus.
- The speed of light is 299 274 km/s.

Opinions

Vague views or feelings that are not exact or have not been proved.

Examples

- I feel that watching TV is good for young people.
- Everyone knows that girls are better than boys at making friends.

Arguments

Reasons given to prove or disprove a statement or viewpoint.

Examples

- TV can be an excellent source of knowledge because many education channels use experts to teach us.
- Athletes are not all "dumb jocks" since many have university degrees.

Read and evaluate the statements below. Compare them to the definitions and examples above. In your notebook, indicate which are facts, which are opinions and which are arguments.

1. Since many animals get the same diseases as human beings, it makes sense to study animals to find a cure for human diseases.
2. I think that using animals for research into human diseases is wrong. There must be a better way to find cures.
3. The University of Toronto uses 98 000 animals a year. Ninety-two per cent are rodents, 1.3 per cent are dogs and cats and .03 per cent are primates such as monkeys.
4. The University of Western Ontario is using fewer animals for research now, since scientists are switching to alternatives such as computer simulations to test new cures.
5. The life of an innocent animal is more important than the life of a person who harms these helpless animals.
6. There are over 250 animal diseases that are similar or identical to human diseases.
7. Animal activists claim that helpless animals are tortured in laboratories and that many experiments are unnecessarily cruel.
8. Ronald Lee of the British Animal Liberation Front said that his group had freed the entire stock of animals from Bromley College of Technology in November 1984.

Projects, Activities and Explorations

1. You might try giving the survey on page 36 to a group of students in your school. If you would like to create your own survey, read the following suggestions:
   a) Choose a topic that you are curious about, such as why students stay in (or drop out of) school.
   b) Write a survey consisting of approximately five questions. Make sure that you pre-test it with a few other students in the class and that you show it to your teacher before you give it to a large group of people.
   c) Once you have all your surveys back, count the number of people who gave certain answers to each of your questions. Express each of these totals as a percentage of the total number of people who answered your survey.
   d) Draw graphs or charts for each of the answers to show your results. Decide what your results mean and present your conclusions in either a written or oral presentation.

2. Collect articles from newspapers and magazines that describe scientific case studies, surveys or experiments. Paste these in a scrapbook and provide the following information in a brief paragraph:
   a) What problem was being studied in each item?
   b) What was the hypothesis?
   c) What methods were used to do the reseach?
   d) What observations were recorded?
   e) What conclusions were stated?
   f) Why is the research important? How might it be useful in your own life? This project could also be done using television shows that deal with scientific topics.

What Have You Learned?

If you have covered everything in this chapter, you should be familar with the following topics:
1. Unscientific sources of knowledge about human behaviour
2. The scientific method of researching human behaviour
3. Ways of gathering data: the experiment (laboratory and field), the case study and the survey
4. The strengths and weaknesses of experiments, case studies and surveys
5. How and why social scientists try to avoid bias in their work

To Help You Study

The following chart will help you review the words, facts and ideas that were introduced in this chapter. Copy the chart into your notebook and fill in the missing information.

Word, Fact, Idea	Example in a Sentence	Page	Definition
bias	The newspaper report was so biased in favour of the hometown team, it didn't even mention that the other team won!	26	opinion formed in advance about people, events, things
frame of reference			
stereotype			
scientific method			
hypothesis			
control group			
experimental group			
observations			
conclusion			
laboratory experiment			
field experiment			
case study			
survey			
random sample			
matched sample			

Studying Human Behaviour

3

What Is Happening in These Pictures?

Carefully examine all the pictures in the collage and answer these questions:

1. What is happening in each of the pictures?
2. What do the pictures have in common?
3. Which pictures seem to go together? Why?

In small groups, compare your findings. Use the following activities to guide your discussion.

1. Divide the pictures into three distinct groups that show:
   a) individuals and their behaviour
   b) groups of people and their behaviour
   c) people of different cultures and their behaviour
2. What focus questions about human behaviour come to mind from viewing these pictures? Write a list of these questions. As you make your way through this book, you will find some answers to these questions.

1

2

3

4

All of the photographs that appear in the collage show human beings behaving — some in familiar ways, others in unfamiliar ways. The pictures were selected to prompt you to do what people do all the time: to become curious about people's behaviour, to ask questions and to suggest possible answers or explanations for the behaviour. This chapter is about the people whose work it is to scientifically unravel the mysteries of human behaviour: psychologists, sociologists and anthropologists.

In a sense, we are all amateur students of behaviour. We are always curious about why people act the way they do. If we weren't, conversation around the cafeteria table would be fairly dull. If you don't believe this, try this little experiment. Keep a mental note of each time you make a statement about your own or someone else's behaviour during the day. You will find that you play social scientist more often than you think.

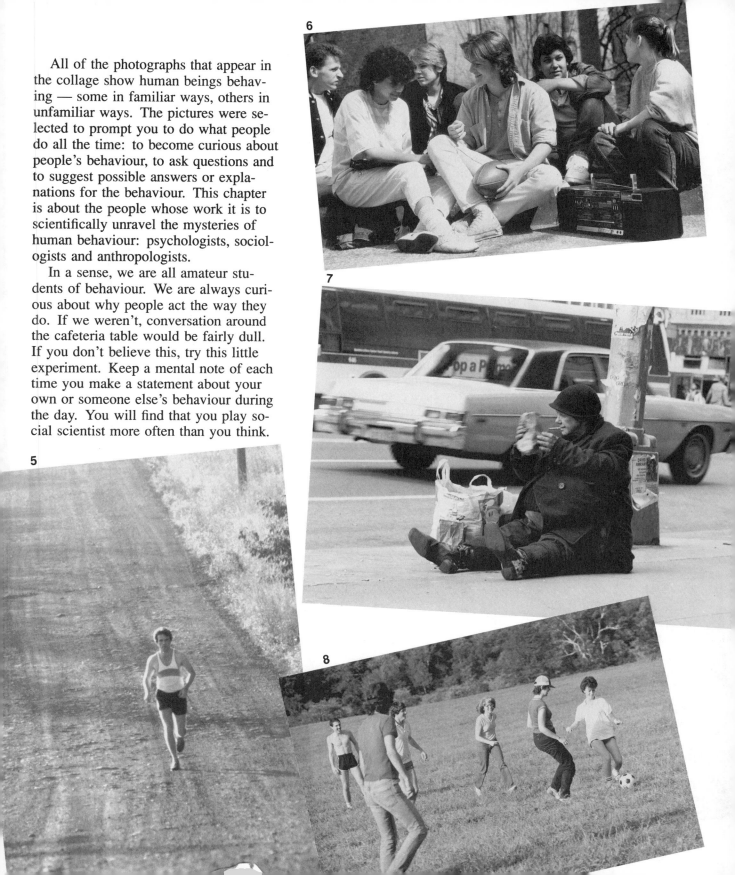

6

7

5

8

Three Ways To Study Human Behaviour

The photographs were especially selected to focus on human behaviour in three different ways. For example, some pictures focus on individuals who are acting alone. In this case, the focus is narrow. You might want to know about the inner workings of the human mind: for example, how an individual's emotions, needs and the brain itself lead to certain behaviour. The social science that focuses on the individual is called **psychology**.

In other pictures, there are people doing things that are usually done in groups. In this case, the focus is broader. You expand your view to include not only the individual, but also the groups and the society in which that person lives. The interest here is in how groups operate to mould the behaviour of their members. The social science that focuses on groups is called **sociology**.

Finally, some pictures show behaviours that involve whole cultures or the entire human race in some way. Clearly, this is the widest focus of all. You are led to discover how and why human beings as a species are both similar and different. This may lead to important questions related to the origins and development of the human race. The social science that focuses on human cultures or the human species is called **anthropology**.

These three viewpoints can be very helpful in focusing your study of human behaviour. You can choose to look at individuals, groups or entire cultures and the species as a whole. Together three social sciences — psychology, sociology and anthropology — explore the actions and motives of people, and give us a total picture of ourselves as human beings.

In this chapter, you will find out about the work of the scientists who study human behaviour from the three different viewpoints described above. You will also discover how their knowledge can be useful in a variety of other, less scientific jobs.

This chapter may get you thinking about your own future career. Can you use your interest in people to make a good living? Read on to find out.

The Psychologist

How Are These Questions Similar?

- Does stress make a person perform better?
- Is punishment a successful way of teaching?
- What happens to a person who is totally isolated from any sights or sounds for many days?
- What causes some people to have accurate memories while others do not?
- What can people do to increase their tolerance to pain without the use of drugs ?

All of the questions above are ones that might be asked by psychologists. Were you able to figure out how these questions are similar?

Interview with a Psychologist

Rather than working with a standard definition and description of psychology, it might be more useful to talk to a psychologist. What follows is part of a conversation with a psychologist who works in a hospital.

Interviewer: What does "psychology" mean to you?

Psychologist: People often say that psychology is hard to define because it deals with so many different aspects of a person. However, if you look at the word "psychology" itself, you will get a good idea of what psychology is about. It comes from two Greek words: *psyche* meaning "mind," and *logos* meaning "the study of."

The ancient Greeks thought that people were affected by two forces: their spiritual nature (the mind, sometimes referred to as the soul) and their physical nature (the body). The way that these two forces function together to produce thoughts and actions in individuals defines what we are interested in as psychologists. In short, I focus on the individual and what is going on in his or her mind.

Interviewer: What do you mean by "focus on the individual"?

Psychologist: Let's take the example of a murderer. As a psychologist, I would ask questions about the motives of this person, what drives him or her to behave in certain ways. I would want to know about this person's emotional makeup and personality. I might compare what I found out about this individual with facts about murderers collected by other psychologists. I would look for similarities and other clues to explain this person's violent behaviour.

Interviewer: What kinds of things do psychologists do?

Psychologists study the thoughts, feelings and behaviour of individuals.

Psychologists study the environment in which people work in order to improve productivity and working conditions.

Psychologist: That's a very hard question to answer because the field is divided into specialities. For example, I'm a **clinical psychologist**. I work in a hospital and sometimes at a local clinic where I diagnose and treat peoples' emotional problems and mental illnesses. I usually only deal with very serious cases that need to be hospitalized.

People with less serious problems usually go to private counsellors who, like myself, have a degree in psychology. They are usually looking for advice in making decisions or solving personal problems.

A common view of the psychologist is of a person in a white coat who pays subjects to take part in experiments. These experiments are designed to test responses or to discover something about the way in which the human brain works to cause behaviour. Scientific efforts such as these create new knowledge and often form the basis of what most other psychologists call fact. These people, not surprisingly, are called **experimental psychologists**.

Then there are **educational psychologists**. These people devote their time to researching how a person learns. They study how the brain takes in and uses information. Their work usually finds its way into the education system, where the knowledge is applied to improve the way that teachers and students work together.

Still another category is **industrial psychology**. People in this branch of psychology deal with the world of business and industry. They study how individuals behave while they are at work. Sometimes industrial psychologists are employed by industries. Generally, their knowledge is used to help a company to be more successful and profitable.

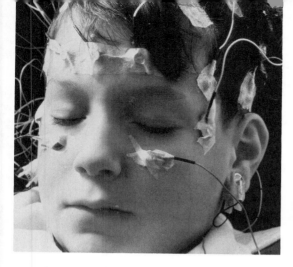

As you can see, there are many different kinds of psychologists. However, we all have basically one thing in common. We are all in the business of searching out facts about what makes individuals think and act the way they do.

Interviewer: It sounds as though anyone who uses the knowledge developed by psychologists could be called a psychologist.

Psychologist: No, that's not really true. Psychology, like sociology and anthropology, is a science. This means that to "do" psychology, you have to be involved in researching human behaviours, publishing the results of your work, and so on. It means following the strict requirements of the scientific method, which include thorough, controlled investigation of the behaviour of human beings. These investigations must use methods that are logical and unbiased. This should produce results which can be reproduced consistently (again and again, in the same way) by other scientists.

Interviewer: So then, people in business who read about the psychological research on the buying behaviour of customers and then use this knowledge to make business decisions...

Psychologist: ...are not psychologists. They may, however, benefit from the knowledge that we've gained.

Interviewer: Why learn about psychology?

Psychologist: Well, it's an occupation for me, but it is useful for all sorts of people. Knowledge about how people generally act and feel in a given situation can help people to predict how others will react. This can assist them to deal more effectively with others.

The ability to predict also suggests that we can control human behaviour and feelings. Some people call this manipulation and consider it dangerous. I personally feel that some people can live happier and better lives if they discover how to control their feelings and reactions.

For example, let's say that I am treating someone who fears leaving his or her own home. I can use my knowledge to reduce or eliminate this fear, which will allow him or her to get back into a normal, active life. So you see, control is not always a bad thing. Knowledge, prediction and control of our behaviour can help us lead more satisfying lives.

From Ideas to Action

1. In your notebook, develop a one-page chart to organize information about the three social sciences. You may wish to use the sample chart below. Fill in the section of your chart dealing with psychology.

Categories of Comparison	Psychology	Sociology	Anthropology
Definition (Focus)			
Activities			
Use of Knowledge			

2. Which of the following questions would a psychologist ask? Explain your answer by referring to the definition (focus) of psychology.
   a) How does a person's level of education relate to the power she or he has in society?
   b) What is the effect of repeated child abuse on its victims?
   c) Does punishment change behaviour?
   d) Are human beings instinctively aggressive?

3. Develop at least two questions that a psychologist might ask about each of the following instances of human behaviour:
   a) People will slow down their cars to get a glimpse of an accident in the opposite lane of a highway.
   b) Some people who have been through major wars get jumpy or even hysterical when sudden, loud noises occur.

4. Look again at the pictures on pages 42 and 43 of this chapter.
   a) Identify those pictures that would interest a psychologist and briefly explain why.
   b) What questions might a psychologist ask about each of your selections?

5. Choose some aspect of your own behaviour that you would like explained. Develop a series of focus questions that a psychologist might ask about this behaviour.

The Sociologist

How Are These Questions Similar?

- How is the family important to a person's social development?
- What factors cause increases in the crime rate in a society?
- What role do schools play in our society?
- How does the social class system in Canada affect our society?
- What happens when people of different ethnic backgrounds live close to each other in a crowded inner city area?

All of the questions above are ones that might be asked by sociologists. Compare these questions with the ones that psychologists ask. Read on to find out how the sociologist with whom we talked sees her job.

Interview with a Sociologist

Interviewer: What does "sociology" mean to you?

Sociologist: The term "sociology" is actually a recent invention. It was coined by the French philosopher Auguste Comte in the mid 1800s. Like many people of his time, he was worried about the effects of the rapid expansion of industry resulting from the Industrial Revolution. People were flooding into the cities to work in the new factories. This led to overcrowding, crime, poverty and, ultimately, to unemployment and social unrest. These problems affected all of society in one way or another.

Because of this early history, the focus of scientists like Comte was on *groups* of people rather than on individuals. From this base came the discipline

Using the Text as a Resource —

The purpose of this exercise is to see if you can use your text effectively. Read sentences 1 to 6 and choose the correct answer.

1. In order to find information on major topics or subtopics in a text, you would look at:
   a) the bibliography b) the index c) the title page(s) d) the table of contents

2. On what pages would you begin to look for information on the following topics:
   a) depression b) alienation c) robotics

3. If you wanted to know when the authors wrote this text you would look at:
   a) the bibliography b) the index c) the copyright page d) the table of contents

4. In order to find information on a *specific* item, idea or person you would look at:
   a) the bibliography b) the index c) the title page(s) d) the table of contents

5. On what pages would you find information on:
   a) field experiments b) Lawrence Kohlberg c) defense mechanisms

6. If you wanted to find other sources, books or articles on a topic you found interesting in this text, you would look at:
   a) the bibliography b) the index c) the title page(s) d) the table of contents

of sociology. Sociologists have always wanted to know what social groups people belong to, why they choose to belong to certain groups, and how they behave while in them. In its most simple form, sociology is the study of how two or more people interact with each other.

Interviewer: You say that you focus on "groups." Please give some examples.

Sociologist: I read your interview with a psychologist. If I compare my interests with those of the psychologist, it might help. He referred to the case of a murderer. The psychologist asks questions designed to get inside the head of that person and others like him or her. Psychologists want to know what makes these individuals tick. They are less concerned about the larger society in which the crime took place.

Well, my interest is society. I want to know how the neighbourhood crime rates have affected the community's feelings, attitudes and actions as a whole. I would research to find out if this sort of case is a national trend, and, if so, how it compares with other countries similar to ours. I would also want to compare the families of convicted murderers to see if there is something common in their backgounds. So you see, it's not individuals but the characteristics of groups, such as families, friends and neighbourhoods, that are of greatest concern to me.

Interviewer: What do sociologists do?

Sociologist: Most of the work I do involves teaching and research. Like the psychologist, I consider it my primary responsibility to use scientific methods to discover general laws of human behaviour. But, in my case, I am interested in human social behaviour, rather than individual behaviour.

What is done with sociological knowledge varies. Like all knowledge generated by social scientists, some of it is written up and published, and is read by other sociologists. Publishing the results of studies makes a valuable contribution to the knowledge of the subject as a whole. But, most important, the results of sociological research can have a real impact on the way people live.

The field of sociology is subdivided into a number of areas that study important social problems. For instance, I am a **social pathologist**. Basically, I study social problems such as crime, delinquency, poverty and racial discrimination. Some of my work has influenced politicians and other decision-makers. They've taken my studies and used them to develop new laws or programs designed to solve some of these serious problems.

Interviewer: You spoke of "a number of areas" in the field of sociology. What are some of these?

Sociologist: Well, **urban sociologists** study the stresses and strains that growing cities have placed on our society. They dig up statistics to see if there are patterns to the sorts of things that happen to city-dwellers that make them distinct from other people. They also try to find out how certain social problems have been created by the rapid growth of cities. Their work can be vital to city planners and politicians. **Criminologists** study the causes of crime and how laws affect society. Their work can be very important not only to law-makers but also to the police.

The psychologist told you that there were industrial psychologists who look into the way the workplace affects individual workers. There are also **industrial sociologists**. They research the group relationships in factories and other businesses. Their studies provide helpful information so that industries can improve worker relations and profit at the same time.

There are many other subdivisions of sociology. However, they all have one thing in common: a desire to find out how and why humans behave as they do when they are in groups. The knowledge that we achieve can affect large numbers of people for the better.

Interviewer: Why study sociology?

Sociologist: The knowledge of sociology can be useful to everyone. We are all born into various groups: family, social class, ethnic group, friends, neighbourhood, city and country. If we know how these groups work, we can better understand our own feelings and actions, and those of the people with whom we interact.

This can be important if we find group interactions difficult or even if we just want to improve the quality of our relationships. I am sure that the students who read my comments have all had some conflicts or disappointments while being part of a group. Perhaps they have had an argument with their mother or father, or have wanted to be liked by their friends. An understanding of the groups in which these events occur can at least make life bearable and may even lead to a way of improving things.

. . . .

From Ideas to Action

1. Add "sociology" to the chart you made previously comparing the social sciences. Make sure you include information about the definition (focus), activities and use of the knowledge of sociology.

2. Which of the following statements would a sociologist make? Explain your answers by referring to the definition (focus) of sociology.
   a) According to research studies, the social class you are born into in Canada seems to suggest the type of job you will be able to get.
   b) In democratic countries, decisions about peoples' behaviour are made by both the state and the individual.
   c) Suicide rates in Canada are lowest in Newfoundland and highest in the Northwest Territories.
   d) Adult prisons may not be a good place for young offenders because there is solid evidence that prisons become "schools for crime."
   e) In order for a student to remember the content of a lesson, learning must be fun.
   f) The most powerful human motivation is the desire and pursuit of pleasure.

3. Look again at the pictures on page 00 of this chapter. Which pictures would be most interesting to a sociologist? Why?

4. Make a list of all the groups of which you are a member. List one or two questions that you would want to ask about each of the groups if you were a sociologist.

5. Imagine that you are a sociologist. You are having a conversation with a psychologist about the following actual case. List all the questions that *each of you* might ask about the case.

At 11:45 one August evening, two police officers were trying to arrest a man seen drinking outside a local arena. The man struggled and began to fight. Within minutes, a crowd of over 300 gathered, drawn from the dance in the arena and from a nearby party. Outnumbered and afraid of attack, the police officers called for help from the crowd. No one came to the aid of the officers and the crowd would not let the officers reach their cruiser. Eventually police from two nearby detachments arrived to assist the outnumbered officers and by 12:30 a.m. two men were arrested and charged with assault.

The Anthropologist

Anthropologists at Work

All of the pictures below show anthropologists studying human beings. How does their work compare with the work of psychologists and sociologists?

Margaret Mead, world renowned American anthropologist, at work in Samoa.

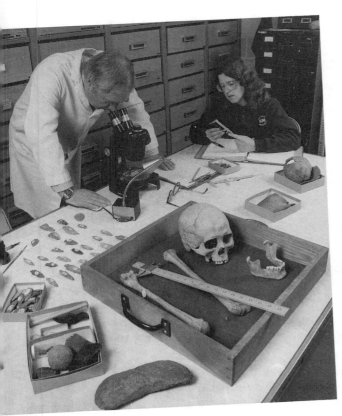

Interview with an Anthropologist

The person who consented to talk with us about the social science of anthropology is now retired. Like most anthropologists, she has seen parts of the world that most people only dream about or see on television. You will discover how her experiences and interests compare with those of psychologists and sociologists.

Anthropologists study human beings in their diverse cultures.

Interviewer: What does "anthropology" mean to you?

Anthropologist: I think it interesting that you have decided to interview me last. Finishing with anthropology makes sense. Psychology is the study of individuals in all of their aspects; sociology is the study of society in all of its aspects; and anthropology is the study of *humankind* in all of its aspects. It's like an onion with its various layers. Anthropology is the outermost layer of the sciences dealing with human behaviour. It has the broadest scope of all.

Interviewer: What do you mean by the "broadest scope"?

Anthropologist: Anthropologists are concerned with all the varieties of human beings existing today, not just the ones closest to home. We are also interested in all periods in history. We begin with the earliest people, millions of years ago, and trace the development of our species right to the present. We not only compare large groups of people, but we also look at their histories.

For example, I spent about a year living with a tribe of people in a rain forest in Brazil. I learned their language. I found out about their customs and beliefs by observing and participating in their daily life. I even developed a certain fondness for cooked insects.

I researched the history of these people through their own stories and I looked over the accounts written by explorers and others, dating back several hundred years. I asked questions and found out about the tribe's social system, religion, dress, customs and the general features of their language. I also noted how their culture had changed over time and offered explanations for those changes.

As you can see, it was not just one snapshot, but the total picture, recorded with as much accuracy, and as little bias, as I could. I then wrote and published my findings, describing and analysing all the aspects of the tribe's life.

To use another example, let's look at the case of the murderer that the psychologist and sociologist discussed. As an anthropologist, I would look for answers to this situation in the attitudes towards violence and authority in western civilization. I might trace the origins of these attitudes into the past as far as I could. I might even compare these attitudes to the views of other cultures on the same subjects elsewhere in the world.

Interviewer: You have given some idea of what *you* did as an anthropologist. Would this be a good description of what all anthropologists do?

Anthropologist: My work was only a part of what anthropologists do. As I've already mentioned, the scope of anthropology is very broad. This has resulted in the development of specialties within the field of anthropology.

At the highest level, anthropology divides into two broad areas of interest. The first is **cultural anthropology,** which generally concerns itself with the ways of thinking and acting that are customary within certain large groups of people.

Cultural anthropology subdivides further into specialties. I, for example, am an **ethnologist. Ethnology,** as you've probably gathered by what I've done, is the study and analysis of the total culture of a particular people: for example, the Cree of Northern Ontario. Ethnologists tend to restrict their activities to societies that do not possess a written language. We usually leave the study of modern, complex societies to the sociologists.

Ethnology usually involves a great deal of travel to places that rarely appear in holiday brochures. You have to participate in the daily life of the people you are studying in order to understand them. This is what I have spent

most of my working life doing — walking around in other peoples' shoes for a while to see how the world looks to them.

Among the other branches of cultural anthropology is **archaeology**. Archaeologists usually study the artifacts or material remains of people who generally no longer exist. Their goal is to reconstruct the customs of these people from such things as pieces of tools, bones from food and burials, and pieces of discarded cloth.

It may sound as though archaeologists study other peoples' garbage. Actually, what people choose to throw out can tell us a great deal about them and their daily lives. In fact, I know of one university professor who teaches archaeology by having his students dig up and analyse local garbage dumps. After all, 2000 years from now what you throw in the trash heap may find its way into a museum as an excellent example of our culture.

Interviewer: And what about the second broad area of interest in anthropology?

55

Scientists Fooled!

The customs, language and artifacts of the Tasadays, a stone-age society living in a remote area of the Philippines, had been the focus of very intensive study by anthropologists. Teams of social scientists descended on these people to research what appeared to be a rare example of early human culture.

However, in February 1986, the government of Ferdinand Marcos of the Philippines fell. When it was replaced by a new government, previously secret files were made available to the public.

The files provided evidence that the Tasadays were really local farmers recruited by the government to play the role of a primitive tribe. They simply acted in a way that anthropologists expected a stone-age group might behave. As a result, the Tasadays were widely written about and filmed.

The Philippine government had hoped that the hoax would boost a sagging tourist industry and also make the Philippines one of the most important anthropological sites in the world (which it did).

Needless to say, the whole affair has left some anthropologists a little red-faced. However, on the positive side, it has served to emphasize the importance of doing thorough scientific research when studying human behaviour. Clearly, social scientists must not only record and analyse what they are observing, but must also question whether the observations themselves are true.

Anthropologist: It's called **physical anthropology**. This field is a very large one, but it is relatively easy to define. It focuses on the evolution of human beings. Beginning millions of years ago, human beings have undergone a great many physical changes. For example, it is generally agreed that we began walking on "all fours" and that gradually we began to walk upright. This process required drastic changes in the bones of the body. Physical anthropologists study physical remains — bones and skeletons — to give us a picture of how and why our species has changed physically over time.

Interviewer: Why study anthropology?

Anthropologist: I can only speak for myself. I think that all the various branches of anthropology contribute to our understanding of ourselves as human beings. I feel that since I live in such a small part of the world, during such a tiny period of time in history, I run the risk of having a very narrow view of human beings.

I am curious to know about other people alive today, or in the past, in different geographic locations, and their ways of living. This helps me to realize that ours is not the only way to do things. In short, it teaches me to tolerate others. It also helps me to appreciate the richness and beauty of human culture.

From Ideas to Action

1. Complete your chart comparing the three major social sciences. Make sure you include information about the definition (focus), activities and uses of the knowledge of anthropology.

2. Which of the following questions would be asked by an anthropologist? Explain your answers by referring to the definition (focus) of anthropology.
   a) How does marriage in North America compare with the same practice in China?
   b) What problems does poverty create in Canada today?
   c) At what point in history has evidence of human religious expression been found?
   d) Does one person interpret an event in the same way another person does?
   e) Do all societies forbid marriage among close relatives?

3. Examine your comparison chart and use it to develop another chart that lists ways in which the social sciences that study human behaviour are similar or different. (This can be done by reading your chart across.)

4. If you were an anthropologist, would you want to be a physical anthropologist or a cultural anthropologist? In a paragraph, explain your answer by referring to the kinds of things that these people do.

Fact, Opinion and Argument — Level 2

SKILLS

The aim of this exercise is to reinforce your understanding of the differences among statements of fact, opinion and argument, and to give you practice in detecting these different kinds of statements.

Examine the definitions below. In your notebook, write whether they define a fact, an opinion or an argument.
1. Vague views that are unproved
2. Reasons one offers to reject a viewpoint
3. Exact things that can be proved
4. Reasons given to prove your side of the case
5. Specific things that can be investigated and shown to be true
6. Beliefs one has that are not established by evidence

After you have discussed the correct answers with your teacher, read the statements below. Determine if they are facts, opinions or arguments. Write your choices in your notebook.
1. Clinical psychologists work in hospitals or clinics, where they diagnose and treat mental illnesses and emotional problems.
2. Pyschology is a much more exciting social science than sociology or anthropology.
3. The word "psychology' comes from two Greek words: *psyche* meaning "mind" and *logos* meaning "the study of."
4. Educational psychologists should work in schools because they can improve the way that teachers and students work together.

5. Sociology grew out of peoples' interest in the social problems of emerging industrial societies in Europe in the 1800s.
6. Sociology can help us get along with people better.
7. Archaeology is a branch of cultural anthropology that studies the material remains of societies that no longer exist.
8. Anthropology is an exciting social science because it usually involves travelling to faraway places and observing different cultures.
9. Anthropology only appeals to people who are interested in living with primitive tribes in jungles.

Social Science and the Work World

What careers exist in the social sciences? Look carefully at the pictures. What job is each person doing? Of what possible use might an understanding of human behaviour be in each of these jobs? Can you see yourself in any of these occupations?

Social scientists are mainly interested in finding out about human behaviour. This has led some people to assume that if one studies "behavioural science," one must be a professional scientist. This is not true. Actually, an understanding of what makes people behave the way they do is very useful in all sorts of interesting jobs that do not require the training necessary to become a scientist.

If you are interested in exploring this further, read the following sections. Your school guidance department can provide you with pamphlets describing specific jobs. Your counsellor can also give you interest inventories designed to give you an idea of your skills and abilities. This information can then be matched with certain careers.

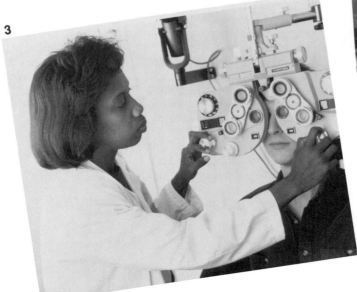

5

6

7

59

A Future Career?

The diagram below is called a career web. It shows only a small number of occupations having an interest in human behaviour as a central feature. Three jobs from the career web are described in detail. You may not want to become a sociologist, but it is important to know what studying sociology can offer you for your future career. The same applies to the other two branches of the social sciences.

Job: Immigration Officer

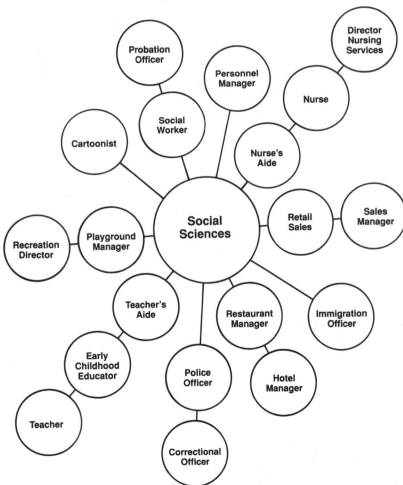

Nature of the Work:

- Interviewing newcomers who wish to stay and make Canada their home
- Reviewing applications of people already in Canada
- Reviewing applications from Canadians who wish to sponsor someone from another country

Training:

- At least two years of high school education
- Experience in any kind of work that involves dealing with people in a firm but sensitive manner (e.g. retail sales return desks)
- Once hired, there is a short training course and then on-the-job training under supervision.

Qualifications:

- An ability to meet people and to treat them with patience and understanding
- An ability to be unbiased and fair
- An ability to ask questions clearly and to adapt to the applicants' needs

Job: Hotel Manager

Nature of the Work:

- Working with and supervising a range of different staff — sales and convention departments, rooms division, financial and accounts departments, advertising and public relations staff, housekeeping, food and beverage departments, personnel
- In large hotels duties are often divided among a number of managers.

Training:

- Previous experience in housekeeping or at the front desk of a hotel, perhaps as a summer job
- Formal training in community colleges that offer courses in Hospitality Services, Hotel Management or Travel and Tourism

Qualifications:

- Must be a willing learner in order to master all the aspects of running a good hotel
- Must have an understanding of people and an ability to be flexible with them
- Must be well organized
- Must be a problem-solver and a decision-maker

Job: Police Officer

Nature of the Work:

- The prevention of crime and protection of property
- Arresting offenders
- Directing traffic

Structure of Police Forces:

- Administrative branch: sets budgets and keeps the department running smoothly (Many employees are not police officers but people with training in administration, finance and computers.)
- Staff operations: controls communication, special investigations and identification; provides services to officers on the streets
- Field operations: comprises all uniformed, traffic and detective personnel in the department (80 per cent of the staff in the average department; has the most contact with the public.)
- Advancement: recruits begin in field operations (Some departments have a "cadet system" that allows young people, aged 17 to 20, who are interested in police work to do routine police activities in the department itself.)

Training:

- Successful completion of at least four years of high school
- General knowledge of Canadian and world affairs (An entrance test that focuses on these subjects is usually required.)
- Some business training, particularly in shorthand and keyboarding
- experience in jobs that require a great deal of contact with the public

Qualifications:

Here are the qualifications listed by some city police forces in Canada.

- Canadian citizen or British subject
- 21 to 35 years of age
- Height and weight standards (This varies from department to department.)
- Passing a physical exam
- Good moral character and habits
- Personality characteristics, such as a sense of humour, and the ability to remain calm in disaster situations and to maintain control over emotions
- An ability to live with an organization that stresses discipline and respect for orders, procedures and authority

Projects, Activities and Explorations

1. Begin a clipping file of newspaper items (photographs, articles, headlines, advertisements and cartoons) that show something about human behaviour. Clip something each day. At the end of each week, present your "item of the week" to the class. Explain to the class which of the social scientists discussed in this book would be most interested in your item and why you chose to present it.

2. Research the life and work of a famous social scientist. The following people are only a sample of many scientists who have contributed to our understanding of human behaviour.
a) Margaret Mead, b) Emile Durkheim, c) Louis or David Leakey, d) Sigmund Freud, e) Auguste Comte, f) Abraham Maslow

3. Create a collage or a mobile to show the focus and activities of the three social sciences that you have learned about in this chapter.

4. Select an isolated society that would be of interest to an anthropologist. Research the society's way of life. Present your findings to the class on bristol board.

5. Role-play the following situation. A psychologist, a sociologist and an anthropologist are asked to debate the question: "Which of the three major behavioural sciences provides the most useful information about human behaviour — psychology, sociology or anthropology?"

6. Discuss how a knowledge of behavioural science is used by advertisers to get you to buy certain products.

7. Ask your guidance counsellor for such career aids as the *Strong-Campbell Interest Inventory, The Career Factory* (a computer program) or the SGIS *(Student Guidance Information Service)*. When you have all the information that you can get from these, ask for detailed job descriptions for occupations related to your interests and abilities. These can be obtained from your guidance counsellor. Share the results of your research with the rest of the class or with a small group of students.

8. If possible, arrange to visit someone doing a job in which you are interested. Take photographs of people working at this job and prepare a photo-collage and a written description for display in your class. Include an outline of qualifications, training and salary.

What Have You Learned?

If you have covered everything in this chapter, you should be familiar with the following topics:
1. Three major ways to study human behaviour: psychology, sociology and anthropology
2. The focus of psychologists
3. The activities of different kinds of psychologists
4. The focus of sociologists
5. The activities of different kinds of sociologists
6. The focus of anthropologists
7. The activities of different kinds of anthropologists
8. Some occupations available for people with an interest in human behaviour

To Help You Study

The following chart will help you to review the words, facts and ideas that were introduced in this chapter. Copy the chart into your notebook and fill in the missing information.

Word, Fact, Idea	Example in a Sentence	Page	Definition
psychology	Psychology is a major social science studying human thoughts emotions and behaviour.	45	scientific study of the human mind
sociology			
anthropology			
clinical psychologist			
experimental psychologist			
educational psychologist			
industrial psychology			
social pathologist			
urban sociologist			
criminologist			
industrial sociologist			
cultural anthropology			
ethnology			
archaeology			
physical anthropology			

Communication

4

How Many Ways Can You Communicate?

In small groups, see how many different ways you can "say" the following things: rebellion, peace, happiness. Be imaginative! Use speech, but also suggest symbols, gestures, body language, facial expressions, pictures, clothes or music that communicate the meaning of the three words.

When your group has at least five ways of communicating each item, share your ideas with the rest of the class. Then answer the following questions:

1. Did each group think of some ways to communicate that were different from the ways in the other groups? If so, why?

2. Were most of your group's ways of communicating *verbal* (using words) or *non-verbal* (using pictures, facial expressions, music, etc.)? Why?

3. Do you think people in other countries could understand your ways of communicating? Why or why not?

By now you probably realize that communication is very complex. This chapter will focus on communication goals; that is, on why and how we communicate, both verbally and non-verbally. It will also look at the role of culture in human communication, as well as the different ways in which communication can break down.

The Goals of Communication

Examine the communication events described below and see if you can figure out why each took place.

a) Rajesh told Danny about the sprained ankle he got playing squash.
b) Nick watched a commercial on TV.
c) Carmela told her friends how great her new stereo was and how lucky she was to have such an expensive sound system.
d) Anne called her girlfriend and suggested going to a movie together.
e) Suzanne complained loudly that she was freezing.
f) Harry read Chapter 10 in his history textbook.
g) Aryta spoke for 20 minutes at her job interview.
h) Carol smiled at Tony as he walked back to his desk with his essay.
i) Rebecca told her sister she looked terrific in her new outfit.
j) François warned his younger brother about the drop-offs in the lake.

When you have figured out the goal, or purpose, of each communication event, discuss your findings with your classmates. Then answer the following questions:

1. How many different types of goals did you identify?
2. Did any of the events have more than one possible goal?
3. Can you think of any reasons for communicating that were not included in the events described above?

Why Do We Communicate?

Human beings share with many animals the need to communicate about **physical needs.** We need food, warmth and safety in order to survive.

Many of our most basic communications are survival-level messages. A calf butts its mother's udder to show its hunger; the mother responds by letting her milk flow. A human baby quickly learns that a cry brings food and attention from parents or caregivers.

Some animals, including human beings, also communicate to satisfy **social needs**. We need to feel loved and accepted. We need to feel that we belong to someone or to a group, as most popular song lyrics tell us. The purpose of much of our communication is to strengthen social bonds. Your long conversations on the telephone or in the school cafeteria are ways of saying to your friends: "I support you. I want to help you." Your friends' responses provide you with the same reassurance. A light slap on the back is another way of expressing friendship and support.

Another social goal satisfied by communication is the need to teach, persuade or control. Your teachers, for example, discuss with their students not just subject matter, but also attitudes, opinions and values. Teachers, counsellors, religious leaders and parents try

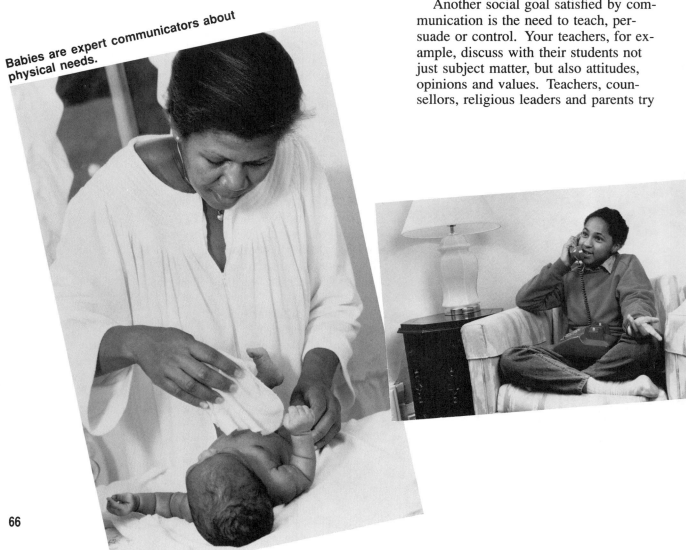

Babies are expert communicators about physical needs.

An important part of human communication is expressing the need to love and be loved.

Acceptance and approval of our individuality is vital to satisfying our ego needs.

to communicate certain social values to the next generation, so that the young may learn to control their behaviour according to these values. Advertisers promoting products to teenagers communicate not only information about the product, but also the promise of popularity and acceptance by one's peer group. Teenagers are not always at the receiving end of persuasion and teaching. They too try to influence their friends, parents, teachers and co-workers.

The third goal of communication is to satisfy **ego needs** — what we need to feel good about ourselves and our behaviour. Each of us wants to be accepted as a member of a group, but at the same time we want to be accepted as individuals, distinct from the group. We want others to understand and confirm that our personal struggles are worthwhile. We seek support from others for decisions we have made: for example, accepting a new job or moving away from home, especially if we feel insecure about the decision. Acceptance and approval are vital ego needs, especially during the sometimes stressful teen years.

Many teenagers experience a lot of frustration of their ego needs. The classic example of this is the "put-down": "Don't do that, you look like a nerd," or "I don't like her, she's weird." Putdowns are not intended to persuade or teach. They are intended to destroy an individual's sense of self-worth and to force that person to conform to some other behaviour.

People of any age feel pain when their value as an individual is rejected. Teenagers, however, are particularly sensitive to criticism. You are already torn between needing and wanting group approval, and needing to be recognized as an individual. Put-downs are hard on your self-esteem, your view of yourself.

67

From Ideas to Action

1. For each situation below, suggest the main goal or purpose of communication:
   a) a marriage proposal
   b) discussing last night's football game with your friends
   c) complaining to your mother about your sore throat
   d) asking your friend's advice about a new girl/boy friend
   e) asking your boss for a raise
   f) checking the newspaper for grocery prices
   g) listening to your sister's disappointment
   h) two runners talking about how they try to reach their personal best
   i) making fun of a classmate who wants to learn French

2. Keep a written record of your longer conversations for a day or so. (This record does not have to be a word-for-word account.) Make a chart in which you record the names of participants, the topics and the goals of these conversations. What are the most common goals of everyday communication?

3. Select a dialogue from a TV serial (use a VCR if you like), or from a play or novel you are reading. Using the chart you made in question 2, analyse the communication goals in the dialogue.

4. How do you generally cope with put-downs, or other kinds of rejection of ego needs? Try to identify both positive and negative reactions to frustration of ego needs. (Think of your own reactions, and those of your friends, in situations in which ego needs were not met.)

How Do We Communicate?

In small groups, play charades. Take turns communicating messages, without saying or writing anything. (Your teacher will secretly tell the first player in each group, and no one else, what the message is.)

Sample Messages:
- "I love tennis and jogging."
- "You're terrific!"
- "I'm bored."
- "Hi! Make yourself at home!"

Now share your experiences with the rest of the class and answer the following questions:

1. Were you able to send all the messages successfully by non-verbal means? What does this suggest about human communication?

2. What kinds of non-verbal communication did you use? Are there other kinds of non-verbal communication you could have used?

3. What percentage of human communication would you estimate is verbal and what percentage is non-verbal? Why do you think so?

The illustration at right demonstrates how human communication takes place. It shows a typical "communication loop." The model applies to both verbal and non-verbal communication. Notice that communication takes place inside each person's frame of reference (all the experiences gained from one's culture, family, religion, education, friends and interests).

We see or hear the message, "You're welcome here!" We then interpret it from our own viewpoint and send a message (a smile) in return to let the first communicator know that we have understood. The last step in the communication process (in this model, a smile) is called **feedback**. Feedback is a verbal or non-verbal response to a message received.

Verbal and Non-verbal Communication

You have seen that there are many ways of communicating with each other. We are most familiar with verbal communication, that involving spoken language. The verbal part of a message, however, is often only a small part of the overall communication. One study found that non-verbal communication made up 93 per cent of the message!

Non-verbal communication has many sources. The most important source is body language. This is the way we use posture, facial expressions, eye movements, gestures and tone of voice to enrich a verbal message. We quickly learn the difference between "Oh, great!" said with a smile, "Oh, great!" said with the eyes rolled upward, and "Oh, great!" said with clenched teeth. You can observe that people usually answer a question first with body language, then with words. Try asking a friend, "Do you like fish?" or "Are you right- or left-handed?" and see if you observe a physical response first.

Use of "social space" is another source of non-verbal communication. Our culture establishes a certain social distance for both casual and formal conversations. Our language reflects this social distance. People who are emotionally close stand physically close to each other. When a relationship is more distant and formal, people stand further apart. If you can say, "He (or she) is a close friend of mine," then you can comfortably cross the invisible social space barrier accepted in your culture.

 Try This Social Distance Experiment.

To demonstrate the importance of social distance, try moving into the social space of someone you don't know very well. Don't be offensive and don't barge into a conversation, but move gently and gradually toward another person over the span of a few minutes. Your behaviour may cause the other person to back right out of the room!

We can also use objects as cues or "props" in non-verbal communication. In some conversations, furniture can play a part in the message. When your principal speaks to you from behind an imposing walnut desk, the message conveyed is different from one in which the principal stands beside the desk or sits casually on its edge.

Besides using physical space and distance, we often communicate by touching one another in appropriate ways. A gentle touch on the arm may convey a great deal of information not easily communicated in verbal form.

 To Touch or Not to Touch?

Recent experiments have tried to gauge the effect of touching in social settings. One experiment examined how touching or not touching the customers in a restaurant affected tips earned by waitresses. (These women were really university psychology students.) Waitresses who touched customers on the upper arm or elbow received much higher tips than those who either touched customers on the shoulder, or did not touch them at all.

Smell is a form of non-verbal communication that we sometimes prefer to ignore! Consumers spend millions of dollars each year to suppress natural body odour and replace it with manufactured scents. The marketing of these deodorants, perfumes and colognes is based on their ability to send messages to others. Certain scents can signal, for example, a healthy, outdoor lifestyle or a chic, seductive personality.

Symbolic Communication

Besides verbal and non-verbal communication, we also use symbolic communication. As you learned in Chapter 1, a symbol is an object, word, action, etc., that a group of people has created to represent something else. We use symbols constantly in everyday life. A plus sign (+) indicates a certain arithmetic operation. A red, six-sided sign communicates a particular message to drivers.

Clothing, jewelry and insignia such as badges can communicate symbolic meanings in our society. Brides traditionally wear white to symbolize purity, for example. People in business wear conservative suits to symbolize a serious, responsible attitude toward their work. Punkers dress in black and decorate themselves with razor blades and safety pins. What does this choice of dress say about them and how they see the world? Uniforms can communicate what a person's role is. We can then respond to that person appropriately. We probably behave differently toward a police officer when he or she wears street clothes rather than a uniform. Similarly, an officer in the armed forces wears insignia: a gold braid on the sleeve, shoulder epaulets and oak leaves on the hat. These symbols communicate high rank, which entitles the officer to respect and obedience from others.

Women in business often adopt the standard business uniform: a business suit and shirt.

From Ideas to Action

1. Identify the kinds of communication (verbal, non-verbal, symbolic) involved in the following situations. (There may be more than one kind of communication involved.)
   a) a boy and girl holding hands
   b) two people sitting side by side, legs crossed away from each other, arms crossed, etc.
   c) a mother gazing at her new-born infant
   d) two people obviously shouting and gesturing at each other
   e) Brian Mulroney holding hands with Ronald Reagan

2. Select a favourite television program and turn off the sound. Write down the various non-verbal ways in which the people in the program communicate.

3. Set up an unusual conversation with a partner. Arrange two chairs so that you are back to back and cannot see one another. What difficulties do you encounter during your conversation?

4. Have another conversation with a friend, but avoid eye contact with the other person. (Do not tell your friend that you're doing this deliberately.) After a few minutes, ask your friend how he or she felt during the conversation.

5. Watch a rock group live or on television. (A VCR might be handy for reviewing television footage.) Carefully analyse how the group's movements, clothing, lighting and other effects communicate certain messages. Now listen closely to the lyrics. Do the verbal and non-verbal messages match?

How To Write an Expository Paragraph — Level 1

The purpose of this exercise is to show you the main parts of an **expository paragraph**. This type of paragraph is used to explain something or to reinforce a viewpoint. The expository paragraph is commonly used by social scientists.

In the right-hand column below you will see an analysis of the expository paragraph presented on the left. Study these main parts as they appear in the sample paragraph.

Read the tips for writing topic sentences and concluding sentences. Then write a topic sentence, two supporting statements, and a concluding statement on a topic of your choice.

Example of an Expository Paragraph

Human beings have developed many verbal and non-verbal ways to communicate. We can speak and write in many different languages. We also use gestures and facial expressions, such as smiles and frowns, to tell others how we feel. Sometimes the kinds of clothes we wear tell others about our occupations. A business suit and an army uniform communicate different things. Our tastes in music, whether rock, country and western, new wave or punk, communicate messages about our values and interests. This variety of communication demonstrates the amazing complexity and creativity of human culture.

Main Parts of an Expository Paragraph

Topic Sentence
(statement of the paragraph's main purpose or idea)

Body of Supporting Statements
(explanations, arguments, facts or examples that reinforce what you are trying to prove)

Concluding Sentence
(summary of what your paragraph is trying to prove)

Analysis of an Expository Paragraph

Human beings have developed many verbal and non-verbal ways to communicate.

We can speak and write in many different languages. We also use gestures and facial expressions, such as smiles and frowns, to tell others how we feel. Sometimes the kinds of clothes we wear tell others about our occupations. A business suit and an army uniform communicate different things. Our tastes in music, whether rock, country and western, new wave or punk, communicate messages about our values and interests.

This variety of communication demonstrates the amazing complexity and creativity of human culture.

Writing Tips

Topic Sentences
Start with a *definite* point of view rather than a vague statement or idea.

Concluding Sentences
Whenever possible, try to use your concluding sentence to reinforce both your topic sentence and the argument you developed in your paragraph.

Examples of Topic Sentences
• You can often tell things about a person just from his or her clothing.

Examples of Concluding Sentences
• Since clothes often communicate clues about our occupations, interests or attitudes, we should choose the right clothes for the right occasion.

• Students' body language and facial expressions often tell a teacher more about the success of a lesson than do words.

• If teachers observe the expressions and body language of their students, they can improve their lessons and maintain student interest.

73

Communication and Culture

Brainstorm About Teenage Culture

As you no doubt realize, teenagers have their own culture, including words, signs, symbols and gestures that are often unfamiliar to their parents. In small groups brainstorm ten items to complete a chart like the one set up below. (One example has been provided. Your teacher will assign one person in your group to copy the chart.)

Here are some guidelines for brainstorming:

1. Write down every suggestion offered by the members of your group.
2. Do not stop to discuss the suggestions.
3. Do not evaluate the suggestions. Assume that every suggestion could lead to something useful.

Word, Sign, Symbol or Gesture	Meaning to Teenager	Meaning to Parent
rad	radical, great, terrific	radiator for a car or house

When your group has filled in the chart, share your items with the rest of the class. Then answer the following questions:

1. Was it difficult to think of ten items? Explain.
2. Would teenagers in other English-speaking countries know the meaning of the items you thought of? Why or why not?
3. What does this exercise reveal about the importance of culture in communication? Explain.

Cultural Differences and Verbal Communication

All human beings speak, hear, think and imagine within the setting of their own culture. Not all cultures can express certain ideas in language. Canada's Inuit have at least 35 different words for snow conditions, while only about ten words for snow conditions exist in English. Early French-speaking Canadians coined a word, *poudrerie*, meaning "dry, blowing snow," This word has no meaning in France because the climate doesn't produce such conditions.

Idioms, or ways of saying things that are unique to a language or culture, are difficult for learners of a second language to master. This is because idioms often arise from a certain historical context that the language learner (and sometimes even a native speaker) does not understand. For example, the expression "dead as a doornail" comes from the rough carpentry practices of our ancestors. If a nail protruded through a door under construction, pioneers would simply bend the tip of the nail and drive it flat to ensure a tight hold. Now, the expression refers to anything lifeless. As the previous brainstorming exercise shows, even idioms in one's own language are not always clearly understood by all the speakers of that language.

Cultural Differences and Non-verbal Communication

Cultural influences colour almost every aspect of non-verbal communication. North Americans, for example, often find the social distance displayed by South Americans in conversation to be uncomfortably close. South Americans are sometimes offended by the greater social distance preferred by North Americans, whom they often view as cold and aloof.

In most cultures, touching conveys strong emotional messages. However, the types of touching appropriate in one culture may be considered offensive in another. With the exception of shaking hands, touching in North American conversations is infrequent, occurring only between relatives and close friends. Males in North America are especially sensitive to being touched by other males, although football players allow bottom-patting and hugging when touchdowns are scored. Football players would be horrified if kissed fully on the lips by a Russian athlete. Russians consider such behaviour a normal and healthy form of congratulating someone, whether male or female.

North Americans are taught to look someone "right in the eye" when conversing. "Looking someone in the eye" is considered a sign of honesty. (Scientific studies have shown, by the way, that people who practise steady eye contact are not necessarily truthful.)

In some cultures, however, eye contact between people of different social ranks is strictly forbidden. In New Zealand, for example, the Maori people believe that those in a lower social position must look away when addressing those of a higher social rank.

Gestures vary widely from culture to culture as well. In North America, nodding the head signifies approval or agreement. We move our heads sideways to signal disagreement or disapproval. In parts of Central Africa, these gestures have the *opposite* meaning!

Different Meaning in Different Cultures

A classic example of a gesture meaning different things in different cultures involved the crew of the U.S. ship, *Pueblo*, captured off North Korea in the late 1960s. North Korea accused the ship of spying. Naturally, Americans at home were worried about the safety and welfare of the *Pueblo*'s crew.

The North Korean captors forced the crew to pose for propaganda photos to make the Americans appear well-treated and in good health. The prisoners obliged, but each one posed with his middle finger pointing upwards. The North Koreans released the photos, not understanding the defiance communicated by the Americans' obscene gesture.

Cultural Differences and Symbols

Some symbols convey powerful messages within a particular culture at a particular time. However, symbols may lose their power over the course of time. For millions of people — especially World War II survivors or relatives of survivors — the Nazi swastika (a cross with the ends bent at right angles) will always symbolize a brutal, oppressive political regime. For many young people, however, the swastika is simply a piece of jewelry or an ornamental design. The swastika's design pre-dates its use in Nazi Germany by several thousand years, for it was once a good luck symbol in China and the Far East.

From Ideas to Action

1. Find the cultural meanings of the following non-verbal forms of communication. Compare what these gestures or behaviours mean in North America.
   a) whistling at a European hockey game
   b) sticking out your tongue in an Arab country
   c) spitting in an Arab country
   d) pretending to slit one's throat in Swaziland
   e) hissing at a stage performance in Japan

2. Make a list of some common hand gestures and their meanings in North America.

3. Look at the following cultural symbols and try to determine their meanings.
   a) Statue of Liberty
   b) Canadian beaver
   c) Soviet hammer and sickle
   d) rising sun on flag of Japan
   e) sacred cow in India
   f) Eiffel Tower in Paris, France
   g) statue of Mao Tse-tung
      (now spelled "Mao Zedong")

How To Write an Expository Paragraph — Level 2

This exercise will give you practice in writing an expository paragraph in the correct form. Below is an incomplete paragraph on the topic, "How Do Cultural Differences Affect Communication?"

Complete this paragraph appropriately in your notebook. Read the existing sentences to get a general idea of what the paragraph is about. Then fill in the missing topic sentence, support statements and conclusion. If you have trouble getting started, you may wish to review Skills: How to Write an Expository Paragraph — Level 1 on page 73.

The Effects of Cultural Differences on Communication

_____
_____ . One example of the impact of these differences is the conflict between some teens and their parents over what punk clothing and hair styles are trying to communicate. Another _____
_____
_____
_____ Hand gestures also _____
_____
_____
_____ While touching among males is normally avoided in North America, Eastern European males do not hesitate to kiss another man as a fond welcome. Given these great differences, _____
_____
_____ .

Effective Communication

Form a Chain Gang

As a class or in a large group, try passing a message of four or five sentences from one person to another in a chain. The message could be a description of a TV program that the first sender of the message had seen the night before. There is one catch to the exercise: *only the sender can speak*. There can be no speech or action on the part of the receiver to make sure that he or she has understood the message. When everyone in the chain has received the message, ask the final receiver to say it aloud.

When you have finished the activity, answer the following questions:

1. What problems, if any, did you have in understanding the message?
2. What were your feelings as you tried to understand and then relay the message?
3. Did the message change as it passed along the chain? If so, why?

Barriers To Effective Communication

Effective communication occurs when the receivers of messages interpret the messages in the way the senders intended. This sounds obvious, but, in fact, the process can be very complex. There are many ways in which the message sending (and receiving) can go astray. The following discussion describes five common reasons for communication breakdown.

One-way Communication

The message-sending activity you just completed points out some of the difficulties we encounter when we communicate in a one-way rather than a two-way direction. One-way communication may take less time, and it may appear more business-like and efficient. However, it is rarely more successful.

Feedback is essential in effective communication. You've probably experienced the frustration of a bad telephone connection, when you could hear the other person on the line, but that person couldn't make out what you were saying. Your inability to feed back your responses disrupted communication. Without your feedback, the other person had no way of telling whether he or she had been heard or understood. Most likely one of you hung up and dialled again, in hopes of a better connection.

A communicator can learn the effectiveness of attempts to communicate by getting feedback from the receiver. He or she can then adjust the language or message accordingly. This process is called two-way communication. By feeding information back and forth about what we have understood, we can be far more effective and precise in two-way communication, rather than one-way communication.

Inadequate Vocabulary and Inattention

From time to time, we find it hard to express our thoughts in clear verbal terms. "I know what I want to say, but I can't say it very well" or "You know what I mean" are familiar expressions of this difficulty. Sometimes we become sloppy and careless in our language habits. Sometimes we simply lack the language ability. Inadequate use of language can cause a breakdown in communication. Look at the following conversation. How could you improve Joe's communication with his supervisor, Ron?

Ron: Hello, Joe. What can I do for you?

Joe: Well, I was just thinking...uh...

Ron: Yes?

Joe: Uh, you see it's like...it's hot, see, and...

Ron: Yes, it's hot. So?

Joe: Well, the other guys, we all thought...

Ron: What do you all think, Joe? Look, I'm awfully busy...

Joe: See, there's this door, I mean the one in the back...

Ron: Joe, there are *five* doors at the back. Which one do you mean? The one on the parking lot side?

Joe: Yeah, that door! Well, it's shut. Uh, it's locked, I looked yesterday.

Ron: Yes, that door *is* locked. What's the deal?

Joe: I thought, if you had a key for that door, it's hot, see and...

Ron: Joe, do you mean you want me to open that door so you can have a cross-breeze through your workroom?

Joe: Yeah, that's it. It's O.K., then? Great!

Miscommunication can also arise from inattention or preoccupation. When a person is "tied up" with concerns that distract from the process of communication, the message may not get through. For example, a Toronto columnist, a frequent guest at cocktail parties, was convinced that a certain socialite was so preoccupied with making a favourable impression in social settings that she did not listen to her guests very well.

To test his hunch, the columnist offered his hostess the following excuse for arriving late at a party: " I'm sorry to be late but I murdered my boss this evening and I had the *hardest* time stuffing his body into the trunk of my car." The hostess beamed and gushed, "Well darling, the important thing is that you have arrived, and now the party can really begin."

Emotional Blocks

Sometimes an emotional block can prevent effective communication. People who are feeling depressed, for example, may misinterpret a neutral observation as a put-down. Examine the communication loop below. Notice how a neutral question was translated into something negative because of the feelings or the "mind-set" of one of the communicators.

Communication also breaks down when we adopt defensive attitudes. We become defensive when we feel threatened by others or when we suspect that others are judging us. As we become more defensive, we spend more time and energy thinking about how we appear to others, how we can win out over others, and how we can impress others. We become too distracted to pay attention to the feelings, attitudes and ideas of other people. The result is poor communication.

Bias

A serious breakdown in communication occurs if we hold preconceived opinions or biases about a person, so that we presume to know beforehand what the person is trying to communicate. We then interpret messages according to these preconceptions and not according to objective statements and events.

Sometimes we can be so strongly prejudiced *in favour* of someone that we accept uncritically anything that person says. In such cases we are reacting not to the objective meaning of the message, but to the qualities we like in the sender. For example, people in love often ignore the wise advice of their friends and family if it doesn't agree with their view of the loved one. The only messages they hear are the ones coming from the loved one.

The plumber wrote back to thank the scientist for the information, saying "I'm glad you approve of the procedure." After several more exchanges, it was clear that the plumber had not understood the message. The research bureau finally wrote: "Don't use hydrochloric acid! It eats the heck out of the pipes!"

This exchange highlights another cause of communication breakdown, that is, the use of **jargon**. Jargon is highly specialized, technical and complicated language. Such language often serves as a communication shortcut within a specialized group. Outside that group, however, the jargon is often not understood.

Jargon can be used to conceal, mislead or deceive. Sometimes people use jargon to impress others with their knowledge and sophistication. Whatever its purpose, jargon often hinders rather than helps communication.

When reception of a message is blocked or changed in some way by emotion, by bias or by jargon, for example, the result is distortion of communication. The only way to find out whether distortion of your original message has occurred is to seek and/or provide feedback.

In the communication loop shown on p. 80, the first communicator can ask for feedback by saying, "Let me get this straight. Do you think I was criticizing you? All I said was...," or "You seem to think that I was criticizing you." At the same time, the communicator is feeding back what she or he has interpreted, so that the other person can either agree or disagree with this interpretation. Feedback of this kind can pinpoint when and how distortion of communication is occurring. Only if both people can agree on what was said or intended can real communication begin.

Jargon

A plumber once wrote a letter of inquiry to a government research bureau. He pointed out that he had successfully used hydrochloric acid to clean out sewer pipes. "Was there any possible harm?" he asked. A government scientist first replied: "The efficacy of hydrochloric acid is indisputable, but the corrosive residue is incompatible with metallic permanence."

From Ideas to Action

1. Identify the type of barrier to communication occurring in each situation below:
   a) You are really angry with your girl/boyfriend. You snap back at your mother when she asks you to do the dishes.
   b) You didn't pay much attention to a female sportscaster when she commented on last night's hockey game. "What do women know about hockey anyway?" you thought.
   c) A group of men are watching Brian Mulroney on TV. They say that they would vote for him because he's a good Irishman.
   d) The teacher continued to lecture to the class, despite a loud disturbance at the back of the room.
   e) The third time the little boy cried "Wolf!" no one listened to him.
   f) The manager's memo stated: "Capitalizing the fixed assets will involve costs determined on the basis of allocations rather than on the basis of resource outflows."

2. Make a list of expressions relating to school, work or recreation that you consider jargon. For what reasons are these terms used?

3. Make a list of any arguments you have had with others recently. Determine the causes of these arguments. How many were due to misunderstanding or poor communication? Where did the communication process go astray?

4. For each of the barriers to effective communication discussed in this chapter, describe a personal situation in which communication was interrupted and/or distorted.

Projects, Activities and Explorations

1. Construct a chart showing some careers requiring especially good communication skills. Describe the particular skills required and the reasons why these skills are needed.

2. View a film or a play and chart the ways in which the scriptwriter and the director communicate the "atmosphere" of the work to the audience. In your chart, suggest other techniques by which the writer or director could have communicated similar ideas or moods.

3. Select any role in a film or play and identify ways in which the actor/actress convey to the audience his or her interpretation of the role.

4. Examine your part-time job from the perspective of communication. To what extent is good communication important in your job? What changes might improve communication at your worksite?

5. Prepare a poster in which you display examples of different communication goals. Use sources such as magazines and newspapers. Here is an example: Social goals of communication:
   a) persuasion →newspaper editorials, political cartoons
   b) teaching →personal advice columns, business and medical columns, carpentry hints and other "how-to" features

6. Set up an experiment to test the hypothesis that clothing styles in school are more important than individual behaviour. Write up a formal experiment, including the problem, hypothesis, method of data collection, analysis and conclusion. If you need help, refer to Chapter 2, especially the section on pages 30–31.

7. Prepare a report based on visual and written material that compares the differences between how teenagers communicate with each other and how they communicate with the adults in their lives. Pay attention to body language, social distance, idioms, symbols and other aspects of communication.

What Have You Learned?

If you have covered everything in this chapter, you should be familiar with the following topics:

1. The various goals of communication
2. How we communicate verbally, non-verbally and with symbols
3. How culture influences the way we communicate
4. How communication can break down
5. How to write an expository paragraph

To Help You Study

The following chart will help you to review the words, facts and ideas introduced in this chapter. Copy the chart into your notebook and fill in the missing information.

Word, Fact, Idea	Example in a Sentence	Page	Definition
feedback	I don't know whether the teacher liked my report because he didn't give me any feedback on it.	69	verbal or non-verbal response to a message received
communication goals			
physical needs			
social needs			
ego needs			
verbal communication			
non-verbal communication			
social distance			
symbolic communication			
idiom			
communication breakdown			
two-way communication			
emotional block			
jargon			
distortion of communication			

The Mass Media

A Glance at the Past

If you could travel back in time to visit a Canadian home of 70 years ago, you would probably see the items shown in the photographs. In small groups or on your own, compare these communication devices with those of today.

Share your comparisons with the rest of the class. Then answer the following questions:

1. Compared to your grandparents, how are you affected by modern communication devices?
2. In terms of communication, what are some advantages of living in the late twentieth century compared to the early twentieth century? What are some disadvantages?
3. Would you prefer to live in the early part of this century, rather than today? Do your reasons have anything to do with modern means of communication?

1

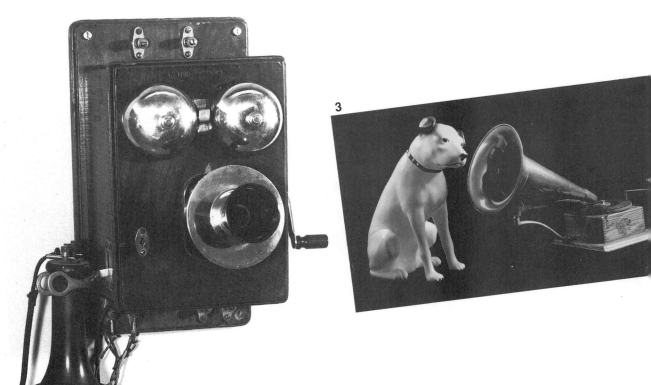

2

3

It is almost impossible to spend a day without using some form of mass media. Your clock radio wakes you in the morning. As you get ready for school, you hear news from around the world, weather forecasts, traffic reports and sports scores. In school, you learn by means of textbooks, magazines, audio cassettes and films. All of these materials are produced for mass audiences. After school, television, videos, films and records entertain you.

The word "media" is the plural of "medium," which means a channel of communication. Television is a medium, radio is another. **Mass media** refer to the various channels of communication we have developed to inform, entertain and educate mass audiences.

In small groups, try to answer the following media trivia questions. Compare your answers with those of other students. Then read the next section on the history of the mass media to check your responses.

1. What new entertainment medium entered Canada from the United States in the early 1900s, replacing vaudeville (live variety shows)?
2. Which medium of the 1980s combines TV and records?
3. When did radio first become popular in Canada?
4. Today, each Canadian household has approximately how many radios:
   a) 1–2   b) 2–3   c) 3–4   d) 4–5?
5. When was TV first introduced in Canada?
6. High school students in North America spend more time watching TV than going to school. True or false?
7. Which entertainment industry spends more money on advertising and promotion than on production?

4

5

A Brief History of the Mass Media

Cinema

Early in this century, silent "moving picture shows" entered Canada from the United States and quickly found a wide audience. As early as 1909, Winnipeg boasted eleven movie theatres. As movies became more and more popular, other forms of entertainment, such as vaudeville and live theatre, began to decline. New movie companies in Hollywood, California, began to churn out feature-length movies. By 1918, Canadians had become regular movie-goers.

Just as radio was becoming popular in the early 1920s, Hollywood developed movies with soundtracks, called "talkies." Canada's first "talking picture" was a black-and-white crime thriller released in 1935. By 1936, Canada's 956 motion picture theatres earned 29 million dollars from 126 million admissions. This represented 12 movie attendances per year for every Canadian. Today, about 500 films a year are produced in North America, at an average cost of 11 million dollars each. At last count, Steven Spielberg's *E.T. The Extra-Terrestrial* had grossed over 200 million dollars worldwide. Canada's most financially successful films to date are comedies about teenage life, *Porky's* and *Meatballs*.

Radio

Most Canadian students know that Guglielmo Marconi, an Italian, made radio history in 1901 when he transmitted a signal in Morse code to England from St. John's, Newfoundland. Less well known is a Canadian, Reginald Fessenden. On Christmas Eve, 1906, Fessenden first transmitted the human voice and music via radio waves. This was much more difficult than sending Morse code signals and made Fessenden the inventor of "real" radio as we know it.

Early radio development was not taken very seriously by the Canadian government. In fact, the Department of the Marine and Fisheries was in charge of issuing operating licences. Despite a shaky beginning, a Canadian radio industry developed in the late 1920s and early 1930s. This industry was fed by popular programs from the United States, and by the establishment in 1932 of a national radio network, the Canadian Radio Broadcasting Commission. Four years later, the Commission disbanded and the Canadian Broadcasting Corporation (CBC) was formed. When the Depression ended in 1939, approximately 75 per cent of Canadian households owned radios. Today, each household has four or five.

Reginald Fessenden

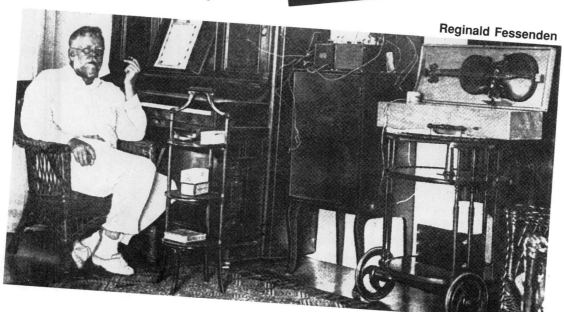

The Recording Industry

Recording media have evolved from scratchy-sounding, one-sided gramophone discs and wax cylinders into crystal-clear cassette tapes and compact discs. The blending of audio recordings and television has produced a new medium, the rock video. The recording industry is perhaps the largest entertainment business in the world. Its estimated annual revenues in North America alone total 5.5 billion dollars.

Record companies spend more money on promotion — packaging, advertising, posters and publicity — than on production. Now that rock videos are so popular with the record-buying public, the recording industry has discovered a new, powerful promotional tool. Not only do videos expose the new material to a wide audience, the broadcasters pay a fee to the record companies to show the videos on television.

Bryan Adams, double Juno Award winner in 1987 and a Canadian recording star

Television

Television was introduced to the North American public following World War II. Public pressure in Canada led to the establishment in September, 1952 of a national television network within the CBC. By the late 1950s, three quarters of Canadian households had television sets.

Within a short time, television began to compete with other mass media for advertising dollars. At first, television "borrowed" much of its entertainment programming from radio, including quiz shows, soap operas, dramas and news. As advertisers transferred their advertising dollars to television, Canadian Saturday newspaper supplements and North American magazine giants such as *Life, Look, The Saturday Evening Post* and *Collier's* began to collapse in the 1960s.

Television is now firmly rooted in North American culture. The technological child of TV and the tape recorder, the VCR, is becoming standard equipment in Canadian households. One study has estimated that by the end of high school, students will have spent an average of 15 000 hours watching TV, compared to about 11 000 classroom hours. In a given week, television now reaches approximately 99 per cent of all Canadians two years and older. On average, Canadians spend 24 hours a week watching TV. With satellite broadcasting, even remote areas of Canada receive a full range of TV programming.

From Ideas to Action

1. Of the various mass media described above, which has the most power to influence how you think and feel? Why do you think so?
2. In your opinion, what kinds of ideas or programs are unlikely to be publicized through the mass media?
3. Keep a log (a record, journal or account) of the number of hours you are exposed to various mass media. What other activities have you perhaps set aside because of this exposure?

How the Mass Media "Create" Reality

In a group or as a class, study first the sequence of photographs, and then the sportscaster's script below. Answer the following questions:
1. In the sequence of photographs, how have the photographs been changed? Why do you think these changes have been made?
2. What ideas or feelings are stressed in the sportscaster's script?

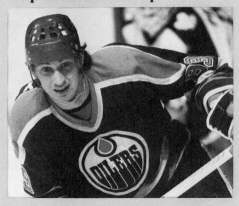

Sportscaster's Script

"The Edmonton Oilers crushed the Philadelphia Flyers 8–2 last night in a bitterly contested rematch of last year's Stanley Cup final. The teams battled to a 2–2 tie until the third period, when the Oilers' awesome offensive power overwhelmed the hard-checking Flyers."

Compare your reactions with the rest of the class:
1. Which photograph did your group find most effective? Why?
2. How could the sportscaster change the message by using other language?

Television Editing

In reporting an event, each medium carefully "creates" its own version of what happened. Although skillfully crafted into what looks like a "seamless" whole, each version of the event is really a blending of many parts. Editing, splicing and piecing together a particular version of the event involves many editorial and technical decisions.

For example, from all the film shot by a camera crew, television editors may select as many "action" scenes as possible. These scenes may not be the most important ones, but action scenes stimulate the viewer. Television editing can reconstruct an action-filled version of an event. In doing so, it may distort what really happened.

Television film footage consists of a series of shots, or "cuts" as they are called in the industry. These "cuts" last only about 3.5 seconds. Each visual technique used in these cuts produces a unique effect. This enables the viewer to "see" the scene in various ways. For example, a television editor may suggest excitement where none existed by using close-ups, over-the-shoulder shots and fast-paced scene changes. By skillfully splicing the film and controlling the length of shots, editors can control the reactions of the viewing audience. A loud soundtrack, rapid cutting and scenes of violence can increase the excitement level of a program or a news report. Commercial television relies on a high level of excitement to maintain the viewer's interest.

Editors can also manipulate the statements of a reporter covering an event. They sometimes do this by splicing commentary from newscasters who weren't even at the scene. Music can be grafted onto the tape. The music's beat, mood and intensity can have a subtle effect on the viewer's emotional responses.

The order in which news stories are presented can influence the viewer's impression of which stories are more important than others. Sometimes the closeness of one story to another can affect how one or both stories are interpreted. For example, a story on the need for a larger budget for a community's police force is strengthened by a nearby news item on increasing burglaries within that community.

Our views of reality are also influenced by the number of times we are exposed to certain topics or events. In a report submitted to the Royal Commission on Bilingualism and Biculturalism, two researchers concluded that English television coverage of Quebec in the 1960s overemphasized crime and anti-social activities. Their analysis showed that between April 1964 and March 1965, about 50 per cent of the

items concerning Quebec that were aired by the English CTV and CBC networks featured violence and criminal behaviour.

Political extremists often seek extensive media coverage to advertise their cause. Could such biased reporting have actually encouraged violent behaviour? Did it have a negative effect on Quebec's relations with the rest of Canada? We may never know the answers to these questions, but we do know that we must be wary of one-sided reporting.

Would You Vote for This Man?

William Lyon MacKenzie King held power longer than any other Canadian Prime Minister, from 1921–1930 and from 1935–1948. If television had existed then, it is unlikely that King would have been elected to office. Even his admirers said that MacKenzie King raised boredom to a new art form.

He had an incredible ability to speak at length without saying very much. Lacking the dynamic and forceful style that looks best on TV, King would have failed miserably today in terms of his media image. Yet, in a pre-TV age, this man held office for almost 22 years.

Print Media: *Tricks of the Trade*

Each medium has its own assortment of mechanical "tricks" used to reconstruct reality. We've looked at some of the tricks used in one electronic medium, TV. Print media (books, magazines, newspapers and other print materials) also use special techniques to manipulate how we react to a story or an event. Like TV editors, book, magazine and newspaper editors also make strategic decisions about what to publish and what to ignore. They select photographs shot at dramatic angles, eye-catching headlines in varying sizes, varying fonts (styles of print), and boxes, borders and other page layout devices. Cover and page design attract our attention. They also create a certain mood and influence our responses to the contents of the print medium.

The Mass Media and Values

The mass media convey messages about what is of value in our society. Are the values we learn at home, in school and on the job reflected in television programs, print media, movies and records?

We are not referring to obvious attempts at persuasion, such as advertising, but to hidden messages. For example, North American TV programs often depict violence as a means of settling disputes. Can we conclude, therefore, that violence is an acceptable form of problem-solving in our society? As another example, afternoon soap operas may convince some viewers of the supreme importance of good looks, clothes, and material comforts.

From Ideas to Action

1. Suppose you work for a television station that is covering a serious accident or a natural disaster. What techniques could you use to sensationalize the news coverage?

2. Watch several episodes of a fast-paced program such as "Miami Vice" or "Night Heat." Write down what values you think are reinforced in the episodes. Pay close attention to the dialogue, the camera shots and the cutting techniques used to communicate these values.
3. Examine a local newspaper. How do the editors attract your attention visually? Do the headlines always match the stories exactly?
4. Listen to several radio programs. What techniques does the DJ or broadcaster use to keep your attention?

How To Write an Expository Paragraph — Level 2

This exercise will give you practice in writing an expository paragraph in the correct form. Below is an incomplete paragraph on the topic "Does the Mass Media Reflect Reality or Falsify It?"

Complete this paragraph appropriately in your notebook. Read the existing sentences to get a general idea of what the paragraph is about. Then fill in the missing topic sentence, supporting statements and conclusion. If you have trouble getting started, you may wish to review Skills: How To Write an Expository Paragraph — Level 1, on page 73.

The Mass Media and Reality

_____

_____. Each medium claims to present total news coverage. In reality, however, editors select only exciting news events and often omit more important but less exciting items. Another _____

_____

_____. One example of a hidden message conveyed by TV is the idea that most North American families are well off. This is simply not true. TV also suggests that

_____
_____
_____In conclusion,
_____
_____
_____.

The Mass Media and Advertising

What Do You See?

In small groups or as a class, examine the following ads. Try to interpret all the messages each ad is communicating. Then answer the follow-up questions.

1. Which of the ads do you think works best at catching the reader's attention and prompting the reader to buy the product? Why?
2. What techniques do the advertisers use to appeal to the reader?
3. Do you think any of these ads have another message besides the claim directly stated by the manufacturer? Explain.
4. Do any of the ads offend you, or strike you as misleading? If so, why?

Who Advertises and Why

A country's economy is based on what is called "the market." The market is not a place, but a process. In this process, people who want to sell things communicate with people who want to buy things, and vice versa. Advertisers participate in this process by trying to persuade the consumer to buy more, or to buy one product rather than another.

The mass media have helped advertising play a larger and larger role in the marketing of products to consumers. An average student, for example, is exposed to about *500* ads per day from various media sources. Advertising was once limited to product labels and to modest, although sometimes misleading, claims and descriptions in catalogues. Modern advertising, however, is varied and sophisticated. Air Canada, for example, has sponsored a climbing expedition up Mt. Everest as part of its advertising campaign. The next section will discuss how advertising is now a subtle but powerful force in shaping our lifestyles, attitudes and values.

Advertising, Values and Social Roles

The ad at the top was published in a magazine in 1972. The ad below was published in magazines in 1987. Study the ads and then answer the follow-up questions.

a) What connection, if any, do you see between the product and the woman in the 1972 advertisement?

b) Do you think the woman's physical appearance and posture were intended to suggest something about women in general? If so, what?

c) Do you find the 1972 ad offensive? If so, why does it offend you?

d) These two ads were published 15 years apart. What changes in attitude toward the consumer do these ads reflect?

Throughout the 1970s, many women began to criticize the ways in which females were portrayed in advertising. They argued that a lot of advertising

1972

1987

was insulting and sexist (that is, it discriminated on the basis of gender). Too often, women were portrayed as passive, emotionally dependent on men, uninformed about issues outside the home and overly concerned with their attractiveness. Advertising also tended to stereotype women. As you learned in Chapter 2, a stereotype is an oversimplified mental picture shared by many people in a group. In stereotyped role depictions, women have traditional, conventional jobs and behave in predictable, conventional ways.

Several studies done in the 1970s seemed to support these criticisms. One study showed that women were seven times more likely than men to appear in ads for bathroom products. The same study found that women were shown in secondary helping roles (as housewives, flight attendants and secretaries) in about 70 per cent of ads involving women. In 1981, a survey of television programs showed that about 60 per cent of the female roles were restricted to motherhood, housekeeping or roles stressing physical appearance. The study identified a relationship between the time of day the ads appeared and the role models depicted. Evening television ads shifted from the housekeeping roles seen in the afternoon to roles centred on attractiveness.

Critics say that members of many other groups can be misrepresented in advertising as well. Men, too, can be the objects of sexist and insulting ads. Members of ethnic and minority groups, and the elderly, are sometimes stereotyped. The few ads involving the elderly often focus on the medical problems associated with aging. Often, they treat the elderly as weak and having no valid role in society.

The elderly have low incomes and have usually bought most of what they

Members of ethnic minority groups are under-represented or misrepresented in advertising.

need. Older people are not, therefore, prime advertising targets for the producers of goods and services. This trend may change, however, as the well-off baby boom generation grows old. Already we are beginning to see some advertisements that show the elderly enjoying healthy and fulfilled lives.

Certain minority groups receive little attention from advertisers, or are negatively stereotyped. The absence of certain ethnic role models in advertising was highlighted in a native Canadian boy's letter to Sears:

> You have no pictures that look like my mom and dad or like my sister or like me. In the catalogue, there are just white people. I'm an Indian. In the next catalogue, could you pick some people who look like me?
> [*The Canadian Press*, 1980]

Because of increased public awareness and concern, the advertising industry has developed a code of ethics to guide advertisers. Many advertisers *do* make an effort to avoid stereotyping and represent Canada's ethnic mix accurately.

Children and Advertising

Look at the ad below and then answer the follow-up questions.

1. What values does this advertisement communicate?
2. Do you think children should be the targets of such advertising?

Many parents and parents' organizations are concerned about the effects of advertising on children. They believe that children's unformed identities, values and behaviour patterns can be strongly moulded by television and television advertising. In Quebec, a ban on childrens' advertising on television was passed in 1980.

Critics of advertising aimed at children have claimed that:
- Childrens' advertising often exposes children to stereotyped role models.
- Children do not understand that ads are designed to market products and services for company profit.
- Children are often disappointed by the exaggerated claims made by advertising.
- Children learn to value possessions and their self-esteem may suffer if they cannot have the things they see advertised.
- Many advertisements promote products which may be harmful to children, such as junk foods and snacks containing sugar.

Much of the research into these claims is inconclusive. Some studies have discovered that even very young children seem to distinguish TV programming from commercials, and that a high percentage of young children can detect the persuasive or selling aspect of TV ads. Other studies have shown that young children cannot distinguish the advertiser's purposes in promoting products to make profits.

The role models in childrens' advertising show an interesting parallel with those in advertising for adults. One 1979 study found that commercials for boys' products featured violent action, a greater variety of scenes and louder sound effects than did commercials for girls' products. Commercials for girls featured softer background music, less action and images of softness, gentleness, and slow, gradual change.

There is some evidence that exposure to advertising showing non-stereotyped role models can have at least a short-term effect on children's attitudes. In a 1977 experiment, for example, children watched television ads portraying women in non-traditional roles (such as courtroom judges). This experimental group was more accepting of such roles than were the control group children who did not see these ads.

The effect of TV advertising on parent-child relationships is difficult to measure. Does advertising influence children to persuade their parents to buy the children's products advertised? One especially careful investigation showed that the more commercial television that children watched at home, the higher the pressure on parents to purchase advertised products. This study also found that 48 per cent of children's requests for products were fulfilled by their parents. The study concluded that television advertising *is* a "vehicle for unhealthy persuasion."

It is impossible to assess here all the claims and counterclaims made about the effects of advertising on children. Evidence suggests, however, that we should pay close attention to both the content of TV advertising aimed at children, and to children's responses to that advertising.

From Ideas to Action

1. Look carefully at some advertisements in magazines and on television.
   a) Is there a relationship between the products advertised on TV and the times of day the ads appear? Who are the targets of the ads?
   b) How often do the ads you see feature ethnic minorities or the elderly? What qualities do the ads associate with people belonging to these two groups? Do the ads stereotype these people?

2. List any stereotyped characters who appear in TV programs you watch frequently. Explain why you think they are stereotypes.

3. Watch some prime-time childrens' programs broadcast between 3 p.m. and 6 p.m. on weekdays and on Saturday and Sunday mornings.
   a) Make a list of the qualities displayed by male and female characters in the advertisements you see.
   b) Categorize the types of products featured in the advertisements. Are they linked to male or female characters in the ads, or to both?
   c) Is aggressive and/or helping behaviour portrayed in the advertisements?
   d) Think about the claims made for products promoted in childrens' advertising. Do you think the claims are realistic or exaggerated?

4. Carefully read or listen to the lyrics of some of your favourite recording artists. What ideas, values and attitudes communicated by the lyrics are hidden or obvious?

Bias and Frame of Reference — Level 2

In this exercise you will learn to detect bias and to connect it to a frame of reference. You will also consider how bias can affect attention to and interpretation of facts.

First read the four definitions below. Decide which describes a) a bias b) a frame of reference c) a fact d) an interpretation.

1. Something exact or specific that can be investigated and that can be proved again and again
2. An opinion, viewpoint or attitude, formed in advance, that can influence how we view people and events
3. A conclusion drawn from a fact or facts
4. A personal perspective based on all the experiences gained from one's culture, family, religion, education, friends and interests

Check your answers with your teacher. Then read the two opposing viewpoints on war toys presented below. Answer the follow-up questions.

Concerned Parents' Viewpoint

As Christmas approaches, many parents are joining the International Day Against War Toys to protest rising war toy sales.

Since the Rambo craze, parents have been increasingly pressured to buy war toys. Many parents feel that such toys convey an unhealthy acceptance of violence and warfare as solutions to problems. Increasing international tensions and the threat of nuclear war have magnified their concerns.

Experiments have shown that war-like games make children less sensitive to the horrors of war, says noted baby doctor, Benjamin Spock. A world threatened by nuclear war cannot say that war is all right, and this is what we are doing, argues Spock, when we buy children war toys.

Some early childhood education specialists believe that action figures such as G.I. Joe, with their predefined roles and characters, stunt a child's opportunities for unstructured creative play.

More and more, parents need guidance in making informed decisions about buying childrens' toys. Besides boycotting war toys, several parent groups are asking Ottawa to ban TV commercials and cartoon shows that feature violent characters.

Toy Manufacturers' Viewpoint

The military toy business is booming, say toy manufacturers. Coleco Industries says its Rambo doll, symbolising patriotism and determination, has become a new American hero admired by both children and parents.

Most toy manufacturers rely on market research to gauge consumer preferences. If there is a demand for war toys, we have to fill it, says Henry Wittenberg, president of the Canadian Toy Manufacturers Association. It is not the manufacturer's job to change the marketplace.

Retail stores agree that the de-

mand for war games and action figures has surged in the 1980s. The manufacturers' promotional campaigns, including successful spin-off cartoons, have had a major impact on sales. Toys such as G.I. Joe *do* help develop imagination and fantasy, says Murray Goldfarb of Hasbro Industries. War toys give children a chance to explore important values, such as good vs. evil.

Industry spokespeople point out that toy soldiers and military make-believe have existed throughout history. As long as the public wants toys and cartoon characters based on them, manufacturers will meet that need in order to make money.

Reprinted with permission — *The Toronto Star Syndicate*

1. Briefly state the bias of the concerned parents regarding war toys.
2. Briefly state the bias of the toy manufacturers regarding war toys.
3. Bias is often obvious when the facts and arguments used to support two opposing viewpoints are compared. Identify two facts or arguments used in each viewpoint above that are not mentioned in the other viewpoint.
4. Bias can lead to different interpretations of the same fact. Show how this occurs in the two viewpoints presented above.
5. Explain how the frame of reference of each opponent may have shaped their biases.

Has Television Encouraged Anti-social Behaviour?

When television broadcasting began in Canada in the early 1950s, many remote communities could not receive signals, sometimes because of geography. One community in British Columbia, surrounded by mountains, was cut off from TV for many years. Media researchers saw an ideal opportunity to study community life before and after the introduction of TV.

Investigators used interview and survey techniques. They explored the level of aggressive behaviour, the level of social interaction, such as church attendance, and student abilities to read and write. When the town acquired TV some years later, the study was repeated.

In 1985, some disturbing research results were published. The study showed that the town's level of violence and aggressive behaviour had increased significantly following the introduction of TV.

There was also a decline in attendance at church and other social gatherings. Finally, childrens' reading levels were lower in the post-TV phase.

1. Do you see any flaws in the set-up of this "experiment"? Are there any reasons why you would reject the study's conclusions?

2. Can you think of any other explanations besides the influence of television to account for the behavioural changes in the townspeople?

3. If you accept that the changes in behaviour were caused by the introduction of television, do you find these results disturbing? Why or why not?

4. Can you think of any other ways to explore the effects of television viewing on social behaviour?

Should Students Be Taught Critical Responses to the Mass Media?

• •

Read the newspaper article below, and then answer the follow-up questions.

Students urged to be critical of media

By Sandro Contenta, *The Toronto Star* [February 20, 1987]

The Ontario government will urge school boards to instruct children how rock videos and other mass media shape and manipulate their lives.

Children from kindergarten to Grade 12 should be taught to deal critically with such powerful media as television, newspapers, films and radio, says a draft of a sweeping teachers' resource book designed by educators and officials from the Ministry of Education.

The shaping of young minds by everything from videos to the hard-sell advertising of toys at Christmas should be taught throughout the curriculum, says the resource book, expected in the schools by September along with a video promoting it.

The government also plans to make so-called media literacy studies mandatory in English courses beginning in Grade 7 as part of an ongoing revision of the Grade 7–12 curriculum.

Growing concern

Although most educators believe a media literacy course is long overdue, the producers of the resource book believe it places Ontario at the forefront of such work.

"The reason we're doing this is because it's needed ... There's been a growing concern by parents and teachers about things like violence and pornography in the media and how it affects the behavior of children," said Jerry George, an education officer in the ministry's curriculum division.

Reinforce sterotypes

Educators have long been concerned about the effects of mass media on children – shorter attention spans, an inclination to resort to overly simplistic, sometimes violent solutions to problems and an inability to distinguish fact from fiction. The resource book gives students examples of potential problem areas.

Videos from so-called heavy-metal bands consistently show women in bondage or wrestling in mud while video glitz queen Madonna – a model for millions of young "Madonna wanna-bes" – has portrayed girls as "boy toys."

While "the potential for this art form remains great," most videos "consistently blur the distinctions between fantasy and reality," the document says.

Children are exposed to more than 500 commercials a day, the report says, and students should realize their purpose is to fuel the consumer society. Beer commercials, the document explains, sell everything from sex to the "good life" while political advertising deals more with creating images than discussing important issues.

TV sitcoms often portray all-knowing parents, for example, that bear no resemblance to real people while information in the news media is often absorbed without a reflection of how economic and editorial biases influence what is portrayed as "the truth," the resource book says.

Educators should also stress the differences between Canadian news, TV shows and films and those made in the United States, it says.

The media makes violence appealing and presents it as a natural form of behaviour, it adds. Educators often point to the popular TV show *The A-Team* as a prime example.

To counter the numbing violence, media literacy studies should teach how special effects and stunts are performed in films and television.

"By taking the pieces apart and seeing how it's made, you in fact demystify the media," said Barry Duncan, an Etobicoke teacher and president of the Toronto-based Association for Media Literacy.

1. What arguments and facts do educators offer to show that students should learn about the manipulative effects of rock videos and other mass media?

2. How might "media literacy" help students?

3. Write a paragraph on your view of media literacy training.

Do We Need Censorship To Control Pornography?

● ●

Read the following two newspaper articles, and then answer the follow-up questions.

10-year terms for kiddie porn under new bill

Ray Hnatyshyn, Justice Minister

By David Vienneau, *The Toronto Star*
[May 5, 1987]

OTTAWA — Tough, new laws that would make it punishable by 10 years in jail to involve anyone under 18 in sexually explicit films, magazines, videos or theatrical performances have been introduced by Justice Minister Ray Hnatyshyn.

The proposed legislation, tabled in the House of Commons yesterday, would also provide maximum 10-year jail terms for anyone who imports, makes, sells or distributes pornographic depictions of children.

The reforms, which still must be approved by Parliament, also call for a maximum of 10 years in prison for anyone convicted of visually depicting sexual violence likely to cause permanent or extended bodily harm...

The bill provides the first legal definition of pornography...

But the bill also attempts to distinguish pornography from erotica and says the production and sale of erotica would be legal as long as it was not displayed publicly or sold to anyone under the age of 18...

The bill also says:
• Possession of kiddie porn would be punishable by up to six months in jail or a $2,000 fine or both.
• Violent pornography including sexual assault, or where physical pain is inflicted, would be punishable by up to five years' imprisonment. The same penalty would apply to depictions of degrading acts...

• People who sell, rent or offer to sell or rent erotica to a person under age 18 would be guilty of an offence punishable by up to six months in jail, a $2,000 fine or both.
• The same penalty would apply to retailers who publicly display erotica and to theatre owners who allow erotica to be presented in front of someone under age 18. Storeowners would be required to post a prominent warning or display the erotica in opaque wrappers or behind barriers.
• Visual depictions of intercourse by adults would be punishable by two years' imprisonment, a $2,000 fine or both.

Reprinted with permission — *The Toronto Star Syndicate*

New porn bill may lump art with 'trash,' critics charge

Statue of Rodin's Adam draped to comply with the new anti-pornography bill.

[May 5, 1987]

OTTAWA (CP) – Canada's art community and groups representing women are relieved that pictures of kissing and hand-holding won't be illegal under the government's new anti-pornography legislation.

But some are still worried that the definitions of pornography and erotica unveiled yesterday are too old-fashioned.

Alan Borovoy of the Canadian Civil Liberties Association said the legislation casts too wide a net.

"The bill incurs a terrific risk of nailing material that would be unconscionable [unreasonable] for a democratic society to suppress," he said.

Some depictions of sexually violent actions are "real trash," but others are works of art that convey a serious social message, Borovoy said...

Artists charged with producing or showing pornography can argue that the work has artistic merit but not if it involves children or extreme sexual violence.

Michelle d'Auray, national director of the Canadian Conference of the Arts, said she is pleased that Justice Minister Ray Hnatyshyn took artists' concerns into account by strengthening the artistic merit defence.

Erotica – which won't be prohibited unless it involves children or is sold to or seen by people under 18 – is defined essentially as nudity. Pornography includes everything from visual depictions of sexual intercourse between consenting adults to extreme sexual violence and degradation.

Lousie Dulude, president of the National Action Committee on the Status of Women, said the definition of erotica is old-fashioned because it excludes healthy, sexual intercourse.

Reprinted with permission — *The Canadian Press*

1. What are the focus questions raised in the articles on pornography?
2. What are the main ideas in each article?
3. What are the supporting statements in each article?
4. What is your position on the issue of pornography? Express your viewpoints in a paragraph. Include the arguments and the facts that most influenced your opinions.

Projects, Activities and Explorations

1. Discuss whether harmful products such as cigarettes or alcohol should be advertised on television or in magazines.

2. Observe some rock videos for evidence of:
   • violent images
   • promotion of drug use
   • stereotyped sex roles

3. Listen to a sample of popular songs in different categories: country and western, rock, punk, new wave, etc. Identify some of the values, ideas and behaviour supported by the lyrics. Present a report on your findings.

4. Develop an outline for a marketing plan to promote a new rock group. Include videos, public appearances and advertising.

5. Develop some ideas for marketing a new cereal. Design the packaging, an advertising plan and a billboard display.

6. Review several episodes of a television program featuring aggression and violence. Present a report on the filming and editing techniques used to depict or suggest violence.

7. Write a TV spot, a radio spot and a magazine or newspaper article that report the same imaginary event. Try to use the characteristics of each medium to best effect. See how far from the "facts" you wander.

8. In groups, prepare a project to compare how various media cover a recent story involving your community. Choose an accident, a fire, a VIP visit or a political event. Clip newspaper and magazine stories about the event. You can also record some radio broadcasts or television footage related to the story. Complete the following chart to compare the coverage of the event by the various media. Try to determine the strengths and weaknesses of each medium. How is your view of reality influenced by each medium.

What Have You Learned?

If you have covered everything in this chapter, you should be familiar with the following topics:

1. A brief history and description of the mass media
2. How each medium manipulates reality
3. The role of advertising in the mass media
4. How television advertising influences children

	Medium			
	TV	Radio	Magazine	Newspaper
Amount and kinds of detail				
Main focus of the story				
Feelings or impressions aroused by the coverage of the story				

To Help You Study

The following chart will help you review the words, facts and ideas that were introduced in this chapter. Copy the chart into your notebook and fill in the missing information.

Word, Fact, Idea	Example in a Sentence	Page	Definition
mass media	It has been shown that exposure to the mass media affects peoples' values and beliefs.	85	the various channels of communication created to inform, entertain, and educate mass audiences
electronic media			
print media			
role model			
editing			

Sensation and Perception

Can You Do These Things — Blindfolded?

Choose a partner or work with a partner assigned by your teacher. One partner in each pair wears a blindfold while trying one or more of the following tasks. The other partner *must* ensure safety! The partners in each pair then switch places.

- Fill a glass of water from a tap or a pitcher.
- Walk to the school cafeteria and back.
- Open your locker and select the books needed for your next class.
- Sharpen a pencil.
- Attend a class and try to participate as usual.

When you have completed some of these tasks, discuss the following questions with classmates who were also blindfolded.

1. How did it feel to be without sight?
2. What kinds of problems or frustrations did you experience?
3. Did you use any other senses to help you adjust to the loss of vision?
4. Suppose that the loss of your sight were permanent rather than temporary. List some ways in which your life would change.

Looking at the Senses

Which Senses Could You Live Without?

Decide which senses listed below you could least easily and most easily do without. In your notebook, rank your choices from 1 to 6, with 1 representing the sense you would find *least* easy to do without. Be prepared to defend your choices in a group discussion.

- your hearing
- your eyesight
- your sense of smell
- your sense of taste
- your sense of touch
- your sense of balance

This chapter will talk about how our senses enable us to cope with and respond to the world around us. It will discuss the different kinds of sensations we experience. It will also discuss perception. This is the complex process in which our brains interpret and organize the information supplied by our senses.

What Are Our Senses?

Do you automatically reach for your sunglasses when you step into bright sunlight? Do you prefer to snack on an apple rather than a lemon? Does the rumble of a jackhammer make you cover your ears? If you wake up in a cold room, do you have trouble getting out of bed? Your answers to these questions depend on your **sensory responses** (how your senses react) to these situations. Most of your behaviour begins with your senses.

Your senses, or more accurately, your **sensory organs**, include your eyes, ears, nose, tongue and skin. These organs are specialized "receivers." They collect information about events taking place both inside and outside your body. This information is also called **sense data.** Any change received, or recorded, by a sensory organ is called a **stimulus**. The plural of stimulus is **stimuli**. For example, when you crawl from under your covers on a cold January morning, the sensory nerves in your skin immediately record the stimulus, a change in temperature. This stimulus is then passed along by electrochemical nerve impulses to a certain area of your brain. You experience this brain activity as **sensation**; in this case, an awareness of cold. You may decide to stay in bed until another stimulus, the alarm clock, transmits another "message" to your brain!

When we experience any kind of sense data — sights, sounds, smells, and so on — we are experiencing sensation. Sensation is awareness of your internal and external environments. This awareness is achieved through the brain's *interpretation* of messages received from various sensory organs.

Psychologists have identified more than ten specific senses in the human body. Specialized sensory organs in the body detect heat, vibration, "light" versus "deep" pressure, and other sensations. You are most familiar, of course, with the following five senses: sight, hearing, taste and smell, touch and balance.

Vision is one of our most important senses. Our eyes record only two stimuli: the length of light waves, which determines colour; and the intensity (or size) of light waves, which determines brightness.

Like vision, hearing also records stimuli in waves of energy known as sound waves. The length and the size of sound waves determine the loudness and the pitch (highness or lowness) of a sound. The ear, of course, is the sensory organ that receives the sound waves.

Your tongue records only four kinds of stimuli: sweetness, sourness, saltiness and bitterness. Your taste sensations are also affected by other senses, mainly the sense of smell. You've probably noticed how food loses its taste when you have a cold and can't smell anything. Familiarity with certain foods also influences your sensations of taste. For example, some people raised on skim milk find that whole milk, which is higher in butterfat, tastes too sweet and rich. Some people raised on whole milk think skim milk tastes like water.

Smell is not as sharp a sense in human beings compared to many animals. We can, however, detect and remember smells better than we can remember sights or sounds. Since smell and taste are so closely linked, they are often considered to be one sense. That is why we are said to have only five senses.

The sense of touch, located in our skin, records four basic types of sensations: warmth, cold, pressure and pain. Any other sensations you feel, such as tickling or itching, are combinations of these four basic sensations. The most pressure-sensitive spot in your body is the tip of your tongue. The least pressure-sensitive area is the sole of your foot.

Braille enables the blind to read using the sense of touch.

The body's sense of balance is located within the inner ear. We often take this sense for granted. Without it, however, we could not stand up without falling over. Colds or infections in the ear can have a disastrous effect on your sense of balance.

If you closed your eyes, stuffed your ears with cotton wool, held your nose and stretched out flat on a soft pad on the floor, you would still experience the functioning of other senses. You could touch your nose with your finger, for example, or stop yourself before you poked a finger in your eye. These other senses tell you where the various parts of your body are in relation to each other. This awareness is called **proprioception**. They also indicate how fast the parts of your body are moving,

an awareness called **kinesthesis**. Sensory nerves located in muscles and joints send messages to the brain about your body's movements. You can imagine how difficult daily life would be without knowing exactly how your body was moving.

Depending on the degree of handicap, people can often lead active and productive lives.

This gymnast is using her sense of proprioception, kinesthesis and balance to complete this routine.

109

"The Disembodied Lady"

The following comes from a case study of Christina, a woman who lost her proprioception because of an extraordinary nerve disease.

> "What I must do then," she said slowly, "is use vision, use my eyes, in every situation where I used – what do you call it? – proprioception before. I've already noticed," she added, musingly, "that I may 'lose' my arms. I think they're one place, and I find they're another. This 'proprioception' is like the eyes of the body, the way the body sees itself. And if it goes, as it's gone with me, *it's like the body's blind*. My body can't 'see' itself if it's lost its eyes, right? So *I* have to watch it – be its eyes. Right?"
> From *The Man Who Mistook His Wife for a Hat & Other Clinical Tales* © 1970, 1971, 1983, 1984, 1985 by Oliver Sacks. Reprinted by permission of Summit Books, a division of Simon & Shuster, Inc.

Christina eventually learned to walk again and to function at home, but in unusual ways. For example, she had to deliberately think about which facial expressions to use in certain situations. She always had to concentrate her remaining senses on how to move her body — on how to sit upright, how to stand, even on how to hold a knife and fork. Christina never recovered from the disturbing feeling that her body was no longer *there*, was no longer a part of herself.

How the Senses Co-operate

Vision, balance, proprioception and kinesthesis work together to give you a sense of your body. Other senses work together too. For instance, your eyes and ears help you to move about in the physical world. Consider the following simple demonstration of this co-operation:

As a child, you probably discovered that if you spun around quickly for a while and then suddenly stopped, things looked as though they were still spinning. As you were spinning, the fluid in your inner ear shifted. (Recall that your body's sense of balance is located within the inner ear.) This shifting told your brain that changes in your body's position were taking place. When you suddenly stopped, the fluid, however, continued to shift. So you still felt as though you were spinning because your ears were "telling" you this, even though your eyes told you you weren't. We interpret this mixed-up sensation as "dizziness."

Dancers and figure skaters spin a great deal. To avoid falling, they take advantage of this co-operation between the eye and the ear. Dancers and figure skaters fix their eyes on one spot for as long as they can each time they spin. When they can no longer see this spot, they "snap" their heads around until the spot is visible again. Because the head motion is so fast and so brief, the fluid in the inner ear doesn't have time to begin to shift. So the brain records very little sensation of motion and a spinning dancer or figure skater doesn't get dizzy.

Elizabeth Manley, Ottawa figure skater, is accustomed to perfect co-operation between the eye and the ear.

From Ideas to Action

1. Identify the senses that are most important to each of the following people. Briefly explain your answers.
a) a guitarist in a rock band b) an airline pilot c) a wine taster d) a gymnast e) a parachutist f) a painter g) a chef

2. Sometimes certain smells bring out strong memories of other sensations. What do the following smells mean to you? What feelings and sensations do they bring out in you?
a) homemade soup simmering on a stove b) newly mown grass c) a gymnasium after a fitness class d) wood smoke e) damp ground during a spring thaw
Make a list of some smells that are personally meaningful to you. What memories of other sensations does each smell arouse?

3. Watch a sports coach at your school teaching an athlete a new physical skill. In what ways do the athlete's senses co-operate as he or she tries to master the new skill?

Focusing the Senses

Stop reading for 30 seconds and try to become *completely* aware of everything in the room — sights, smells, sounds and textures. Now list about ten of your observations. Compare your list with the lists of at least two classmates. What do you notice? How can you explain the differences in the sensations that were listed?

Suppose you are at a school dance. The music is blasting and hundreds of people are talking and laughing at once. It's hard to hear what your friends are saying. Strangely though, despite all the noise, you suddenly overhear your name in a coversation, as clear as a bell.

This common occurrence illustrates how the brain first *selects*, and then uses, the information it receives from the senses. In this case, your ears transmit all the sound waves they "pick up," much like a microphone picks up every sound within its range. The music, the conversations, the laughter, the shuffle of feet on the dance floor — every sound wave is converted into a nerve impulse and transmitted from your ears to your brain.

Can you imagine what your experience at a dance would be like if you were fully aware of *all* the sounds transmitted to your brain? You would probably run screaming from the building with your hands over your ears. You could not stand intense awareness of all the sounds. Similarly, if you were constantly aware of the sensations of your clothing next to your skin, it would "drive you crazy."

There are *countless* sensations stimulating your sensory organs at any given moment. You may have heard the terms "sensory bombardment" or "sensory assault" used to describe this constant stimulation of the senses. To prevent sensory "overload," your brain selects and uses only some information, and ignores other information that it does not need.

This **selective attention** on the part of your brain narrows your focus to specific stimuli in the environment. When you shift your attention, your brain selects and emphasizes other information. This reaction enables you to respond better to events around you. So, when your teacher tells you to "Pay attention!" what he or she really means is: "Tell your brain to ignore the visual and auditory (hearing-related) stimuli of the sportscar in the parking lot, and refocus your attention on the cassette-filmstrip I'm showing."

"Paying attention" means ignoring some stimuli in favour of other stimuli. Paying attention may or may not be conscious. Consciously paying attention to something involves *voluntary* control of the brain's natural, *involuntary* tendency to focus attention. Paying attention is part of the process called perception.

Insights into Blindness

Bob Fenton wants to run for Canada in the 1988 Olympics in Korea. The 20-year-old Wilfred Laurier University student has participated in international track and field meets. When Bob's not running, he may be skiing, water skiing, playing hockey or teaching kids how to use a computer. He won't be driving a car, though. Bob Fenton has been blind since birth.

Learning to cope with his blindness has not been easy for Bob, despite the advantages of a supportive family and a sharp mind. What he has learned with such difficulty can guide us all.

Bob's parents have never pushed any of their three sons, of whom Bob is the oldest, into excelling. Instead, they have supported involvement in sports, cultural and school activities in a way that encourages but does not pressure their children. Bob thinks some parents "baby" their blind children, never encouraging them to try things on their own. Worse off are handicapped kids who are ignored by their families as lost causes. Bob hopes that both kinds of families can learn from kids like him, who are trying to be as independent as possible. It's all a matter of education.

Bob's own formal education began in a school he loved, the W. Ross MacDonald School for the Blind in Brantford, Ontario. His experience in grade 13 in a regular high school was "academically worthwhile, but socially not so good." Walking into a new school and trying to make new friends in one year is tough, even when you *can* see them. Bob found some students were shy about approaching him. They were unable to make the first move, and were perhaps intimidated by his high marks. And there were other problems.

Blind students' needs, says Bob, aren't always understood by teachers or fellow students. Some of those needs, such as requiring material to be read off the board for him, may annoy other students. Because of these difficulties, Bob thinks blind people have to assert themselves to get an education. "When in doubt, ask. They [people] may look at you kind of funny, but you can't see that!"

As part of his adaptation to the absence of vision, Bob "remembers" his way through the world. He says all his other senses are more focused to inform him of his surroundings. He gets along just fine, with the exception of loud music, which really disorients him. "I can't move, I can't tell where tables are. If I left the room I couldn't find my way back to the people I left." Loud music distracts his attention from the "map" he creates in his mind in order to get from one place to another.

There is little chance that Bob Fenton's blindness will be cured, but he's not waiting around. Instead, he's actively seeking an independent and satisfying life. The motivation burns in him to communicate, to learn and to succeed. And when things get rough? "You've got to keep going forward, going on. I have no respect for quitters, no matter what."

Bob Fenton (*l.***) running with his guide**

How to Write an Expository Paragraph — Level 4

Identify the four mistakes in the following paragraph. These are not factual or spelling mistakes, but mistakes in structuring an expository paragraph.

The Importance of Your Sense of Taste

Some people do not give much thought to their sense of taste, and consider their sense of sight or hearing much more important.

The sense of taste is vital, because without it we might swallow harmful substances, for example. You might also argue the our sense of sight can protect us because we can read the warning labels on bottles containing drugs and dangerous household products. Our ability to taste is also a great source of pleasure. Think how boring meals would be if you could not taste your food! Mealtime would become a nagging chore, not a satisfying experience.

Is your sense of taste as important or more important than other senses?

1. What are the four errors in the structure of the paragraph? If you have difficulty spotting the errors, review "How to Write an Expository Paragraph — Level 1," on page 73 of Chapter 4.

2. Correct the mistakes and re-write the paragraph properly.

3. Now write an expository paragraph on the topic "Which of my senses I would least like to lose, and why."

Sensation versus Perception

Look at Figure A. What do you see at first glance? As you continue to look, do you see anything else?

Figure A

Look at Figure B. Do you recognize these fragments as a horse and rider?

Figure B

Using a ruler, draw two vertical lines of equal length side by side. (See Figure C.) At both ends of one line, draw arrowheads. At both ends of the other line, draw reversed arrowheads. (See Figure D.) What do you notice? The lines that you know are of equal length now *appear* to be unequal.

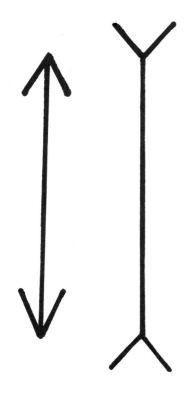

Figure C   Figure D

The first part of this chapter discussed sensation, the process by which we experience a variety of sense data — sound, smell, touch, taste, and so on. Our sensory organs receive various kinds of stimuli and transmit this information to the brain in the form of electrochemical nerve impulses.

At this point, the process of perception comes into play. We often use the word "perception" to mean a viewpoint or interpretation. The question "What's your perception of what happened last night?" uses this meaning of the word. In psychology, however, perception has a different meaning. When used by psychologists, **perception** refers to the process in which our brains *select, organize* and *interpret* (make sense of) the huge amounts of information assaulting our senses. For example, when you looked at the scattered shapes in Figure B, your brain "saw," or interpreted, a horse and rider, and not just random (disorganized) shapes.

The brain combines sensory information. In other words, it combines the various separate "pieces" of sense data into an understandable pattern. This process is happening right now as you read this page. Your brain is combining the black lines and curves of separate letters printed on the page into meaningful patterns known as words. Perception imposes an organization or meaning upon the sensory information our brains receive, so that we understand events in our environment.

To sum up, the process of perception involves the selection and organization of sense data so that we can understand our environment, and then respond in appropriate ways.

Perceptual Consistency

Psychologists believe that our brains have a natural tendency to perceive things in consistent (predictable) ways. For example, the brain tends to interpret complex patterns as simple patterns. Our brains strive to perceive consistent, recognizable patterns within the "raw," disorganized sense data they receive.

Figure A, for instance, illustrates the brain's tendency to recognize patterns or figures in the foreground first, and patterns in the background second. Your brain tends to select the figure of the vase first, while ignoring the background. You perceive the figures in the background only if you consciously direct your mind to ignore the figure of the vase and to focus on the background. Similarly, you can carry on a conversation with a friend in a noisy room because you focus on your friend's voice, which becomes the "figure." All other sounds become the "background."

In the same way, you can perceive a musical theme in a song despite all the other notes you are hearing at the same time.

The brain also strives for consistency in perceiving the sizes of objects that are near or far away from you. For example, as you watch a friend walking away from you, the visual image of that person shrinks in size. But you do not perceive your friend as actually getting smaller. This is because your brain is processing other meaningful information, that is, the fact that distance from your friend is increasing. This other information helps you interpret why your friend's image appears to be shrinking. Therefore, you can maintain a realistic perception of your friend's actual size. The two pieces of information — the changing size of the visual image and increasing distance from the image — are integrated by your brain. This lets you perceive that a person walking away from you remains the same size.

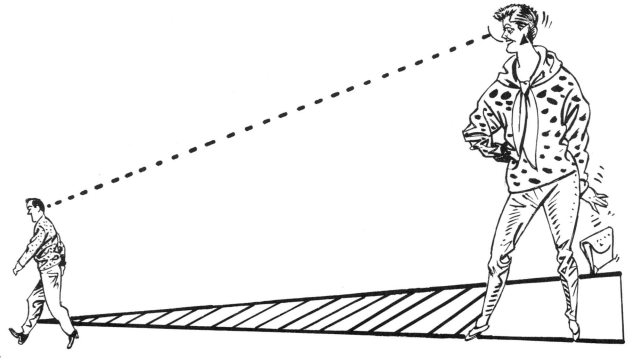

Why Is Perception Important?

Perception is important in two ways. First, in perception, the brain adds information that really isn't there. Second, it ignores meaningless or unnecessary information. These two functions of adding and ignoring information are vital to human beings. Although human beings have the most complex brains of any animal on Earth, we also have a limited attention span and a limited immediate memory. Therefore, we rely on perception to "economize" our mental efforts. We narrow our attention to focus on important things. We record information in our brains by "recoding" it into simple formulas that omit what isn't needed. Finally, we use certain devices to help us notice and recall important information. For example, the presence of rhyme in poetry helps us to remember the lines better. All these perceptual responses help us make sense of the information overload bombarding us.

. . . .

From Ideas to Action

1. List the ways in which you focus your attention in the following situations.
   a) reading a book on the bus
   b) talking to a friend in a noisy, crowded room
   c) remembering an important name or address
   d) writing a test in class

2. Explain which meaning of the word "perception" (viewpoint or process of organization, selection and interpretation) is used in each of the following sentences.
   a) The driver's perception of speed was impaired by alcohol.
   b) Colette's actions were guided by her perception of duty to her parents.
   c) During the experiment, John's visual perception was altered by the use of drugs.
   d) I read the latest book on extra-sensory perception, but I'm very sceptical of the claims made in it.
   e) What's your perception of the government's new policy?

3. How do you think magicians take advantage of the brain's tendency to see consistent, predictable patterns? If possible, learn a simple magic trick and perform it for the class.

4. Research some ways in which people who are deaf or blind learn to adapt to their sensory loss. If possible, either interview or invite to your class someone who is blind or hearing-impaired. Ask the person to comment on his or her emotional reaction to the sensory loss, and how the loss affected the person's lifestyle. Discuss as well the unique challenges that sense-impaired people face in our society. Can technological aids help them to cope with these challenges?

5. Select a public building such as a shopping mall, a government building or your school. Could a blind person use the building easily? What changes could you suggest to make the building more manageable for blind people? You may wish to write up your findings and suggestions and send them to the person in charge of the building.

Influences on Our Perception

Subjective Influences

What does this cartoon suggest to you about how we interpret what we see? Read on to discover individual factors that influence how we interpret the sensory data we receive. These factors are called **subjective influences** upon perception. A subjective influence comes from moods, attitudes or opinions.

The first subjective influence is known as **perceptual set**. This refers to what we *expect* to see, hear, taste or touch. For example, quickly read aloud the phrases in these triangles.

Try it again. You may need to read them several times before you see the repeated words.

Perceptual Set Alters Perception

There are many examples of perceptual set altering our perceptions. Think of a food that once made you violently sick. It is possible that you will avoid not only that food in future, but also any food that looks, smells or tastes similar to the one that made you sick. You *expect* these other foods to make you sick too, and they just might.

Another curious example of perceptual set involves how we look at each other. People who are important to us tend to appear larger than people who are unimportant. Bigger may not be better, but better definitely *seems* bigger.

Another subjective influence upon perception is **emotional state**. In one experiment, subjects viewed some pictures placed behind a ground-glass screen. The screen made it difficult to see the pictures clearly. The longer the subjects were deprived of food, the hungrier and more frustrated they became.

As the subjects grew hungrier and more frustrated, the more likely they were to associate the blurred images with food.

Some days when you are feeling unhappy, the whole world looks bleak. Everyone around you is hostile and critical of your behaviour. A neutral "How are things?" becomes an unwelcome invasion of your privacy, so you snap back "Get lost!" The feelings inside of you cause you to perceive an innocent question as a hostile one.

 ## The Bagby Experiment

J.W. Bagby of New York's Roosevelt Hospital devised an experiment in which American and Mexican school teachers looked into a device that presented a different visual image for each eye at the same time. One eye saw a picture of a baseball player, and the other eye saw a picture of a bullfighter. Most American teachers "saw" only the baseball player, while most Mexican teachers "saw" only the bullfighter.

From Ideas to Action

1. For each situation below, identify the subjective influence, either the perceptual set or emotional state, that is influencing perception. Briefly explain how the influence changes perception.
   a) As the chairperson of a community organization, you must appoint a secretary to keep records of decisions. You ask a female member of the committee to be the secretary, although there are lots of men available.
   b) Waves washing gently against a beach create a peaceful mood.
   c) When North American Indians first saw firearms in use, they thought that Europeans were able to throw lightning.
   d) A thirsty desert traveller sees water and palm trees on the shimmering sands ahead.
   e) When asked how tall the bank robber was, every eyewitness to the robbery gave a different height.

2. Write briefly about a personal experience involving subjective influences upon perception.

3. Imagine a scene showing a stand of tall white pines. Try to imagine how each of the following people would perceive the trees:
   a) a scientist who studies trees
   b) someone interested in preserving the environment c) a person in the lumber industry d) a poet e) a highway engineer

ESP — Fact or Fiction?

• •

Read the following article entitled "Probing the inexplicable" and also the book excerpt entitled "ESP is a problem for science." Then answer the follow-up questions.

Probing the inexplicable

By Carol Howes, *The Calgary Herald* (February 13, 1982)

Unexplainable.

Some scientists are mumbling that word over their breakfast coffee these days as they thumb through their files on psychic phenomena.

Despite all their effort to leave the subject alone, and despite efforts to convince the public it's just a bunch of hocus-pocus, the popularity of extrasensory perception and other psychic phenomena has been steadily growing...

"Culturally people are beginning to question materialism, immediate existence, life after death," explains University of Calgary professor Greg Fouts. "There's been a sharp increase in younger people wanting to know the meaning of life."

Fouts was one of the few Calgary scientists who jumped on the controversial bandwagon 10 years ago, when the surge of public interest in the subject had Calgarians on the university doorstep demanding information. Some were just curious; others claimed they had psychic abilities.

"A growing shift in the public view of science over the past decade has resulted in more and more people turning to other sources for answers," he says. "There's been a real shift in public mood — anti-scientific," he explains.

"Science usually raises a lot of hopes but it's let a lot of people down. They don't believe science any more."

Fouts has always considered himself a "healthy skeptic" and has conducted his research on psychic phenomena with an "open door" attitude. But like many who have delved into the subject, he has found himself torn between proof and the unexplainable.

The limited research that has been done in the area has not been very supportive, he says, and he has yet to find duplication in his experiments to convince him the phenomenon exists. Yet, he adds, "there have been instances I have no explanation for. I will basically use a psychic explanation because I don't know how else to explain it.

"We know one out of every 20 studies will come out significant," he explains. "But the science world needs consistency to make any conclusions," he adds.

Psychic phenomena include a wide variety of areas, most commonly described as anything "that goes beyond the ability of the five senses."

It includes extrasensory perception — telepathy (mind-to-mind communication); clairvoyance (reading future or distant events); psychokinesis (moving or altering physical objects with the mind); and sending messages to people across great distances.

Ghosts, faith healing and reincarnation are some of the other concepts that are commonly associated [with extrasensory perception]...

One particular case Fouts checked involved someone who phoned him complaining of hearing footsteps in an attic. Equipped with a tape recorder to record his conversation with the complainant, he investigated the situation, but to no avail. When he later played back the tape recording, he found the tape had been mysteriously wiped of all conversation that had taken place during the search.

"I don't know the explanation but I'm not willing to buy an easy one which is psychic," he says.

Since he began his investigations, Fouts says he's found only one of the approximately 50 people who claimed to be psychic and were willing to be tested, whose answers proved to be better than just chance.

The other stories he hears are written off as coincidences. A few are actually a result of emotional or psychological problems...

[Says] Ann Fohmzway, author of three books on psychic phenomena: "I don't profess to be 100-per-cent accurate; I'm not that vain. There's a lot of charlatans out there to make a big buck. Most of them are into body language which doesn't take much," she says. "They give the good ones a bad name."

A reporter who got readings from a number of psychics found most of them were accurate at general descriptions — current emotional and physical problems, career decisions, personality traits. Some were even dead accurate about past life experiences.

But when it came to the future, the readings varied greatly in detail.

"Psychics can only pick up general tendencies around you," explains [Calgary astrologer Pat] Kirst. "And depending on your emotional state that can change."

Other psychics offer a number of reasons why predictions of the future vary from reading to reading.

Like Kirst, Fohmzway agrees: "If you're down one day it's going to show up and if you're in a good mood it's going to change."

One psychic even maintains that if a subject is sick or upset his energy vibrations are weaker and harder to receive.

But psychic Lorna Levett says future decision-making and other unaccounted factors play a major role in limiting predictions.

"Destiny itself is like a pathway with potholes, and depending on what actions or inactions you take you can change it," she says.

For this reason many psychics limit their predictions to only a few years down the road.

Time is definitely a problem for most psychics.

Some say they receive answers in the form of pictures; yet they have no idea if these pictures are in the past, present or future. Others receive answers through physical feeling, "or just straight through as an answer.". . .

Their true ability they describe as a "gift" or an "awareness" from a higher source. They agree that everyone has the ability to develop this "sixth sense," although they differ as to why some are capable of developing it more than others.

Some, such as [psychic Hugh] Vickers, describe psychic ability as "genetically aware," while others describe it as "spiritually advanced."

Other psychics however, as well as Fouts, describe it as intuition. "Some people are just very good at reading people. How they sit, carry themselves, can tell you a lot. . .

Used by permission of *The Calgary Herald*

What appears to be a ghost in this photo is in fact the result of a photographic accident.

ISSUES

ESP is a problem for science

In his book, *Extrasensory Deception,* Toronto magician, columnist and broadcaster Henry Gordon criticizes the claims made by supporters of ESP.

...But one thing more than anything else convinces many that ESP does exist — the strange experiences we sometimes encounter. Whenever I lecture on ESP I get more questions on that aspect of it than anything else. "I had a dream about Aunt Clara in Vancouver. She was very ill. The next day they phoned me from there. It really happened. Can you explain that?" Or "My husband didn't come home at the usual time. I knew he was in a car accident. It turned out to be true." Perhaps you've had a strange experience. You were at a cocktail party. Suddenly, for no apparent reason, you thought of a friend you hadn't seen for twenty years. Nothing too strange there — these things can happen. But ten minutes later, as you navigate your way through the milling crowd, who do you come face to face with? That's right, the long-lost acquaintance. Shakes you up, doesn't it? File it away in your computer under "paranormal phenomena."

But, ... there is a statistical argument. Consider the millions of people who are worrying at any one time about the welfare of an absent relative. We never hear about the countless cases where nothing happens. But the odd case where something does happen is the one we always hear about. Just take the extremely small percentage of these cases as against the unreported ones. Isn't it more likely to be a coincidence than a case of ESP, which is highly improbable?

To which I might add the shower phenomenon. When you're in the shower and the phone rings, how many times have you said in exasperation, "Every time I'm in the shower the phone rings." Have you ever considered the number of times you've showered when the phone *didn't* ring? There's more than coincidence involved here. There's the matter of memory, which is very often unreliable.

Almost any psychology textbook will mention that distortions of memory are very common. These distortions are caused by many factors: omissions of certain details of an experience, distortions in one's perceptions of an event caused by built-in beliefs, and distortions caused by the passage of time.

The passage of time — this is the type of case that comes up constantly. Almost every psychic experience I hear about is one that happened ten, twenty, thirty years ago. How many distortions have accumulated in these anecdotes over the years, even when recounted by sincere people? We'll never know. But I can tell you this — I seldom hear of a case that has just happened, that can be immediately investigated with some chance of coming up with definite explanations.

To get back to your cocktail party experience — perhaps I can come up with a rational explanation. Have you heard of subliminal perception? That is your reception of a sensory memory without conscious awareness. Remember the "Eat Popcorn" messages flashed at high speed on drive-in movie screens? You got the message without realizing it. Well, here you are in this crowded room filled with the babble of voices. You hear this familiar voice from across the room, but it doesn't immediately dawn on your consciousness. It does make you think of the former friend, however, without realizing why.

When you finally see him or her it's a shocker. Another psychic anecdote has been added to that huge storehouse of the unexplained.

Reprinted from *Extra-Sensory Deception* © 1987 by Henry Gordon with permission of Prometheus Books, Buffalo, New York.

1. Name and describe the various types of extrasensory perception (ESP) and extrasensory phenomena.
2. What explanations are offered for these phenomena a) by psychics, and b) by Henry Gordon?
3. Why is it so difficult to prove that psychic powers do or do not exist?
4. How do psychics explain their "abilities"?
5. Write a paragraph on the topic "Do human beings possess psychic abilities?"

122

Detecting and Testing a Hypothesis — Level 1

The Social Scientist's Method

This exercise will reinforce your understanding of the method a social scientist uses to answer a question or to solve a problem. As you learned in Chapter 2, a social scientist first defines a problem to be examined. He or she then states a hypothesis that might solve the problem. The next step is to gather facts and to arrange the facts into a meaningful pattern. When the facts have been analysed, the scientist states certain interpretations or conclusions based on these facts. Read the following short case. The questions that follow will help you decide whether the facts in the case support the hypothesis.

The Extrasensory Perception Hypothesis

Do human beings have extrasensory powers? One story that seems to support this hypothesis concerns a sick woman's predictions of doom for herself and her family.

Lying ill in bed one night, Lilly told her husband that two misfortunes were about to strike. First, she predicted that she would die the next day at three o'clock. Then, turning to her eldest son, she said, "You are going to run off and get married this very evening, against our wishes."

Naturally, her son denied that this was so. And her husband assured Lilly that she would recover and live a long life. But the next day Lilly died at the appointed time and her son did get married that day, as she had foretold.

Later, Lilly's husband tried to make some sense of this strange occurrence. His doctor suggested that people can seem to will themselves to die. Lilly's apparent prediction was more likely just a self-fulfilled prophecy. Likewise, her comment to her son perhaps encouraged him to do something he had only dreamed of doing before.

Lilly's best friend, Gail, claimed that Lilly was a gifted person who could read minds and see into the future. Hence, Lilly knew what her son was thinking and could sense her own fate.

A psychologist argued that Lilly was probably just good at reading body language and at guessing. From the way her husband was looking at her, she had guessed that death was near. She could also tell that her son was anxious and guilty. She used this observation and what he had said before to guess that he wanted to run off and get married against his parents' wishes.

Definition of Hypothesis

A possible answer;
an educated guess;
an assumption that
directs your search for
an answer

Examples

1. People who are more important to us appear larger than people who are less important.

2. Dizziness can occur if sense data received through the eyes is contradicted by the body's balance mechanism, located in the inner ear.

1. Which of the following states the "extrasensory perception hypothesis" for Lilly's "predictions"?
   a) Lilly was good at guessing and at "reading" body language.
   b) Lilly could see into the future and read minds.
   c) Lilly told her husband when she would die and she predicted that her son would run off and get married.
   d) Lilly encouraged her son to run away and get married by planting this idea in his mind.

2. Read the following statements. Then write in your notebook whether each statement supports the extrasensory perception hypothesis (S), rejects the hypothesis (R), or neither supports nor rejects the hypothesis (N).
   a) The limited scientific research into ESP has not been supportive. Only one in 20 studies supports ESP.
   b) Psychoanalyst Logan Stanfield claims to have seen "energy healings."
   c) Some psychic believers claim that modern equipment is not sophisticated enough to prove the existence of ESP.
   d) Calgary professor Greg Fouts says he has been unable to duplicate ESP phenomena in his own experiments.
   e) Fouts says he has found that only one out of 50 people who claimed to be psychic and who were willing to be tested provided answers that proved to be better than chance.

3. Do you believe the extrasensory perception hypothesis is valid? Why or why not? What additional information would you need in order to change your opinion about this hypothesis?

Projects, Activities and Explorations

1. Create an imaginative display or a series of diagrams which illustrates the process of perception.

2. Locate photographs of scenes or people that have also been painted by famous Canadian artists. Compare these photographs with the paintings. In what important ways do the paintings differ from the photographs? How would you explain the differences?

3. Do some research to discover how physical beauty is defined in several different cultures. What characteristics are perceived as attractive in males and females in these cultures? How do you explain the differences, if any?

4. Watch a sports event, such as a hockey match or a basketball game. Write a detailed report of the game, making very careful observations. Compare your report with two or three newspaper accounts of the same game. Do the accounts differ from yours? If so, how and why?

5. Contact some organizations that help sense-impaired people to function in society. Ask for some information sheets, booklets and brochures. Then describe some ways in which sense-impaired people can be helped to cope with their sensory loss. Include special services, technological aids, government regulations, training programs, and anything else you discover in doing your research.

6. Try this classic test for ESP. Make a deck of 25 cards using five basic symbols. Each symbol will be shown on five cards. For example, you might use the symbols: X, O, OO, ? and !. A "sender" concentrates on one card at a time in one deck. A "receiver," who has a second deck and is out of sight of the "sender", guesses which card he or she thinks the sender has in mind. With simple luck, or chance, a receiver should be able to guess about five cards in the deck correctly each time. Test a group of students to see if any can score more than five correct guesses. Can the test be repeated successfully with the high scorers? If not, what do you conclude?

What Have You Learned?

If you have covered everything in this chapter you should be familiar with the following topics:

1. How we experience sensation – awareness of our internal and external environments – through our various sensory organs

2. How certain senses co-operate as we move about in the physical world

3. How the brain selectively focuses attention upon sensory stimuli

4. The difference between sensation and perception

5. Perceptual consistency (the brain's tendency to perceive similar patterns and to translate complex patterns into simple ones)

6. Subjective factors (including perceptual set and emotional state) that influence perception

7. How to write an expository paragraph

8. How to detect and test a hypothesis

To Help You Study

The following chart will help you review the words, facts and ideas that were introduced in this chapter. Copy the chart into your notebook and fill in the missing information.

Word, Fact, Idea	Example in a Sentence	Page	Definition
sense/sensory organ	The nose is the sensory organ for the sense of smell.	107	a specialized "receiver" that collects information about events taking place both inside and outside the body
stimulus			
sensory response			
sensation			
sense data			
proprioception			
kinesthesis			
selective attention			
perception			
perceptual consistency			
subjective influence			
perceptual set			
emotional state			

Learning 7

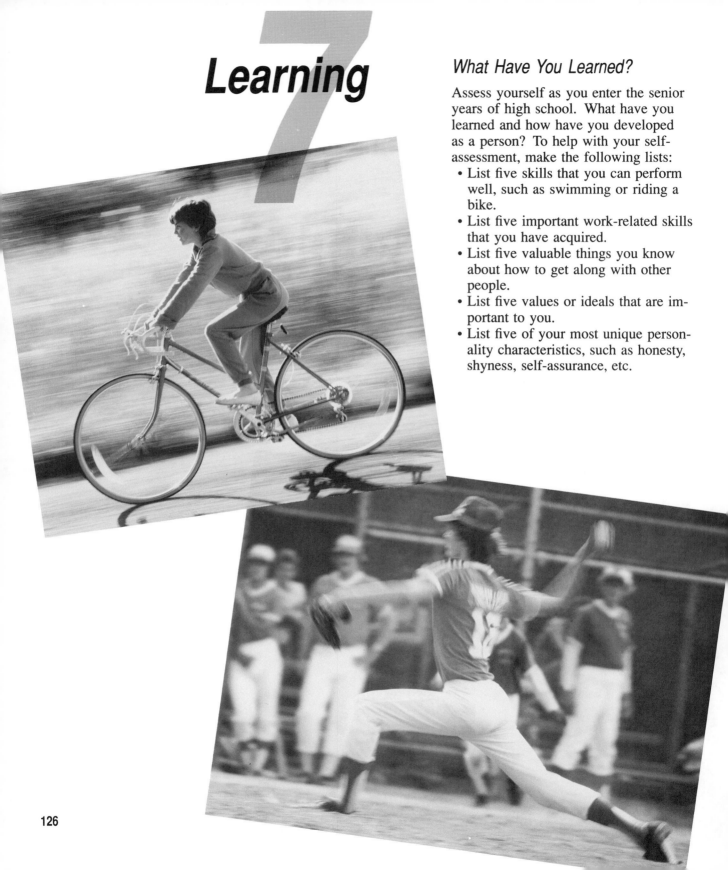

What Have You Learned?

Assess yourself as you enter the senior years of high school. What have you learned and how have you developed as a person? To help with your self-assessment, make the following lists:

- List five skills that you can perform well, such as swimming or riding a bike.
- List five important work-related skills that you have acquired.
- List five valuable things you know about how to get along with other people.
- List five values or ideals that are important to you.
- List five of your most unique personality characteristics, such as honesty, shyness, self-assurance, etc.

In small groups, discuss the following questions:

1. Were your lists different from those of other students? If so, why do you think they differ?
2. Which of the skills, abilities and personality characteristics that you listed do you think you were born with?
3. How do you think your life experiences have shaped the characteristics and abilities you now possess?
4. How many of the skills you listed were learned in school?

The self-assessment you just did points to the kinds of learning you have experienced, and the sources of that learning. Learning is a fundamental process in human development. Psychologists have been studying and arguing about learning for almost 100 years.

In this chapter you will find out what psychologists know about learning. You will also discover some ways to use this knowledge to help you change your behaviour and that of others.

Learning and Intelligence

What Is Learning?

Learning takes place when we come to recognize a connection between two events that had not been connected previously in our minds. In psychology, **learning** is defined as a change in human behaviour (what you do) or capacity (what you are able to do). This change comes about through repeated experience of certain associations. For example, if we experience a connection or an association between a hot stove and pain, we learn to avoid touching hot objects. Or, if we experience an association between a long wind-up and power, we learn to perform a successful slapshot in hockey.

Some behaviours do not have to be taught at all. These are called **reflex behaviours**. When light shines into your eye, the pupil of the eye automatically gets smaller. You do not have to be taught this pupil-contracting reflex. You do it perfectly from birth.

Generally speaking, early changes in human behaviour or capacity are part of a "built-in," or innate, plan for growth and development. Whether a baby is born in Tokyo or Trenton, she will lift her head at about three months. She will begin to crawl and to pull herself upright at eight or nine months, and she will take her first unsteady steps at about twelve months. Language skills develop in a similar step-by-step fashion. The gradual development that takes place in the brains, nerves and muscles of infants and young children is called **maturation**. The maturation process makes human learning possible.

The rate of maturation is unique to each child. There is no single schedule of events. Babies develop at different rates because, for one thing, they differ in temperament. Some are active, while others are quiet. Babies' surroundings also influence the rate of maturation. For example, in learning how to walk, a child needs a suitable space to explore and move about in, with safe objects and furniture to use as supports. In learning to talk, a baby needs someone in his or her environment to listen and to respond to verbally.

This child's rate of maturation is influenced by her mother's attention and conversation.

The Development of Intelligence

Many psychologists think there are *stages* of human maturation and development, and that these stages are important to learning. One of the most influential researchers was a Swiss psychologist, Jean Piaget (1895–1980). Piaget started out as a biologist studying plant and animal life. He spent most of his life, however, studying the development of intelligence in children. **Intelligence** is the ability to learn and know. It is also the ability to use abstract thought to deal with new situations and to solve problems. Piaget concluded that a child's mental development can be divided into four stages. The stages are *cumulative*. This means that a child must have reached the capabilities of one stage before progressing to the next stage. A brief summary of Piaget's theory of development is shown in the chart on the next page.

Jean Piaget in 1973

Stage	Age	Characteristics	
Stage One	Birth to 2 years	A child learns to distinguish parts of himself from other objects in his environment. For example, he learns that his hands are part of him, but that a wooden boat is not. He also gradually learns that when the boat is hidden under a blanket, it still exists. He will therefore search for it. This shows he has reached the stage of recognizing a difference between himself and the outer world.	
Stage Two	2 to 6 years	A child begins to speak, can visualize things in her mind and can draw pictures. Although she is beginning to use symbols such as words and pictures, she must still act out a problem in order to solve it. For example, she can easily choose a square peg to fit into a square hole, but she cannot explain how she knows that this is the correct choice.	
Stage Three	6 to 12 years	A child can solve simple arithmetic problems. He can also understand that when two cups of water are poured into a tall, thin glass, the volume of water is the same as when two cups are poured into a low dish. He stills needs to work through this kind of puzzle with the actual objects — two cups of water, a glass and a dish. He can't yet figure out the solution in his head.	
Stage Four	12 years to Adulthood	A teenager begins to understand connections between abstract things as well as concrete things. She can form a hypothesis about a problem, for example, by associating doing homework and getting high grades. She can then systematically test this hypothesis. She learns about cause and effect in the physical world, as well as in the world of values, attitudes and emotions. She begins to question previously accepted values.	

From Ideas to Action

1. Explain whether or not each of the following are examples of learning.
   a) After years at a gym club, Sandy has developed her skills in gymnastics.
   b) Little Colin seemed to be behind the other children in the playgroup. He was very clumsy and did not speak as well as the other children in the room. However, by the time he was three, he was just as co-ordinated and verbal as the other children.
   c) Karl put his hand on the stove accidently. He pulled his hand away rapidly.
   d) Alicia, who grew up in a large family, is able to get the students she works with in groups to co-operate.

2. The behaviours of three children at different stages of development are described below. In which of Piaget's stages would you place each child?

   a) This child can see that two plasticine balls of the same mass remain equal in mass, even if one is squashed flat. The child can observe differences in the sizes of objects, and can order the objects from largest to smallest. The child can also count objects in boxes, and can say which group of boxes contains the greatest number of objects.
   b) This child enjoys placing his fingers and toes in his mouth. The child is very responsive to finger-snapping, and will follow this sound closely. The child can reach out and hit an object suspended above his bed. He enjoys the sound made when this happens. The child will search for an object, even though the object is out of sight.
   c) This child can solve a wooden jigsaw puzzle. She fits the pieces randomly in the spaces and discards the ones that don't work.

3. As an assistant manager in a toy store, you are expected to help shoppers choose gifts for their children. Using Piaget's theory of development, list some types of toys that you would recommend for each stage of development. What would the child learn when playing with each toy?

4. Suppose that your parents have given you permission to decorate the new baby's room. With Piaget's first stage of development in mind, how would you decorate the nursery? What furniture or objects do you think would be appropriate?

How Learning Takes Place

Have you ever had the experiences described below? Think about the situations, and then answer the follow-up questions.

- You pretend to give your dog a treat. You call your pet and snap your fingers, just as you do when you have a treat for it. The dog sits up and begs several times, even though you don't feed it anything.
- When the end-of-class bell rings, you unthinkingly slap your books closed and pick them up. You then realize that the student presenting her paper is still in mid-sentence.
- For several weeks you have been playing cards for money on Friday nights. You are thinking of giving it up, though, because you never seem to win. Then, one night, you win nearly every hand. For weeks afterwards, you are keen to play cards.

1. Why does your dog react in the way described above?
2. Why do you sometimes respond to the bell in the way described above?
3. Why would you be keen to continue playing cards if you began to win a lot?
4. Think of other situations in which your behaviour, or that of another person or animal, seemed "programmed" in some way.

Compare your experiences with those of other students. Then discuss the following questions:

1. In the situations described above, certain types of behaviour have been learned. What do these learning situations have in common with each other?
2. How do you think this type of learning works?
3. Do you think this is an effective type of learning? Why or why not?

Classical Conditioning

Conditioning is a result of learning. In sports, an athlete may spend hours every day in training. Through this training, the athlete's body learns to respond to the demands of the sport. We say that the athlete is well conditioned. Without training, the body will not learn the proper responses and we would say that the athlete is unconditioned. In psychology and in sports, conditioning refers to what is learned.

All learning involves a **stimulus** and a **response**. For a hungry dog, food is a stimulus. No one has to train a dog to eat food, so the food is called an **unconditioned** stimulus. A dog also naturally salivates at the sight of food. This behaviour is called a **response** and because no one trained the dog to salivate, it's called an **unconditioned response**.

A whistle is also a stimulus. To your dog, it is a **neutral stimulus**, that is, it has no particular meaning. It is just a sound.

However, if you whistle every time you feed your dog, the whistling becomes connected to food in your dog's mind. Soon your dog will respond to your whistle by running to its food dish. The whistle is now called a **conditioned stimulus**, because your dog has *learned* the connnection between whistling and food. The response of running to the food dish is now called a **conditioned response** because the response has been learned or conditioned.

Look at the following cartoon sequence. Explain what is happening in each frame using the terms of classical conditioning.

Some psychologists claim that many human fears are learned through this process of conditioning.

From Ideas to Action

1. For each of the following examples, identify the unconditioned stimulus (US), the unconditioned response (UR), the conditioned stimulus (CS) and the conditioned response (CR).

   a) Sally was a subject in a conditioning experiment. She sat on a chair with a special pair of glasses on. The glasses were connected to a tube that would blow a puff of air into her eye. This always made her blink. During the experiment, the experimenter tapped a pencil on the desk just before the puff of air was delivered to her eye. After a while the experimenter would just tap the pencil. In time, Sally would blink to the tapping pencil alone.

   b) Bill was just learning his position as a receiver on the football team. One day in practice he was not wearing his helmet when he failed to catch a ball thrown to him. It slipped through his fingers and hit him directly in the face. From that day onwards his coaches could not get him to stop closing his eyes whenever the ball was near his head.

2. Suppose your pet is conditioned to the sound of the fridge door opening. It responds by running into the kitchen at the sound. Could you condition your pet to respond in the same way to a second conditioned stimulus, such as a bell ringing? How would you go about this?

3. Explain how an association could be learned between a) people in white coats and pain b) new kinds of food and disgust c) snakes and fear. Draw a diagram like the one on page 130 to help you chart and label the steps in the learning process.

4. Find information in your school library about Ivan Pavlov's research into classical conditioning. Present your findings to the class. Include diagrams if you like.

Learning to Kick the Habit

Some therapists use a type of classical conditioning to trick cigarette smokers into quitting. The technique involves having a smoker learn an association between smoking and an extremely unpleasant experience. Sometimes a drug that causes nausea can be associated with cigarettes, if the smoker smokes cigarettes and takes the drug at the same time. In this way, the client may learn an association between the unpleasant drug (unconditioned stimulus) and smoking (conditioned stimulus). If this association is learned, the client will experience nausea (the conditioned response) upon lighting up a cigarette. If the therapy is successful, the client, once conditioned, will experience nausea whenever he or she attempts to smoke.

Operant Conditioning

Study the illustrations below and answer the following questions:
1. What is happening in these illustrations?
2. What is causing the cat's behaviour?
3. If the cat were put back in the cage again several times how do you think its behaviour would change?
4. This kind of learning is called **trial and error.** From the experience of the cat, what do you conclude about trial and error learning?

The cat in the illustrations hit the release device more and more quickly each time it was put back into the cage. It had learned that a certain behaviour brings a reward. This reward encouraged the cat to repeat its behaviour when in the cage. This kind of learning is called **operant conditioning**.

B.F. Skinner and Operant Conditioning

An American psychologist, B.F. Skinner, used operant conditioning to train pigeons to walk in circles, and eventually to dance. Skinner observed a pigeon as it turned and walked about in its cage. He rewarded the bird with food (the stimulus) *only* when it turned clockwise (the desired response). The food reward (stimulus) strengthened the connection in the bird's mind between the stimulus and the desired response (turning clockwise). As this association became stronger, the bird was soon turning in circles.

In operant conditioning, each time a subject performs a desired response, the subject receives a **positive reinforcement** (reward) for that behaviour. A **positive reinforcement** is any stimulus that causes the desired behaviour to be repeated.

The subject being conditioned must value the stimulus for that stimulus to act as a positive reinforcement. For example, reinforcement with food will probably be ineffective for an animal already satisfied with food. A child who dislikes sweet foods is not likely to be reinforced by candy. Rewards in the form of high marks or academic praise will be effective *only* if a student values academic rewards to begin with.

Learning is often more effective if the reinforcement follows the desired response immediately. This means, for example, that students should receive the results of tests as soon as possible. In this case, the correct answers on a test are the desired response. The test, marked by the teacher and returned to the students, is the reinforcement.

Once learning has taken place, people and animals will continue to perform the desired behaviours even though they

B.F. Skinner at Harvard University

may not be reinforced for the behaviour every time. The change from external control of behaviour to internal control by the individual has happened. The behaviour has been learned.

Behaviour Modification

Behaviour modification is an application of learning using operant conditioning. It involves a specific program of rewards designed to change behaviour permanently. An important part of the reward program is praise. Praise helps the subject feel good about the desired behaviour and learn to make it part of his or her own behaviour. Eventually, no rewards or praise from other people will be needed as reinforcement. The steps described on the next page are used in behaviour modification to teach a desired behaviour.

Steps in Behaviour Modification

1. Define *precisely* the behaviour to be modified.	• Example of precise definition: *Maria leaves her clothes in piles all over her room.* Example of imprecise definition: *Maria is too messy.*
2. Determine how often the behaviour occurs and how often the desired behaviour should occur.	• Maria never picks up her clothes until one of her parents yells at her. She should pick up her clothes every day.
3. Design a specific program of rewards. Decide how long the program is to continue.	• Maria will receive 50 cents toward a new poster for her bedroom each time she remembers to pick up her clothes and put them away. The program will continue for three weeks.
4. Ensure that the program is understood and agreed to by both parties.	• Maria understands exactly what the consequences of her behaviour will be in terms of rewards.
5. Carry out the agreement consistently for the agreed length of time.	• Maria wants the poster, so she earns the necessary money by cleaning up her room. By the end of three weeks she is behaving as desired every day. She has learned to associate a certain desired response (cleaning up her room) with a certain stimulus (the money for a poster). Praise makes her feel positive about her own behaviour and willing to continue without the money reward.

From Ideas to Action

1. Decide whether classical or operant conditioning is involved in each of the following situations:

   a) Robert doesn't like math. He had a bad experience with math in grade 6 and hasn't liked it since then.

   b) Every time Martin does his chores, his father gives him a hug.

   c) Some babysitters bribe the children in their care with rewards for good behaviour.

   d) Many pets are afraid of thunder and lightning. Some dogs also display fear of rain.

   e) Tony and his shop teacher worked out a plan to help Tony improve his marks. He did extra work after school, for which he received bonus credits.

   f) Schools award prizes to students achieving high marks.

2. Explain how you might use classical or operant conditioning to modify behaviour in the following situations. Use a diagram if you like.

   a) teaching your dog to fetch a newspaper

   b) encouraging someone to cook healthier meals

   c) making sure students attend classes

   d) making sure a young child puts toys in the toy box after playing with them

3. Imagine you are a teacher. One of your students is having difficulty in your subject. The student is skipping class, is not paying attention and is disrupting your lessons. How could you use behaviour modification techniques to change the student's undesirable behaviour to desirable behaviour? You might role-play the techniques with a classmate.

Learning and Punishment

How Effective Are Punishments?

List some punishments intended to change behaviour a) at school b) at home c) at work. Which punishments do you think are effective? Which ones do you think are ineffective?

When you have completed your list, compare your findings with those of other students. Then answer the following questions:

1. Group the punishments you listed into three categories: "very effective," "somewhat effective" and "not very effective." How are the punishments in each category similar? How are they different?

2. Do any of the punishments seem to cause more problems than they solve? Explain your answer.

3. Do you think punishments are more or less effective than rewards in changing behaviour? Think of some examples to support your viewpoint.

Our culture has several well-known sayings that support the value of punishment. One old saying is "Spare the rod and spoil the child." In the types of learning discussed so far, reinforcement in the form of rewards has been used to *increase the likelihood of a response*. The goal of punishment is precisely the opposite: *to reduce the likelihood of a response* (for example, being late for school).

Punishment can take the form of an unpleasant stimulus. This is the kind of punishment involved when a child is sent to its room for playing on the street. Punishment can also be the removal of a pleasant stimulus. Losing access to the family car for staying out too late is an example of this kind of punishment.

There are some basic ideas to keep in mind when you are trying to decide if punishment might be effective in a learning situation:

a) Consistency: Punishment should be applied *every* time an undesirable behaviour occurs. If this is not done, the behaviour becomes even harder to change.

b) Timing: To be effective, punishment should follow the undesirable behaviour as soon as possible.

c) Intensity: People and animals can become accustomed to punishment over time. Psychologists say that punishment should be as severe as is necessary to change the behaviour. For example, you should not begin to discipline your dog with a minor punishment (such as a stern look) and increase to a more severe punishment. If you do, you allow your dog to become accustomed to the undesirable behaviour while the punishment is light.

Problems Caused by Punishment

The use of punishment to change behaviour is a controversial issue. Punishment can have harmful side-effects and some definite disadvantages. First, the results achieved through punishment are not as predictable as are the results achieved through rewards. A study of the effects of punishment in toilet training young children showed that punishment actually *contributed* to bed-wetting. Another study found that children who were punished for aggressive behaviour only became more aggressive. Many observers argue that when punished, people will often hide, rather than change, the undesirable behaviour.

Often the person who punishes a child — a teacher or a parent — is also responsible for teaching that child. A child who has been punished may try to avoid the person who has given the punishment, instead of changing the undesirable behaviour. This means that the child may lose out on opportunities to be taught healthy, appropriate behaviours.

Many people feel that when an adult physically punishes a child, an example for aggressive behaviour is set up. For the child, a slap can become deeply engraved as an acceptable form of behaviour. The verbal part of the lesson, which should tell the child how to behave, can get lost in the act of punishment.

From Ideas to Action

1. Choose at least six different behaviours that you have observed during a typical school day. State how each behaviour is positively reinforced (rewarded).

2. a) Observe and take notes on how one of your teachers reinforces (rewards) appropriate behaviour. Be sure to observe both verbal and non-verbal forms of reinforcement.
   b) To what extent does the teacher use punishments rather than rewards in shaping students' behaviour?

3. Examine a copy of your school's code of behaviour, the school's official policy on enforcing rules. To what extent does the school rely on punishments or other means to control students' behaviour? Do you think the school's policy is effective in changing behaviour? Why or why not?

4. You have just bought a dog. Develop a training program, based on conditioning principles, that will teach your dog to:
   a) roll over and play dead
   b) sit up and beg for food
   c) fetch you the newspaper from the front door

Cognitive Learning

Can you solve this word puzzle? Unscramble the four jumbled words below. Then rearrange them into a sentence.

GINSOLV KESTA SUZZLEP ORTFFE

In small groups, discuss the following questions:
1. How did you go about solving the puzzle? What *kind* of thinking would you say you used?
2. Did all the students in your group solve the puzzle in the same way? Can you detect different methods by which other students solved the puzzle?
3. Do you think you could use conditioning to teach the kind of learning needed to solve word puzzles? Why or why not?

Another approach to learning comes from a branch of psychology which sees learning as a **cognitive** process. The word "cognitive" refers to a broad range of behaviours that we identify as "thinking". These behaviours include problem solving, decision making, classifying, perceiving, labelling and interpreting. These behaviours are usually considered "thought processes."

Thus far, we have looked at learning solely in terms of conditioning. In classical conditioning, a person or an animal learns a response by associating a new stimulus with an existing stimulus. In operant conditioning, new behaviour is learned because the behaviour is rewarded.

Let's illustrate the difference between the two approaches to learning, conditioning and cognitive learning, by looking at how math operations are learned. It is *possible* that 3 + 4 = 7 could be learned through conditioning. This would mean repeated reinforcement of the correct response. In other words, the stimulus "3 + 4" could be reinforced consistently to produce the response "7." But what happens when you try to solve more complex math problems, such as 6244 − 2890? It is unlikely that reinforcement could teach the correct responses to problems such as these. What must be learned in order to perform complex math operations is a set of mathematical principles.

Learning Through Insight

Try solving these problems.
1. Below is a conversation in code between a waiter and a customer in a restaurant. Try to discover what the customer is ordering by quickly saying each separate letter and number aloud.
   Customer: FUNEX?
      Waiter: SVFX.
   Customer: NEM?
      Waiter: SVFM2.
   Customer: DUFT?
      Waiter: ST2.
   Customer: LFMNXNT.

2. The sentence below does not seem to make any sense. Can you put in punctuation marks so that the sentence *does* make sense?

   it was and I said not but

You can see that the kind of thinking required to solve problems such as these is very complex. The stimulus-response association in conditioning is simple in comparison. Notice that the learner is very involved during cognitive learning. Rather than simply receiving a stimulus, the learner actively plays with it, trying to see what it can become, organizing and reorganizing thoughts and reactions to it until a solution is reached.

Kohler's experiments highlighted the role of insight in learning. **Insight** is a relatively sudden form of cognitive learning that occurs when the subject recognizes a new relationship or connection between certain elements in the environment. Sultan was not trained to see the relationship between the sticks and the bananas. Instead, he experienced a flash of insight that enabled him to perceive the sticks placed in his environment in a new and creative way.

We often experience insightful learning. To give an everyday example, it is common to substitute one tool for another if the correct tool is not available. If you don't have the correct tool for taking the tire off a bicycle wheel, you

This dog cannot apply problem-solving to solve its problem. It will try various activities until it eventually discovers the solution.

In the mid 1920s, a German psychologist, Wolfgang Kohler, discovered that chimps could learn to solve problems. Sultan, Kohler's most intelligent ape, learned to stack boxes in order to reach bananas that were placed out of his grasp. In a second experiment, Sultan had two sticks placed in his cage. By joining two lengths of sticks together, like a fishing pole, he could reach the fruit. At first the ape had little success, and he appeared to give up. Later, however, while playing with the sticks, Sultan accidentally lined them up with one another. In a flash, the ape understood the relationship between the sticks and the bananas and he quickly secured the reward.

might substitute the handle of a pair of pliers.

Scientists have discovered that insightful learning depends on a variety of factors. These include:

1. *Experience.* The broader the range of your experience, the more likely you are to experience insightful learning.

2. *Organization of the learning experience.* Ideally, all the elements of the learning event should be present or available. We might not be able to substitute an alternative tool unless it is clearly within sight.

3. *Trial and error.* Insightful learning is often accompanied by trial and error activities, involving random, disorganized behaviour.

Learning by Modelling

We don't always have to experience a situation first-hand in order to learn. We can learn new responses by observing the responses of others before we experience them ourselves. This form of cognitive learning through observation is called **modelling**.

Imitation is a form of modelling that occurs when, after observing a behaviour, you can then perform the behaviour yourself. Examples of imitation are learning dance steps from an instructor, or learning how to use a skateboard by watching others. "How-to" books and films are based on this kind of learning. Much of the learning that takes place in school involves conscious imitation of examples.

Modelling can be a very efficient way of learning some behaviours. To explain to someone verbally how to drive from your house to the nearest bank could be confusing. Drawing a map — a visual model, an imitation of reality — to show someone how to get to the bank is much more effective. Think about the many skills that are easy to demonstrate visually, but are too complicated to be explained verbally. Two examples are gymnastics movements and dance routines.

Parents are often frustrated to discover that their children are learning behaviours by watching rather than by listening. If parents advise against speeding and dangerous driving, for instance, but continue to do both themselves, their children will imitate parental *behaviour*, rather than parental advice. The old saying, "Do as I say, not as I do" just doesn't work.

From Ideas to Action

1. Identify each of the examples below as either conditioning or cognitive learning. Briefly explain your answers by refering to the characteristics of conditioned and cognitive learning.

   a) Fred had a serious car accident when he was a child. When he reached an age where he could learn how to drive, he was reluctant to take lessons.

   b) One day Eli Whitney was watching a cat trying to catch a bird by reaching its claws through a hole in a picket fence. The bird escaped and the cat caught only a few feathers in its claws. Whitney realized that this illustrated the answer to the problem of how to separate cotton wool from the seeds in the cotton plant. He built a machine that duplicated the cat, the fence and the bird.

   c) The Johnsons were teaching their son to clean his room. Each time he picked up an article of clothing, they gave him a hug. Eventually he would clean his whole room.

   d) The tennis star was having a hard time against a young opponent. The youngster seemed to have developed a new kind of serve. The star tried various combinations of return shots that had worked well in the past. She soon realized that one combination kept the youngster off balance. The star went on to win the match.

2. Identify the kind of cognitive learning (insight or modelling) involved in each situation:

   a) The students are building a three-dimensional model of Vancouver Island based on maps that show the contours of the land.

   b) Joe stared at the puzzle for ten minutes, then suddenly saw the solution.

   c) On her first day at a new school, Yvette tagged along behind a group of students who weren't new to the school.

   d) Rita discovered she could use a pair of pliers instead of the missing wrench to remove the handlebar nut from her bicycle.

   e) The teacher did not punish Vic and Sue for their misbehaviour. Soon the other kids in the class began to misbehave too.

3. Recall the exercise you did at the beginning of this chapter. Now list some of your skills, characteristics and abilities that have resulted from modelling. For example, writing, eating with a knife and fork, and skating are skills. Honesty and timidity are characteristics.

How to Ace a Test

Here are some learning tips that can help you study and remember more effectively:

1. Behaviours that are positively reinforced are more likely to be repeated. Give yourself a small reward such as a snack each time you successfully complete a learning task.

2. Sheer repetition, without signs of improvement or without reinforcement, is a poor way to learn. Always be careful to identify what you are not doing correctly, and then try to correct your errors. Have your teacher go over a test or an assignment with you to provide immediate feedback on your progress.

3. The period of most rapid forgetting occurs immediately after you have learned something. Recalling information by going over your notes after school will reduce the amount of material forgotten. Frequent review is much more valuable than cramming sessions.

4. Learning by reading is more effective if you spend time recalling what you have read, rather than rereading.

5. When you are learning a idea, try to apply it to something outside the classroom that you do in everyday life. For example, if you are trying to learn about positive reinforcements, think about all the things you have learned by being rewarded.

6. Avoid memorizing new material by itself. You will be more successful if you relate the new material to concepts you already understand. For example, when you study operant conditioning, compare these new ideas to classical conditioning, which you learned earlier.

7. Make sure you *understand* what you are learning. If you are not sure of something, check with your teacher. Experiments have shown that material that is understood is more easily recalled than information that is not understood or merely memorized.

8. You learn more effectively if you break up the learning period into short, brief sessions. Don't study in one long cram session.

9. There is evidence that learning is more effective when followed by sleep instead of another activity!

Challenge: Choose one of these nine learning tips and put it into practice as much as you can. Compare your results on tests before using this tip to your results after you have used it for a while.

Using the Library — Level 1

An important skill that can help you become a more effective learner is knowing how to use a library. This exercise will teach you how to use library resources and research tools.

1. The **subject catalogue** lists books in the library according to topic. An example of a subject heading in this type of catalogue is: "Psychology."

   Use the subject catalogue to find the *authors* and *titles* of some books on the following topics: child abuse, stress, learning.

2. The **author/title catalogue** lists books in the library alphabetically by the author's last name and/or the title of the book.

   a) Use the author/title catalogue to find the *titles* of books about the future by authors Alvin Toffler and John Naisbitt.

   b) Now use the author/title catalogue to find the *author* and *title* of a book whose title contains one of these words: sociology, psychology, social problems, anthropology.

3. The **vertical file** is a collection of newspaper and magazine articles filed alphabetically by subject area, for example, "Learning."

   Use the vertical file to find the *title, date* and *source* (for example, *The Toronto Star*) of an article on one of these topics: television, suicide, cults, the elderly.

4. **Encyclopedias** are sets of books that give brief overviews of topics. Generally, these books are organized according to subject headings listed alphabetically. Refer to the encyclopedia's index to find the volume and the pages for the subject you're interested in.

   Use an encyclopedia to list the *volume* and the *pages* of material on these topics: pornography, heredity, crime.

5. A library also has **reference books** that provide basic background information on certain topics, rather than detailed analyses. Examples of reference books are the *Canadian Senior Dictionary* and *The Canadian Almanac*.

   Use one of the following reference books to look up the *pages* containing material on the topic in brackets.
   Canada Year Book (health)
   KWIC Index To Your Ontario Government Services (prejudice)
   A Dictionary of Psychology (perception)
   Directory of Community Services (youth)

6. All school and public libraries use a numbering system called the **Dewey Decimal System** to arrange books on the shelves according to subject. For example, 540 is the number for chemistry.

   Use the subject catalogue to find the *range of numbers* for pyschology, sociology and anthropology.

How Reliable Are Intelligence Tests?

You have probably taken a version of an I.Q. test. How well did you do? Did the test determine which school program you would enrol in? Where you ever told the test results? Read the article below and then answer the follow-up questions.

IQ tests: Battle still rages over their use

By Elaine Carey, *The Toronto Star*
[October 20, 1985]

In two high schools in North York, psychologist Mike Luther is taking students who are failing miserably and teaching them how to improve their scores on intelligence tests.

The simple fact is that middle class kids do well on IQ tests and disadvantaged kids don't, he argues, because they lack the skills needed to do the tests — organization, precision and fast thinking.

So Luther, who went to Israel for the North York Board of Education to study a unique program developed there, teaches those students how to slow down, be less impulsive in answering the questions and get organized.

"We teach the kids how to do better on the tests we eventually have to give them," he said.

Many of the students end up with a higher intelligence score which allows Luther to pull them out of the vocational programs they have been streamed into or prevent them from being placed there in the first place.

Is Luther allowing the real intelligence of the students to come through, as he argues, or is he simply teaching the test?

It is the latest round in the ongoing battle over intelligence and the value of IQ tests in measuring

Mike Luther, North York Board of Education

it that has raged throughout the twentieth century.

Opinion is so divided that two of the largest school boards in Metro — Etobicoke and Scarborough — still administer IQ or similar intelligence tests to all elementary students while the rest, including North York and Toronto, don't routinely test children at all.

IQ tests began to fall out of favor in the late 60s and early 70s with the arrival of immigrants, particularly West Indians, who scored poorly on the tests and were put in vocational streams and schools for the retarded.

They argued the tests were culturally biased and loaded with questions on language and vocabulary that a child who had grown up in another country could not hope to answer.

Test defenders argued that intelligence was innate and some groups were genetically inferior, launching the still hotly contested battle over whether intelligence is born or bred...

A report to the [Toronto] board in 1978 said IQ tests should be discouraged because while they identify what areas a student may be weak in, it's a myth they measure intelligence. The tests measure skills important in school, it said, but they don't test other aspects of intelligence like memory, human understanding and creativity...

Others argue IQ tests are still the best indicator of success in school and later life.

"They are one of the most important contributions to psychology in this century," said Colin MacLeod, associate professor of psychology at the University of Toronto. "I can't think of a better way to decide who should be admitted to gifted programs."

School boards that drop testing because it's a political hot potato are "bowing to any influence that comes along," he said. "The idea of dropping something because it shows you have a problem to me is ridiculous. It's like not using a thermometer because it shows some people are sick."

But he admits an IQ score does not show creativity, music ability or even genius. Psychologists still don't know how to measure those qualities.

"You can have very bright people who will never compose a symphony," he said. "And a genius is probably someone who is very bright but they have got to have a lot more than that."

Harvard University psychologist Howard Gardner argues there are actually seven intelligences including social grace, athletic skill, musical ability and self-knowledge as well as the standard verbal, mathematical and spatial abilities.

"There are too many people who are brilliant at short answer quizzes and yet failures at life for that talent to be important," he said in his book, *Frames of Mind.* "Even the newer IQ tests last only a few hours and it may be impossible to draw a realistic picture of a human being in that time."

But Tony Vernon, a psychologist at the University of Western Ontario, calls the IQ score "the single best predictor of numerous different things including scholastic achievement and occupational success. It doesn't predict with better than a 50 per cent accuracy, but it's the best we have."

Vernon argues that intelligence is inbred and the most a good environment can do is bring a child up to his or her potential. Any attempt to improve an IQ score — like the North York program — is simply teaching the test...

Children do get put in the wrong program because of their IQ score, he admits, "but you just have to hope that teachers can spot them. Using an IQ score per se [by itself] is not a satisfactory thing."

And even Vernon, a leading intelligence researcher, cautions that tests should be confined to individual problem cases, not used on a group...

The first modern IQ test was developed in 1905 by French psychologist Alfred Binet to help the government identify schoolchildren in need of remedial education.

His test was taken up enthusiastically by American psychologists and in 1916 Lewis Terman of Stanford University produced an expanded version called the

Stanford-Binet test, still one of the most popular measures used today.

Terman called the final score an Intelligence Quotient — calculated by dividing a subject's mental age by his physical age and multiplying by 100. A six-year old performing at a six-year-old level would then have an IQ of 100; if he performed at the nine-year-old level, he would have an IQ of 150.

Psychologists insist they analyze the various parts of the IQ test to get a picture of a person and how he learns. But they admit the general public latches on to the final score as a label to be saddled with for life — bright, average or stupid.

Quarter says IQ tests came into fashion because teachers needed something objective, beyond their own assessment, for classifying kids.

"Basically what it's used for is to classify people, and schools want some politically safe way to do it," he said. "If you're referring a child to a special education class because he's doing poorly,

this is a more powerful type of judgment.

"Psychologists say they can save some kids because they scored high in IQ even though they were doing poorly in class," he said. "But for every one they save, ten go under."

The Toronto Board uses academic prowess [ability], creative thinking and commitment to specific tasks in determining who should be admitted to gifted programs because psychological studies show those qualities go hand-in-hand with superior intelligence...

The North York board took a differnt approach. After complaints from the West Indian community, it decided to look for better ways to measure the intelligence of disadvantaged kids.

Luther was sent to Israel two years ago to study under psychologist Reuven Feurstein who developed the Learning Potential Assessment Device after he was asked to assess the IQ of Third World children coming into Israel and found all of them were scoring very poorly.

The program, unique to Israel and North York, "teaches kids the basics they have to know to approach these tests," said Luther. "We're really trying to get at their learning ability — are they teachable. I.Q. tests don't look at that. They look at what you learned in the past. I think this is a better predictor of how well a child will do in the future than a regular IQ test. It helps us decide who we should spend our limited resources on reeducating."

So far, the pilot program has been a success, he said.

"The kids we have been able to have leave vocational school have by and large done well in regular schools. We're able to change teachers' perceptions that these kids are retarded."

"An IQ test simply tells you how a kid is functioning at a particular time in a particular culture," he said. "It measures fast thinking and there really aren't many places where you need to think fast, except maybe a war."

Reprinted with permission — The Toronto Star Syndicate

1. What does "I.Q." mean? How is it determined for children?

2. What is a "culture-biased" I.Q. test?

3. Design two questions that are not culture-biased. Is this difficult to do? If so, why?

4. Make two headings in your notebook:
   a) arguments supporting the use of I.Q. tests
   b) arguments rejecting the use of I.Q. tests
   Use the information presented in the article to summarize the arguments for both sides.

5. How would you respond to the following situations, based on what you have learned about I.Q. tests?
   a) You are a teacher with the Toronto Board of Education. A parent of one of your fifth graders is concerned about his child's progress and wants the child to have an I.Q. test. What would you say to this parent?
   b) You have just applied for a job with Angus Computers of Canada. They inform you that you must take an I.Q. test if you want an interview for the job. How would you react, and why?

Detecting and Testing a Hypothesis — Level 2

The purpose of this exercise is to help you first detect a hypothesis, and then practise your ability to find evidence (facts and arguments) to support the hypothesis. You may wish to refer to Chapter 2, page 30 to review what a hypothesis is and how social scientists use hypotheses.

Read the **Hypotheses** and the **Supporting Statements** about intelligence tests. Then answer the follow-up questions.

Hypotheses

a) Intelligence tests are not accurate. The tests include many questions using vocabulary that may be unfamiliar to a child from a cultural background or social class different from that of the people who designed the test. As a result, these children will not score well on the I.Q. test even though they may be quite bright.

b) Intelligence tests are useful in predicting a person's abilities and chances for success in life. A person is born with a certain intelligence. The environment plays only a small part in shaping a person's overall potential. Intelligence tests are essential in helping to diagnose students' learning problems and then placing those students in appropriate programs.

c) Intelligence tests should be avoided because they do not measure important kinds of intelligence such as memory, musical ability, creativity, self- knowledge, athletic ability and human understanding. As well, factors such as emotional conflicts and poor motivation may affect a child's I.Q. scores. Hence I.Q. tests may not give a very true picture of a child's potential.

Supporting Statements

a) Studies suggest that there is really very little association between I.Q. score and success in life.

b) Associate professor of psychology Colin MacLeod says that I.Q. tests are the best method of selecting students for gifted programs.

c) Some new immigrants to Canada score poorly on I.Q. tests when they first arrive, but tend to improve as they become culturally adjusted.

d) Psychologist Tony Vernon says the I.Q. test is the single best method of predicting future school achievement and success in the work world. The test is not perfect, but it is 50 per cent accurate, he claims.

e) A Georgetown University medical study found that increased stress could cause students' I.Q. scores to decrease by as much as 45 per cent.

f) Psychologist Mike Luther found that middle class children did much better on I.Q. tests than children from disadvantaged homes, who lacked the skills needed to succeed on I.Q. tests. But disadvantaged children can be taught the skills required to perform well on these tests.

1. In your own words, briefly state each hypothesis presented above. Check your statements with your teacher before you proceed to the next question.

2. Which of the statements above could be used to support each hypothesis? Write your choices, and your reasons for these choices in your notebook.

3. Which of the three hypotheses do you find most convincing, and why?

Projects, Activities and Explorations

1. As a member of your school's student council, prepare a brochure welcoming new students to the school. Include a section on learning strategies and study skills.
2. For students who babysit young children: write up a comparison of techniques that parents use to teach their children the following:
   a) toilet training
   b) eating with a spoon
   c) picking up toys
   d) being polite to visitors
3. Visit a Montessori or a private school, or a school for developmentally handicapped or exceptionally gifted students. Write a report comparing the different teaching techniques used with students with special needs.
4. How is classical or operant conditioning used in teaching sports?
5. Invite the principal or vice-principal of your school to your class to explain how the school uses reinforcements to teach correct student behaviour.

What Have You Learned?

If you have covered everything in this chapter, you should be familiar with the following topics:
1. What learning is, and how it takes place
2. The stages of development known as *maturation*
3. Three kinds of learning: classical conditioning, operant conditioning and cognitive learning
4. The principles involved in behaviour modification
5. The effectiveness of rewards and punishments in changing behaviour
6. How to use the library
7. How to detect and test a hypothesis.

Answers to puzzles on page 140

1. *Customer*: Have you any eggs?
   Waiter:　Yes, we have eggs.
   Customer: Any ham?
   Waiter:　Yes, we have ham too.
   Customer: Do you have tea?
   Waiter:　Yes, tea too.
   Customer: I'll have ham and eggs and tea.
2. It was "and" I said, not "but".

To Help You Study

The following chart will help you
to review the words, facts and
ideas introduced in this chapter.
Copy the chart into your notebook
and fill in the missing information.

Word, Fact, Idea	Example in a Sentence	Page	Definition
learning	Learning is a fundamental process in human development.	128	a more or less permanent change in human behaviour, in which an association is made between two events previously unrelated in our minds
maturation			
classical conditioning			
unconditioned stimulus			
unconditioned response			
neutral stimulus			
conditioned stimulus			
conditioned response			
trial and error			
operant conditioning			
positive reinforcement			
behaviour modification			
cognitive learning			
insight			
modelling			

Motivation and Emotions

8

1

Figure Out These Scenes

Examine the pictures below. What are the people doing in each scene and why are they doing it?

Compare your views with those of your classmates. Then, as a class, answer these questions:

1. Did you agree on what people were doing in most of these scenes?

2. Did you agree on *why* they were doing it? Why might it be more difficult to agree on the reasons for people's behaviour?

3. What general comments can you make about people's reasons for acting the way they do?

2

3

4

It is very difficult to pinpoint what makes people act the way they do. You probably concluded that there were a combination of reasons for the behaviour of each person. In the case of the burglar, you may have tried, like a good detective, to imagine a *motive* for his crime. In the case of the athlete and the student, you may have wondered why they were so highly *motivated*, what made them push themselves so hard.

The words "motive" and "motivated" both have to do with what gets people *moving*. When social scientists try to discover what moves people to act, they are involved in the study of **motivation**. The goal of this chapter is to show how motivation influences peoples' behaviour.

5

6

Basic Motives: Needs and Drives

What Motivates You?

Test your awareness of your own motivations by answering the following questionnaire in your notebooks. You will find that your **needs** often motivate your behaviour. How often do the following needs motivate actions or decisions in your life? Copy the list into your notebook. Rank your most common motivating needs in order of their importance to you (1 for first place, 2 for second place, etc.).

need for water	need for praise or recognition
need for food	need for affection
need to be included	need for independence
need to feel secure	need to reach your full potential
need to feel capable	need to understand the world

When you have finished, compare your results with other students. Then, as a class, answer these questions:

1. Which of the above needs are basic to your survival or to the survival of the human race?

2. Which of the above needs are important, but not basic to your survival?

You probably found this task difficult, because all the above needs are important to human beings at different times and in different situations. But some needs are more important, because they are basic and instinctive for everyone.

Drives and Human Behaviour

Your body signals to you that it has basic physical needs. These include the instinctive needs for food, water and reproduction. These **needs** are things we require to survive and function adequately. If your need for food is not satisfied, the proper functioning of your body is upset and you feel tense and uncomfortable. The tension created is called hunger. If your need for drink is not satisfied, the tension created in your body is called thirst.

Psychologists refer to thirst, hunger and sex as drives. Drives are instinctive and unlearned. A **drive** is a physical urge to act, caused by tension or imbalance in the body. To reduce the tension, you do something to satisfy your drive. For example, when you feel the drive of hunger, you may run out to get a hamburger. Your body returns to its state of balance and relaxation when the drive has been reduced by eating the hamburger.

Some psychologists believe that human beings have another instinctive drive related to survival: aggression. They suggest that we have all inherited this urge to be violent from our earliest ancestors. In those early times, the survival of the individual may have depended on the willingness of a person to fight and to compete with others.

Today, we are rarely physically threatened. However, the struggle to compete for a job promotion or to keep your boyfriend or girlfriend from dropping you for someone else may seem like personal threats. It has been argued that these situations may trigger an instinctive drive to defend yourself aggressively.

It is worth noting that other psychologists do not think that people are instinctively aggressive. They feel that we are not born with the drive to be aggressive. Instead we have learned our aggressive behaviours from sources such as our parents, our society or even from television and the movies. If you are interested in this controversy, you could turn to Chapter 15 for further details.

Freud and his Theories of Motivation

Sigmund Freud (1856–1939) began his career as a physician specializing in nervous diseases. To the conservative, well-mannered society of the early 1900s, Freud's writing on the subject of sex was a scandal. This was a time when sex was not openly discussed.

Freud made three assumptions about human behaviour:

1. People have two basic drives that motivate all their behaviour: sexuality and aggression. Society tries to control these instinctive urges. The needs to reproduce and to defend ourselves in order to reproduce are normal, healthy needs. But these drives often make us feel guilty and anxious, and we are therefore likely to hide them, not just from others but also from ourselves.

2. All behaviour has a meaning and a reason behind it. People may try to hide the reasons for their behaviour from others and from themselves. However, their real motives can be uncovered with some analytical guidance.

3. The part of our mind where we hide our drives for sex and aggression is called the **unconscious** mind. We are not aware of the contents of our unconscious mind. Urges and desires are hidden because they involve behaviour that is strictly forbidden by society. To think of them would make us feel guilty.

In Freud's view, many of our desires are sexual. Freud believed that very young children experience a strong attraction to parents of the opposite sex. Since such a feeling is strongly disapproved of in almost every society, children learn to hide it even from themselves. They lock it away in a part of their mind where they cannot find it. Freud called this part of the mind the **unconscious**.

Freud believed that the contents of our unconscious can motivate us to behave in ways which we do not understand. For example, we may become involved with someone who reminds us of our father or mother. We are later disappointed in that person, when it becomes clear that the person is in fact *not* a carbon copy of our real parent. In this situation, we will probably be unaware of the reasons for our disappointment and the behaviour that results.

It is easy to see why Freud's theory made him very unpopular during his time. His view of hidden drives motivating human behaviour upset the view that people are completely rational beings. Even today, there is a great deal of argument about the accuracy of his ideas. Yet, Freud did succeed in opening the human mind to scientific study. His studies led to the modern field of psychiatry, which combines counselling and drugs to treat people with mental or emotional problems.

Austrian psychoanalyst
Sigmund Freud

Sigmund Freud's famous couch in his house in London

From Ideas to Action

1. Examine the following list of behaviours. In each case, name the drive that is motivating the individual.
   a) The shipwrecked man began drinking sea water.
   b) Sam was furious when he discovered that he had to give up his room to his visiting cousin.
   c) Carol missed both breakfast and lunch. When she got home from school, she yelled at her brother because he had forgotten to prepare dinner.

2. Clip some newspaper articles that describe situations based on human needs and drives. Watch a favourite television program and observe how needs and drives motivate behaviour. Write down your observations.

Curiosity as a Motivator

The drives to satisfy physical needs are easy to understand. But physical drives do not explain all human behaviour. Curiosity, for example, is a non-physical, innate motivation in human beings. We like to explore new experiences. Some animals, notably primates (apes and monkeys) as well as dogs and cats, are curious too. In fact, monkeys will often ignore a favourite food in favour of an activity that is interesting to them, such as solving a puzzle. Human beings are easily bored by repetitive work or a monotonous routine. We need change and seek it out. This seeking of new experience is the basis of human learning.

Emotional Motivations

Can You Explain the Orphanage Mysteries?

What is the mystery in each of the following cases? How would you explain what happened?

Case One:
In the early 1900s, people who worked in orphanages noticed something strange. The death rate among infants in such institutions was much higher than it was for infants raised in families. This seemed to make little sense. After all, the orphans were fed and changed regularly, and were kept warm.

One orphanage tried something a little different. Usually the children spent most of their days in their cribs. The only human contact they had was when they were fed. As an experiment, when the children were fed or changed the orphanage worker would take a few minutes to hold each baby, cuddle it and talk to it rather than immediately putting it down. Almost immediately the death rate for infants in that orphange dropped to levels normal for infants raised in families.

Case Two:
French scientists noticed that orphanages had large numbers of what appeared to be mentally retarded children. The intelligence of these children was very low.

As an experiment, some of these retarded children were taken from their orphanages and given to mentally retarded women to raise and care for as they would their own children. Curiously, although their new mothers were often just as mentally retarded as they were, the I.Q. scores of many of the children climbed to almost normal levels.

Compare your explanations for these mysteries with the explanations of your classmates. Then discuss the following questions:

1. What negative effects were experienced by the children in each orphanage?

2. What positive change did each orphanage make to help the children?

3. What do children need in order to survive and develop normally, as suggested by these orphanage experiments?

The Mysteries Explained

Both cases above stress a single point about human beings: the satisfaction of basic physical needs is not enough to guarantee normal development or even survival. Even when the institutional environment of infants is enriched with pictures, mobiles and other kinds of sensory stimulation, these things do not replace physical contact, love and affection. Human beings are motivated not only by biological drives but also by powerful emotional needs as well.

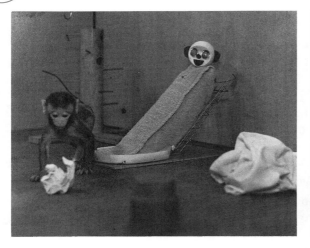

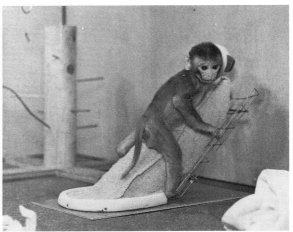

These infant monkeys were taken away from their mothers and given the models above as replacements. The infants became very attached to the cloth-covered model rather than the one that fed them. When frightened, they would run and cling to the cloth model. They would feed from the wire model while holding onto the cloth one. Monkeys raised only with the wire model became very withdrawn as adults, unable to relate to other monkeys. They were also poor mothers, neglecting or even abusing their young. However, when monkeys who started life this way were given a a normal baby monkey playmate while they were still relatively young, they developed into normal adults. Are there any lessons to be learned by human beings from these experiments?

What Are Your Emotions?

Most people think of emotions as feelings that we experience. There are the emotions of love, joy and happiness that make us feel good. There are also the emotions of hate, fear, anger and sadness that may make us feel bad and cause problems in our relationships with others.

These feelings are accompanied by physical experiences — love with a pounding heart, sadness with a lump in the throat, fear with "butterflies" in the stomach. Often the physical states are similar for several emotions. For example, a rapid heart rate, sweating palms and an increased rate of breathing can accompany the emotions of love, hate or fear. How do we distinguish between emotions? The situation tells us which emotion is being experienced.

What Are Your Emotional Needs?

Read about the following emotional needs and identify the degree to which each one motivates your behaviour. When you have done this, rank the emotional needs in order of their importance to you. When you have finished, compare your rankings with those of other students in your class.

1. **The Need for Security**

   Everyone needs a stable, predictable life and a place to come home to. You probably get uneasy when you have to move your home or change schools or friends. Most people feel better when they know and trust the people and the environment around them.

2. **The Need for Affection**

   You need love and attention from relatives and close friends. In fact, people who come from homes where they received little affection often have personality problems. They may cling to others, constantly seeking the affection they missed as children. Or they may become isolated, lonely and unable to form relationships.

3. **The Need for Acceptance**

   You need to feel that others accept you for who you are. As children, we want the approval of our parents. In later life, we may still want and need acceptance of our actions and ourselves from the people who are important to us.

4. **The Need for Self-esteem**

   This need involves two things: self-respect and the respect of others. You need to feel that you are a worthwhile person and that others think highly of you. When you feel these things, you are self-confident. When you don't feel these things, you may feel inferior, weak and inadequate.

5. **Competence**

   You need to feel capable of handling life's daily problems and challenges. Mastering new skills and learning from new experiences are some of the challenges. You need to feel that your efforts to learn are succeeding. If you can meet these challenges you will feel competent *and* self-confident.

6. **The Need for Independence**

   As you grow older, you need (and demand) greater and greater amounts of personal freedom. This begins when you are an infant and you first realize that you can influence the things and people around you. As a teenager, you may feel that your chief goal is to break away from your family.

Maslow's Hierarchy of Needs

Abraham Maslow (1908–1970), an American psychologist, developed a framework for classifying human needs, ranging from the most basic to the most difficult to achieve. His hierarchy of needs, first published in 1968, has influenced a variety of fields, such as nursing and business.

Abraham Maslow

Maslow listed five levels of human needs in the following order:

Level 1: Basic Physical Needs:
   air, food, water, etc.

Level 2: Fundamental Needs (safety):
   the need for shelter

Level 3: Belonging Needs:
   the need to belong to a group, the need to be accepted or loved for who you are

Level 4: Psychological Needs (esteem and status):
   the need to be respected by others, to have a special status or position within a group, to be competent

Level 5: Self-actualization Needs (fulfillment):
   the need to live up to your full potential as a human being; the need to be challenged and to explore the limits of your true abilities and talents

Maslow believed that motivation for human behaviour comes from many sources. He felt that our motivations change depending on where we find ourselves in life. If we are clutching to the lowest rung of the ladder, struggling to feed and clothe ourselves and

Albert Einstein solving puzzles in 1944

Marc Garneau, Canada's first astronaut

to keep a roof over our heads, these needs occupy all our time and attention. However, once we are warm, well-fed and safe, we can move up a few rungs. There the social need to belong to a group and the psychological need to be respected by that group motivate our behaviour. Once we are loved, accepted and respected, the highest rung on the ladder now challenges us, the need to reach our full potential as human beings.

Adler and the Struggle for Competence

Alfred Adler (1870–1937), a student of Freud, developed his own theories about motivation. He believed the real motive in life is the struggle for competence. In his view, this motivation is a response to our childhood, when we are totally dependent, inferior and incompetent. As we grow older, we try to change this state.

For some people, achieving a sense of competence is not easy. Some people are born with physical problems. Others are neglected by their parents. Sometimes conquering the things that make people feel inferior is difficult, if not impossible. If this is the case, they may develop what Adler called an *inferiority complex*. People who have an inferiority complex have strong feelings of incompetence and often feel that they cannot solve their daily problems.

From Ideas to Action

1. Identify the physical sensations you experience with the following emotions:
   a) fear b) anger c) love d) worry
   e) sadness f) joy

2. Although your body reacts in the same physical way to many emotions, you do not always *feel* the same. How do you account for this?

3. What level of needs are each of the following people trying to satisfy? (physical, safety, belonging, esteem and status fulfillment) For each case, explain your answer.
   a) Out of work for two years, John turned to crime.
   b) The famous scientist, Albert Einstein, spent the last years of his life trying to develop a theory to explain the way the universe worked. His friends argued that the task was impossible. He died without ever having achieved his goal.
   c) Jessica was a new student in the school. She hung around the cafeteria, trying to meet people.
   d) Marc Garneau, Canada's first astronaut, was a very successful officer in the Canadian navy before he decided to apply for the space program.
   e) Sandy had just been transferred to a new job in a new town. She spent a very frustrating day looking for an affordable place to live.

   f) Stranded on a mountain for weeks, the survivors of the plane crash resorted to eating the bodies of those who had died.
   g) When Frank made the football team, he began an intensive program of weight lifting. He wanted to be the biggest and strongest lineman in the city league.

4. a) Observe the behaviour of your family or friends on at least five different occasions. Identify what needs might be motivating their behaviour. Make a simple chart like the one below to record your observations.

Behaviour Observed	Needs Motivating Behaviour
eating breakfast	hunger

   b) When you have completed your observations, check your answers by asking the people you observed to explain the reasons for their behaviour.
   c) Did your observations match the explanations of the people you observed? How would you account for the difference(s) in your interpretations?

Achievement, Motivation and Competition

The following poem is often used by amateur and professional coaches to motivate their athletes. Do you find it effective? Why or why not?

If you think you're beaten, you are,
If you think you dare not, you don't,
If you'd like to win, but you think
   you can't
It'a almost a "cinch" you won't.
If you think you'll lose, you've lost,
For out in the world you'll find
Success begins with a person's will —
It's all in the state of mind.

For many a race is lost
Before even a step is run,
And many a coward falls
Before even the work's begun.
Think big, and your deeds will grow,
Think small and you'll fall behind;
Think that you can and you will
It's all in the state of mind.

If you think you're outclassed,
   you are,
You've got to think high to rise,
You've got to be sure of yourself
   before
You can even win the prize.
Life's battles don't always go
To those on top of the hill,
But sooner or later the people
   who win,
Are those who think they will.

(Anonymous)

Stress and the Frustration of Needs

The word **frustration** means a feeling of discouragement and anger. Frustration also means a situation in which people are prevented from doing what they want to do.

Frustration has visible effects as well as effects that are not as easily seen. **Stress** is a natural physical reaction to any real or imagined threat. It has sometimes been called the "**fight or flight response**," since the body automatically prepares to either defend itself or to escape from a threatening situation. As the body becomes aroused, the

Hans Selye, a Canadian scientist, known as the father of the theory of stress

heart rate and blood pressure increase to drive blood to the large muscles of the arms and legs. If no action is possible, or if the action does not cause the frustrating situation to end, the body stays geared up. As a result, the arousal level also stays well above its normal level. If you maintain a high level of arousal for a long period of time, your mental and physical health are likely to suffer.

A Canadian scientist, Hans Selye, developed the following three-stage theory of stress:

Stage One: Alarm

Your body prepares for action. You experience all the changes associated with physical arousal.

For example, Reema is in her car, caught in a traffic jam, and is late for work. This concerns her because she has a new job. She is trying to make a good impression on the manager by arriving at work on time. In this case, her need for acceptance and self-esteem are powerful motivations for her behaviour. She sees the people in other cars as frustrating her desire to satisfy these important emotional needs.

While this is certainly not a life-threatening situation, it is nevertheless recognized by the body as a threat. Automatically, Reema's body becomes physically aroused. Her heart begins to pound, her breathing becomes rapid and she feels hot as blood is pumped into her face. She interprets these uncomfortable sensations as anger and begins to mutter unflattering comments to the motorist ahead of her.

Stage Two: Resistance

If stress continues for more than a few minutes, the extreme symptoms of arousal disappear. However, to meet the ongoing challenge, your body continues to function at well above its normal level.

Reema cannot hit the gas pedal of her car and ram the car in front of her because it is in her way. This would land her in jail. Nor can she get off the highway and escape the traffic. This will take her miles out of her way. Instead, she sits motionless in her car, thinking about the trouble she is going to be in when she gets to work. The energy and the chemicals that were produced to deal with the threat will not be used and will stay in her system. By the time she gets to work, she will be so upset, tense and uncomfortable that she will be unable to do her job properly.

Stage Three: Exhaustion

Your body can tolerate these high levels of performance for only so long. If you do not overcome your frustration over a long period of time, you may develop one of a number of stress-related diseases. These include stomach ulcers, headaches, high blood pressure and even heart attacks. Some scientists have suggested that there may be a link between stress and some forms of cancer. Too much stress — with no time for the body to relax and recover — can eventually kill you.

• • • • • • • • • • • • • • • • • •

From Ideas to Action

1. For each of the following situations, identify the stage of stress at which each person is operating.
   a) People were amazed at Cindy's ability to turn out quality work, while working 12-hour days during the company's busiest time of year.
   b) Sam was threatened by two men with knives. He turned and ran. He suddenly became aware that he had never run so fast.
   c) Six months after the death of her husband, Joanne, who had always been very healthy, had a heart attack and died.
   d) Fred usually got two major colds a year. Strangely, they usually hit him a week after football season was over and shortly after exams.

2. When were the last few times that you were ill? Try to recall what you were doing in the weeks before these illnesses. To what degree might the frustration of needs and stress explain the timing of your illnesses?

Conducting an Interview or Questionnaire

Not all topics can be researched easily in a library. Some are too current or are just not available. To gather information on a current or difficult topic, you can interview people and/or have them answer a questionnaire that you have prepared on the topic. This exercise will help you learn how to design, conduct and write up the results of an interview or a questionnaire.

Purpose of Your Interview or Questionnaire

Why are you conducting your interview or questionnaire? You may be gathering information to test a hypothesis. For example:

Hypothesis: Teenagers are motivated to succeed in school by their desires to pursue a career.

Or you may just wish to understand other people's views on a topic. For example:

Interview parents or teachers about their views on teenage motivation.

Types of Questions

In your interview or questionnaire, you can ask open or closed questions. *Closed questions* have a fixed number of responses, a yes/no answer or a number of choices to rank in order of importance.

In an interview, closed questions help you focus on some basic information you need. You can then go on to ask *open questions*. These allow your subjects to answer in their own words. In an interview, you can ask other questions to expand on an answer already given or to direct the subject's attention to an area overlooked in the answer. In a questionnaire, you must rely on the printed question to be answered as fully as possible.

Closed Questions

Interview

- Do you know what career you want?

- Can you tell me how many hours per day you study?

- What is more important to you, money or friendship?

Questionnaire

- Do you know what career you want?
Yes _____ No _____

- How many hours per day do you study?
0 h _____ 1/2 h _____
1 h _____ 2 h _____
more _____

- Rank from 1 to 5 the following factors that motivate you in school. (1 = most important, 5 = least important) a) future career b) peers c) parents d) teachers e) money

Open Questions

Interview

- What is the key factor motivating teens? What are other factors?

- How did you react when you failed the exam? Why did you behave that way?

Questionnaire

- Explain in detail what you think motivates teens.

- Describe how you reacted when you failed the exam. Explain what motivated your behaviour.

Hints for Conducting Interviews

1. Prepare more questions than you actually need. Test them out on several people and select the best questions.

2. Make sure your questions are clear, direct, concise, well organized and inoffensive. They must give you the information you need, and should be easy for respondents to answer.

3. Practice asking questions and recording answers.

166

4. For most questions, it is wise not to comment on your subjects' answers. You might influence the answer.

5. For most interviews, arrange an appointment and explain your purpose.

6. If you plan to use a tape recorder, ask your subjects' permission first.

7. Above all, be polite and friendly. Your subjects are helping you and you want them to be relaxed. Introduce yourself and briefly explain the format. Be patient and, if you have to, interrupt politely. Thank your subjects for their help.

Writing Up the Results of Your Interview or Questionnaire

How you write up the results of your interviews or questionnaires will depend on your purpose and format. Questionnaires can be reported as social science experiments with the problem, the hypothesis, the method used to gather information, the analysis of the observations and a conclusion. They can also be reported as a set of tables. Another approach is to write an essay using the data collected from a questionnaire, or quotes from an interview. A magazine-style, descriptive article may be the best way to record an unstructured interview.

Suggestions for Interviews

1. Interview high school students to find out the kinds of things they find most stressful.

2. Interview someone whom you consider successful about their motivation to succeed. Write an article based on your interview.

3. Interview someone with a very stressful job or hobby. Report on the motivation behind the stressful activity. Write an article for your school newspaper.

Analysing a Problem

There are many problems in our society. If we are going to deal with them, we must first learn to identify them and to understand their seriousness. We must know their causes, possible solutions and how to choose the most effective solution. This exercise will give you a method for analysing problems.

Step One: What is the Problem?

First, identify the problem. This involves defining the problem, and indicating its basic characteristics and the symptoms or signs which show that someone is experiencing the problem. If we can recognize when someone is having a problem, friends, family or professionals may be able to prevent something more serious from happening. For example:

Problem: Stress is a natural body reaction to threats you perceive. It is how your body releases extra energy to defend itself or to escape. Too much stress, however, can lead to anxiety, tension and even illness.

Symptoms: tense muscles, sore back and headaches, a pounding heart, shortness of breath, irritability, lack of concentration, loss of sleep, absenteeism from work or school, depression, increased use of alcohol or drugs, ulcers and less ability to fight off infections.

Step Two: How Serious is the Problem?

In this step, we find statistical and other evidence of the problem. This will help us know the extent, location and other features of the problem. For example:

One symptom of the incredible increase in teenage stress is the 400 per cent increase in teenage suicide since 1970. Medical studies suggest that more than 70 per cent of all illnesses are stress-related.

Step Three: What Are the Causes of the Problem?

In this step, we try to discover the reasons why the problem exists. Understanding the causes will help us select an appropriate solution. For example, stress can be caused by:

- sudden and serious events, such as an accident or family death
- daily events such as writing a test or getting into a fight
- a gradual buildup of long-term frustrations in our lives, such as fear that we will not meet our high expectations at school or on a job

Step Four: What Are the Solutions to the Problem?

This is the most difficult stage of analysis, but it is also the most important. There are three basic approaches that are often used to explore solutions to problems. The chart below shows these approaches and how they apply to the problem of stress.

You will find that one approach may suggest several solutions to the problem. For example, if your approach is to prevent the problem of stress, you may think of more ways to solve the problem than the two examples given.

Approaches	*Example of a solution*
1. Prevention: Create programs or take steps to see that the problem does not develop in the first place.	• Set realistic goals that will not frustrate you. • Join a health club and exercise regularly.
2. Rehabilitation: Adopt some type of program to help with problem situation.	• Discuss the problem with a psychologist to help you discover what is causing your stress. • Take a course on how to reduce stress.
3. Punishment: Apply a law to control the situation or punish people who cause the problems and to prevent others from becoming involved.	• The law punishes abusive parents. Child abuse is very stressful for children. The child may be taken away from an abusive parent.

Step Five: How Do We Decide What To Do?

This step involves weighing all the advantages and disadvantages of each solution.

You could develop an organizer to help you make more effective decisions. Here is an example. For each possible solution to the problem, you might consider the financial cost, the time and the number of people required to carry out the solution, and the effectiveness of the solution. The following chart has been filled in for the first two approaches to the problem of stress. When you have completed your chart, examine the advantages and disadvantages of each solution and rank order each solution. Explain your reasons for choosing the best solution. Take into account the cost, time, people needed and the effectiveness of each solution.

Advantages and Disadvantages of Each Solution			
Solution	Cost	Time/People Needed	Effectiveness
Prevention			
Join a health club	$100	4hr per wk	– reduces stress; doesn't eliminate cause
Set realistic goals	0	minimum	– may reduce stress, does eliminate cause
Rehabilitation			
Take a course in stress reduction	$250	1hr per wk for 10 wks	– helps to remove cause of stress
Discuss problems with psychologist	$500 – $700	1hr per wk for 10 wks	– helps reduce stress and may remove cause

Starving to Death for Beauty?

• •

Read the following article on anorexia nervosa and then complete the follow-up exercise.

Needless Diet Sparked Anorexia

Lynda Hurst, *Toronto Star*
May 27, 1983

It began innocently enough in the summer of Maryanne's 15th year. She wanted to lose 10 pounds and exercise just enough to firm herself up. Something went wrong, however, after the 10 pounds were lost. In Maryanne's words, she seemed to break through a wall. Although she was thinner, she somehow looked larger. And so she kept on with her diet. Between July and October, her weight dropped from 120 to 99 pounds. She is 5 foot 6.

Maryanne returned to school that fall, a private Roman Catholic girls' school where she was known as a straight A student, if a somewhat snooty, aloof classmate. She didn't like school, she says; no matter how well she did, she felt it wasn't good enough — not for herself, not for her parents...

When her parents grew alarmed by her weight loss and placed her in hospital, she was pleased. It meant no more school; it meant

getting away from the family. No one involved knew it then, but that hospital admission was to be the first of 19 over the next 11 years...

Three weeks after her release her weight dropped to 77 pounds. By that point, Maryanne says she was scared to eat. The smallest mouthful, she thought, would make her balloon. She began to exercise compulsively while her parents watched helplessly. Within a month she was back in hospital, first to Women's College and then to the Clarke Institute of Psychiatry....

By then, Maryanne's anorexia had developed into bulimia. She binged and then forced herself to vomit. Eight fruitless months later, she was released, and within weeks of returning home, her weight skyrocketed to 185.

"I felt alienated at home. I didn't fit in anymore. I quit school, worked at a few jobs, but I

couldn't keep them because of my eating. I stayed for two months with relatives in the States, lived for a while in a group home, and when I finally came back, it was only to find out that my dad had cancer. That made everything worse."

The hospital admissions continued. Maryanne grew out of her teens and into her 20s. Then finally, in 1981, a doctor at Women's College pulled the rug out.

"They kicked me out. Looking back, I don't blame them. I made people hate me. I wasn't trying to help myself. But I did want to stay in hospital — it meant I didn't have to face the world outside. I was furious when they wouldn't let me stay.

"I tried to sign up for a six-month program at Mt. Sinai, but even they wouldn't have me. I guess they knew my record."

Denied the security of an institutional existence, Maryanne was forced to confront what she was doing to her life. She moved in with an aunt and gradually began to realize she was, as she puts it, tired of being sick.

"It sounds strange, I know, but suddenly I realized I had no choice but to get better. I got a job as a clerk, and I told the boss my entire history. He agreed to take me on only if I promised to stay well. So I promised."

It was a slow but steady recovery. Maryanne trained herself to eat properly and after a few setbacks, learned to control the urge to vomit. For the first time in her life, she says, she had money to spend on clothes, movies, anything she wanted. Previously, it had always been spent on food.

Last year, Maryanne helped set up an anorexia nervosa self-help group that meets every Monday. The case histories, she says, are all different, but the same bodily obsession runs like a thread through each woman's conversation. Many are still in the clutches of the disease, still binging and dosing themselves with laxatives.

"I've got to stop myself from shouting at them, begging them to quit. They're not ready though. They don't know yet that they 'chose' to be sick, and they can choose to be well. Everything is still distorted with them: they're skin and bone but when they look in the mirror, all they see is fat. I know what that feels like.". . .

Maryanne used to believe the illness was caused by psychological factors, in her case an unhappy home life and an obsession with excelling at school. Today, she's more inclined to think a hormone or brain chemical is at fault. Once a person loses a certain amount of weight very quickly, she theorizes, the brain switches gears and spews out false perceptions.

Indeed, the latest research appears to support this line of thinking. According to researchers at the U.S. National Institute of Health, irregularities in the secretion of a hormone called vasopressin could be the key. Vasopressin regulates the body's water balance and in healthy people goes to work when they eat salt.

In anorexics, however, the control mechanism is distorted and with salt intake, vasopressin levels fluctuate wildly. It's thought this fluctuation somehow may turn ordinary dieting into a catastrophic obsession and in so doing, alter the thinking process.

"I don't know for sure what happens or why," says Maryanne, "but I do know that if I hadn't started on that unnecessary diet when I was 15, none of this would have happened. I might have had other problems, but not this hell. If only teenage girls would realize that dieting is no way to solve anything."

Reprinted with permission — *The Toronto Star Syndicate*

After you have read this article on anorexia nervosa, make notes on this problem using the guide outlined in Skills: Analysing a Problem, on pages 168–9. Compare your notes with other students. How different or similar are they? Why?

Projects, Activities and Explorations

1. Create a clipping file. Collect articles, pictures, advertisements and cartoons from newspapers that show people trying to satisfy their needs. Use the items to create a collage that deals with human needs.

2. Find some poems that deal with human needs. In groups of three, read your selections to each other. Then have the group determine what needs each poem is expressing.

3. Interview the manager of a successful local business. Find out how this person motivates the employees to work hard and enthusiastically. You might also want to interview some of the employees later to determine how successful the manager's motivational techniques are. After you have completed your research, share your results with the class. (If you are really interested in this topic, you may wish to read the book *In Search of Excellence* by T. Peters and R. Waterman, Jr., Harper & Row, 1982. It deals with the problems of motivating people to perform enthusiastically in the workplace.)

4. Make a mobile that expresses the needs that you are currently trying to satisfy or the greatest areas of frustration in your life. These mobiles may be hung anonymously or explained to your classmates, after they have tried to determine the meaning of your sculpture.

5. Role-play Sigmund Freud, Alfred Adler and Abraham Maslow with two other students. Choose some recent cases of interesting human behaviour for which you feel you would like to have some explanation. (Scanning the front page of the newspaper is a good source for this.) Explain from your character's point of view the motivations of the people in your selected cases. Remember, you must stick to your role throughout the discussion.

6. Research the life of a famous person who interests you. Write a short biography that explains the motivations of the person. Were these people self-actualizing? If you are interested in finding out more about Maslow's research into people who he felt were self-actualizing, refer to his book *Motivation and Personality*, 2nd ed. New York: Harper & Row, 1970.

7. Research how advertising uses an understanding of people's motivations to encourage them to buy. You might wish to select examples of ads that clearly appeal to certain human needs studied in this chapter. Which ads are most successful? Do human needs play a role in the success of ads?

What Have You Learned?

If you have covered everything in this chapter, you should be familiar with the following topics:

1. The nature of basic needs and drives

2. Some theories explaining the motivations behind all human behaviour (Sigmund Freud and Abraham Maslow)

3. Types of emotional needs

4. The effects of the frustration of needs (stress)

5. How to design and conduct an interview or a questionnaire

6. How to analyse a social problem

To Help You Study

The following chart will help you to review the words, facts and ideas that were introduced in this chapter. Copy the chart into your notebook and fill in the missing information.

Word, Fact, Idea	Example in a Sentence	Page	Definition
need	Humans have a need for food, water and love	153	something required to ensure survival or growth
motivation			
drive			
emotions			
frustration			
stress			
flight or flight response			

Exploring Your Personality

Try This Experiment

Study the Personality Profile Form on the opposite page.

Each line represents a scale for a personal characteristic. Make a copy of the form. Circle the number on each line that you feel best describes you. For example, the first line deals with a range of behaviour from very quiet to very outgoing. If you think you are "sort of quiet," you might circle the number 2 or 3 on this line. If you think you are usually the life of the party, you might circle the number 7. After you have finished, try the following:

1. Join all your circles with lines to give you a profile of your personality.

2. Put your profile aside without showing it to anyone.

3. The class will then be divided into groups of three. Fill out a profile for each of the other two students in your group. Do not talk to these students while you fill out the profiles for the other two students.

4. After everyone has finished, the forms should be returned to the subjects of the profiles. Now fill in the other students' views of you on your original Personality Profile Form, using different colours or different kinds of lines. The colours will highlight the differences and similarities in opinions.

5. Compare your profile of yourself with the profiles of you created by others.

Personality Profile Form

	1	2	3	4	5	6	7	
Quiet	1	2	3	4	5	6	7	Outgoing
Serious	1	2	3	4	5	6	7	Happy-go-lucky
Timid	1	2	3	4	5	6	7	Aggressive
Tough-minded	1	2	3	4	5	6	7	Sensitive
Trusting	1	2	3	4	5	6	7	Suspicious
Conservative	1	2	3	4	5	6		Experimenting
Dependent on Others	1	2	3					Self-sufficient
Relaxed	1	2	3	4	5	6	7	Tense
Practical	1	2	3	4	5		7	Imaginative

175

Now in a group or as a class, discuss the following questions to see what you have discovered about human personalities:

1. How do the various profiles of you compare? How would you account for the differences and similarities?

2. Which is the more accurate view of you: the view that you have of yourself or the view that others have of you? Why do you think so?

3. Why do you think it is important to study the personalities of others?

In this chapter, you will learn that the study of personality is not an easy one. As the activity above shows, even defining your own personality is a very tricky task. There is also controversy over how personality is formed. These are the problems that face psychologists who study personality. This chapter will try to provide you with some of the answers.

Why Study Personality?

Many people love to read horoscope profiles and to fill out so-called "personality tests" in popular magazines. We like to know about ourselves and we are also fascinated by the personalities of other people.Knowing about ourselves and others is interesting, but what we choose to do with this information is even more important. We often use our knowledge of the personalities of individuals to make decisions. For example, personality plays a big part in choosing a job. If you have been told that you are an impatient person, you might decide not to apply for a job that requires a great deal of patience. Smart employers often try to discover as much as possible about an applicant's personality before offering him or her a job. In fact, the most common beginning to a job interview is, "Tell me about yourself." Your responses may lead the employer to predict your success as an employee.

Whether we use our knowledge of personality to understand ourselves, to find and keep friends or to succeed at our jobs, the study of personality forms the basis of our insights into human behaviour.

I gotta be me, ♫
oh I just gotta be me... ♫

"The Far Side" is reprinted with permission of Chronicle Features.

The Study of Personality Formation

In 1936, two psychologists discovered that there are more than 17 000 words in the English language that describe personality characteristics. They also found more than 50 different definitions for human "personality." Today, most psychologists agree that **personality** is the unique pattern of thoughts and behaviours that characterize an individual. The study of personality stresses understanding the individual and what makes the individual unique.

The word "personality" comes from the Latin word *persona*, which refers to the masks that Roman actors wore in plays. A small number of actors could take many parts in the same play simply by putting on different masks and changing their voices. When they changed masks, their roles in the play changed, and so did their personalities.

In the same way, people often "change" the kind of person they are, depending on the situation in which they find themselves. For example, at home your family may think of you as a relaxed and lazy person. Your room may look like a jungle. However, at school your fellow students and teachers may see you as a neat and efficient person. You are quick to complete your work, and your assignments are always neat and well organized. You have put on different "masks" depending on the **role** (part) you play in your daily life. Your roles depend on who you are with and what you are doing. Sometimes you become the person that others expect you to be. For example, the professional soldier may be a mild-mannered family person at home. On the battlefield this person is a trained killer. As situations change, so may your personality.

You also have certain **personality traits**, which are characteristics or inner qualities that tend to be stable and permanent. Just because you are touchy one moment and calm the next doesn't mean you have totally changed your personality. We all possess personality traits that seem at times to contradict one another.

The study of personality has a long and colourful history. Greeks and Romans believed that the four elements — earth, air, fire and water — were present in four basic human personalities. These were the *melancholic* (sad) personality, the *sanquine* (happy) personality, the

Many cultures portray spiritual powers through the use of masks in ceremonies.

177

choleric (violent) personality and the *phlegmatic* (calm) personality. An early twentieth-century theory suggested that body type (fat, muscular or thin) controlled your personality. Fat people were thought to be jolly and friendly. Thin people were seductive and intense. Muscular people were active and violent.

Modern theories of personality formation use more scientific methods and analyses. In this chapter we will look at three modern theories of personality formation: psychodynamic theory, social learning theory and humanistic theory. Which one will you find most convincing?

. . . .

From Ideas to Action

1. In the previous pages, you learned that knowledge of human personality is frequently used to make important decisions. For each of the following jobs, decide if you would like to do them. What is it about your personality that would make the work interesting for you? What is it about your personality that would make you reject the other types of work?
a) salesperson b) social worker c) office filing clerk d) computer operator e) forestry worker f) bus driver g) lawyer h) childcare worker

2. How would knowledge of someone's personality be useful in each of these situations:
a) deciding whom to accept for police training
b) hiring an airline pilot
c) hiring a new teacher for a school
d) deciding whether or not to promote a worker to the position of supervisor
e) selecting an astronaut for a space flight

3. Draw a horizontal line to represent your life. At one end, write your birth date. As you go along the line, enter key events in your life that you think had an important effect on the kind of person that you are today.

SKILLS

Making Notes From A Text

The purpose of this exercise is to give you an effective method of getting the most out of your reading and notetaking. This method is called **SQRS**. Try the following steps on the next section of this chapter.

Skim — Skim through the section reading the first and last paragraphs, the heads and sub-heads, and the questions at the section end.

Question — Make up your own questions to answer about the section.

Read and Record — Read to find the answers to your questions and record them in your notes.

Summarize — Examine your notes and pick out the main ideas and the important supporting statements. Learn these.

Psychodynamic Theory

Read the following cases and decide how you would act in each situation.

Situation 1

Some of your friends are driving to Montreal for a rock concert and want you to go with them. This would mean an overnight trip and you don't think your parents would approve. However, they are also going away that weekend. Would you a) go and not tell your parents b) worry about the plan, feel guilty and finally tell your parents or c) assess your school work and financial situation and decide whether you can afford the trip?

Situation 2

You are standing in front of a display of stereo equipment that is on sale. You have a paycheque in your pocket. Would you a) march right in and buy the equipment b) worry about spending too much money because you never know when you might need it or c) compare stereo equipment prices in several stores and then make your decision?

Situation 3

It's the first real spring day after a long winter. Your friends want to skip classes in the afternoon and just cruise around. Do you a) grab your jacket and head for the door b) worry about breaking the school's rules or c) try to decide what would happen if you skipped classes and make your decision accordingly?

In groups or as a class, discuss your results. Then answer the following questions:

1. Did everyone have the same responses to the situations? Why do you think there were differences?
2. Would you always have the same responses to these situations?

The exercise you have just finished uses the "voices" of three different parts of a personality as described by Sigmund Freud. These three parts function together to create our unique personalities.

Freud and Psychodynamic Theory

As you learned in Chapter 8, Freud explored personality in terms of unconscious motives, sexuality and aggression. His ideas became the basis of psychodynamic theory, used in both psychology and psychiatry.

Freud believed that personality characteristics and personality disorders grow out of conflicts resulting from drives (instinctive urges to act). These conflicts occur mostly in the unconscious mind. The unconscious mind is where painful memories are hidden so that they do not interfere with daily life.

Freud believed that there were two parts of the personality at war with one another in the unconscious: the id and the superego. The **id** is the part of our personality with which we are born. It is the source of our primitive, animal urges, such as sex and aggression. It seeks immediate pleasure. Have you suddenly felt the almost uncontrollable urge to do something that you shouldn't? Have you ever "pigged out" on some food even though you were already full? Freud would say that these are examples of your id guiding your behaviour. When you are an infant, the id is the only developed part of your personality. It has no sense of what is right or wrong, possible or impossible. It just knows what it wants and that it wants it *now*! When you are an adult, your id continues to influence you.

Constantly fighting with the id is the **superego**. The superego is the part of our personality that tries to control our behaviour. It emerges as our id drives us to demand things that others around us think are wrong. Parents scold children with "Don't do that again; it's dirty," or "Nice children don't do that." Their goal is to make us feel guilty enough to control our behaviour.

Here is an example of the battle between id and superego: you might be very angry at someone and want to hurt him or her. Your id insists that this will reduce your tension and will make you feel better. Your superego insists that you have always been taught that injuring another person is wrong. You now have a problem: which part of your hidden personality will finally decide your actual behaviour?

The decision will likely be made by the third part of your personality, referred to by Freud as the ego. The **ego** emerges during the first few years of life. Unlike the id and the superego, it is not hidden in the unconscious mind. This part of us is in touch with reality. It is the part of our personality of which we are aware.

The ego develops as we gradually come to realize that there are ways to get what we want that will not make us feel guilty. For instance, the hungry child eventually realizes that it will be fed if it waits for supper. This avoids the exhausting screaming that its id would normally have insisted upon.

The ego also develops ways to balance the demands of the struggling parts of our personality. It tames our animal desires. It also prevents us from feeling

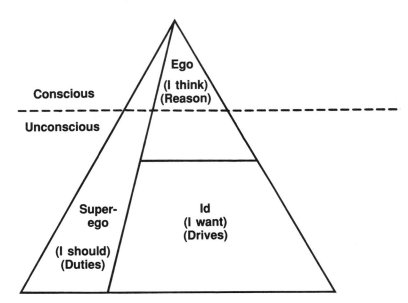

A diagram of the human personality, as theorized by Sigmund Freud. Notice the amount of activity going on at an *unconscious* level.

guilty every time we satisfy our basic needs. The ego enables us to have a well-adjusted personality that can function successfully in society.

Freud made some important additions to our understanding of personality. But many people disagree with his views. They point out that most of his ideas were formed while studying people who were emotionally disturbed. Therefore, his theories may not explain the personalities of "normal" people very well. However, he did show that we are very complicated beings. He also made the important suggestion that we are not always what we appear to be, not even to ourselves. There may be a very private, unknown self in each of us that has to come to grips with the demands of the real world.

Defense Mechanisms

Sometimes the demands of the id and the commands of the superego cannot be balanced. In this case, the ego has failed to perform its function and we will face feelings of frustration, conflict and failure. According to Freud, we defend our ego against these feelings by using mental devices to distort reality. These devices are called **defense mechanisms**.

Defense mechanisms have three characteristics:

1. They are *reactions* to feelings of frustration, tension and worry. They help reduce some of these unpleasant feelings.
2. They are unconscious. This means that we are not aware of taking these actions to protect ourselves.
3. They distort our view of reality. If what is happening to us is too painful or too shocking to think about, we protect ourselves by changing our view of the painful situation into one that is less painful to bear.

Defense mechanisms serve a useful purpose. The distortion of reality helps relieve us of stress and confusion. This gives us time to work out solutions to problems that first appeared impossible to solve. However, if people continually deceive themselves about their real situations and real feelings, they will not be able to realistically solve their problems.

As you read the following chart, try to see why each is called a defense mechanism. Ask yourself if you have ever used any of these methods to deal with frustrating or painful situations.

Defense Mechanism	Example
1. Rationalization: An excuse is invented to explain a failure, error, loss or bad behaviour. The excuse is considered reasonable by the person who invents it.	You have been rejected by someone you really wanted to date. In reaction, you say to yourself "Oh well, he wasn't all that bright any way!"
2. Repression: Unpleasant urges or thoughts are pushed out of our conscious minds down into the unconscious. They can no longer be recalled and remembered but may surface.	Someone who hates a brother or sister will say 'I don't hate you, sis.' but the unconscious anger will perhaps surface in sarcasm or unkind behaviour.
3. Displacement: Direct aggression against the actual cause of our frustration may not be socially acceptable. Instead, we take out our desire to be aggressive on some innocent person or thing.	Frank has had a terrible day at work. His boss made fun of him, and Frank had to put up with it. When he gets home he explodes at his daughter over some minor wrongdoing.
4. Projection: We see traits and feelings in other people that we sense in ourselves but can not admit openly. Just as the movie projector "projects" the images inside of it onto a screen, we project our inner feelings onto other people.	Susan was an abused child. She has grown up hostile and angry. She trusts no one and has no friends. She thinks that everyone is trying to harm her. She sees in others the anger and hostility that is inside of her.

From Ideas to Action

1. Label each of the following statements as examples of id, superego or ego.

   a) I want that chocolate bar.
   b) I love you.
   c) Stealing is bad.
   d) Rather than stealing that record, I'll wait for my next paycheque and then buy it.
   e) That's a pornographic movie.
   f) Staying in school is probably a better idea than dropping out.

2. Explain how the diagram below shows the psychodynamic theory of personality.

3. Identify each defense mechanism being used in the following situations. Explain your answer.

   a) Kim had tried unsuccessfully to get on the school basketball team for two years. When asked if she had been cut she replied, "Yes, but the coach hates me. In fact he hated my brother too."
   b) Soo Ling's boss was criticising him for his use of English. Soo Ling could not defend himself against these attacks and felt humiliated. His sister suggested he buy a new coat during the January sale and he angrily told her to leave him alone.
   c) As a young child, _____ was physically abused by his parents. He does not remember the abuse but has always feared any display of emotion, either in love or in anger.
   d) Pierre, who is extremely jealous of his girlfriend's other friends, says loudly, "I'm not jealous — she's the one who follows me around to see who I'm talking to!"

4. In the situations described in question 3, which defense mechanisms would you consider appropriate to the situation and which defense mechanism might cause more problems than it solves?

5. For a period of one or two weeks, keep an accurate record of the frustrations, conflicts and anxieties you are experiencing. These situations may involve schoolwork, conflicts with parents, anxiety over girl/boyfriends and sports. For each one, indicate the way you responded to the situations. Then explain how well you think you handled each situation, and whether you might have responded in a more effective way.

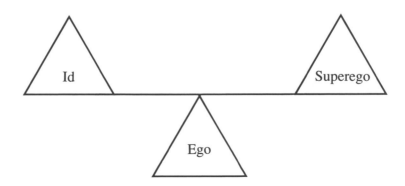

Social Learning Theory

Do We Learn Personality?

Consider the following situations.

- You see a wallet drop from the pocket of a pedestrian. Picking up the wallet, you run to catch up with its owner. The owner looks at you as if you are a thief, grabs the wallet from your hand and walks away. Several days later, a student ahead of you in the cafeteria line-up forgets her change on her lunch tray. Would you return the money to the student? Explain your reason.
- For many weeks you work hard on a major school project. But when you have completed it, no one seems to notice your efforts. Your teacher simply gives you a grade without any comment. Would you make this effort on your next assignment for this teacher? Explain your reason.
- Some time ago you went to a party that you hadn't wanted to go to. You met many interesting people and had a great time. You met one special person there. You are now living in another city where you know almost no one. There's a party on Friday night to which you have been invited. Would you go to this party? Explain your reason.

Now compare your reactions to the above situations with the reactions of other students. Then answer the following questions:

1. If you are often rewarded, not rewarded or punished, how does it affect how you will react in similar situations in the future? Could it eventually affect personality traits, such as your honesty, your desire to work hard or your ability to take risks in new situations? If so, why?

2. Would everyone have the same feelings and reactions to being rewarded, not being rewarded or being punished for honesty, hard work or risk-taking? Why?

3. What does this suggest to you about how personality is formed? Can you see any problems with this explanation of how our personalities develop?

Human beings grow up surrounded by other people. We are constantly learning from our experiences with other people. Some psychologists believe that we also learn all the thoughts and behaviours that make up our personalities. Read on to find out how you may have learned your personality.

Skinner and Social Learning Theory

In Chapter 7, you read about the American psychologist, B.F. Skinner. Skinner spent many years studying how animals learn behaviour. He discovered that animals will repeat behaviour that is rewarded. This seems like a simple observation. But Skinner also applied his theory to how human beings learn thoughts and behaviours. He felt that human personality is formed by the same process of learning and remembering. He called this "social learning" because it happens within a society.

People who favour social learning theory doubt that you were born with any personality. They believe that your personality is the sum of all your experiences. You are not like an iceberg with most of your personality hidden beneath the surface. Instead, you are like an empty container. As you go through life, you learn how to act in various situations. Each new experience is poured into the empty container that is you and is added to your memory.

According to social learning theory, the search for the "hidden you" is a complete waste of time. After all, it is impossible to accurately measure what cannot be seen. It is more worthwhile to study how you behave and then to search for the ways in which you learned your behaviour. As a result, those who favour this view of human personality study how people and events in the environment influence and teach us to behave.

How Reinforcement and Punishment Affects Personality

How do you learn your personality? Reinforcements are the key to the whole process. As you learned in Chapter 7, a reinforcement is anything that causes a behaviour to be continued or repeated. Punishment is anything that causes a behaviour to be reduced or to stop. According to learning theory, we learn to behave in certain ways because we usually want to receive rewards and avoid punishments.

Aspects of our personalities are moulded by the positive or negative reactions to our behaviour. Some people are hard workers. At some point in their lives, they may have been rewarded for some extra effort they put into something. As a result, they frequently repeated this behaviour that got them a reward. Eventually, they repeated this behaviour so often that it became a habit. They then no longer needed anyone to actually reward them. Working hard and accomplishing tasks made them feel good, and this was reward enough.

On the other hand, suppose you worked hard at something and your efforts were criticized, which is a punishment. People usually try to avoid punishment. This might cause you to avoid working hard again. In another case, you might have put a special effort into something, but no one noticed. While this is neither a punishment nor a reward, you may decide that the effort was not worth it. The rewards were not enough and eventually you stopped trying.

Reinforcement occurs in two ways, directly or indirectly. When someone openly gives you either a punishment or a reward for your behaviour, it is **direct reinforcement**. This will cause you either to reduce or to repeat the behaviour. You receive **indirect reinforcement** when you see someone else being rewarded or punished for behaving in a certain way. If they are rewarded, you may imitate them in hopes of getting the same reward. If they are punished, you may avoid doing what they did.

In a way, a long prison sentence for a serious crime is both a direct and an indirect reinforcement. It gives a direct punishment to the convicted person. This should teach the criminal to avoid repeating the act that resulted in the imprisonment. The sentence is also an indirect reinforcement, because it may discourage others from committing a similar crime.

Some people find social learning theory disturbing. It seems to suggest that personality is something taught by others. You simply sit and learn the lessons. If this is true, then we have little control over the kind of person that we become.

In fact, if social learning theory is correct, personality is nothing more than a set of masks that we slip on and off. We have been taught to know which masks are the right ones in certain situations. For example, timid people can be trained to be assertive when the situation calls for it. A mild-mannered attendant working in the emergency ward of a busy hospital soon learns to give orders quickly and clearly. If he or she doesn't, lives will be lost. Thus, our personalities may be somewhat fluid, changing as the circumstances and environment change.

From Ideas to Action

1. For each situation below, do the following:
   a) Identify the reinforcement(s) used.
   b) Determine whether the reinforcement(s) is(are) direct or indirect. In each case, explain why.
   c) Predict what the likely outcome of each situation will be.

Situation 1

John was new at the school. He felt lonely and a little out of place. One day in the cafeteria, he saw a popular person with a new haircut. People from other tables came over to compliment the haircut.

Situation 2

Sally was a "pain" in class. She would rarely sit at her desk. She always bothered her neighbours when they were trying to work. The teacher had tried detentions after school and had phoned Sally's parents. This seemed to *increase* Sally's bad behaviour. The teacher learned that Sally simply wanted attention. She would take it in any form that she could get it, including detentions and scoldings from her parents.

Situation 3

In order to change Sally's behaviour, the teacher decided to ignore Sally's bad behaviour. Instead, she decided to give attention to a good student who sat near Sally. Each time this student did something good, the teacher would praise the student in a voice loud enough for Sally to hear.

2. Suggest reinforcements that might be used to get someone to learn the following behaviours:
   a) getting someone to study regularly
   b) getting someone to school on time in the morning
   c) getting a child to stop stealing
   d) getting an adolescent to stop stealing
   e) getting someone to control a violent temper

3. For each case below, do the following:
   a) Identify the problem behaviour.
   b) If you were a parent who wanted to use your knowledge of social learning theory, what actions might you take?

c) For each action that you think of, predict the likely outcome on the childrens' personalities.

Case 1

In a family of three children, there is a constant battle for attention. The children fight to see who will help their mother bake cookies. At other times, they fight for the right to select a program on TV. On other occasions, they seem to fight just to get one of the parents to come running to stop the disturbance.

Case 2

William was a very stubborn boy. One day his parents had promised him a visit to the zoo. At the last minute, the parents got a call from some family friends inviting the whole family over for dinner. William was furious. He pouted all the way over in the car. Once they had arrived, he refused to come into the house. The family went into the house, leaving William in the car. They sent his sister to try to persuade him to come in. He refused to budge. This was only one of a long list of stand-offs that William had won.

4. Here is an opportunity to try to change some aspect of your own personality. Select some habit that you have been trying to break. Now, develop a plan for changing that behaviour using a program of reinforcements. If possible, carry out your plan. If you feel comfortable about it, share the results of your program with the rest of the class. If the program was unsuccessful, how would you explain this? How might you have improved your plan?

Humanistic Theory

What Makes Personalities Change?

Look at the numbered photographs and answer the following question in your notebook:

Why are these people behaving the way they are?

1

2

3

4

5

6

The problem with both the psychodynamic theory and the social learning theory of personality is that they both imply that we don't have control over who we are. Freud says that inner forces drive us, Skinner says that external forces manipulate us. Either way, there doesn't seem to be much room for the individual to control or change his or her personality.

Maslow and Humanistic Theory

Abraham Maslow, an American psychologist, believed that individuals *can* control and change their personalities. As you learned in Chapter 8, Maslow said that the most important factor in human motivation is the need to live to the "fullest potential." Every person's fullest potential is different, because we are all different. We can't all be the world's greatest singer or typist. However, we can try to become as good as we can be, as capable as we are able, and as tolerant and understanding of other people as possible. In our own ways, we can reach our fullest potential.

People who support the humanistic theory of personality believe that we are basically good, thinking individuals who want to become better human beings in the course of our lives. They do not believe that we are driven by uncontrollable forces nor that we are exactly what experience has taught us. We strive to reach our fullest potential, and it is our striving which shapes our personalities.

. . . .

From Ideas to Action

1) Decide whether each situation below is an example of unconscious drives (psychodynamic theory), learned behaviour (social learning theory) or striving to reach full potential (humanistic theory).

a) To teach Sarah to be punctual, her parents scolded her every time she was late for meals.

b) Sylvia's greatest joy in life is trying to better her own personal best on the track.

c) Brad can't ever relax and just have fun. He always feels guilty about not working hard enough.

d) Susan loves to have friends around her, because they share many happy experiences together. Her friends think of her as a warm and friendly person.

e) Enrico has managed to overcome a serious stutter and is now a confident, self-assured young person.

Making an Oral Presentation

The purpose of this exercise is to help you make a more effective oral presentation. Below you will find a suggested structure for oral presentations and an example of a presentation on the topic "Learning Your Personality."

The Structure

Introduction:
State the main questions you will discuss and your hypothesis (what your presentation will attempt to prove).

Content or Knowledge:
Research enough facts, opinions and arguments to prove your hypothesis. Be certain that this information is accurate and of interest to your audience.

Illustrations:
These should be used to clarify your ideas, to support your arguments and to engage your audience. They may be written (quotes, poems, or stories) or pictures, charts, slides, maps or films.

Summary:
You should have a final statement that sums up what you have been trying to prove. You may also wish to raise new questions that developed out of your presentation.

Example

Is your personality learned? Some psychologists believe that external forces "teach" us our personalities.

1. How people learn.
2. The role of reinforcement
   a) Direct reinforcement
   b) Indirect reinforcement
3. How we learn to change.

1. Describe some experiments on learning and reinforcement (from textbooks or experience).
2. Use anecdotes (true stories) about watching brothers and sisters learning personality traits.
3. Make a chart showing how reinforcement works.
4. Display a photo of B.F. Skinner.
5. Mention case studies on personality.

Personality can be learned from external sources, as shown in experiments and case studies. Does your personality change as you grow older?

Additional Hints

1. Do not merely read your presentation. Instead, explain your ideas in your own words, so that you teach your audience. You can refer briefly to point-form notes to keep yourself organized or to quote examples.

2. Sit or stand straight so that you maintain eye contact with your audience. Make your audience feel that you are talking to each person individually.

3. Show enthusiasm for your topic. If you enjoy it, your audience will too.

4. Insist that students listen to your presentation and give you their full attention. You may wish to provide a class set of notes at the end of your presentation. This will avoid the distraction of note-taking during the presentation itself.

5. Speak clearly and use language that is understandable. Where necessary, explain difficult terms slowly and carefully.

6. Use short sentences to repeat key ideas, but avoid constant repetition.

7. Try to make your presentation relevant to your audience. Questions that cause them to think about their viewpoints is one way to do this.

Try making a presentation on one of these topics:
1. What do baby doctors, such as Benjamin Spock, Frederick W. Rutherford and Haim G. Ginott, have to say about personality development in very young children?
2. Reseach the theories of child-raising specialists, such as those of Dr. Fitzhugh Dodson in his book *How to Parent*, those of Dr. Lee Salk in *Your Child in Adolescence* or those of Thomas Gordon in *Parent Effectiveness Training*. What do these experts say about the role of parents in the development of their childrens' personalities?
3. How valid are the following methods of testing personality: reading a person's palm, handwriting analysis, horoscope readings?

Can We Change Our Personalities?

● ●

The following case studies will help you explore the issue of how personality might be shaped and changed. Some people argue that personality is the result of internal forces. Others favour the idea that personality can be moulded or changed by outside forces. When you have read the case studies, answer the follow-up questions.

The Edith Project

On August 16, 1952, Aaron Stern called a press conference. He proudly pointed to a baby in a nearby crib. "Meet my daughter, Edith. She is going to be a genius. I shall make her into a perfect human being."

He called his method "total educational immersion." He felt that people begin learning the day they are born and that they do not stop learning until the day they die. The trick is to make their world stimulating and challenging. Only this will result in the growth of outstanding intelligence.

Aaron Stern did not work because of ill health. He spent each minute of the day teaching and playing with Edith. If they passed a construction site during a walk, he would teach her about physics. If they passed a group of people on strike, he would seize the opportunity to teach her about government or labour relations. From the day that she was born, she heard nothing but classical music. "Classical music shall beautify her soul," stated Stern.

Baby talk was forbidden. Edith was spoken to in complete, adult sentences at all times. Her crib was filled with multi-racial dolls and the walls of her room were plastered with posters of the wonders of the world. In time, these were replaced by pictures of the world's greatest thinkers, such as Gandhi, Tolstoy and Einstein.

At eleven months, Stern asked Edith how old she was. She reached into her crib and picked up a flash card with the number 10 on it and held it up. He waited. Then she raised a chubby forefinger beside it and she counted aloud, "1, 2, 3, 4, 5 ...." Stern kissed her many times. Kisses and candy were the rewards for good performance.

At age one, Edith spoke simple sentences and identified letters on flash cards. At two, she knew the entire alphabet. Stern claims that she had read through all the volumes of the *Encyclopaedia Britannica* by the age of four-and-a-half. By the time she entered school at the age of six, she was reading two books and *The New York Times* every day.

Edith skipped alternate grades through to grade 8 and then skipped high school altogether, enrolling in college at the age of twelve. Aaron Stern drove the school system crazy throughout this period. He would make unscheduled visits to her classes. He sent a constant stream of complaint letters to the school board.

Edith had few friends. She cared little for her appearance and rapidly gained weight. The only time that she became popular was during exams, when other students would ask her for help in their studies. In fact, her only real companion throughout her early life was her father. She saw little of her mother because her father had insisted on being the one who fed her. Besides, since his health prohibited him from working, her mother had to go out and work to support the family.

By the age of fifteen Edith was teaching higher mathematics at Michigan State University and was working on her Ph.D. She consistently scored over 200 on intelligence tests (150 is considered genius).

Some say that Stern robbed his daughter of her childhood and that her development was abnormally fast. Stern stated, however, "Every parent has the desire to fulfill himself through his child. It's not unusual. Ask Edith if she missed anything. Those who say I stole my daughter's infancy are wrong. I didn't restrict her; I added to her life."

Stern was asked if he was content with the results of his "project." After some thought he said, "I am not very impressed with Edith. She could have been much more given what the input has been. I don't believe she has reached the plateau of Einstein or that she is a genius. She will be a genius when she makes a contribution."

(Adapted from: "The Edith Project" by Jack McClintock. *Harper's*, March 1977.)

The Case of Elizabeth von R.

Sigmund Freud believed that the abnormal conditions and feelings that people reported were often caused by parts of their personalities hidden deep in their unconscious minds. Only after these people could be made aware of these inner conflicts would their outward symptoms go away.

The case of Elizabeth von R. provides a good example of Freud's way of getting at the hidden self. Elizabeth complained of pains in her legs. She said that she sometimes felt very cold. Although both her legs were extremely sensitive to pain, the centre of the pains seemed to be the front of the right thigh. She walked with difficulty and tired easily. Otherwise, she was a cheerful, bright young woman.

She did not respond to regular medical treatments for the physical symptoms that she was experiencing. As a result, Freud suggested that she allow him to explore the hidden reaches of her mind for the source of her pain. She consented.

In the sessions that followed, Elizabeth lay on a couch with her eyes closed and talked about her memories. Her story centred on the events of the past few years. These were times of great sorrow for her. Her father, with whom she had always been close, had been very ill. During the 18 months that he had spent in bed before his death, she had remained by him. During this period, she experienced some pains in her legs, but these always went away.

During treatment, Freud would put his hand on her head. He told Elizabeth that when she felt the pressure on her head, a thought would pass through her mind.

The first time he tried this method, she remembered that she had been persuaded to leave her father's side only a few times during his illness. One night, she went to a party where she spent the evening with a young man whom she had known for years. She felt very attracted to him and she believed that he loved her. When she returned home she found that her father's condition had become much worse. She blamed herself for having left his side for her own pleasure. She rarely saw the young man again.

Elizabeth also remembered the many times that she would run to her sick father in the middle of the night. The floor was cold beneath her bare feet. She also recalled that her father's condition made one of his legs swell. It was necessary to bandage the leg, and while she did this, his leg rested on her right thigh.

Freud concluded that a conflict had been created in Elizabeth between her feelings for the young man and her guilt. As a result of the conflict, Freud believed that the sexual energy that she felt towards the young man was turned into the pain that she felt in her legs.

The precise centre of the pain was connected with the place where her father's bad leg rested, the right thigh. Her feelings of coldness probably began with the cold floors. The pain itself was possibly caused by exhaustion from the long hours of sitting up with her father and the cold of the floors. This real pain was then increased by the sexual energy that she hid and denied. In time, the pains were no longer caused by any physical problem. Instead, the causes were now purely in her mind, the result of memories that were too painful to call up.

Once the possible reasons for her pains were revealed, Elizabeth's suffering began to lessen. After another period of therapy, the pains disappeared altogether.

(Adapted from: American Psychological Association, *Studying Personality: An Instructional Unit. The Human Behaviour Curriculum Project*, pp. 8–13. New York: Teachers College Press, Columbia University.)

1. In groups of two or three, prepare an oral report based on the case studies you have read. Your presentation should include:
   a) a description of the problem or situation
   b) a description of the personality theory that is being studied
   c) how the theory was applied
   If you have any difficulty organizing your oral report, refer to the skills exercise "Making an Oral Presentation" on page 189.

2. What evidence is there in the case studies that we can change our personalities?

3. Under what circumstances should personality be changed? Who has the right to make this decision? Why?

Projects, Activities and Explorations

1. Organize a "Non-science Fair." Research various unscientific methods of personality testing, such as:
   a) handwriting analysis,
   b) horoscope reading, c) palmistry, d) phrenology, e) physiognomy

   Set up booths with a display that tells about the history and the basic principles of the various methods. Offer to tell people about their personalities, using the method set up at each booth. After "clients" have been through all the booths, ask them to discuss how the various readings compared and how accurate the readings seemed to be in describing their personalities. You can vary this project by adding a booth where an objective-style personality test is offered.

2. Many centuries ago, people put their personal symbols onto their shields when they went into battle. These soon became family coats-of-arms. Below is a sample of what a coat-of-arms might look like. Create your own coat-of-arms. Draw or paste pictures into the sections of the coat-of-arms that say something important about you. If possible, come up with a short "motto" or saying to go at the bottom of the coat-of-arms, that would sum up everything on the shield.

3. A Zen Buddhist monk was once asked what was the most difficult and important task for a person to accomplish in a lifetime. Without hesitating, the monk smiled and answered, "To know yourself." Do you agree or disagree with this statement? Use evidence from this chapter to support your view.

4. a) Examine the art of two famous artists. Is there any pattern in their subjects or in the way that they have portrayed them? If so, does this reveal anything about the personalities of the artists? Research the lives of the artists that you have chosen to study. Were your original impressions about their personalities accurate?

   b) You may wish to present your findings to the class by showing slides of some of the artists' pictures. Begin your presentation by asking the students in the class to look at the pictures and to guess about each artist's personality. After the students have given their opinions, reveal the results of your research.

   c) Find out how psychologists learn about personality by means of the pictures that their clients and patients draw. This method is often used when the patients are young children who cannot express themselves in words. You may wish to report your findings to the class.

What Have You Learned?

If you have covered everything in this chapter, you should be familiar with the following topics:

1. The definition of personality
2. Why we study personality
3. The psychodynamic theory of personality formation (id, superego, ego)
4. The social learning theory of personality formation
5. The humanistic theory of personality formation
6. How to make an oral presentation

To Help You Study

The following chart will help you to review the words, facts and ideas that were introduced in this chapter. Copy the chart into your notebook and fill in the missing information.

Word, Fact, Idea	Example in a Sentence	Page	Definition
personality	Murderers may have serious personality problems.	177	the unique pattern of thoughts and behaviours that characterize an individual
role			
personality traits			
id			
superego			
ego			
defense mechanisms			
direct reinforcement			
indirect reinforcement			

Human Beings in Groups

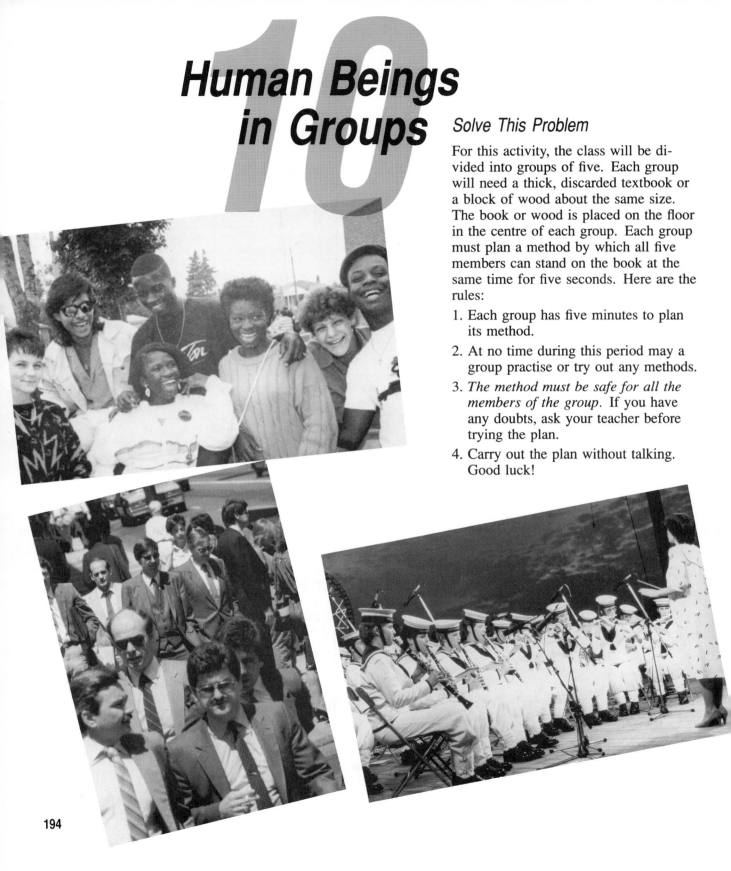

Solve This Problem

For this activity, the class will be divided into groups of five. Each group will need a thick, discarded textbook or a block of wood about the same size. The book or wood is placed on the floor in the centre of each group. Each group must plan a method by which all five members can stand on the book at the same time for five seconds. Here are the rules:

1. Each group has five minutes to plan its method.

2. At no time during this period may a group practise or try out any methods.

3. *The method must be safe for all the members of the group.* If you have any doubts, ask your teacher before trying the plan.

4. Carry out the plan without talking. Good luck!

When each group has completed the activity, discuss the following questions:

1. If your group was successful, what enabled it to do well?

2. If your group was unsuccessful, what interfered with success?

3. How could your group's performance have been improved?

4. Think of other groups that you belong to. Have the same kinds of things that occurred in this activity happened in these groups as well? Give some examples.

5. Why do you belong to certain groups? Why do you think most people choose to be in a group rather than being alone?

Groups are very important to human beings. Chapter 3 mentioned how we are all born into various groups: family, friends, ethnic group, neighbourhood, etc. You spend a great deal of your time in groups, and they affect you in both positive and negative ways. Groups can help you to achieve and to grow. But they can also restrict and even harm you. In this chapter you will learn about the types of groups you belong to. You will also discover how and why these groups affect you as they do.

What Is a Group?

Which Pictures Show a Group?

Compare your answers with those of your classmates. Did you agree about which pictures showed groups? Why or why not? What do you think are some characteristics of a group?

Characteristics of a Group

Your teacher has just announced that everyone has to do a presentation in front of the class. Do you suddenly feel like leaving the planet? Would you feel better if you could do the presentation with some other students?

Why do we feel so nervous when we must perform in front of others? And why do we feel more secure when we can perform with other people? If you have ever felt these things or asked these questions, you have experienced the power of groups on human beings.

A **group** has two basic characteristics:

1. It consists of two or more people.
2. Members of a group interact in such a way that each person *influences* other people in the group.

Your class is a group. Obviously, it has more than one person in it. The members of your class also influence each other. For example, when you rehearse a presentation at home, you don't feel very nervous. But when you stand in front of your classmates, your palms may sweat, your voice may shake and your stomach may have butterflies.

Groups can also have positive effects. Suppose you prepare a presentation for your class with some other students instead of working by yourself. This also forms a group. The members of this group influence each other by suggesting different ways of doing the presentation. You finally agree on the best approach, divide the work required, and then make the presentation. This group effort reduces your fear because you are "on stage" for only a few minutes. By working together in a group, you and your classmates produce a presentation that is probably better than one you could do on your own.

Types of Groups

Categorize These Groups

Place the groups listed below into any logical categories you can think of (e.g. social, professional, etc.). Be prepared to explain your choices.

a) your family
b) this class
c) the school volleyball team
d) the company you work for part-time
e) the people you hang around with in your spare time
f) a club you belong to
g) you and your girl/boyfriend

Now as a class or in small groups, discuss the following questions:

1. How did you categorize the groups? Why did you choose these categories?
2. Suggest other groups that would fit the categories you selected. Why would they fit?
3. If you have not done so, how could you reduce the number of categories to only two?

Both your family and the people you work with are groups. Each of these groups is made up of more than two people who constantly influence your behaviour. These two groups are quite different, however. Sociologists divide groups into two basic categories: primary groups and secondary groups. Each type of group influences you in different ways.

Characteristics of Primary Groups

Primary groups share these common features:

1. They involve close personal relationships. Each member of the group is interested in each other member as a whole person.
2. Usually the members get to know each other well and share not only information, but also feelings.
3. Communication is usually, although not always, face-to-face.
4. Members of the group are usually difficult or impossible to replace.

Your family and the group of friends you spend most of your time with are both primary groups. The members of these two groups are concerned about you as a total person. You probably spend more time communicating with these people than with any others. When you are down, they are most likely to notice and to ask you what is wrong. They would also be painfully aware of your absence. Your family and close friends realize that if you were to disappear, there is no one quite like you who could fill the empty space.

You do and feel all these things for the people in your primary groups as well. Since you care for each other, you are more likely to feel secure and relaxed with these people. You are also more likely to share your most secret feelings and hopes. For these reasons, primary groups are usually highly valued by their members.

The closeness, warmth, support and security created within primary groups give them great power over their members. These groups often require their

members to adopt certain ways of thinking and acting. If you dress out of step with the accepted style, for example, your friends might give you a hard time. This would probably influence your choice of clothing in the future. We all want and need to fit in with the groups that are most important to us, so we often give in to the demands that primary groups make of us.

Problems Created by Primary Groups

Belonging to two or more primary groups can sometimes cause conflict, because what is expected by one primary group may be unacceptable to another. Your friends may insist that you dress in a certain way. Your parents may react to your style of dress with phrases such as, "No child of mine is leaving the house dressed like that!" or "While in this house, you will live by our rules!" This puts you in a difficult position. Since both your friends and your family are primary groups, you need and value each group and cannot easily choose between them.

Sometimes primary groups demand that their members behave in ways disapproved of by the rest of society. Gang behaviour is a good example of this. The members of a gang may encourage each other to steal or to vandalize, which causes other social groups to reject the gang.

Finally, primary groups reduce the independence of their members. Generally, everyone in a primary group must consider the feelings and opinions of the others before acting. If you really value your independence, this can be frustrating. You may come to resent the group's demands, and be forced to decide whether or not to remain in a group that is restricting you too much. Leaving a family or a group of friends, however, is never easy.

Characteristics of Secondary Groups

Secondary groups share these common features:

1. They are not interested in the whole person. Because only a few aspects of each member are considered important, relationships among the members are often not close or personal.

2. The group members usually know little about each other. They share information, but they rarely talk about their deepest feelings.

3. Communication is not always face-to-face. Members often communicate by written notes or by phone. They may never actually meet each other.

4. Since only a few aspects of each member are important to the group, members can be fairly easily replaced.

If you have a part-time job, you are in a secondary group. This group is probably interested only in your ability to perform the task for which you were hired. If you are constantly late, or ask for fewer hours because you are having trouble at school or at home, you may be laid off. While your manager may feel sorry for you, you are merely an employee and must do the job assigned to you. Other examples of secondary groups you might belong to are a soccer team and a drama group.

Relationships in secondary groups can be very impersonal. For example, managers do not usually take the rest of your life or your emotions into account when dealing with you. If you can't do the job, you will be replaced by someone who can.

Communication in secondary groups also tends to be formal and impersonal. The manager may pass instructions to you in the form of a memo or through another employee. You may never meet the workers at other outlets owned by the same company, but simply get information from them over the phone.

It is unlikely you would talk to the members of a secondary group about something that is bothering you outside of work. The members of such a group often do not know each other well enough to talk about personal matters.

A Positive Side to Secondary Groups

The workplace, sports teams and other secondary groups are not always cold and impersonal because, in some cases, they *can* overlap with primary groups. Occasionally, friendships develop in the workplace, for example, and these friends take an interest in each other's personal lives. If one friend is under a great deal of stress, the others may "cover" for that person. Friends may swap hours to help each other out. And you can always "let off steam" with friends in the workplace.

In playing or working together, people often get to know each other as they *really* are, with their good *and* bad points. The secondary group can therefore provide an opportunity to form new friendships. These friendships can help you to develop, both as a member of the secondary group and as a person. For this reason, secondary groups can be just as valuable to their members as primary groups are.

From Ideas to Action

1. Which of the following are groups and which are not? Explain briefly.
   a) a soccer team
   b) people waiting in an elevator for their floor
   c) a person waiting outside an elevator
   d) people in an elevator moments after one of the passengers has collapsed from an apparent heart attack
   e) your family
   f) you and your closest friend
   g) the people on your shift at the company where you have worked for the past four years

2. a) Identify which groups in question 1 are primary and which are secondary, and briefly explain why.
   b) Which group or groups might involve both primary and secondary groups at the same time?

3. Make a chart like the following to compare the characteristics of primary and secondary groups.

	Primary Groups	Secondary Groups
Focus of Interest		
Emotional Closeness		
Communication		
Replacement of Members		
Positive Aspects		
Negative Aspects		

4. Some people believe that the primary groups in our society are breaking down and are being gradually replaced by secondary groups. Do you agree with this view? If this trend does exist, how might it affect individuals and society in the long run?

5. Imagine that you have never been in a group of any kind. How would your life be different? How do you suppose your personality would differ? Answer these questions in any of the following ways:
   a) a poem b) a drawing c) a collage
   d) a series of diary entries

The Effects of Groups

Complete This Survey

Respond to the survey below. Copy the letters a) to k) in your notebook. Then rate the following situations according to how nervous you would feel. Use the following rating scale:

1 = relaxed, 2 = slightly nervous, 3 = moderately nervous, 4 = very nervous

When everyone in the class is finished, compare the results and try to explain any differences and similarities.

a) You are told to research and give a talk with three other students.
b) On your own, you must research and give a talk to four other students.
c) On your own, you must research and give a talk to a class of 30 students.
d) You must tape a talk that will be played later to a group. You will not be present when the tape is played.
e) On your own, you must give a talk to a group sitting three feet away from you.
f) On your own, you must give a talk to a group seated 20 feet away from you.
g) On your own, you must give a talk to a group of parents and teachers.
h) You are practising your talk alone in your room.
i) You are giving your talk with two other students who prepared the presentation with you.
j) You are giving your talk on your own. Several other students will also give talks. The teacher will choose the best presentation, and the winner's name will appear in the local newspaper.

k) Each presenter in your group of three is being given a mark and the total of your marks will be your group mark. There will be an individual prize and a group prize awarded. The other two in your group have given good presentations and now it is your turn.

Now do the following:

A. Reread the situations and put a check-mark (√) beside the ones that would make you feel competitive. Put an asterisk (*) beside the ones that would lead to co-operation.
B. Reread the situations and put a "W" beside the ones in which you would probably perform well. Place a "P" beside those in which you would probably perform poorly.

As a class or in small groups, discuss the following questions:

1. What factors seem to influence how nervous people feel? Why?
2. What factors seem to influence people to be either competitive or co-operative? Why?
3. What factors seem to improve a person's performance? What factors seem to hinder a person's performance? Try to explain how these factors work.

Audiences, Tension and Performance

When performing in front of people in some situations, you may have felt very nervous. In other situations, you may have felt calm and confident. Perhaps at times you performed extremely well, but at other times felt that your performances were disasters. Is it possible to predict how people will perform in front of certain audiences?

Four factors affect your feelings of tension and your performance in front of an audience. These are:

1. The *number of people* in the audience. Usually, the larger the audience, the more nervous you feel. You are probably not as nervous when you present a project to a small group of students instead of to the whole class.

2. The *distance* between you and the audience. The greater the distance, the more tense you may feel. You often feel more comfortable when your audience is close enough to make eye contact with you. You feel more in control of your audience's attention and reactions. This also helps to make the group seem smaller.

3. The greater the *power or status of the people watching you,* the greater your tension. If you could choose to do a presentation in front of a group of teachers, or a group of students, you would probably choose an audience of students because this would be less threatening.

4. The *degree to which the task* you are expected to perform *is well learned or well practised.* You have probably heard the saying "Practice makes per-fect." If you perform a task that you have practised to the point where it has become automatic, you will probably give an outstanding performance. But if you are trying something fairly new under the pressure to perform, you will probably perform poorly.

In practice sessions, professional athletes may drop a ball or miss an easy shot at a net. However, in front of 30 000 screaming fans, they often seem superhuman. The opposite would probably happen to you. Although you might catch a ball or skate fairly well, in front of 30 000 sports fans, your nervousness under pressure would seriously hinder your performance.

So, the next time you have to perform in front of an audience, practise well beforehand. You may be pleasantly surprised by the results.

Co-operation and Competition

What happens when people stop being an audience and become an active group working towards a goal? In other words, instead of simply watching you, they become participants in your performance. This situation can result in two kinds of behaviour: co-operation or competition.

Co-operation occurs when members of a group work together towards a common goal. This usually happens because everybody in the group realizes that accomplishing the task would be impossible without the help of each group member.

For example, a class project might be too difficult for you to do on your own. Suppose the assignment requires some art work and you can't draw very well. Someone else in the group who is artistic can take on this task. Also, by dividing the assignment into separate tasks, the work load is lessened and the project can be completed on time. Co-operation benefits everyone in the group.

Co-operation does not always mean that everyone benefits equally, however. In a business, for example, everyone from the owner to the sales staff helps to make the company a success. The owner and the workers know that they need to co-operate with each other to make the company profitable. The profits are not shared equally, though. The owner might make 200 000 dollars a year, while a salesperson might earn 18 000 dollars.

Competition occurs when members of a group are all trying to gain something that is in short supply. Promotions, money and jobs are all things that many people would like to have. Unfortunately, there are never enough of these things for everyone. People must compete for these rewards, and there will always be winners and losers.

Competition can have both positive and negative effects on people in groups. Competition usually makes people strive

to perform well. If you and a co-worker both want the same promotion, both of you will try to out-perform the other person. You might even set a new company sales record in order to win the promotion. In situations such as this, competition affects both you and the company in a positive way.

But competition can also hurt people. In competitive situations, someone has to lose. If you lose often, your self-esteem can suffer. You might begin to label yourself a "loser." Your negative self-image might cause you to avoid competitive situations. But if you never compete, you will lessen your chances of becoming a winner. This could make your negative self-image even harder to erase. For this reason, competition can damage capable people.

Competition can also hinder the performance of a group as a whole. When tasks are very complicated, everyone's willing effort is needed. If competition in the group is fierce, however, some individuals may decide that the struggle is not worthwhile. They may withdraw their special skills from the group. This reduces the likelihood that the group will do its best. In circumstances such as these, co-operation rather than competition would produce better results.

From Ideas to Action

1. For each case below, predict how nervous the individual is likely to feel. Also predict whether a good or a poor performance is likely. Justify your answers using information presented in this chapter.
   a) You are about to take your driver's test after four lessons with a driving instructor.
   b) You are playing on your school's hockey team during a championship game.
   c) You are having an interview for a job with a company you have been researching for months.
   d) You have written a song and are playing it in front of a few friends.
   e) You have been practising with a new performing group. Tonight your group will make its first public appearance.

2. Each situation below might involve mainly co-operation, mainly competition, or both co-operation and competition. Determine which condition would best fit the situation. Briefly explain your answers.
   a) working as a firefighter to put out a dangerous blaze
   b) working in a fast food restaurant
   c) selling clothes in a department store
   d) climbing on a team that is trying to reach the summit of a mountain never before attempted
   e) playing on a soccer team during the playoffs

3. For each case above involving competition, state whether the competition would have positive or negative effects. Briefly explain your answers.

4. As an experiment, on the next test for this course, set up a competition with someone else in the class. Decide on a prize of value to both of you (two tickets to a movie, for example). The person scoring the higher mark will win the prize. Compare your mark on this test with your previous test results. How would you account for any differences?

Writing an Essay — Level 1

The purpose of this exercise is to introduce you to the main features of an expository style of essay. This is the type of essay you write when you are trying to explain something or prove a particular point of view on a topic. It is the most common type of essay for social scientists to write.

On the left you will see an explanation of the essay and on the right you will see a very brief example of this style of essay.

Expository Essay Structure

Introduction
State the essay's purpose or main question.
Indicate the essay topics in the order you are going to examine them.
State your thesis — what you are going to prove in your essay.

Body Paragraphs
Use a separate paragraph for each main topic of your essay.

In each of these paragraphs, state the supporting arguments and facts that relate to this topic.

Be certain to connect each topic to your overall argument or thesis. The first or last sentence of each topic paragraph should do this.

The Conclusion
Clearly re-state your thesis and summarize all the main arguments you used to develop it. Use at least one sentence for each topic. As a final point, build on your thesis by applying it to the present or near future.

Example of an Expository Essay

Title: The Use of Group Work in the Classroom.

Is group work an effective approach to learning in a classroom? To answer this, it is necessary to examine the impact of groups on student involvement, productivity and preparation for the working world. This will show that group work is an excellent learning technique with many benefits.

Group work creates a higher level of involvement in lessons than does more traditional teacher centered methods. Where teachers ask all the questions to individual students, few students actually get to express their ideas. In groups, nearly all students will get to ask, answer and discuss the questions. It is difficult for them to remain uninvolved in small groups that have a specific task to complete.

Group work is a more productive approach to some learning tasks. If large amounts of research are needed, a group could accomplish this by sharing the load where individuals would fail. A presentation that involves dramatic talents, artistic skills and good written abilities, can be handled more easily by drawing on the many skills that a group may possess but that no individual would likely have to the same degree.

Group or co-operative learning situations are excellent preparation for the working world. Businesses need people who have learned to work effectively in groups. Co-operative skills such as listening attentively, sharing ideas and assigned work are necessary for any business to prosper. These are skills that can and must be taught as part of classroom group work.

Group work is a very effective approach to learning. It provides great opportunities for student involvement. The sharing of group skills and effort makes it very productive. It can give students co-operative skills needed for future jobs. Perhaps more of our classes should use group work.

Now you try to write a brief four to six paragraph essay on one of the following topics:

1. The impact of teenage gangs or cliques in schools.
2. The conflict between family groups and peer groups for teens.
3. Individual rights and group pressures.
4. The role of co-operation and competition in our society.

Groups At Work

Groups or Individuals: Which Work Better?

Decide whether each activity below could be done better by an individual or by a group.

a) building a house
b) lighting a fire
c) publishing a school yearbook
d) writing a poem
e) making a cup of tea
f) studying for a final exam
g) painting a picture
h) designing electrical circuits for an office tower
i) organizing a high school conference on social issues

Compare your responses with those of other students and then answer the following questions:

1. Generally, when are group efforts more effective than individual efforts? Why do you think so?
2. When are individual efforts more effective than group efforts? Why do you think so?
3. Can you think of times when group efforts ought to be better than individual efforts at school? Why do these group efforts not always work out as well as they should?

It is often said that groups are better at solving problems or getting things done, compared to individuals. Is this true? Research tells us that the answer is both "yes" and "no." It depends, for one thing, on the type of task or job involved.

Large or Complicated Jobs: Yes!
Groups are better at tasks requiring the labour of many people at once. You couldn't pull your friend's car out of the ditch by yourself. But a group of twenty people with a strong rope could do it easily.

Groups are also better at some complex tasks, such as assembling an automobile. Each worker on the assembly line is given a single task and becomes an expert in doing that one thing. Checking the quality of the work done by specific workers is much easier than if the entire job were done by one person. Groups are more suited to large, complicated tasks than are individuals, because groups can work more quickly and have access to more resources.

Creative or Simple Jobs: No!
For creative tasks, it is not as clear that groups are superior to individuals. For instance, in a brainstorming session, a group gets together and tries to think of as many new, creative solutions to a problem as possible. It was once thought that groups could brainstorm more and better ideas than could individuals. But this is not what always happens. Often a group tends to favour one solution, which can steer thinking away from other creative ideas.

Finally, when groups try to solve simple problems, they often *appear* to do better than individuals. But what is happening here has nothing to do with the group. One person in the group usually hits on the solution first. This is either due to luck, or because the person is an expert in the kind of problem facing the group. So the group's success has more to do with an individual than with the strength of the group as a whole.

Roles in Groups

Read the following conversation:

Sanjay: So, what are we going to do Saturday night?

Mykhail: I don't know.

Sanjay: What do you think, Charlene?

Charlene: I want to see that new movie we talked about yesterday.

Sanjay: Or we could go to the school dance. I hear they have a good group.

Charlene: Only losers go to school dances. I wouldn't be caught dead at one!

Mykhail: OK, OK, let's lighten up. Sanjay was only making a suggestion. Remember — we're all friends just trying to plan something fun.

Sanjay: Well, what else could we do?

Charlene: Make all the suggestions you like, but I'm going to the movie — with or without you two.

Mykhail: Charlene, you seem upset today. Is there something bothering you? Is there anything we can do?

Charlene: No, I'm fine. I just don't like to feel pressured into doing something I don't want to do.

Mykhail: OK, we have two choices so far: a movie and the dance. Is there any way we can combine things so everyone will be happy?

Sanjay: How about going to the video dance at the community centre? That way we can dance and see a movie too! I can pick you all up at the school. Chalene, will you be finished work in time or will you have to take the bus?

Mykhail: Listen, Sanjay, maybe we shouldn't push Charlene to decide today...

Each person in this group is affecting the way the group interacts, but in different ways. Each person represents one of the three types of roles commonly seen in groups.

The Task-centred Role

Sanjay is playing the **task-centred role**. People in this role are most concerned with accomplishing the group's goal. They may take charge, start the discussions in the group and ask the opinions of other group members. They also tend to try to organize the group once a decision has been reached because they want to make sure decisions are put into action. Sanjay begins the discussion and asks for ideas from Charlene and Mykhail. He later tries to put a plan into action by offering to do the driving. For people like Sanjay, the group must first and foremost accomplish its goal.

This role is both good and bad for a group. On the positive side, task-centred people make things happen. Groups can spend hours chatting about what to do and never really accomplish anything. On the negative side, task-centred people are often aggressive and can rush the group into making a decision. This can make other members unhappy, so that they decide to offer nothing further. If this happens, the task-centred person may have to do the task alone. If the task is complicated, however, this may be impossible and the goal will not be reached.

Task-centered people must ensure that everyone in the group has some input into the final decision. They must sense when it is wise to slow down the decision-making and allow for more discussion. They must also be able to speed up the group when things seem to be going nowhere. This role is not an easy one, but it can be vital to the success of a group.

The Maintenance Role

If you live in an apartment, you know there is always someone around who does the maintenance for the building. This person's job is to keep the building running if something breaks down.

In the same way, Mykhail plays the **maintenance role** for the group. People in this role are most concerned with how the group members are getting along with each other. Mykhail points out that Charlene feels pressured. He also tries to head off a fight between Charlene and Sanjay. People playing this role want everyone to feel good about being in the group. If someone seems to feel ignored or if tempers flare, the person in the maintenance role jumps in to repair the damage.

The maintenance role can be very important in a group. Sometimes group members may decide to back away from the group. They may be angry or feel that their views are not respected by the others. But these members may have special talents that the group needs in order to put its final decision into action. People in the maintenance role use their sensitivity to others to encourage these people to get involved again. People who play this role may not be seen as leaders, but, without them, groups can quickly fall apart.

The Self-centred Role

People playing a **self-centred role** are concerned only with themselves and are rarely interested in what the group wants to do if it clashes with their wishes. Charlene plays this role as she stubbornly refuses to consider any of Sanjay's suggestions.

People playing the self-centred role may do everything they can to block the efforts of the members playing the task-centred and maintenance roles. They may deliberately look for small things that might be wrong with various ideas.

They are often the jokers in the group, constantly interrupting by trying to be funny. They may sit and doodle on a pad of paper, or play with paperclips. They often cause distraction just as the group seems to be getting somewhere. In the end, they may destroy the group's ability to accomplish anything. These people can pose a serious problem for a group.

However, they can also have ideas and skills that could benefit the group. Perhaps these people have had bad experiences in groups. They may have felt ignored or put down. Other group members must show the self-centred person that his or her opinions are needed and respected, and that he or she can make a positive contribution to the group.

From Ideas to Action

1. Which task below would be done better by an individual, and which would be done better by a group? Briefly explain your answers.
   a) solving a math problem
   b) starting a new business
   c) finding out what is wrong with a stalled car
   d) taking notes quickly on a section in a textbook
   e) building a log cabin
   f) designing a good oral presentation

2. Below is a list of behaviours you might see exhibited by people in groups. Classify each behaviour as either task-centred, maintenance or self-centred. In each case, briefly explain your answer.
   a) *Initiator*: helps to start the group discussion; organizes the group; introduces new ideas and raises new questions
   b) *Dominator*: talks a lot; tries to manipulate the group in order to show his or her personal authority or superiority
   c) *Clarifier*: asks for additional information; requests a definition of terms and perhaps a clearer explanation of goals or opinions
   d) *Distractor*: clowns around; carries on side conversations; is generally uninvolved in the group's efforts
   e) *Harmonizer*: attempts to smooth out disagreements and reduce tensions; helps others to explore their differences

   f) *Encourager*: encourages silent members of the group to get involved and to offer their opinions; rephrases the ideas of others in positive terms to clarify thoughts and feelings
   g) *Summarizer*: sums up how much the group has accomplished; ties together related ideas; points out areas of agreement and disagreement
   h) *Silent Member*: says little or nothing; does not participate in the group's activities

3. a) Which behaviours listed in question 2 would be positive for a group? Why? Which ones would be negative? Why?
   b) What could you do to make the people displaying negative behaviour in a group become more positive and productive?

4. Redo the group decision-making activity presented on page 194. When the activity has been completed, have the members of the group identify which role(s) each person (including themselves) played. (You may wish to refer to the list of behaviours described in question 2.) When all group members have compared their choices, each member should explain why he or she associated a certain role with a certain member of the group.

Should Cults Be Controlled?

● ●

When a group seems drastically different from other groups in a society, it may be seen as a *cult*. Carroll Stoner and Jo Anne Parke, authors of *All God's Children, The Cult Experience — Salvation or Slavery?* suggest the following criteria for identifying cults:

1. A cult has a leader (either living or dead) and the doctrine is based on his (or her) revelations, which supplement or replace traditional religious scriptures.

2. The cult leader is an authoritarian and the sole judge of his (or her) members' faith. He (or she) often lives like a king while the followers live in poverty.

3. The cult promises that its members will work to save the world, yet sponsors no community improvement programs.

4. Cult members are required to perform demeaning tasks that utilise little or no talent or education.

5. Cults are exclusive social systems that claim their members will achieve salvation and will thereby be superior to outsiders.

6. To join a cult, one must cut him/herself off from society — job, friends and family.

7. Cults use ego-destruction and thought control to recruit and indoctrinate.

8. Cult practices can be psychologically unwholesome and, in some cases, physically dangerous.

Read the following two articles and then answer the follow-up questions.

Brainwash or belief?

By Bill Dampler *Toronto Star* [March 8, 1980]

On Friday, Feb. 8, 1980, a girl we will call Shirley Caine left home. She is 18 years old, a slow learner who had never been able to find a full-time job.

She left suddenly and without explanation.

Her mother, Mrs. Susan Caine, had gone to work that morning as usual. Shirley had an appointment to see about a federal retraining program — "the one where they give you $100 a week while you're learning" — and phoned midway through the morning to say she was going to the Canada Manpower office. She did not keep the appointment, and she didn't return home that night.

"There was no note, nothing," Mrs. Caine said at the time. "We didn't sleep all weekend. We imagined all the worst things that can happen to a girl that age."

Shirley phoned the following evening and said she was well, that she was staying with friends, and was not going to come home. When her mother asked where she was, she hung up.

Mrs. Caine worried for a few days, then called the police. The officer who spoke to her was courteous, but he explained carefully there was nothing he could do.

Her daughter is 18, and deemed to be an adult, the officer said. If he located her and she did not want her parents to know where she was staying, he would not be able to tell them.

Two days later, Mrs. Caine called the police again and an officer came to the house.

"He wasn't pleasant to me," Mrs. Caine recalls. "His manner seemed to say 'Well, she's 18, there's nothing I can do, why are you wasting my time?'

"Shirley is 18, but she's not very mature for her age. She's not as mature as some girls are at 14.

"Eventually he told me that I had a problem, that I was the one who needed help."

A week after her daughter disappeared, Mrs. Caine learned that she was living in a temple on Avenue Road owned by the International Society for Krishna Consciousness — the Hare Krishnas. She also learned, to her surprise, that a neighbour's son was a devotee of the sect, and had been taking Shirley to meetings there for some months.

When she next saw her daughter, it was at the Hare Krishna temple, under the careful eyes of half a dozen sect members.

"Shirley came in, wearing a long blue dress and a cowl on her head, and she had lost about 10 pounds, just in that short time.

"I put my arm around her and kissed her and it was like kissing

a board. There was no response at all. She was like a robot. She never looked me right in the eyes, not once."

Shirley's parents, who live in a mobile home outside Toronto, are by their own description "not a wealthy family. We don't have any money to hire a deprogrammer. And there isn't anything here in Canada to help us. There's nowhere to turn." So it is only by the barest chance that Mrs. Caine got her daughter back.

Shirley phoned her mother about a week later, sounding happy and unusually elated. She wanted her mother to send her flannelette pyjamas and a dress. She said she needed the pyjamas because it was cold where she was sleeping — on a mat on a cement floor. She needed the dress for sam-kirtan — selling Krishna literature on the street to unbelievers.

In the normal course of events, Mrs. Caine might not have heard from her daughter again. But in this particular case an accident intervened: Shirley got sick.

Two weeks after she had moved into their temple, members of the group checked Shirley into the Women's College Hospital. Two days later she called her parents in tears and asked them to come and get her.

They found their daughter in a room decorated with pictures of the sect's leader and gods, festooned with garlands of flowers. Sect members had left a tape recorder of Krishna chants, and books for her to read. They had also brought special vegetarian food, which they said Shirley must eat.

The Caines learned their daughter was suffering from severe malnutrition and incipient phlebitis.

"Her legs and knees were all swollen," Mrs. Caine says, "and she was very weak. She couldn't bathe herself or wash her hair. We had to help her."

Shirley had changed in other ways as well, Mrs. Caine says.

"She's much more child-like than she was before. She needs someone to hold onto, to hold her hand, and she's terrified they're going to come and take her back.

"We took her to her grandmother's house, and she couldn't sleep until her brother went outside and walked all around the house. She thought there was someone hiding outside.

"'Mom, I hear noises,' she said. 'They're going to come and get me.'

"And there's something else wrong with her, something I can't really explain. She'll be talking and smiling and cheery, and then something you say, or something in the conversation will set her off. Her eyelids droop and her face goes blank, as if she's in some kind of trance."

Shirley has since been readmitted to hospital, on the orders of the family physician — but a different hospital, and with her name deleted from the register because the family fears cult members will try to reach her again. They have already phoned four times, asking where Shirley is being kept.

Mrs. Caine says Shirley told her "she wanted to leave" the temple but "she had one of the whatchamacallit — devotees — with her all the time, even when she was talking to me on the telephone."

The Hare Krishnas say, however, that Shirley was at the temple voluntarily and could have left at any time.

Mrs. Caine says the cult kept $160 Shirley took with her when she entered the temple — "they say she made a contribution to the church" — and they still have the dress Mrs. Caine sent her daughter to wear when she went out begging.

But Mrs. Caine has her daughter.

Reprinted with permission — *The Toronto Star Syndicate*

Sects and Sanity

By Sandy Rovner *Washington Post* [reprinted in the *Kitchener-Waterloo Record*, Saturday, April 30, 1983]

WASHINGTON — From the persistent airport flower (sales) children to the grotesque Jonestown tragedy . . . from the paddling death of a toddler in a country commune, to bizarre-looking dress on city streets . . . from mass-marrying Moonies to blank faces and hooded eyes on the street . . .

The very word "cult," which evokes these images, has become synonymous with eerie, whether brutal or benign.

There also are the perceptions of personal tragedy, of young people brainwashed, their minds "controlled" . . . of parents kidnapping even adult children from temples or communes, of deprogramming . . . of shattered families and conflict and heartbreak. And most pervasive of all is the image of crazed young people, somehow unhinged: "weirdos" or "schizzies."

Although negative connotations of some cults are obviously warranted, some new studies are suggesting that fairly large numbers of young people — in some of the so-called cults or sects — may be happier and better adjusted than they had been in the "real world."

Latest of these studies, appearing in the April issue of *The American Journal of Psychiatry,* reports on 42 members of the Hare Krishna Temple in Melbourne, Australia. The investigator, Michael W. Ross, Ph.D., of the department of Psychiatry of Flinders University Medical School in Bedford Park, Australia, found that in standard mental-health tests the "scores and findings were within the normal range."

His findings, he writes, "do not support the popular view that many members of the Hare Krishna movement are mentally disordered."

He also found that the longer the members of the group had been in the temple, the better adjusted they became. (He makes the point that Hare Krishna is a well-established traditional Hindu faith that dates to the second century, B.C., and is still practised by millions of Indians.)

"I cannot emphasize too strongly," he writes, "that it is inappropriate to label all apparently new and non-conforming movements as cults. . . ."

"In short," he concludes from his study, "the popular view of Hare Krishna devotees as brainwashed and poorly adjusted individuals is not true."

If a group of 41 Hare Krishnas on the other side of the world seems somewhat removed from home, consider a New York psychiatrist who has studied cults, sects and their members in the U.S. and has reached some similar conclusions.

Dr. Marc Galanter, a psychiatrist at the Albert Einstein College of Medicine in New York City, has found that "groups may offer psychological support and meaning to life (to those who join) and in that respect the members may feel more secure than a lot of their friends who lead what is perceived as purposeless lives.

"People today tend not to have a lot of direction in their lives, and that generates a measure of anxiety which has been described as characteristic of our century." Success of the groups, Galanter believes, is in their ability to provide a belief system and stability "that harkens back to a period when people had more certainty about the reasons that the world turned."

Both Galanter and Ross have found that it is not uncommon for members of charismatic groups to have had pre-group psychological problems. Among the Australians, Ross writes, 27 had experiences with "addictive and hallucinogenic drugs" and only 10 had no previous drug experience.

In a December article in *The American Journal of Psychiatry*, Galanter says he found 38 per cent of members of the Divine Light Mission (adherents of the Maharaj Ji) had sought professional help before they joined the group and nine per cent had been in institu-

tions. Of a group of members of the Rev. Sun Myung Moon's Unification Church, 30 per cent had previously sought help and six per cent had been hospitalized.

Galanter refers to other reports indicating that alcohol and drug abuse declines markedly among individuals after joining sects. Galanter and his associates found two sects in which "both mild and heavy use of drugs declined."

Ross found the same thing among the Melbourne Hare Krishnas. "Since the movement eschews [avoids, shuns] all drugs (including such mild stimulants as tea and coffee)," he writes, "this history of abstinence after joining the movement must rate as one of the more successful rehabilitation programs."

Writes Galanter, "the apparent potential of charismatic groups for enforcing new behavioral norms is ... well illustrated."

Galanter, considered one of the top U.S. authorities in the field, also specializes in treating substance abusers. He suggests that there is a similarity between the success of such programs as AA and the decline of substance abuse within many cult groups.

The structure of the group and the stability of its leadership has a great influence on the emotional health of its members, says Galanter, "but you cannot make a judgment that groups are ... good or bad. One has to judge these, like any other social groups, by

what they do, and every citizen is entitled to make that judgment."

He recognizes that they also may be judged in terms of one's own belief systems. This can result in the kind of parent-child conflict over membership that in turn leads to such radical procedures as kidnapping and deprogramming.

"It is not," he notes, "that the parent or the group is right or wrong," but the potential for conflict exists.

Both Galanter and Ross see, as Galanter puts it, "unusual behavior and attitudes as obligatory characteristics of a cohesive group — things that define it and set it apart. It may look strange to us, but it tends to stablilize the group's cohesiveness, and establish its boundaries."

He also suggests that findings in which converts appeared, as one researcher writes, "drab and dreamy outside the group, and somewhat expressionless..." may be no more than other manifestations of boundary-setting: a deliberately blank public face.

Writes Ross, "It may be that mental-health professionals are paying too much attention to conformity in a social and religious sense without recognizing that most established religions began in a manner similar to today's fringe religions..."

1. What is the view of cults presented in each article?
2. What arguments are used to defend the articles' main ideas?
3. What facts do the articles use to support their arguments?
4. An Ontario Royal Commission has decided that our present provincial laws are adequate to deal with any problems related to cults. Do you agree with this ruling? To do further research on cults, you could investigate the following areas:
   a) Histories and descriptions of several cults
   b) The methods cults use to attract and hold members
   c) Characteristics of people attracted to cults
   d) A study of deprogramming and its successes and failures
   e) Is deprogramming a greater threat to civil rights than are the activities of cults?

Writing an Essay — Level 2

This exercise will give you practice in writing a brief expository essay.

Below is an incomplete, four-paragraph essay on the topic "Are Cults Harmful?" This particular essay takes the stance that cults *are* harmful: other points of view are possible. Complete this essay appropriately in your notebook. Read the existing sentences to get a general idea of what the essay is about. Then fill in the missing sentences. You may wish to review "Skills: How to Write an Essay — Level 1" on page 206.

Are Cults Harmful?

_____

_____. To discuss this question involves examining the effects of cults on family relationships. Also, _____

_____. When these factors are considered, it is clear that some cults can be extremely harmful.

Cults are often organized in such a way that maintaining a good relationship with the cult member's family is impossible. One example of this is the case of Shirley Caine. She _____

_____. Other problems centre on the harsh discipline of young children in some cults. For example, _____

_____

_____.

The case of Shirley Caine provides solid evidence of the negative effect of cults. After her experience with a cult, Shirley became more child-like and more dependent, and felt terrified that the cult might kidnap her. Although some studies suggest that sects or cults may not have harmful psychological effects, Shirley's mother claims that the cult

_____.

Cults can endanger society. The impact on family life _____. Cults can also have a negative effect on the mental health and development of teenagers, because cults

_____

_____.

Projects, Activities and Explorations

1. Make a collage or a mobile showing all the groups you are currently involved in. Include both primary and secondary groups.

2. In this creative group activity, you will need a lot of old newspapers, tape, string and scissors. The goal is to construct a shelter large enough for all the members of your group to sit in comfortably. You will have 15 minutes to plan the shelter, and 20 minutes to build it. One member of your group should act as an observer and make notes on the following:
   a) evidence of co-operation and/or competition within the group
   b) the presence and effect of a group leader
   c) the time taken to design and build the shelter
   d) the roles played by the group members
   e) the pattern(s) of communication within the group
   f) the satisfaction of each group member
   g) the quality of the final product (appearance, structure, size, etc.)

3. Research the attitudes of some other cultures towards co-operation and competition. Compare these views with those of your own culture. Some suggestions are:
   a) the bushmen of the Kalahari Desert
   b) Canada's native peoples
   c) the Japanese
   d) the Russians
   e) the Chinese
   Present your findings in a written report or as an oral presentation.

4. Keep a co-operation/competition log for a group you are involved in. Over a period of time, note examples of various forms of behaviour. Later, decide which form of behaviour dominated the group. How would you account for this?

5. Hold a group decision-making olympics. Divide the class into teams of equal size. Design tasks that are challenging but not dangerous. For example, mark an area on the floor about 2 meters across. Announce that this section is an electrified floor and must be avoided. Each group must figure out how to get everyone to the other side. If anyone touches the floor, the entire group must begin again. Provide any materials that might help to solve the problem (pieces of wood, rope, etc.). Whatever the problem set up for your group, it should be possible to solve it, and it should be a *safe* activity! Score the teams according to the amount of time taken to complete the task successfully. The team taking the least amount of time is the winner. After the olympics, ask the groups to discuss how well they worked together.

6. Write a mini-biography or do a presentation on a famous rock group. If possible, use both pictures and music in your presentation. Based on what you have learned in this chapter, discuss whether the band has been successful as a *group* (besides being successful, perhaps, in terms of fame and earnings). Try to discover how well the members of the group get along with each other. What advice might help them improve how they work together?

What Have You Learned?

If you have covered everything in this chapter, you should be familiar with the following topics:

1. The characteristics of a group

2. The differences between primary and secondary groups

3. How primary and secondary groups affect their members

4. How groups affect an individual's performance

5. The effects of co-operation and competition on both groups and individuals

6. How and when groups perform better than individuals

7. The types and effects of some roles played within groups

8. How to write an essay.

To Help You Study

The following chart will help you
to review the words, facts and
ideas introduced in this chapter.
Copy the chart into your notebook
and fill in the missing information.

Word, Fact, Idea	Example in a Sentence	Page	Definition
group	A family is a group.	196	two or more people who influence each other as they interact
primary groups			
secondary groups			
co-operation			
competition			
task-centered role			
maintenance role			
self-centred role			

11

Socialization and Social Institutions

How Is This Girl Different From You?

Read the short article below. List all the ways you can think of in which the girl in the article differs from you. Try to explain why she is different.

Girl in Coop Acts Like Chicken

In the summer of 1980, newspapers carried the story of Isabel Queresma, a nine-year-old girl who had spent most of her days in a chicken coop. She lived with her mentally retarded mother in a village near Coimbra, in central Portugal. For more than eight years, the mother locked Isabel in a chicken coop in the mornings, gave her the same chicken feed (corn and cabbage), and went off to work in the fields. As the mother explained: "Where else could I leave her? I couldn't take her with me, though I feel sorry for her. But she tears and breaks everything up."

After spending most of her waking hours in the company of chickens, Isabel acted like one. She could not talk and made only squealing sounds, took very small and quick steps, and flapped her arms like wings. Isabel was brought to an institution for the severely retarded in Lisbon, but she showed no real progress there.

Several questions arise: Is such an institution the right place for her? What behaviours will, or can, she learn from the other children? Would your family be a better place for her?

Reprinted with permission — The Canadian Press

As a class or in small groups, discuss the following questions:

1. In what ways does Isabel seem not to be a human being?

2. Do you think it was a good idea to put Isabel into an institution for severely retarded children? Why or why not?

3. What other ways to help Isabel enter human society could you suggest? How would these alternatives have helped her?

4. List some things a person needs to function well in a society. Why does a person need each of these things?

The story of Isabel is true. There have been other reports of children who were isolated from human beings at an early age. Often these children behave more like wild animals than people. In some cases, they sit or lie motionless and seem like empty shells.

You are quite different from these children. You know who you are and how you fit into society. You know how to behave in social situations. You have goals in life and you know accepted ways to achieve these goals. You will make a contribution to society someday.

The main difference between you and Isabel is that you have experienced the process of socialization, which she did not. This chapter will discuss how we learn to interact successfully with other human beings within a society.

What Is a Society?

A **society** is a large group of people existing in a certain geographic area who often share a distinct, inherited culture. You learned in Chapter 1 that culture is the huge body of knowledge, skills and attitudes we learn in order to survive and to be accepted by other human beings. Culture prescribes certain ways of thinking, feeling and acting. Generally, a society creates ways to ensure its survival and to pass along its culture to the next generation. Governments, laws, police forces, families, schools and social services are a few examples of these survival mechanisms.

Canada is a society that blends many different cultures. The francophone culture in Quebec and Canada's native cultures are just two examples. Canada is called, therefore, a multicultural society.

The Process of Socialization

In Chapter 1 you learned that culture is one factor that makes human beings unique on this earth. We acquire culture by being socialized. **Socialization** is a complicated process in which people learn, from a very early age, how to participate in and contribute to a particular society. In the course of socialization, our contact with others gradually teaches us acceptable ways of thinking and behaving. What is considered acceptable thinking and behaviour varies from one society to another. Through socialization, we discover who we are and how we fit into our society. Socialization also involves learning the knowledge and skills needed to survive and to function effectively within a particular society.

Because Isabel had never been socialized (that is, had never undergone a hu-

man socialization process), she could not possibly fit into and participate in her Portuguese society. On the other hand, because you have been socialized to fit into Canadian society, you, too, would have trouble coping in a society other than your own.

What Is Learned Through Socialization?

As you grow up and are socialized you will learn four fundamental things:

1. *Basic skills*: These include social activities such as how to eat, dress and converse in acceptable ways.

2. *Goals*: Every society values and promotes certain goals. For example, finding a good job and a comfortable home are central goals in our society.

3. *Knowledge and education*: These provide you with the means to attain the goals that society promotes as desirable. For example, many jobs require the ability to read and write. Other jobs require specific skills, such as word processing.

4. *Roles*: You have learned that roles in society are the parts you play in your life. You have learned a number of roles: family member, student, worker, friend, and so on. Your society considers certain behaviours appropriate for each of these roles. These expected behaviours are called **norms**. For example, as a worker, you are expected to arrive on time for work. Punctuality is, therefore, a norm of the Canadian workplace.

When people adjust their behaviour to coincide with the norms of a society or a group, they are said to conform. **Conformity** is obedience to the codes of behaviour and ways of thinking established by a certain group. If you consciously dress the same way as most of your friends do in order to be accepted, you are conforming. Skipping school because your friends do is another example of conformity.

Conformity serves a very practical purpose in every society. As long as people conform to social norms, everyone in the society understands what to expect from each other. They know that some behaviours, such as a handshake as a greeting, are acceptable and that other behaviours, such as violence against children, are not acceptable. This kind of conformity makes life in society and cooperation among its members much easier.

People also tend to conform because they want to avoid looking "out of step" or strange to others. If we appear strange and different, we risk being rejected by the group. We all want to fit into and to be accepted by groups that are important to us. Being accepted by a group means having to conform to the group's norms.

Roles also demand that you learn and at least appear to accept certain values. A value is a particular belief or attitude that a society considers important. You cannot see or touch a value. It exists in the mind and guides behaviour. For example, the value of loyalty to friends prompts us to support those close to us during a crisis.

Values are useful because they can guide your behaviour in specific situations. For example, if you value honesty, you will turn in a wallet that you find instead of keeping it. In this way, values can shape the norms of a society. Norms and values can differ enormously

from one society to another. For example, in many African countries, having many children is considered desirable. In Canada, however, having two children is considered desirable by many families.

How Lessons Are Taught

Socialization teaches you in two ways: directly or indirectly. Direct teaching occurs when someone deliberately instruct's you concerning the norms and values of society. A parent showing a child how to eat properly or discussing the importance of kindness is involved in direct teaching.

In sociology, the rewards or punishments you receive as part of this teaching process are called **sanctions**. A **positive sanction** is a reward, such as a hug or a raise in your allowance. A **negative sanction** is a punishment, such as a one-week grounding or a school de-

tention. Both types of sanctions have the same objective: to encourage you to obey the accepted rules of behaviour in your society.

Indirect methods of socialization include what you learn simply by observing how other people think and behave. For example, suppose you overhear your parents discussing how to cheat on their income tax returns. Your parents would probably never teach you directly to cheat. Yet, in this case their behaviour would teach you indirectly that in some situations, cheating seems to be acceptable.

Why Is Socialization Important?

Socialization is important for both you and for society. On the personal level, socialization teaches you the skills and the knowledge you need to function in society. It also shapes your sense of self. It gives you the confidence to play

roles in society. Because you experience socialization, you learn how to act and learn how to win the approval of the people around you.

You can also feel secure with other people because *they* have been socialized as well and, therefore, share some common norms and values. This means that many people in a society will react in similar ways and that you can predict the behaviour of others to some extent. Imagine how stressful life would be if, when you met someone, you could not anticipate whether that person was going to shake your hand or do something totally unpredictable, perhaps tickling you or sticking out their tongue. Socialization reduces the need for worrisome guesswork in our interactions with others.

Socialization benefits society too. It helps to reduce conflicts among people by establishing certain agreed-upon, acceptable behaviours and values. It also sets up mechanisms allowing individuals in the society to express disagreement over behaviours and values, in non-destructive ways.

Socialization also ensures a society's survival, by preparing children to eventually replace adults who die. Through socialization, a society's culture, skills and knowledge are passed on to the next generation. Our society needs people such as police officers, teachers, factory workers, health-care professionals, skilled labourers and technicians in order to function from day to day.

. . . .

From Ideas to Action

1. Which of the following groups could be considered societies? Explain your answers by referring to the characteristics of a society.

   a) a remote fishing village in New-foundland
   b) your school
   c) the people you work with
   d) your family
   e) the residents of Australia

2. a) Write the following headings in your notebook:
   i) Basic Skills ii) Goals iii) Knowledge and Education iv) Roles
   List some things that you have learned through socialization.

3. a) List all the roles you are expected to play in your daily life.

   b) List some expected behaviours (norms) associated with each of your roles.

   c) Look carefully at the list you made for b). Are you sometimes expected to behave in a certain way in one role, and in the opposite way in another role? If so, draw lines to connect the behavioural norms that seem to conflict with each other.

   d) Are there any roles you are expected to play that always conflict with one another? What problems does this create for you? How do you deal with these conflicts? In what other ways might you deal effectively with role conflicts?

4. Which of the following are norms and which are values?

   a) respect for others
   b) hiring the most qualified person for a job
   c) equality
   d) not smoking in elevators
   e) friendship
   f) refusing to gossip about people who are close to you

5. How do each of the following situations illustrate the idea of conformity?

   a) Lin was new on the job. The factory he worked in required him to put parts on the frame for a new television. He soon mastered the skill required to do the job. He found that he could easily finish 20 televisions a day. This fact came to the attention of the older workers on the assembly line. They had all agreed to assemble no more than 12 per day. This pace allowed them to work a little over-time once in a while and made their jobs secure. At first they suggested that Lin "slow it down." He refused. They began to ignore him and soon refused to even talk to him. After several weeks of this, Lin's production had dropped to 12 televisions per day.

   b) Anita came from a small town where drinking was not the norm. However, when her family moved into a suburb she discovered that drinking heavily was considered a normal and sometimes required part of teenage social life. She knew that her parents trusted her and would never check on what she did. She also wanted desperately to avoid disappointing them. In the end, she decided to drink with her new friends.

6. You have learned that values are the basis of norms, and that values and norms serve to guide and mould our behaviour. The values and norms in question 4 can be paired so that each value would lead logically to a certain behavioural norm. Identify the pairs and explain your choices. Suggest any other pairs of values and norms you can think of.

Agents of Socialization

Match the items in the column on the left with the items on the right. More than one match may be possible.

People and Things That Influence Us	What We Learn
1. your family	a) how to select a job or career
2. your friends	b) how to behave in a restaurant
3. your school	c) how to speak properly
4. television	d) what kinds of clothes to wear
5. musical groups	e) how to show love and affection
6. movies	f) how to show anger or frustration
7. your church/syna-gogue/mosque	g) religious beliefs
	h) respect for the law
	i) honesty
	j) the difference between an attractive and an unattractive person
	k) what it means to be a Canadian
	l) how to behave in the workplace

Now as a class or in small groups, discuss the following questions:

1. Name some other things you learn from each of the influences in the column on the left.

2. List some ways in which the knowledge, skills, values and behaviours in the right-hand column are taught to you. Are these things always taught in a deliberate, formal way?

3. Which influence do you think is most essential to society? Why? Which is the next most essential influence? Why?

The influences listed in the left-hand column above are called **agents of socialization**. Family, friends, school and the media — these and other agents help to shape the kind of person you are.

They also teach the skills, knowledge, values and behaviours you rely on in performing your various social roles. Some of these agents are formal social institutions; some are informal groups.

Social Institutions

Look at the following list of words and group them into two categories in your notebook.

religion
education
friends
family
government
volleyball team
economy
high school band

As a class or in small groups, discuss the following questions:

1. How did you decide on the two categories?
2. What are the major differences you see between the two categories?

This exercise points to the difference between social institutions and informal groups in society. **Social institutions** are not buildings. They are social practices or behaviours that a society has agreed to support and obey. Religion, education, government, the legal system and politics are examples of social institutions. When we speak of government as an institution, we do not mean any one particular political party in power. We mean all the behaviours and customs and relationships of any group of people who govern and we call this group a government. In this section you will learn about the characteristics of social institutions and concentrate on two very important institutions in the life of every member of society: the family and education.

As social institutions, religions teach moral values to each new generation in a society.

Characteristics of Social Institutions

As different as a family and a government or a legal system may seem, they all share these characteristics of social institutions:

a) Social institutions last a long time once they have been established. The family in its many forms around the world has existed for thousands of years.

b) Social institutions change gradually and very slowly, and some change more slowly than others. For example, it took many years for schools to cease using physical punishment to discipline students.

c) Social institutions have formal and often written codes of behaviour. For example, schools all have codes of behaviour for their students to follow. Family law describes the specific duties and responsibilities that family members have to each other.

d) Social institutions have various kinds of structures. In a school, the roles of the principal, vice-principal, department head and teacher are easy to identify. In the military, roles are even more rigidly defined by different ranks. Families, on the other hand, often have very loose structures with family members playing various roles. There may be several "bread-winners," or a wife may earn the family income while the husband takes care of the children. Grandparents may be involved as caregivers while a parent is working.

All these characteristics can be observed in the social institutions of any society in the world. They make social institutions very different from other agents of socialization, such as peer groups. We will look at two social institutions in greater detail.

The Family

Look at the diagram below. What needs does the family fill in society?

1. The family is the main unit responsible for the reproduction and rearing of children.

2. The family feeds, clothes and protects its members.

3. The family gives its members a certain social place in society, e.g. you may start out life as the son or daughter of a factory worker or a lawyer.

4. The family is responsible for socialization. It teaches almost all basic skills such as hygiene, eating habits, language and fundamental concepts of right and wrong.

In simple or primitive societies, the family handles almost all of a child's socialization. In complex societies such as ours, however, it is usually impossible for the family to do this. There are too many skills and too much knowledge to be mastered by children growing up in our society. Therefore, other agents, such as peer groups and schools play an important role in socialization as well.

The Family and Gender Roles

In a famous experiment to test assumptions about gender, the same child was dressed in a pink outfit, a blue outfit and a yellow outfit. The child was then given to the adult subjects to play with. Remarkable differences in behaviour toward the pink, blue and yellow 'babies' were noticed.

Those people who thought the baby was a girl cooed and hugged her a lot and talked to the child. Those who thought the child was a boy spoke to him less, put him on the floor and gave him different toys while watching him play. Those who were unsure of the sex were uncomfortable with not knowing and soon peeked in the diaper to see what sex the baby was. When satisfied, they then behaved toward the child in the same manner as the previous subjects.

This experiment seems to indicate that there are norms (expectations of behaviour) about how males and females ought to behave and that parents were passing them along. These patterns of behaviour for males and females are called **gender roles**. Gender roles are stereotypes and many people are now working to erase these stereotypes from Canadian society. For example the entire school curriculum is now available to both boys and girls. Most textbooks are careful to illustrate men and women in a variety of roles, not just those traditionally assigned to them.

Ways of Classifying the Family

Families can be classified by the members that are included in the family group and by the form of marriage. A

Weddings are important events in most cultures, and brides often wear elaborate clothing.

nuclear family consists of a husband, a wife and children. It may also be a single parent and children or a couple without children. An **extended** family consists of a husband, a wife, children and other family members related by blood, such as grandparents or aunts and uncles. In this kind of family, the responsibility for the rearing and socialization of the children are spread among many family members. A **polygamous** family consists of several spouses, either a man with several wives, or a wife with several husbands. Though illegal in North America, polygamous families still exist in many societies around the world.

Education

Look at the diagram below. What needs does education fill in society?

1. Education, along with other social institutions, is responsible for the teaching of culture, that is, our beliefs, attitudes and behaviours.
2. Education is responsible for producing skilled people capable of entering the workforce.
3. Education is designed to encourage creative thinking that may result in new discoveries and inventions that change society.
4. Education helps each individual in his or her own personal development.

Society relies on schools to teach not only essential knowledge and skills but also to reinforce the norms of the community. When social norms change, school norms do too. A Canadian teacher 40 years ago might have disciplined a student with a ruler or a strap. Today, society does not accept such behaviour and teachers do not strap their students.

Schools emphasize certain values that society considers important. These values tend to be traditional ones. For example, many schools begin the day by playing the national anthem. Students are expected to stand in respectful silence. This is designed to teach the values of patriotism and love for one's country. Societies need ways to create a feeling of unity, and schools rather than families are primarily responsible for promoting these values.

Sometimes schools have a difficult time accepting change in social norms and values. They tend to hold more traditional points of view than the rest of society. Thus, when longer hair for boys was more or less accepted by society in the 1960s, some schools struggled to keep student hair short or expelled students for growing mustaches.

The increasing involvement of schools in socialization has led to some conflict. Where should a school's responsibility begin and end? Should schools teach information or values to the children of parents who do not want these lessons taught to their children? With more and more parents working, how involved in the upbringing of children should the school become? In a rapidly changing technological society, how can we agree on what schools should be teaching to prepare students for the future? These are difficult questions for parents, teachers and school administrators.

From Ideas to Action

1. Identify the characteristics of social institutions described in the following sentences.
   a) Christianity holds the Ten Commandments to be the basis of good behaviour.
   b) Despite the high divorce rate in Canada, people are getting married in increasing numbers.
   c) British judges and lawyers continue the 200-year-old custom of wearing wigs and gowns.
   d) In the Canadian armed forces a private must salute all officers superior in rank.

2. Where do you find stereotypes of gender roles (different behaviours for males and females) in society? Do you think it is important to teach gender roles? Explain your answer with examples.

3. Identify the function performed by education in the following situations:
   a) René had just finished a diploma in computer programming and was preparing job application forms.
   b) Ukranian-Canadian children researched and presented a discussion of their Christmas customs in Canada.
   c) Lois is taking saxophone lessons after school and wants to become a professional musician.
   d) Young children in kindergarten are encouraged to play games that involve co-operation and team work.
   e) Canadian scientists Banting and Best were the first people to discover insulin.

4. What positive sanctions are used to encourage conforming to norms in a) your school b) your religion c) your family

Adolescence and Socialization

How Do You Differ From Children and Adults?

In small groups, brainstorm two lists. First, list all the ways you can think of in which you, as teenagers, are different from children. Focus on differences in the way that you are treated and in what people expect of you. Then list some differences between you and adults.

Now as a class or in groups, discuss the following questions:

1. In what essential ways are you different from children? From adults?

2. In our society are teenagers treated more like children or more like adults? Upon what evidence do you base your answer?

3. Do you think our society could "skip" adolescence as a stage of life altogether? Why or why not?

The Peer Group

Your peers are those friends or people you associate with who are roughly the same age as you are. Your peer group changes constantly throughout your life. As you grow older, peers gradually become more important to you. Eventually, they may replace the family as the most important influence in your life.

The peer group frequently expands the socialization provided by the family. Sometimes the lessons taught by the peer group are ones that the family is unable or unwilling to teach. For example, children need to know acceptable ways to deal with their sexual feelings. This is a topic some parents find difficult to discuss openly. Children therefore may turn to the peer group for information on this subject.

The peer group tends to convey knowledge and attitudes that are less traditional than those taught by the family. For instance, some women in our society face opposition from their families if they decide to postpone marriage or children in order to further their careers. Friends and co-workers, however, tend to support such non-traditional choices. Generally, the peer group helps individuals break away from their families and develop more independence.

Discontinuous Cultures

Some cultures throughout the world do not have "teenagers." These are called **discontinuous cultures** because members of these cultures simply discontinue childhood and begin adulthood immediately. There is no stop-over period of adolescence.

Most people in these societies live simply, depending on whatever the land will provide. Often their survival hinges on raising domestic animals. A young person needs relatively little knowledge and few skills to survive and to be successful in such a society. The young can be taught how to hunt and to gather food by the age of 13. Once they are physically able to have children, young people can do everything adults do. At this point, therefore, childhood ends.

Around the time of puberty — age 12 or 13 — a boy or girl goes through a series of ceremonies that signal the end of childhood and the beginning of adulthood. Ceremonies that mark the transition from one stage of life to another are called **rites of passage**. These ceremonies sometimes involve trials of skill or pain. Rites of passage notify everyone that the young person has officially entered the adult world.

In discontinuous cultures, entry into adulthood happens in a matter of hours or days. Young people suddenly have all the rights and responsibilities of adults. They can participate in major decisions, get married and have a family.

Continuous Cultures

Our society is an example of a **continuous culture**. The move into adulthood is very gradual. The lines between childhood, adolescence and adulthood are often blurred. For example, you are told to "act your age" one moment, and then told to "be in the house by 11 p.m." You are permitted to drive a machine that can kill people by the age of 16, but you cannot vote until you are 18. Life for a teenager in a continuous culture can be confusing.

Why does our society have such a long period of adolescence? Some social scientists argue that in a society as complex as ours, young people need a long time to learn the knowledge, skills and values necessary for survival and success. Years of training are often needed in order to find a job that will pay enough to allow independence.

Other social scientists point out that in a society with high unemployment, we perhaps cannot afford to treat teenagers as adults. In the eighteenth century, young people began to compete for the same factory jobs as adults. Young people tended to lose out because they did not have families to support.

Schools helped to solve the problem of unemployed youth. It was argued that a long period of adolescence was good for society because it prevented tension in the workplace. An adolescence spent in school also allowed young people to receive specialized training for future employment.

Rules for Film Censorship, 1925

The following are forbidden in films:

1. cruelty to animals
2. sexual relations
3. insulting views of public figures (such as politicians)
4. methods used by criminals
5. false information about the methods used by police (such as the use of force)
6. the use of bad language
7. the use of drugs

The behaviours listed above were censored in movies seen in Canada in 1925. What values were these rules trying to support? Are these values still important in our society? Which of these censorship rules still exist? What behaviours are censored in movies today?

Reprinted with permission from *Maclean's*, November 1, 1925.

. . . .

From Ideas to Action

1. Which agent(s) of socialization is (are) *most* responsible for preparing you for the following experiences? Briefly explain your answers.
   a) marriage
   b) dating
   c) eating in a restaurant
   d) attending a graduation dance
   e) raising and caring for children
   f) choosing your clothing

2. In what ways are the knowledge and skills implied in question 1 taught to you directly? In what ways are they taught indirectly?

3. In your notebook, label each of the following as either a positive or a negative sanction.
   a) a promotion
   b) a speeding ticket
   c) a suspension from school
   d) inclusion on your school's honour roll
   e) getting bonus points for good attendance
   f) the "silent treatment"

4. a) Brainstorm a list of all the things schools try to teach you, both directly and indirectly.

   b) Organize your list in a chart with the headings "Skills," "Knowledge," "Norms," and "Values."

   c) Examine your chart. Do you think that school is preparing you adequately to participate in society in the future? If not, what categories or items do you think should be added to the chart?

5. Decide which of the following could be considered aspects of either discontinuous or continuous cultures. Briefly explain your responses.

   a) By the age of 19, most people in Canada may drink alcohol legally.

   b) For a week, the young boy had to live separately from his family in a hut with other boys his age. He then took his place at the elders' fire.

   c) Young people are often told that the intense attraction they feel towards someone of the opposite sex is only "puppy love."

6. Rites of passage are common in discontinuous cultures. Can you suggest any ceremonies that take place in a continuous culture that might be considered rites of passage?

Using the Library — Level 2

This exercise will help you learn to find books and articles in the library on a specific topic. If you look in the subject card catalogue for your topic, you are likely to find little or no information. This exercise will show you how to solve this problem.

Method

Step One
Read about your topic in a text or an encyclopaedia to discover:
1. alternate names for your topic
2. subtopics connected to it

Step Two
Use the information you gained about other names and related subtopics to find books in the subject card catalogue on your topic. Note the call number, author and title of the books. Check the catalogue card and book index or table of contents to see if it is useful.

Step Three
Some of the books you located in step two will have suggested readings or bibliographies on your specific topic. Look up the ones that seem relevant and interesting.

Step Four
If your topic is a relatively recent one, or has been in the newspapers lately, you may find articles in the vertical file. Vertical files hold file folders containing magazine and newspaper clippings.

Step Five
To find recent articles on your topic, use the periodical index, which lists by subject articles in many magazines your school may have.

Step Six
A a last measure, ask your teacher or librarian to suggest other sources.

Example: What is socialization?

Child or human development, psychology of learning, personality development, conformity, social institutions, family and peers

Child Development: 301.15, ELK; Elkin, F., *The Child and Society: the process of socialization.*
Human Development: 155, HUR; Hurlock, E.R., *Developmental Psychology.*
Learning, Psychology of: 370, REY; Reynolds, H., *Learning in Society*

Suggested Readings
Dreitzel, Hans Peter (ed.), *Childhood and Socialization*

Child Development: "Growing Pains", Goody Teachman Gerna, *MacLean's*, September 7, 1987.

Child Psychology: "Why kids act the way they do.", O. Westheimenr, *Ladies Home Journal*, 103:96, November, 1986.

Librarian: "Have you thought of looking in *Annual Editions: Early Childhood Education*?"

Complete the following questions for a topic of your own choosing or a topic given to you by your teacher.

1. List several alternate names for your topic, and several people and subtopics associated with your topic.

2. Use the subject catalogue to find three books for your topic. List the books in your notebook.

3. Use the suggested readings or bibliography from one of the books you found for question 2, to find at least one more book for your topic.

4. Use the vertical file and the periodical index to find two articles on your topic.

233

Projects, Activities and Explorations

1. With your teacher's help, arrange a field trip to an elementary school to observe ways in which children are taught the norms and values of society. Try to identify exactly which norms and values the teacher is trying to teach. Is the teaching direct, indirect or both? Do you think the methods of socialization the teacher uses are effective? Why or why not? You may wish to compare a summary of your observations with those of other students.

2. Try this experiment. Warn your parents beforehand that you are going to adopt the behaviour of a house guest for a few days instead of your normal behaviour. Discuss the results of this experiment with the rest of the class.

3. Collect some comic strips that show a variety of values, norms and social roles.

4. Design the perfect school for the year 2010. Make decisions about the design of the school and the kinds of equipment it should have. What subjects will be compulsory? What will the school's evaluation policy be? How will students qualify for graduation from your school? When you have completed the project, you may wish to share your ideas with your principal or with a school board official responsible for future planning of schools.

5. Help organize a panel discussion to explore the effectiveness of schools in preparing young people to take their places in adult society. Invite students, teachers, your principal, a school superintendent, a school trustee, parents and an employer who regularly hires young people.

6. Research a ceremony or ceremonies practised by a specific social or religious group to symbolize that a child has become an adult. Report your findings to the class. If possible, try to suggest other reasons why these ceremonies might be important to that particular group.

What Have You Learned?

If you have covered everything in this chapter, you should be familiar with the following topics:

1. The meaning of the term "society"

2. The process and purpose of socialization

3. How socialization benefits both the individual and society

4. Social Institutions: The Family and Education

5. Informal Groups: Peer Group

6. Adolescence in continuous and discontinuous societies

To Help You Study

The following chart will help you
to review the words, facts and
ideas introduced in this chapter.
Copy the chart into your notebook
and fill in the missing information.

Word, Fact, Idea	Example in a Sentence	Page	Definition
society	The people of Canada are a society.	219	a large group living in a certain geographic location, with a distinct culture, and the means to pass its culture on to future generations
socialization			
norms			
agent of socialization			
social institutions			
positive sanction			
negative sanction			
conformity			
nuclear family			
extended family			
polygamous family			

Social Deviance

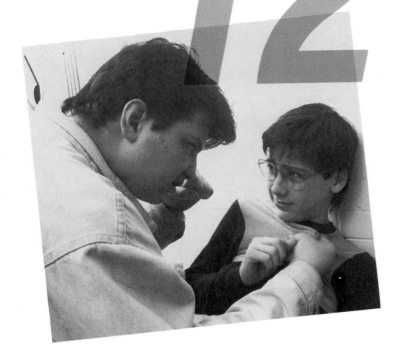

Compare Your Reactions

Rate your reaction to each situation below. Use the following rating scale: 1 = strong approval, 2 = moderate approval, 3 = no reaction, 4 = moderate disapproval, 5 = strong disapproval.

a) You see a big grade 12 student threatening a small grade 9 student with physical violence.

b) A new student with a "Mohawk" haircut and razor-blade earrings joins your class.

c) You see a student putting a cassette of a classical opera into his portable tape recorder.

d) You hear some students planning a wild party at a house where the parents will be away for the weekend.

e) You see someone in the school parking lot buying illegal drugs.

f) You see someone breaking into another person's locker.

g) You find a group of students smoking in the school washroom.

h) Someone you know tells you she is going to skip Friday's classes.

Now as a class or in a group, discuss the following questions:

1. Make a chart to compare the ratings assigned to the situations by various students. How would you account for any differences and similarities in reactions?

2. What kinds of behaviours met with the most negative reactions? Why?

3. Are the ratings given by students to some of the situations very different from each other? If so, why?

4. How do you think the chart would differ, if your reactions had been compared to those of your parents or the school vice-principal?

5. What can you conclude about how society views acceptable and unacceptable behaviour?

What is Deviance?

Deviance is any behaviour that breaks a society's rules or norms or that clashes with a society's definition of appropriate behaviour. A person who breaks, or deviates from, society's rules is called a **deviant**. Deviance involves a failure to conform to social norms. Defining deviance, however, is much easier than determining which behaviours are deviant and which are not.

The problem is that the definition of deviance varies depending on the time, place and situation. For instance, early in this century women who demanded the right to vote were considered deviant by the rest of society and were thrown into jail. Today, a woman is not only entitled, but is expected, to exercise her right to vote. In some cultures it is considered appropriate for a wealthy man to have more than one wife. Having more than one spouse in Canada is against the law. And as a final example, if a civilian kills someone, other than in self-defence, society considers this act a serious crime. However, a soldier who kills the enemy in battle may receive a hero's medal. To sum up, deviance is a *relative*, not an *absolute*, term.

Within any society, there is often wide disagreement as to what is "right" and "wrong" behaviour. What you regard as deviant and what your vice-principal regards as deviant are probably quite different. Most societies have agreed, however, that certain behaviours are always deviant: theft, murder and incest, for example.

Which of the behaviours shown on these pages could be considered deviant?

How Criminals Define Deviance

Curiously, people labelled "deviant" by society often have their own distinct definitions of deviance. For example, convicted criminals classify other criminals into categories of acceptable and unacceptable behaviour:

- "Rounders" are professional thieves. In the same way that a non-criminal is dedicated to his or her job, the rounder is committed to crime. The behaviour of rounders is reliable. They are careful, avoid violence wherever possible, and plan their "jobs" down to the smallest detail. To receive full rounder status, a criminal usually has to "do time" in a major federal prison in Canada, where he or she can meet the best thieves and learn the finer points of the craft. Rounders are given the highest status in the world of crime and are not regarded as at all deviant by fellow criminals.

- "Dope fiends" and "alkies" are drug addicts and alcoholics. These criminals are given a lower status than rounders because they do not steal for stealing's sake, but to maintain their habits. Alkies are usually seen as bunglers who will eventually make a serious mistake while doing a job. Dope fiends are often seen as skillful and daring. However, both categories are seen as highly unreliable compared to rounders.

- "Bums" are thieves who do not plan their jobs at all. In the opinion of rounders, a bum's methods are sloppy. Bums are the type of thieves who kick in a door to gain entry to a house. They may panic and harm someone while doing a job. They are also the type who steals occasionally and may live off a prostitute the rest of the time. Like dope fiends and alkies, bums are seen as unreliable. However, they are regarded as more deviant because they are not really committed to stealing as a way of life.

- "Rapos" are rapists and other criminals who use violence against women, children or the elderly. Rapos are placed at the bottom of a prison's social ladder. No self-respecting criminal would ever associate with one. Rapos are the real deviants in the criminal world.

Adapted from *Crime As Work* by Peter Letkemann © 1973. Reprinted by permission of the publisher, Prentice-Hall Inc., Englewood Cliffs, N.J.

What Causes Deviance?

The Search For the Deviant Personality

For years social scientists searched for what they called the deviant personality. They thought that there was a certain kind of person who was more likely to be deviant. Some scientists thought that deviance was genetic and was passed from one generation to the next, in much the same way as hair colour or eye colour. If a person's father was violent or a criminal, the child's chances of becoming the same were judged to be very high. However, the deviant personality hypothesis yielded little supporting evidence. Most social scientists now reject this explanation of what causes deviance.

New Approaches to Understanding Deviance

The study of deviance no longer focuses on deviant personality types, but on the deviant behaviour itself. Most social scientists do not view deviance as the result of some inherited personality flaw. Instead, they look at the conditions that lead people to behave deviantly. Even so, there is not much agreement concerning the causes of deviance. The one thing social scientists do agree on is that deviant behaviour is learned in the same way people learn all other behaviour. For example, children misbehave and discover that this makes their parents upset. For a child who feels neglected, this reaction wins their parent's attention, which is a reward. To continue to win this attention, a deprived child will repeat deviant behaviours. Thus, deviant behaviour is reinforced and rewarded.

Below are a few current views concerning the sources of deviance. Which do you think are the most reasonable explanations?

1. There are deviant subcultures. A **subculture** is a group within the larger culture of a society that has a specific set of norms and values all its own. Inner-city gangs are a subculture. These groups develop their own social norms. Although these norms are seen as deviant by the rest of society, the members of the gang regard them as desirable. Therefore,

239

gang members support and encourage each other's deviant behaviour. Stealing a car or beating someone may be regarded as normal and desirable behaviour from the perspective of a subculture such as this.

2. Deviant behaviour is a result of a person's weak **attachment** to society. If we are strongly attached to family and friends, we will consider their feelings and wishes when we are trying to decide how to behave. We are also "attached" to the values of society to the extent that we support or believe in them. According to this view, then, stealing a car results from a poor attachment to society and its values.

3. **Labelling** can lead to deviance. If society decides to label certain people deviant, this can affect the way these people see themselves and how they choose to behave. For example, unemployed teenagers who hang around a shopping mall may be labelled and treated as deviants by shop owners. The management at the mall may take steps to bar the teenagers from the mall. Being labelled and treated like deviants could make the teenagers feel rejected, angry and isolated. These feelings cause the group to draw closer together and to find ways to get back at those who they feel are punishing them unjustly. Eventually, these teenagers will come to see themselves as deviant — which was not the case originally — and they will behave in deviant ways.

4. In Canada and other industrialized nations, there is **social pressure** to become successful financially. Success is symbolized by the kind of car you drive and the house you live in. But society does not provide everyone with the means to achieve these

Society must avoid labelling poor people as deviant just because the poor live with substandard conditions.

goals. There are not enough high-paying jobs to go around, and educational programs that could qualify a person for a better job have limited enrollments. Under pressure to live up to social expectations, some people may turn to crime to gain the material symbols of success defined by society. Other people may reject the pursuit of success as defined by society in order to pursue their own, less visible, goals, such as artistic excellence.

Explaining what causes some people to become deviant is not a straightforward task. The explanations presented above may be valid for some individuals or groups, but not for others. Also, the factors described above may interact in some cases. In order to understand why someone is behaving deviantly, the individual, the individual's environment and the deviant behaviour itself must be studied and analysed in great detail.

240

Can Deviance Have Some Useful Consequences?

How can behaviour that most people label "bad" sometimes have "good" consequences? Some experts argue that certain forms of deviance may actually benefit a society. James Teevan, a noted Canadian sociologist, offers the following analysis:

• Deviance and those who deviate are viewed and labelled negatively by society. Deviants do not conform. They are placed, therefore, on the bottom rung of society. This leads people who *do* conform — the majority of a society's members — to feel good about themselves. If they are not labelled deviants, then the people who conform can see themselves as good and worthy individuals.

• Deviance may serve as an early warning system, alerting a society to a growing social problem. People who first protest against some form of injustice — for example, racism — are initially seen as deviant. In time, however, other people in the society begin to wonder if the so-called deviant may not be right. When these people begin to explore the reasons for the protest, they may discover that the deviants have a valid cause. Steps can then be taken to try to solve the problem.

Similarly, an increase in certain kinds of crime can signal to a society that all is not well. The crime could be the result of a larger problem, such as poor housing or unemployment. The increasing crime rate may shock the rest of society into paying attention to a serious social problem.

• Some deviants provide a society with a fresh direction and new leadership. They may dare to offer new and bet-

R.C.M.P. officers read the criminal code to a group of Haida Indians blocking a logger's road.

These people are protesting the nuclear arms race.

241

ter approaches to solving problems than the ones — perhaps worn out — that already exist. Many great religious and social leaders, such as Jesus and Gandhi, were viewed as deviants by the societies they lived in.

- Minor forms of deviance may serve as safety valves. To let off steam, some people may break a few rules to express their independence and to reassure themselves that they have some control over their lives. This can help to reduce tension. Otherwise, mounting tension could cause an explosion of destructive behaviour in some people.

From Ideas to Action

1. Which of the following behaviours do you consider deviant? Why?

   a) swearing
   b) smoking cigarettes
   c) men wearing long hair to their shoulders
   d) a student carrying a switchblade
   e) drinking alcohol when under age
   f) telling dirty jokes
   g) kissing in public
   h) wearing very short shorts in May and June
   i) physically attacking another student

Ralph Abernathy and Martin Luther King Jr. lead a protest march for civil rights for blacks in Alabama in 1963.

2. In the section you just read, you learned about some possible explanations for deviant behaviour. Which of these hypotheses would best explain each of the following cases?

a) Four teenagers who are always in conflict with their school's administration break into the school one night and vandalize it.

b) People who join motorcycle gangs such as the Hell's Angels are expected to take part in the clubs' many illegal activities. Most participate willingly and see nothing wrong with what they are doing. In fact, bikers often complain that it is the rest of society that is deviant.

c) Many young men and women who leave small towns to look for jobs in large cities have been unable to get them. Either these jobs do not exist, or the job-seekers are not sufficiently qualified. In time, some of these young people turn to crime to make a living.

d) The young man who tried to assassinate U.S. President Ronald Reagan in March, 1981, claimed that his hero was the main character in the film *Taxi Driver*. As the movie's climax, the hero goes on a killing spree in which he shoots down many people he sees as the scum of society.

3. Examine a copy of your school's code of behaviour. List the behaviours that the school considers deviant. What does your school see as the worst forms of deviance? How can you judge this? What appears to be the relationship between deviance and punishment? Do you think the methods of punishment enforced by your school reduce the amount of deviance? Why or why not? What improvements to the code of behaviour could you suggest?

4. a) Suppose you felt strongly about some form of injustice in society. What would you be prepared to do to try to get society to change? Select some strategies from the possibilities below, or suggest some methods of your own.

   i) Complain about the problem to a friend or neighbour.
   ii) Sign a petition.
   iii) Call or write to a local newspaper.
   iv) Write to an elected official (the Mayor, a City Councillor, your Member of Parliament, etc.).
   v) Help to organize a protest march.
   vi) Participate in a protest march.
   vii) Chain yourself to a building or participate in a sit-in, even though you know you will probably be arrested for doing so.
   viii) Plant explosives to draw attention to your cause.

b) Some of the actions listed above are clearly deviant. Can you think of any circumstances in which the use of violence is acceptable in the effort to right a social wrong?

Writing an Essay — Level 3

This exercise will give you practice in writing an expository essay in the correct form. Below are two paragraphs of a five-paragraph essay on the topic, "Does Non-conformity Always Harm Society?"

In your notebook, (1) write an introductory paragraph, (2) complete the third body paragraph and (3) write a concluding paragraph for this essay.

The introduction should:

a) briefly state the essay's purpose
b) state the topics clearly in the order in which they will be developed
c) state the hypothesis (what will be proved) clearly.

Each body paragraph should:

a) relate to the hypothesis
b) provide arguments supported by facts and examples to prove your hypothesis.

The conclusion should:

a) restate your hypothesis
b) summarize your major arguments — about one sentence for each one — to reinforce your hypothesis
c) feature a forceful final sentence that builds on your hypothesis.

Nellie McClung

Does Non-conformity Always Harm Society?

[Write an introductory paragraph in your notebook.]

New developments and inventions are often created by the non-conformists in a society. What would we be driving today, without the work of those social deviants who insisted on experimenting with noisy, unreliable horseless carriages, the forerunners of today's automobiles? The Wright brothers were scorned and laughed at for their attempts to build flying machines. Many people thought Alexander Graham Bell was wasting his time trying to invent a long-distance communication device. Deviants such as these, who break with tradition, benefit society by discovering better ways of doing things.

Defenders of human rights often use non-conformist means to achieve just ends. The Canadian feminist activist Nellie McClung and her friends staged a shocking play in which women who ran the government denied human rights to men. McClung used an unconventional way to show the unfairness of excluding women from politics in Manitoba in the 1910s. During the 1950s and '60s, Martin Luther King Jr. used civil disobedience — peaceful law-breaking — to help win equality for black Americans. Several Canadian native groups have staged illegal sit-ins on government property to protest what they view as unfair handling of their treaty rights by the government. It seems that social deviance is sometimes needed in order to achieve social change.

Some forms of non-conformity may not harm society at all. For example, rock and roll. . .
[Complete this paragraph in your notebook.]

[Now write a concluding paragraph in your notebook.]

• •

Deviants who break laws must be punished. Few would dispute this statement. But deciding on methods of punishment for young offenders causes much disagreement. How should young offenders be punished? Should criminal records of young offenders stay with them as they grow up? Consider these basic questions as you read the following article and answer the follow-up questions.

Young Offenders Act
Growing pains for new law

Charles A. White, *Canada and the World* [December, 1985]

The Juvenile Delinquents Act was long overdue for renewal. However, as Charles A. White reports, its replacement is not without its problems.

Eleven-year-old Danny attempts to snatch an elderly woman's purse and knifes her when she resists. He cannot be prosecuted. Rick, 15, is going berserk, armed with a loaded shotgun and driving a stolen car. Police cannot broadcast his description or identity to aid in tracking him down. Both boys are protected by the Young Offenders Act. The act, which replaces the Juvenile Delinquents Act, went fully into force on April 1, 1985.

The philosophy of the old act was paternal. The wrongdoer was thought of "not as a criminal but as a misdirected child." The judge acted as a kindly but firm parent who prescribed "treatment" for the child for as long as it took to "cure" the delinquency. Sentencing was open-ended and flexible and applied to young people from ages seven to 15. Beyond that age, young people were tried in adult courts.

The purpose of the Young Offenders Act is to make young lawbreakers more accountable for their actions. The vague term "delinquency" disappears, and offences such as impaired driving, sexual assault, manslaughter, breaking and entering, and drug dealing are clearly defined. Judges are now given sentencing options, including fines of up to $1,000, payments or services to victims, probation, and open or secure custody for a maximum of three years. The age limits are now 12 to 17. Children below the age of 12 are considered too young to be held morally responsible for criminal acts. The 16- and 17-year-olds, like other young offenders, are now to be tried in youth courts.

The former act gave youths no adult rights. Under the new law, however, young people must be told that they are under no obligation to give a statement and that "any statement given by you may be used as evidence in proceedings against you." An arrested youth must also be given the right "to consult with counsel or a parent."

Two clauses in the Young Offenders Act are intended as protection for suspects or those who have been sentenced. The first prevents police from publicly identifying suspects such as Rick in the example above. The second requires the destruction of criminal records of a young offender five years after completion of the sentence.

Until 1984, when the new act began to come into use, young wrongdoers were sometimes sent to adult jails where they rubbed shoulders with hardened criminals. The Young Offenders Act requires their separation in buildings or space of their own. Where open custody is the sentence, group homes are to be provided.

This short summary of the act contains the seeds of most of the criticism which has grown out of it so far. Here are points made by police and others:

• Police argue that while the vast majority of offending children under age 12 may be no real danger to society there is a hard core of exceptions. Take the case of one 10-year-old who has already been caught in acts of theft and assult. He was caught again after stealing his aunt's car, terrorizing the neighbourhood, and pulling fire alarms in a highrise apartment. He laughed at police who could do nothing but take him home to his mother.

- There are also predictions that Fagins, of Oliver Twist fame, may set up in business. With young untouchables available for crime, adult criminals could use them in the drug racket or for break and enter offences. Older juvenile offenders could teach children the tricks of the trade, knowing the youngsters can not be prosecuted.
- The act hands the problem of what to do with the under-12 group to provincial child welfare acts. Robert Kaplan, former federal solicitor-general, singles out Ontario as the only province "that hasn't acted to bring this age group under child welfare laws where they can be dealt with." Critics, however, say that local children's agencies can't handle really violent offenders, and that the law should allow the worst cases to be brought before a Family Court judge who can decide whether to lay a charge.
- Another criticism is that the maximum three-year sentence is not severe enough for serious crimes. A 17-year-old who commits murder could be out to do it again at the age of 20; in adult court, a year later, the same crime could draw a 25-year sentence. The three-year maximum is simply not enough to protect society from such crimes as murder, sexual assault, or hostage taking, say critics.
- Many involved in running the new system don't like the rules for creating, keeping confidential, and destroying the records of young offenders. Destruction of the records is meant to protect young people from living with a permanent criminal stigma, but it may generate problems. If, for example, an offender is found not guilty by reason of insanity, documents which may be essential if he or she later needs more treatment or commits other offences will no longer exist. Some lawyers believe the law should be amended so that records will be kept confidential without actually being destroyed.

1. What was the main purpose of the Juvenile Delinquents Act? How did that purpose change with the Young Offenders Act?

2. Make a chart comparing the two acts.

3. What are the main criticisms of the act? Do you agree with these criticisms? Explain your reasons.

4. What changes would you make to the Young Offenders Act to correct its flaws?

"Cruel" solitary confinement still common Prison exper

By Joanna Morgan, *The Canadian Press* [November 10, 1983]

TORONTO — Eight years after the Federal Court of Canada ruled solitary confinement can constitute "cruel and unusual punishment," a Vancouver lawyer says prisoners in Canada are still widely subjected to it.

Michael Jackson, a professor of law at the University of British Columbia, has monitored the situation in prisons since the December, 1975, ruling he obtained for seven prisoners at the B.C. Penitentiary. It stemmed from a request by inmate Jack McCann, who had spent more than two years in one stretch of solitary confinement....

Many prisoners in despair, with no idea how long they'll be condemned to such isolation or what they would have to do to be released from it, try to kill themselves by hanging, setting their cells on fire, or slashing their wrists.

In his new book, *Prisoners of Isolation*, Jackson maintains inmates of maximum-security prisons are still too often condemned to many months or years at a stretch in their isolation units. He says many are put there for the vague reason that they pose a threat to "maintenance of good order and discipline in the institution," a loosely interpreted section in the Penitentiary Service Regulations.

In the super-security Millhaven and Laval SHUs, a phased program exists on paper whereby a prisoner may progress toward more privileges such as increased exercise or creature comforts. In reality, says Jackson, it is a sham because inmates don't know what they must do to qualify.

Conditions in the institutions vary, but Jackson describes grim surroundings in recent years — such as lights burning 23 hours a day in cells, bad ventilation, windowless cells, confinement to cells 23 1/2 hours a day, no access to reading material, and inadequate or no medical or psychiatric aid.

The horror of suicide attempts, Jackson recounts, is common.

"I was at Kent last week," he said in an interview. "One prisoner tried to hang himself, two other prisoners slashed up [attempted suicide].

"The guy who hung himself wasn't even removed from his cell. They just stripped the cell of anything else he could use and left him. This is in the segregation unit at Kent — H unit. The prisoners were extremely upset.

"It's a recurring phenomenon. Whenever other prisoners slash up, or attempt suicide, the other prisoners get extremely alarmed because it's their own insanity, and their potential for self-destruction, made manifest."

Jackson says he wrote the book for the same reason he became involved in the McCann case — "to put a stop to practices that no man should impose upon another." And to stop these, he urges that prisons adopt a segregation code that would be fair to both prison administrators and inmates.

He agrees wardens should be empowered to segregate prisoners implicated in episodes such as escape attempts, possession of dangerous contraband or threats of violence to other inmates.

But there should be set time limits and the prisoner should be informed of the reasons for the actions and have access to legal help at hearings where their cases would be heard by an outside adjudicator.

The professor says reaction is divided when he appears on hotline radio and TV shows.

"People say you're a bleeding heart. These guys are criminals, they're dangerous. Whatever we do to them can't be bad enough.

"Or, the other kind of calls are usually from people who have worked in prisons or been in prisons and are now out."

One of them which he found "disturbing" came recently from a man who 15 years ago had been put in solitary confinement in a juvenile detention center for two weeks. He has since gone straight and has a family.

But, "he was almost crying, on the phone, remembering what it was like."

Prisoner's humour — graffiti on a cell wall

1. What is solitary confinement? Why is it used?

2. What impact does it have on inmates? Why?

3. Should solitary confinement be used in our prisons? Defend your answer.

Convicts face peril of "jungle justice"

Kathleen Kena, *Toronto Star* [October 14, 1986]

"It was bound to happen sooner or later," he said, with a shrug. "I figured I was spending the rest of my life in jail anyway, so whether I lived or died didn't matter."

"Besides, those are the rules. You just accept them."

Those rules are part of the inmate code, the unwritten law known as "jungle justice." It delivers judgment and punishment inside prison more swiftly and

savagely than any court on the outside.

"It's a law that's turned upside down," said Kingston crown attorney Rhys Morgan. "Basically everything that's bad on the outside is good on the inside."

It is an often merciless law — described as a "code of ethics" by some inmates — that exacts capital punishment for anyone even suspected of being an informant, a sexual offender or someone convicted of crimes against children.

"Through all of this, there's a

twisted sense of fairness, of what's right and wrong," said Millhaven Warden Al Stevenson, 41, explaining that sex-related crimes or crimes against women are especially loathed because male inmates feel helpless to protect their families from harm while they're imprisoned.

The code can dictate murder or injury for seeming trifles, such as refusing to keep body or cell clean, to the more major "crimes" of gambling debts, failure to deliver drugs, theft and refusal of sexual advances. Revenge for wrongs committed on the outside, whether against the attacker or his friends or family, is another motive.

"One of the weird things about the inmate code is that you're not supposed to rip people off; all the rules change in jail," said Dennis Curtis, Ontario spokesman for the federal correctional service.

"You could be killed for a debt, but the funny thing is, this is probably a guy who has never repaid a debt in his life. It's probably the reason he's in prison in the first place."

The code also orders a beating, and sometimes death, for an insult. Calling someone a goof guarantees a fight, or worse.

"It has to do with pride," said Bob, a 29-year-old Collins Bay inmate who has been in trouble with the law since the age of 10 and is near the end of a 13-year sentence for counterfeiting and assault. (He asked that his surname be withheld, to protect his family.)

"That's why most of us end up in the joint in the first place. People get into conflicts and confrontations inside because of their pride."

The climate of paranoia, intimidation and fear in prisons often means attacks are a response to the attitude of getting the enemy, real or perceived, before he gets you, several inmates and ex-cons said.

"If you have a serious argument with a guy, you pretty well have to kill him, because if you just beat him up, he's not going anywhere," Wildman said. "A lot of it is just to show how tough you are."

Sixty-three inmates have been murdered by fellow prisoners in Canadian prisons since 1980, including 24 in Ontario. In the past six years, there has been an average of eight inmate murders every year — double the annual rate for the preceding 10 years....

What the statistics don't show is the number of near-misses, as in Wildman's case.

Officials from the federal correctional service admit their records don't give an accurate picture of the problem either.

Prison workers are required to report incidents involving serious injuries, but penitentiary officials say many assaults are never recorded because they're not witnessed by staff, and the inmates, no matter how seriously wounded, usually refuse to squeal on each other.

"The lifer has to care, because he's got to live here a lot longer, so we try to keep the joint quiet so guys can just do their time,"

said John Hypolite, 38, serving a life sentence at Collins Bay prison.

A Millhaven inmate, who asked to be identified only by his first name of Bob, said younger cons hide their fear about what might happen to them in prison by being violent before someone gets them.

Prison authorities say the large number of lifers — 34 per cent at Millhaven — is another reason for violence, because inmates get despondent about their families and the hopelessness of ever re-entering society.

And inmates with good behaviour records used to be released automatically after serving two-thirds of their sentences, but the new law — passed by a special sitting of Parliament in July — allows the parole board to revoke that privilege for those who might be considered prone to violence.

"Parole is the only thing we have to look forward to," said Bill Brooks, a 33-year-old lifer at Kingston prison. "It's just like being a sailor and having your shore leave revoked after you've been waiting for it, counting on it.

"We're going to see mutiny on the ship."

A study by the federal solicitor-general's office in late 1984 shows that serious assaults in Canadian prisons have skyrocketed since such statistics started being recorded on a regular basis in 1978.

Although record-keeping methods have changed over the years and most assaults aren't reported, the study shows 53 such assaults in 1978, and a steady increase from 152 in 1979 to almost 500 in 1984. The prison population

increased to about 12 300 from 9 300 in the same period.

Correctional service officials say violence in Canadian prisons has increased in the past few years, but this is only a reflection of the outside world.

"Institutions don't exist in a vacuum. They're appendages of outside society," said Irving Kulik, the service's director of inmate custody and control. "The rate of violence in the community has gone up about 15 per cent in the past six years, with a pretty continuous curve going upward...."

Boredom, frustration and the hopelessness of long terms can build to a boiling point, said Sam, a 31-year-old Millhaven inmate who has served two years of a life sentence. (He asked that his surname be withheld.)

"A lot of us are here forever, so sometimes the frustration becomes a confrontation. I've looked close at a person and stalked him for a day or two and I thought I was going to kill him.

"If he had come near me, I probably would have, but a friend talked me out of it. Haven't you ever thought of killing somebody, maybe planned it in your mind, even though you know you wouldn't do it?"

But inmates and prison authorities say it's only a minority that will murder in prison. They point to the large increase in the number of young and first-time offenders — half the population at Collins Bay and Millhaven is under 30 — who not only don't know the "solid" or older con's code, but refuse to acknowledge it.

Reprinted with permission — *The Toronto Star Syndicate*

1. Explain what is meant by "jungle justice."
2. What impact does jungle justice have on the lives of prison inmates?

3. a) Why does a system of jungle justice develop in prisons?
   b) How does it affect chances of helping the inmates?

249

Projects, Activities and Explorations

1. Study the school attendance records of your school. What factors do you think contribute to truancy?

2. Study the use of deviance in entertainment to sell products such as rock videos, films or situation comedies.

3. Research some methods used to rehabilitate criminal offenders, such as probation, community service orders, conjugal visits and temporary passes to leave custody.

4. Study protest groups that sometimes use deviant means to achieve social change, such as Greenpeace or animal rights activists. Try to discover how these groups view their activities.

5. Examine the differences in maximum, medium and minimum security prisons. Explain why the differences exist and whether they are intended to punish or rehabilitate criminals.

What Have You Learned?

If you have covered everything in this chapter, you should be familiar with the following topics:

1. Problems in defining deviance

2. Some insights into possible causes of deviance

3. Some possible beneficial by-products of deviance

4. Further information on how to write an essay

To Help You Study

The following chart will help you to review the words, facts and ideas introduced in this chapter. Copy the chart into your notebook and fill in the missing information.

Word, Fact, Idea	Example in a Sentence	Page	Definition
deviance	Studying deviance is a requirement for jobs in the fields of law enforcement and criminology	237	any behaviour that breaks society's rules or norms
subculture			
labelling (as applied to deviant behaviour)			
social pressure (as important to deviant behaviour)			
attachment (as applied to deviant behaviour)			

Human Beings Alone

Do you think you could squeeze in some time to write me? ... There's a rumor in my mind that says you don't much care for me any more. My problem is that I believe it whether it's true or not ... I don't think I've ever been so lonely in my life!!! ... Sorry to be so gloomy.

From Vivienne: The Life and Suicide of an Adolescent Girl by John E. Mack & Holly Hickler © 1981 by David Loomis & Paulette Loomis. Reprinted by permission of Little, Brown and Company.

What Does This Collage Communicate?

Look carefully at the items in the collage and answer these questions:

1. What do all the items in the collage have in common?
2. Describe the feelings communicated by the pictures and the poems.
3. Do you ever experience feelings like these? What causes these feelings?

In groups or as a class, share your responses and then discuss the following questions:

1. List some ways in which people try to cope with the feelings you identified in the collage. Divide your list into two categories: "successful ways of coping" and "unsuccessful ways of coping." Explain why you placed each item in your list in one category or the other.
2. Why do you think social scientists consider studying the feelings you identified in this activity important?

Each item in the collage expresses feelings of loneliness and isolation from other people. It is normal to feel lonely and isolated at certain times in our lives. Such feelings do not usually lead to serious problems. However, some of the poems and diary entries in the collage were written by people your age who eventually committed suicide. These writings show the deep despair of human beings who feel painfully isolated.

This chapter will explore some explanations for and responses to human loneliness and isolation. It will also suggest ways of coping with these feelings in yourself and in others.

You reach for a smile
But there is no one there
To reflect it.
You are utterly and absolutely
Alone.

Will there never be a hand
To grasp at yours within the mirror?
Will there never be an arm
To hold you tight amidst the terror?

From *Vivienne: The Life and Suicide of an Adolescent Girl*
by John E. Mack & Holly Hickler © 1981 by David Loomis
& Paulette Loomis. Reprinted by permission of Little, Brown
and Company.

It was a terrible experience.
This is the way I would describe how
I felt when my best boy-friend moved.
Up until this point in my life, he
seemed to be the only *real* friend I had
— oh, I had other boy-friends, but to
me, he seemed just like a brother.
The period from the day he left to
about a week after was about the worst
for me. I felt that life was all over for
me, and there seemed to be nothing to
look forward to.
Nothing seemed to go right for me,
and I felt that no one in the world could
possibly be as lonely as I was.
I was beginning to hope that the
world would come to an end.
— I didn't care.

From *Loneliness* by Clark E. Moustakas © 1961. Reprinted
by permission of the publisher, Prentice-Hall Inc., Englewood
Cliffs, N.J.

When loneliness strikes I feel thoroughly abandoned.
To me, loneliness seems to have different stages. At first I usually feel
somewhat mad, even a little bitter toward the person who caused my loneliness. Many things pass through my
mind when I'm lonely. After a while
I sometimes begin to wonder — is our
friendship really worth these countless,
tormenting hours?
It seems almost as though a transparent barrier has separated my world from
that of my friend. A barrier too high
to scale and too solid to get through.
Therefore I'm a captive of loneliness
until it chooses to release me.

From *Loneliness* by Clark E. Moustakas © 1961. Reprinted
by permission of the publisher, Prentice-Hall Inc., Englewood
Cliffs, N.J.

253

Loneliness vs Aloneness

What is the difference between loneliness and aloneness?

a) In your notebook, describe three situations in which you have felt lonely.
b) Describe three situations in which you have been alone.

In small groups or as a class, compare your experiences and then discuss the following questions:

1. In the first three situations you described, could someone have noticed you were lonely just by looking at you? Why or why not?
2. What causes people to feel lonely? What are the effects of loneliness?
3. Is the experience of being alone sometimes a positive one? Explain your answer.
4. Does everyone who is alone necessarily feel lonely? What is the difference between loneliness and aloneness?

We cannot assume that a person feels lonely simply because the person is alone. For example, someone can be just as lonely in the midst of a party as when he or she is alone at home. The outward signs of loneliness are not always easy to observe.

Loneliness usually results from disturbed social relationships. Losses such as moving to a new school or breaking up with a boyfriend or girlfriend, difficulty relating to parents or teachers, and other disrupted social relationships can cause loneliness and isolation.

Loneliness is always an unpleasant experience. Lonely people often feel panicky or helpless. They may also feel bored and depressed. If they ask themselves why they feel lonely, they may conclude that something is wrong with them, or that they are unworthy of friends. Conclusions such as these only make a lonely person feel worse.

Aloneness, however, is not necessarily an unpleasant experience. In fact, it can be healthy and refreshing. We all need some time to ourselves just to think, or to do things that interest us. People who choose to avoid companionship for a while are not necessarily experiencing problems with friends or family.

254

Who Experiences Loneliness?

Look carefully at the graph below. What relationship does it show between age and feelings of loneliness? How would you explain this relationship? Which of the age groups would you *expect* to express feelings of loneliness?

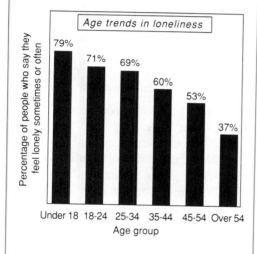

Age trends in loneliness

Under 18: 79%
18-24: 71%
25-34: 69%
35-44: 60%
45-54: 53%
Over 54: 37%

Percentage of people who say they feel lonely sometimes or often

Age group

To find out if someone is lonely, you have to interact with that person, talking, listening, and observing carefully. Even then, some lonely people are very good at masking their feelings of pain. Unfortunately, the old saying that someone can be "laughing on the outside and crying on the inside" contains a great deal of truth.

Causes of Loneliness: Emotional and Social Isolation

Social scientists group the causes of loneliness under two broad categories: emotional isolation and social isolation. **Emotional isolation** usually occurs when a person has no one special to share experiences, feelings and concerns with. A lack of close ties to another person or persons can lead to deep feelings of loneliness.

Social isolation occurs when a person has no group of friends, relatives, or colleagues to relate to. People can feel socially isolated when they move from one city, school or job to another.

Reactions to emotional and social isolation vary. Some people see their isolation as something more or less permanent. This is called **trait loneliness**. People usually experience trait loneliness if they blame themselves — some fault or shortcoming — for their isolation. For example, some people may (falsely) assume that they cannot make close friends because they are not attractive enough.

Other people see their loneliness as a temporary condition. This is called **state loneliness**. It is usually experienced when people realize that their loneliness is caused by external factors, and not by some personal flaw. Suppose you begin a new job in a new city. You feel lonely, but you know that you are basically a likeable and capable person. You feel reasonably sure that you will, in time, make new friends. Thus, you make the effort to meet new people and your loneliness gradually disappears.

Coping with loneliness and its causes depends to some degree on how people feel about themselves. People who are unsure of their own worth are especially likely to feel long-term loneliness. This lack of self-esteem prevents people from doing something to relieve their loneliness. Relatively self-assured people also experience loneliness. However, they are more likely to do something to reduce or eliminate their feelings of isolation.

Six Months of Solitude

The famous explorer Admiral Richard E. Byrd needed to escape the public eye for awhile. He decided to spend six months doing scientific research in a tiny, isolated station in the Antarctic — completely alone.

At first, Byrd found being alone peaceful and satisfying, as this excerpt from his diary shows:

The day is dying, the night being born — but with great peace. Here were the great forces of the universe in action. They are harmonious and beautiful. That's it, harmony. That was what came out of the silence — a gentle rhythm... In that instant I could feel no doubt of human oneness with the universe...

Byrd soon began to experience the less pleasant aspects of isolation: loneliness and boredom. He tried to fill his days with careful scientific tasks that demanded concentration. However, he became less and less able to concentrate, and at times his loneliness threatened to overwhelm him.

Finally, he experienced real terror in this dark and hostile environment. Sometimes, in temperatures of -50°C and lower, his eyes would freeze shut, blinding him. He once nearly died from carbon monoxide poisoning. Sick, and painfully aware of each passing moment, he struggled to stay sane as the months dragged on.

Later, Byrd wrote that he had sunk to the bottom of what it was to be human and had discovered what being alive really meant. He noted that, before his ordeal, he had often failed to see the simple beauty in things and the importance of human relationships. His grim experience in the Antarctic led this strong and resourceful human being to form a new set of humble values.

From Ideas to Action

1. Identify which of the following cases involve loneliness, and which involve aloneness. If a case involves loneliness, state which cases show a) emotional isolation b) social isolation c) trait loneliness and d) state loneliness. Briefly explain your answers.

   a) Chan would retreat into a private world in his room, where he could freely read and write and where no one could bother him. He had always been a loner. He felt awkward around other people, and seemed to find life easier if he avoided them.

   b) Eduardo had just moved to a new town. It was Friday night. He paced up and down in his room. There was nothing on television. He could feel a hollow tension in the pit of his stomach. Finally, he ran downstairs and threw on his coat. Even though he didn't know anyone there, he had decided to go to the school dance.

   c) Sarah's best friend Alisha had moved away. This was hard on Sarah, since she had always found it difficult to make close friends. She had plenty of people to hang around with, but there was no one she could really talk to. She found going to parties a waste of time. Conversations at these parties never seemed to get beyond "How are you?" Her relationships now seemed so meaningless.

   d) Ted was in the hospital for surgery. Summer — what a terrible time to be cooped up in a hospital! To keep himself busy, he toured the hospital floors in a wheelchair. Other patients had their own problems and he didn't feel he could bother them. Ted could hardly wait for visiting hours, when his parents and friends would come to see him.

2. Copy the following chart into your notebook. Log in your activities for a few days. At hourly intervals, record what you are doing. Use a checkmark ($\sqrt{}$) to show whether you feel lonely, and how lonely you feel, as you do these activities. Then answer the follow-up questions.

Time	Activity	Do You Feel Lonely?			
		Not At All	A Little	Moderately	Very Much
7 a.m.					
8 a.m. Etc.					

   a) How often are you alone during the day?
   b) How often do you feel lonely?
   c) Is there any pattern to the times when you feel lonely?
   d) Are there circumstances in which you are more likely to feel very lonely? Moderately lonely? A little lonely? Not lonely?
   e) Is being alone generally a pleasant experience for you? Why or why not?
   f) If you feel lonely sometimes, what can you do about it? (List several possibilities.)

Alienation

Have you ever experienced feelings like the ones described below?

a) "I'm not sure that life has any real meaning anymore. Years ago, when someone said they were your friend or that they cared, they really meant it. Today, people are fakes. They just want to be successful, to get ahead. They have no real concern for others. They'll tell you they are your friend, when they really just want to use you in some way. The old values that made life worthwhile are long gone."

b) "I am totally powerless. I don't really have any control over what happens to me. The government, the police, my parents, my teachers, and my boss all tell me what to do and what I am supposed to think. It seems that I'm just a small and insignificant part of a very large machine that doesn't work very well. There is nothing I can do to change my life, let alone make the world a better place."

c) "Who am I? Why am I here? Sometimes I imagine I am floating above myself, watching myself go through the day. I see that I have little or no control over my life. I watch myself working to reach meaningless goals that everyone else thinks are important. I smile and pretend to like what I am doing and that my life is worthwhile. I just don't know who I am anymore or where I fit into society."

In small groups or as a class, share your responses and then discuss the following questions:

1. In what ways are the feelings expressed in each quotation similar?
2. What do you think might cause such feelings?
3. How might someone be helped to overcome these feelings?

In science fiction, an "alien" is a being from another planet. The word "alien" also means someone newly arrived from another country. In both cases, an alien is someone who probably feels "out of place" in our world and, therefore, lonely and confused.

Generally, people experiencing **alienation** feel uninvolved in and perhaps rejected by society. They cannot interact with others in a meaningful way, and therefore feel detached from society. They also feel detached from themselves, and often wonder what the purpose of their existence is. They drift through life, frustrated by their inability to overcome these feelings of detachment.

What Causes Alienation?: Marx's Explanation

Why do some people come to feel that life is meaningless and that they are powerless to change things? Why do these people begin to question their identities and their self-worth? Almost any answer to these complicated questions would be oversimplified. However, it might help to summarize the ideas of one of the first social philosophers to recognize that alienation was a problem for modern society.

Karl Marx

The German philosopher Karl Marx (1818–1883) witnessed the birth of modern industrial society, with its cities, factories, and big business. He observed that with industrialization, the way society was organized was changing. How people related to each other and to themselves was changing as well. These changes, he argued, led to feelings of alienation.

Marx noted that in the days before industrialization, people tended to live in small, rural communities where everyone knew each other. They survived by farming and by selling home-crafted articles. During a bad time, such as a poor growing season, a community pulled together to ensure the survival of the group.

But with the creation of large factories and wealthy business owners, society changed for the worse, according to Marx. People left the country to find factory jobs in large, impersonal cities. They worked for factory owners who paid them survival-level wages. People did not co-operate with each other. Instead, they had to compete for fewer jobs when factory owners laid off workers.

Marx believed that factory workers had little control over their daily lives. They were powerless employees dependent on a boss for their livelihood. Each worker was assigned to a job and the owner made all the decisions. Without any say in how the factory produced goods, workers were bored and frustrated in their monotonous jobs. They also had little or no involvement in the goods they produced.

Because the owners were in total control, the powerless workers felt alienated from their jobs, their communities, and themselves. Marx saw this as the central problem, and the greatest tragedy, of modern industrialized society.

Many people argue that Marx's ideas do not apply today. They point out that labour unions now ensure that workers have some decision-making power in the workplace.

They also insist that people do have meaningful contact with others in cities. Many families have managed to thrive in cities. And most people living in cities form a network of close and meaningful relationships. Many community organizations and support groups tackle problems related to urban living. Governments, churches and other agencies have assistance programs for those in need.

Anomie

The French social scientist Emile Durkheim (1858–1917) wrote about the connection between suicide and social norms.

According to Durkheim, society sets desirable goals and acceptable ways of achieving those goals. Supposedly, if a person follows the rules and behaves exactly as he or she is expected to, then these goals will be achieved. If society itself becomes disorganized, however, as in times of rapid change, the rules don't work anymore. This situation is known as **anomie** or "lack of norms." People become confused and frustrated because they can't achieve their goals by following the rules.

Let's apply the idea of anomie today. Society seems to stress the goal of "success." It judges whether you have achieved this goal by material assets such as your house, your income or the kind of car you drive. It also tells you how to achieve success: working hard, obeying the law and getting a good education.

Even when people do follow the rules

Would you like to own these things? Why or why not? How could you acquire these things?

for success, it is obvious that many never achieve this goal. Young people graduate from colleges and universities and discover that there are few good jobs. Getting a good job may depend more on who you know than on your education and how hard you've worked. Furthermore, someone who breaks the law may become rich. There are many indications that conforming to social norms does not necessarily lead to rewards.

This contradiction can lead some people to feel that there are no stable, reliable social norms. They may decide that the goals established by society are meaningless. These people may simply drop out of the daily struggle to pursue socially prescribed goals. For these people, nothing is worth striving for. This causes a state of anomie.

Feelings of anomie are similar to feelings of alienation. A person experiencing anomie is likely to feel detached and powerless. He or she sees no point in following rules that will not lead to desirable goals. They may doubt that the goals themselves are meaningful. Thus, the person experiencing anomie may also develop feelings of alienation.

· ·

From Ideas to Action

1. Decide if each of the following cases are examples of alienation. Be prepared to defend your decisions.

   a) Rashad was the sales manager for a large department store. He'd been in this position for more than ten years. He felt, however, that he'd been unable to make any changes in the way the business was run. He went to work each day asking himself, "Why am I bothering with all of this frustration?" One day he put his house up for sale and moved to a cabin in the mountains.

   b) Tina was fed up with the day-to-day grind of school. She wanted to get away, to do something exciting. She knew that she ought to get a good education, but why now? She decided to take an extra week's holiday with her parents at Christmas.

   c) Rex had no idea why he was in school. There were no jobs worth going after, as far as he could see. Besides, he didn't know what he wanted to do. He questioned the motives for people's behaviour. In his view, everyone walked around with masks on, pretending to be what they were not. All in all, there seemed to be so little caring in the world, so little purpose, and so little that he could do about it.

2. In the 1920s some American writers living in Paris referred to the youth of that time as the "Lost Generation." Do you feel that this description could be applied to teenagers today? Why or why not?

3. In your notebook, make a chart like the one below to compare how Marx and Durkheim analysed alienation.

	Marx	Durkheim
Similarities Causes of Alienation		
Effects of Alienation		
Differences Causes of Alienation		
Effects of Alienation		

Suicide

In a group, spend ten minutes brainstorming answers to the problem below.

The Problem:
Human beings have a powerful urge to survive. Nevertheless, some people decide to override this urge and attempt to kill themselves. Why?
After your brainstorming session, discuss the following questions:

1. How do people commonly explain suicide?
2. Are there any circumstances in which you feel it is understandable for a person to commit suicide? If so, what are these circumstances?
3. If you know or suspect that someone is going to attempt suicide, should you try to stop the person? If so, how? If not, why not?
4. Why should we learn about suicide?

Suicide in History

Since the beginning of history, human beings have taken their own lives. Society has reacted to suicide in two opposing ways. In certain situations, the act of suicide has been tolerated. However, most societies have strongly condemned suicide, considering it "self-murder."

Societies that have tolerated suicide have done so only in rare circumstances. At one time, for example, the Inuit practised suicide as a way of ensuring the survival of the group. When food became scarce, people too old or sick to contribute to the group's well-being sometimes wandered off into the cold. By intentionally freezing to death, they eliminated one more mouth to feed in a harsh environment.

Some societies tolerated suicide as long as a person chose to die in order to uphold religious beliefs or principles. In ancient Rome, military officers took their own life after a defeat in battle. This act was seen as the honourable thing to do. In the past in Japan, the warrior class, called the samurai, committed a ritual suicide called *hara-kiri*. This act was committed when a warrior felt he had been disgraced or when he had been sentenced to death.

Throughout history, societies have generally disapproved of suicide. Organized religions have spoken out against it. In ancient Greece, suicide was seen as the coward's way out. A suicide was denied an honorable burial within his or her city. The hand that had committed the act was cut off and buried separately.

Christians regarded human life as a gift from God. Life was not something that an individual had the right to make decisions about. Final decisions concerning life and death rested entirely with God. Suicide ranked alongside murder and was seen as a sin. Christian suicides, therefore, could not receive a religious burial.

Influenced by religious opposition to suicide, governments began to pass laws to punish suicide. What was originally seen as a sin against God was seen as a sin against society as well. In England, for example, all the property belonging to a suicide victim was automatically seized by the government.

Facts About Suicide

- Attempted suicides have been estimated to occur as much as 50 to 100 times more often than completed suicides.

- Girls are more likely to attempt suicide than boys.

- Boys are more likely to complete the act of suicide than are girls. In Toronto, for example, between 1970 and 1977, three times as many adolescent girls compared to boys tried to kill themselves, but four times as many boys succeeded.

- Girls tended to use methods such as pills, while boys use more violent means, such as firearms, or jumping from high places or in front of trains. However, recent data seems to indicate that girls are using methods similar to boys.

- The area of Canada with the highest rate of suicide is the North, while Prince Edward Island has the lowest rate.

- Monday morning is the most common time for males to attempt suicide.

- The Christmas and New Year holiday season is a common time for attempted suicide.

- The "suicidal crisis" is the point at which the suicidal person feels the strongest urge to kill himself or herself. Experts estimate that, for most people, this period lasts no longer than ten minutes at any given time.

Canadian Attitudes Towards Suicide

Generally speaking, Canada disapproves of suicide, even though it is no longer a crime to attempt suicide in this country. In some ways, however, society still punishes those who take their own lives. Insurance companies, for instance, will not pay insurance money to the family of a suicide victim if the policy has been in effect for less than two years. Companies will refuse to pay disability benefits if the suicide attempt causes injury but not death.

People are beginning to realize that suicide is a serious social problem. In most provinces of Canada, suicides now account for the third largest number of

deaths annually. Suicide is exceeded only by traffic accidents and cancer as the greatest killer of Canadians. The numbers are highest among young people aged 14 to 25. We no longer simply condemn those who commit suicide. Instead, our society is now trying to understand what compels a person to attempt suicide.

Why Do People Commit Suicide?

Durkheim's Theory
Emile Durkheim was the first social scientist to study suicide seriously. He examined thousands of cases of suicide in France. He eventually identified four types of suicide:

1. **Egoistic Suicide**
   These people are usually isolated, lonely, alienated from society and see no reason for living. They tend to have few ties with the communities they live in.

2. **Anomic Suicide**
   These people have undergone drastic changes. The rules which used to regulate their lives have broken down. They are therefore unsure of how to act, or how to deal with new and stressful situations. An astronaut who has trained for years for a single mission, and then retires, might experience such feelings. It might seem afterwards that there is nothing worth striving for.

3. **Altruistic Suicide**
   These people sacrifice their lives for others or for some important principle. Unlike the egoistic and anomic suicide, these people care very much about society and the well-being of its members. Soldiers who give their lives to save comrades during combat fit this category. So, too, do members of certain religious groups who kill themselves to draw attention to social and political problems. For example, in the 1960s Buddhist monks in South Vietnam set themselves on fire to protest discrimination against their religion.

4. **Fatalistic Suicide**
   Those who commit suicide because they feel their lives are unbearably controlled by others fit this category. For example, slaves and prisoners may decide that death is preferable to hopelessness and oppression.

Some social scientists have criticised Durkheim's work because his methods of collecting and interpreting information were often not very scientific. However, he did succeed in focussing attention on suicide. He also offered an important insight: that the suicide rate was directly related to the health of society as a whole. According to Durkheim, suicide results not from some shortcoming within the suicidal person, but from the person's environment. Therefore, if society is changed for the better, the number of suicides will decrease.

Adler's Theory

The Swiss psychologist Alfred Adler (1870–1937) was a friend and colleague of Freud and for awhile worked closely with him. He hypothesized that people kill themselves because they are abnormally distressed by personal shortcomings. He labelled these feelings of personal inadequacy an **inferiority complex**.

A person with an inferiority complex finds it difficult to relate to other people. Individuals suffering from this complex are convinced they are unworthy of friendship. By killing themselves, they seek to prove that they are not worth caring about. In some cases, however, suicide may be an attempt to *conquer* feelings of inferiority. Killing oneself shows that one has ultimate power over life and death.

Adler's ideas are related to the idea of "psychological wounding." Wounding occurs when someone is rejected by parents or friends. It can also result from a series of experiences that leads an individual to conclude that he or she is incapable or stupid. A sense of total incompetence in solving problems can lead to feelings of helplessness and powerlessness. When the distress becomes acute, an individual is in danger of committing suicide.

A Behavioral Perspective

One theory about suicide concerns the importance of reinforcement in a person's life. As you remember from the chapter on Learning, a reinforcement is anything that makes you repeat an activity. What if people lose their reinforcements in life, the things that make them feel good, such as a job, their health, friends, money and so on? They may feel they will never have these reinforcements again. They may loose the desire to continue living and may commit suicide.

Truths and Falsehoods about Suicide

The statements below about suicide are either true or false. Write the numbers from 1 to 11 in your notebooks and indicate by "T" or "F" whether you think the statement is true or false. The correct answers and a discussion of each statement are on page 268.

True or False?

1. Suicide usually happens without warning.
2. When trying to assess suicidal intent, direct questioning should be avoided. Asking someone if they are suicidal might give them ideas.
3. People who attempt suicide really don't want to die.
4. People who talk about suicide rarely mean it and can be considered to be a low risk.
5. Suicide is inherited or "runs in the family".
6. Suicide occurs more frequently in lower socio-economic groups.
7. A person who has attempted suicide is at a lower risk of a second attempt.
8. Once a person is suicidal, he or she is suicidal forever.
9. Following a suicide attempt we witness tremendous improvement. This indicates that the risk is dissipating.
10. Substance abusers rarely attempt suicide; they have, in a sense, found a different outlet to deal with their difficulties.
11. Suicidal people are mentally ill.

By Monty Laskin, M.S.W., Jewish Family and Child Service of Greater Toronto.

Interpreting a Table — Level 1

This exercise will teach you how to read a table and use the data presented in it. Like charts and graphs, tables are shorthand ways of presenting information. In the left-hand column below, you will see an analysis of the table presented on the right. Study these main parts as they appear in the sample table.

Main Parts of a Table

Title
This states the purpose of the table. It also states the range or limits of the information the table contains.

Units
The units represented by the figures in the table are often indicated in the title. The units can also be indicated in the row titles or column titles, as in the table shown. For example, in this table units are given as totals *and* as per 100 000 of the population.

Columns
These present information vertically. In the table shown the first column lists areas in Canada.

Rows
These present information horizontally. In the table shown, the first row presents suicide figures for all of Canada.

Example

Suicide (Male-Female Ratio): Totals and per 100 000 for Canada and Provinces and Territories, 1985 (Source: Statistics Canada)

Area	Total number of suicides Male	Female	Per 100 000 of population Male	Female
Canada	2566	693	20.5	5.4
Nfld	23	0	7.9	0.0
PEI	3	2	4.7	3.1
NS	90	16	20.6	3.6
NB	73	13	20.5	3.6
Que	879	245	27.2	7.3
Ont	790	248	17.7	5.4
Man	102	25	19.3	4.6
Sask	106	27	20.8	5.3
Alta	243 *	53	20.4	4.6
BC	238	62	16.6	4.3
Yukon	7	1	59.3	9.1
NWT	12	1	44.9	4.1

* estimated figure

Comparing Figures in Columns and Rows

To interpret increases or decreases in the figures shown in a table, you have to make comparisons. For example, the table shown is organized by area in Canada. To see a trend from one area to another, you must read down the columns. But to see which sex had more total suicides, or the highest rate for males or females per 100 000 people, you must read across the rows.

Data Sources

Statistics Canada provides extremely accurate information, but other sources might be less reliable. Remember too that data changes over time, so that what is correct data now will probably not be correct in a few years.

Now answer the following questions:

1. Briefly state the purpose of the sample table shown.
2. State two limitations to the table's usefulness.
3. What two units are presented in the table?
4. Briefly explain what column 4 of the table tells you.
5. Briefly explain what row 7 of the table tells you.
6. Briefly explain what the figure in column 4, row 2 tells you.
7. Is the rate of suicide in Canada higher among men or women?
8. Which area of Canada has the highest rate of male suicides?
9. Which area of Canada has the lowest rate of female suicides?
10. What can you conclude from this table about the geographic distribution of suicide in Canada? How might this be explained?

Questionnaire Discussion

Following is a discussion of the true and false statements from page 266. Compare the answers with yours.

1. *False:* Suicidal people give many clues and warnings regarding their suicidal intentions, e.g., giving away possessions, a change in mood, etc.

2. *False:* Allowing individuals to discuss their feelings and plans is imperative. Direct questioning, in a gentle manner that conveys a caring attitude, will often bring relief to someone who is contemplating suicide. It can indicate to that individual that someone has actually recognized his or her despair. Verbalizing hopelessness is the first step in crisis intervention.

3. *True:* A staggering majority of people who attempt suicide *do not want* to die. Their primary wish is to somehow rid themselves of their emotional pain; thus, they seek relief at any cost. We often hear people speak of an individual who attempts suicide as an "attention seeker". Indeed this may be accurate but only insofar as attention will result in discovery and help. With respect to adolescents, research has taught us that they often have no concept of the finality of death.

4. *False:* Nearly 85% of people who have committed suicide demonstrate warning signs; one of the major warning signs is talking about suicide.

5. *False:* Suicide is an individual pattern. However, families in which a member has committed suicide are prone to different dynamics of guilt and blame.

6. *False:* Suicide is represented proportionally among all levels of society, rich and poor alike. There is no "*type*".

7. *False:* Once individuals attempt suicide, they are at a greater risk for attempting again. An attempt is a cry for help. Eighty per cent of those who have completed suicide have previously attempted suicide.

8. *False:* Intervention *does* help. People who are suicidal have lost hope; support services are effective and can greatly reduce the risk of a second attempt.

9. *False:* Most suicides occur within 3 months following the beginning of marked improvement. The individual now has the energy to put his or her ideas into action.

10. *False:* It is reasonable to suggest that an individual who is a substance abuser is at a higher risk for committing suicide. Suicidal risk increases in direct proportion to the decreasing size of one's support network. Alcoholics and drug users are frequently alienated from their family and friends. One out of four alcoholics attempts suicide.

11. *False:* Although the suicidal person is extremely unhappy, he or she is not necessarily mentally ill. An overpowering feeling of hopelessness can result, for example, from a temporary emotional upset or from a long illness.

The Warning Signs

Contrary to popular belief, there *are* warning signals when someone is considering suicide. Here are the specific signs that merit action on your part.

- Expression of suicidal thoughts such as, "I won't be around to bother you much longer," or "I can't stand it anymore, I'm going to end it all."
- Talk indicating helplessness, unhappiness, pessimism.
- Giving away prized possessions such as a record collection, terminating important things in life, making a will or other final arrangements.
- The recent suicide of a friend or relative.
- A previous suicide attempt.
- An extreme change in eating habits or sleeping patterns — too much or too little.
- Withdrawal from friends or family, or other major behaviour change.
- Changes in school performance — lower marks, quitting activities, dropping out.
- Personality changes — the shy person becomes a thrill seeker, the extrovert becomes withdrawn, unfriendly or uninterested; increasing apathy about appearance and heatlh.
- Excessive use of alcohol or drugs. (One study showed 80 per cent of people who committed suicide had been drinking at the time.)

By Sally Armstrong, *Canadian Living.*

From Ideas to Action

1. In your notebook make a chart to compare Durkheim's, Adler's and the behavioural perspective on suicide.

2. Why do you think Durkheim developed a classification of types of suicide? What problem was he trying to address?

3. Durkheim's work is also important because he connected suicide to the environment and the question of a healthy society. Do you believe Durkheim was correct? Explain.

Teenage Suicide

• •

Our society tends to regard youth as a carefree time when the world is opening up and life is just beginning. A teen suicide, therefore, comes as a great shock. In both Canada and the United States, suicide among the young is increasing. Sometimes, outbreaks of suicide seem to follow one another. Today, people tend to be more open about discussing problems, and experts are available to deal with troubled adolescents. Why, then, is suicide on the rise? What are the signs to look for in someone who is considering suicide? What possible solutions are there for this social problem?

The following two articles suggest ways this problem can be dealt with. Research the ways in which suicide is being dealt with in your community.

Home restores hope for suicidal teen

By Paul Watson, *Toronto Star*
[September 30, 1986]

Richard is ready to leave home again, and this time he's headed for a promising future.

The 19-year-old Toronto man, who has tried suicide numerous times, has spent almost two years in Delisle house, a home for troubled teens.

But next week he'll be leaving for a new life, thanks to Delisle Youth Services...

Richard was admitted to the psychiatric ward at Sunnybrook Medical Centre for the second time last year after trying to commit suicide by taking an overdose of drugs and slashing his wrists.

"I was going with a girl who broke up with me in early January and I tried to keep things together for as long as I could," Richard recalls. "By February I just couldn't take it any more."

It was Richard's fifth "serious" suicide attempt among "scads of little ones," but now he is looking forward to life.

He has a good job in a record store and he'll move into his own apartment. But most important, Richard says, he regrets "dancing with death — it just shouldn't have to come to that alternative."

At Delisle house, a staff member is in the house 24 hours a day to handle emergencies. But residents, who stay about a year, have to cook group meals, keep the place clean and try to settle their own disputes.

House head Gail Martin says it's part of making teens — with a variety of emotional, behavioral and psychiatric problems — "learn from becoming dependent on each other."

The two-storey house in the Yonge St.-St. Clair Ave. area was once a church minister's home, but for the last 16 years it's been a refuge for teenagers like Richard who have had troubles coping with life — and paren

"My parents always have been fabulous people, but they've never been very good parents. After what I went through, I needed someone to say, 'We're sorry, too,' but I couldn't get that," Richard says. "Just by being away from them and talking to the staff here, I can feel it's over now — that it's been dealt with."

That quiet confidence wasn't there when he first arrived on the Delisle house doorstep after a frightening two week wait in a downtown youth hoste

"It was scary because it was full of some pretty tough kids," he recalls. "I'm street smart, but I'm not a street kid."

Reprinted with permission — *The Toronto Star Synd.*

How to Help

By Sally Armstrong *Canadian Living* (March 21, 1987)

If someone confides in you that he or she is thinking of committing suicide or shows other signs of being suicidal, talk about it. Your questions will help your friend know that someone is willing to listen. Your interest may give your friend hope at a time when that is exactly what he or she needs. Here's what to say, what not to say and where to get help.

- If someone is givng you clues — "The world would be better off without me; I can't stand this any longer" — but can't say the words directly, you need to speak them for them. Say, "Are you thinking of harming yourself?"
- Ask, "How long have you been feeling this way? Do you know why you feel this way?"
- Say, "You aren't alone. You aren't crazy. There is help available."
- Ask how the person intends to end his or her life: "Do you have a plan? How would you do it?"
- Don't use platitudes such as, "Think how much better off you are than most people," or "You should appreciate how lucky you are." That will end the conversation and make the person, who is already feeling guilty about having suicidal thoughts, feel even more guilty. It's not helpful and may even be harmful. Don't do it.
- The answers to your questions will give you an indication of how serious the risk is. For instance, if someone says, "I intend to shoot myself and I have a gun hidden in the garage," you know that he or she is in imminent danger and should not be left alone. On the other hand, if the person doesn't have a concrete plan, the risk is probably not as great. However, the evaluation of the risk should be made by a professional, not by you.
- No matter what else you do, make sure he or she gets help. The most obvious source is the family physician or clergy person. If that isn't suitable, call the emergency department of the local hospital and ask for the number of the distress centre, crisis centre or suicide prevention center in your area. If there isn't one, call the public health department (look under municipal government in the blue pages for the phone number) or Canadian Mental Health Association (see the white pages) in your city or town. If your friend refuses help, explain the situation to a reliable member of the family or make the call to a crisis centre yourself.
- Keep the lines of communication open, talk calmly and don't be judgmental.

Projects, Activities and Explorations

1. Collect some poems, music and pictures that communicate loneliness and/or alienation. You could display your collection in a slide and tape presentation.

2. Research the lives of people who have experienced alienation, for example:
   a) Socrates b) Karl Marx
   c) Ernest Hemingway,
   d) Thomas Paine e) "punkers"
   f) "skinheads"

3. Arrange a visit to a crisis intervention centre in your area. Observe how the volunteers at the centre handle calls from people in distress. If possible, find out how these volunteers are trained. Report your findings to the class.

4. Develop a crisis intervention telephone directory. Using a telephone book, and with the help of your guidance department, list a variety of social agencies that help people in crisis. Research and write brief descriptions of the services provided by each agency. Type up your directory and ask to have it displayed in your school guidance office for the use of students.

5. Invite a member of your school guidance department, a psychologist or a social worker to visit your class to discuss how to handle a distressed friend who might be suicidal.

6. Research and compare the statistics for suicide in various countries. Try to determine how each country defines suicide. This might seriously affect the number of suicides reported.

What Have You Learned?

If you have covered everything in this chapter, you should be familiar with the following topics :

1. The difference between loneliness and aloneness
2. The causes of loneliness (emotional and social isolation)
3. Two types of loneliness (trait and state)
4. The characteristics of alienation
5. Some theories explaining what causes alienation
6. Attitudes toward suicide in the past
7. How Durkheim, Adler and behaviorists explained the causes of suicide
8. Youth suicide: causes and prevention
9. How to read and use a table

To Help You Study

The following chart will help you
to review the words, facts and
ideas introduced in this chapter.
Copy the chart into your notebook
and fill in the missing information.

Word, Fact, Idea	Example in a Sentence	Page	Definition
loneliness	When a close relationship ends, feelings of loneliness arise.	254	an unpleasant feeling of isolation, often associated with disrupted or inadequate relationships with others
aloneness			
emotional isolation			
social isolation			
trait loneliness			
state loneliness			
alienation			
anomie			
egoistic suicide			
anomic suicide			
altruistic suicide			
fatalistic suicide			
inferiority complex			

Prosocial Behaviour

14

1

Compare These Emergency Situations

- In which situation(s) is a person in need being helped?
- In which situation(s) are the people helping rewarded financially for doing so?
- In which situation(s) are people acting unselfishly?

Now as a class or in a group, answer the following questions:

1. What factors help people decide whether or not to assist others who are in distress?
2. Why do some people risk their lives to help others?
3. Can people truly act in unselfish ways, or is there always some hidden self-interest?

3

2

4. How are people affected when they are willingly helped by others?

All the pictures on these pages show an emergency in which someone needs help. It is obvious that people react differently in situations such as these. Why do some people choose to offer their help, often at great risk or cost to themselves, while others decide to do nothing? This is the key question raised in this chapter.

This chapter also discusses how and why people actually decide to offer their help in certain circumstances. It will explore something that is rarely studied: the effects of helping on those who are helped. Finally, you will be challenged to decide if, and how, we can create a society in which people are more helpful than aggressive towards each other.

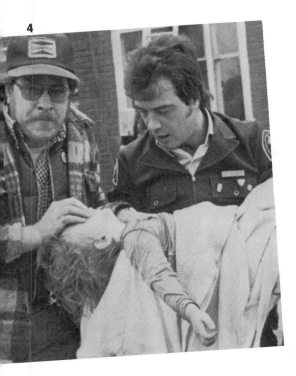

4

What Is Prosocial Behaviour?

When parts of Edmonton, Alberta were devastated by a tornado in August 1987, the response from Albertans and from people all over Canada was swift and generous. Money and goods of all kinds poured into relief centres. People offered their time and their skills to help the tornado victims put their lives back together.

In late August 1987, a Toronto couple radioed to shore that their sailboat had sprung a leak and was sinking in the middle of Lake Ontario. Soon a flotilla of small boats and several small planes began to criss-cross the western end of the lake looking for the survivors. Some of the searchers knew the couple, but many, knowing the lake and how cold the water was, just wanted to help.

Emergency situations such as these tend to dramatize the role of helping behaviour. Whether the situation is dangerous or critical or routine, action that helps or benefits others is called **prosocial behaviour**. Some people, such as nurses or firefighters, are paid for their prosocial behaviour. Other people act prosocially out of a simple desire to help others.

Altruistic Behaviour

Offering to give a confused-looking grade nine student some directions, or lending your calculator to a classmate who is about to take an important exam are examples of prosocial behaviour. Clearly, both people helped have benefitted from your behaviour.

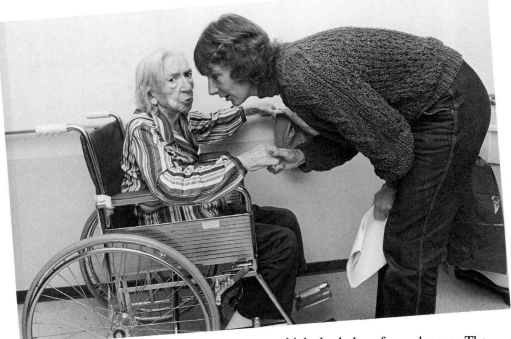

When people voluntarily give to a person or to a cause more time or money than they can reasonably expect in return, their behaviour is called **altruism**. Altruism comes from the Latin word *alter* meaning "other," and is a form of prosocial behaviour.

Society needs prosocial behaviour and is willing to reward police officers and social workers for behaving prosocially. But society also relies on the altruistic behaviour of volunteers. Thousands of organizations across Canada rely on volunteers to deliver meals to people who are housebound, to canvass for charities, to answer telephones in crisis centres or to act as Big Brothers or Big Sisters to young people who need stable, supportive relationships.

Volunteers function in almost every aspect of society in which hard work, enthusiasm and knowledge can be of use. Society benefits enormously from these altruistic activities. We could never begin to repay volunteers for their time and talent.

Heroic behaviour is altruism in which the helper faces danger. The passerby who leaps into a freezing river to rescue a trapped motorist, or someone who at great personal risk enters a burning building to save the occupants, is acting heroically, as well as altruistically.

Some social scientists doubt that human beings are capable of true altruism. These scientists are concerned with the hidden motives for people's behaviour. They argue that perhaps people help themselves when they help others, and are really acting out of self-interest rather than self-sacrifice. For example, these scientists would ask, why did the passerby jump into the river? Perhaps he thought that by saving someone he would get his name in the newspapers and become a local hero.

If you have a positive view of human nature, you may believe that people are capable of great personal sacrifice. If you have a negative view of human nature you may doubt that people will put themselves at serious risk to help others unless there is a significant reward for doing so. In the end, the decision is yours.

From Ideas to Action

1. Which of the following are examples of altruistic behaviour? In each case, explain your answer.

   a) You offer to mow someone's lawn for $5.00.

   b) You are late for your graduation ceremony, but you stop your car to help someone change a flat tire.

   c) The life guard at a pool jumps in to save someone who is drowning.

   d) You offer to help with his or her homework someone who usually bullies you at school.

   e) You witness a student that you do not know cheating on an exam. Later, a teacher asks if you saw the student cheating. You say no.

   f) You are not an expert swimmer, but you swim towards your friend who seems to be in trouble in deep water.

   g) You call the police when you see someone breaking into your neighbour's house.

   h) You spend ten hours a week as a volunteer answering the telephone at an institute for the blind.

2. Which of the cases above did you find difficult to assess? Why? What additional information would have helped?

3. Which of the cases above might also be called heroic? Why?

4. a) Examine the story of the "good Samaritan" in the Bible, Luke 10:29–37. Is this story a good example of altruism? Why or why not?

   b) Find stories in other religions that are examples of altruism.

 ### Are Whales and Dolphins Altruistic?

Whales and dolphins have been observed to offer help, not only to their own kind, but also to other species. They seem to clearly recognize when a creature is in trouble and will act to help, even if helping endangers their own lives. A whale or dolphin will either remain by a victim until the emergency has passed, or swim beneath it and support it so that it can breathe. A whale or dolphin helping in this way will pause only to breathe, will not eat and will not stop helping until the stricken animal either dies or is able to move off on its own.

Whales and dolphins have also been seen swimming between an attacker — a shark or a human, for example — and its intended prey. At great risk to themselves, they sometimes bite or attack capture vessels, and even try to chew through nets to free a captured animal.

The Origins of Prosocial Behaviour

Social scientists are divided on the subject of prosocial behaviour. As you will see, the two key points upon which they disagree are the origins of prosocial behaviour in human beings, and the motives for prosocial behaviour. The major theories that deal with the origins of prosocial behaviour are:

- Instinctive Theory
- Social Learning Theory
- Developmental Theory

Instinctive Theory

Why do female worker bees labour tirelessly on behalf of the one fertile queen in the hive? Why do they attack and sting intruders, an act that defends the hive but results in their own deaths? Why do ground squirrels whistle a warning when a predator approaches? This act saves other ground squirrels nearby, but also calls attention to the whistler. Why does a mother leap in front of a passing car to save her child?

Some social scientists and some biologists explain these altruistic behaviours in terms of instinct. They believe that animals, including humans, act instinctively to ensure the survival of the genes shared by themselves and their relatives. Worker bees are all sisters of their queen; ground squirrel colonies are interrelated by breeding. A mother contributes one half of her child's genetic material. The continuing life of the hive, the clan and the family is more important than the survival of any one individual.

This instinctive theory of altruism seems to contradict the "survival of the fittest" theory of evolution. But some biologists and social scientists think that in this case, altruism improves the chances of *all* the individuals in the group to survive. The "fitness" of the group is therefore improved. The gene for altruism is preserved and passed on to succeeding generations. As a result, altruistic behaviour will increase, according to this theory.

Social Learning Theory

According to the Social Learning Theory of prosocial behaviour, people learn to be helpful by watching prosocial models. For example, people are more likely to stop and help a stranded motorist if previously they have seen someone else doing the same thing.

Do we learn helping behaviour by following the example set by others?

As children, we are taught how, where and when to be helpful. There is nothing instinctive about helping behaviour according to social learning theorists. We learn it in much the same way that we learn other behaviours. We tend to repeat actions that result in some form of reward. We tend not to repeat behaviour that results in negative consequences.

At first, we are directly rewarded for acting correctly. "It was very good of you to offer to help clean the house," says your mother as she hugs you. As we grow older, we learn to find being helpful rewarding in itself. This kind of subtle, private reward becomes enough to make us want to continue being prosocial. Again, we are selfish when we are helpful. We are simply acting to get the rewards that result from being prosocial.

Developmental Theory

According to the Developmental Theory, prosocial behaviour is due to the gradual development of the ability to reason about morals and values. Children must mature to a certain stage of moral development before they can be truly prosocial.

At first, children will act prosocially only if they are ordered to do so by some authority figure. They associate helping with reward and punishment. This stage usually lasts until about age 11. After this stage, children act helpfully because they know that it is expected of all people, or because it is their duty to do so. They cannot reason about why they are helping, or what the results of their helping are. This stage usually lasts until the early teenage years.

Later, people help one another because they recognize that their actions can increase the well-being of another person and that this is good. Eventually an individual helps on the basis of her or his own ideas of what is right or wrong rather than of those of the rest of society. Deciding what is right and wrong is called **moral reasoning**. At this stage, people are altruistic. They are prepared to help in ways that might be regarded by others as unwise or crazy, because they believe it is the right thing to do. They don't expect a reward. In fact, they are probably aware that they may suffer for their actions.

Although theories about the origins of prosocial behaviour appear very different, some of them in fact work together. People who support the developmental theory, for example, also believe that behaviour is learned, but only when the child is mature enough to learn it. Social learning supporters admit that very young children do not learn altruistic behaviour. However, they would probably disagree with developmental theory supporters that the stages are as well defined as developmental theorists say they are.

Moral Reasoning

Lawrence Kohlberg, an American psychologist, believed in the developmental theory of prosocial behaviour. In the 1960s he devised a method of measuring the level of **moral reasoning** at which a person was operating. According to Kohlberg, there were six stages of moral development, ranging from little understanding of helping, to pure altruism.

Kohlberg's Six Stages of Moral Reasoning

Stage 1: Punishment and Obedience Phase

You judge whether an action is good or bad depending on whether you are punished or rewarded. For example, an act that harms someone else, but doesn't affect you, would not be seen as bad.

Stage 2: Self-Centred Phase

Actions that satisfy a person's needs are seen as good. Actions that do not satisfy needs are seen as bad. At this stage, people help only to get something in return, not out of loyalty or a sense of justice.

Stage 3: Good Boy–Nice Girl Phase

Actions that are approved of by others are seen as good. Those that are disapproved of are seen as bad. At this stage, the good intentions of a person are becoming important. Although an action may have negative results, the fact that the person who acted "meant well" is important.

Stage 4: Law and Order Phase

Actions in which a person "does his or her duty" are considered good. At this stage, a good person is one who respects and upholds authority and the laws of society.

Stage 5: Social Contract Phase

An action is good or bad depending on whether it violates another person's rights. If the rights of others are violated, then the action is judged to be bad. Society has critically debated and agreed upon certain standards of behaviour and, if practical, these should be upheld. However, if it can be shown that these generally accepted rules must be broken or altered, then doing so is good.

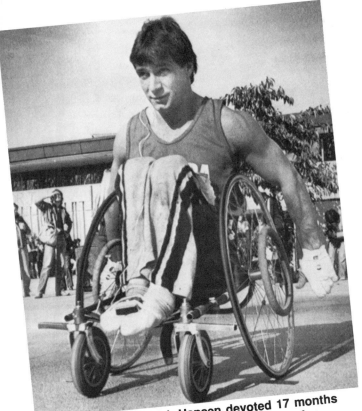

Wheelchair athlete Rick Hansen devoted 17 months to a round-the-world journey to raise money for spinal research.

Stage 6: Universal Principles Phase

Individuals do not base judgements of right and wrong on the general rules of society. Instead, they act in ways that fit with their own personal views of good and bad. At this stage, such universal principles as justice, equality of all people and the dignity of each human being are more important than society's rules.

[Adapted from *How to Assess the Moral Reasoning of Students.* Nancy Porter, Nancy Taylor. OISE Press, The Ontario Institute for Studies in Education, 1972.]

From Ideas to Action

1. Answer the following questions and compare your answers with the descriptions of each of Kohlberg's six stages of moral reasoning. Try to decide at which stage you are operating.

   a) In the gym change room, you see a friend steal a wallet. Your friend is not aware that you saw this. At the end of class, the teacher asks for information about the stolen wallet. What will you do?

   b) You are at an out-of-town party with your best friend. Your friend drinks too much but insists on driving home. You want to grab the keys, but how will you get home? You do not have your permanent driver's licence and if you phone either set of parents you will be grounded, neither of you was supposed to be at this party. What will you do?

2. Make a chart like the one below to organize your notes about the three theories explaining the origins of prosocial behaviour.

	Instinctive Theory	Social Learning Theory	Developmental Theory
Origins of Prosocial Behaviour			

3. Which theory or combination of theories for the origins of prosocial behaviour would explain the following cases?

   a) A person volunteers to go to a remote area to work with people suffering from a deadly disease.

   b) A rock group gives a benefit concert in aid of famine relief.

   c) A parent helps a child find a permanent job after the child has finished school.

   d) A father returns to his burning home to save his children trapped inside.

   e) A woman, whose father is a decorated war hero, tackles a man who has just stolen another woman's purse.

   f) A wealthy business person works hard to make millions of dollars and in the last few weeks of life donates the entire fortune to several charities.

4. Research and present a history of "Band Aid" or "Northern Lights" for African famine relief. In your presentation, discuss the reasons why the performers gave so freely of their time to participate in the project.

5. Think of your usual reasons for helping someone. Which theory or combination of theories for the origins of prosocial behaviour do you think would best explain your behaviour? Why?

Clarifying and Analysing Values

The purpose of this exercise is to give you a method for more clearly understanding and making decisions about value issues.

Read the following hypothetical case study. Then complete the Values Discussion Worksheet that follows. It will help you to clarify and analyse your values.

The Case of Vito S.

You have known Vito S. since grade two. By grade eight, you and he had become friends. You did track and field together, belonged to the same church and often hung around with the same group at the local mall. Lately, however, you have grown apart. Vito seems moody and withdrawn, and he no longer seems interested in sports or other activities. He often talks about life being useless and not worth living.

None of this makes much sense to you, until you study teenage suicide in class. Suddenly it all fits. You feel you should tell Vito's parents or at least contact the school social worker, but you are afraid of becoming involved. Vito's parents don't like outsiders interfering in family problems. It could all become very embarrassing, especially if you are wrong. Yet you really like Vito and feel that his life could be in danger.

Now complete the following worksheet in small groups of two or three students. Then, as a class, discuss your answers.

Values Discussion Worksheet

Values Question: Complete the following question suggested by this case study, "Should you ..."

Your View: State your view on the above question and explain why you feel this way. Begin with: "I think that ..."

Results: What would be the results if you did as you suggested above? What would be the results if you made the opposite decision?

Role Reversal: Put yourself in the place of the person most affected by your decision. How would he feel about this decision? Why?

Application to You: Have you, your family or friends ever had to make a decision like this one? What did you or they do? Why? What happened?

Analogies: What if Vito S. were a member of your family? What if he were only a casual aquaintance? Would your views remain the same?

General Principle: What is the general rule or truth on which you are basing your decision?

Reasons for Helping

In each of the following cases, decide if you would be likely to help.

- A fellow student asks to borrow one of your many extra pens so that he or she can write an important test that must be written in pen.
- Your brother wants to borrow your sports car because he would like to see how fast it will go.
- You see a friend being beaten up by two older and stronger teenagers.
- A classmate who is failing a course badly wants to copy your essay so she or he can pass at least one assignment this term.

Now in small groups or as a class, discuss the following questions:

1. What was similar about the cases in which you would find it easy to decide to help?
2. What was similar about the cases in which you would find it difficult to decide to help?
3. In the cases referred to in question 2, state why it would be a difficult decision to decide to help.?

The Costs of Helping

There are many different factors that influence people's willingness to help. Let's first consider the benefits and costs

In November 1985, some of Canada's top recording artists under the name Northern Lights recorded *Tears Are Not Enough* for Ethiopian famine relief.

of helping. This may provide a way of explaining why people help in certain circumstances, and not in others.

The basic idea is very simple. It states that you mentally calculate two costs before deciding whether or not to give your help. First, you figure out what the cost of direct help would be to yourself. Will you have to risk your life (high cost)? Or will you simply have to spend a few moments to give someone directions (low cost)? Second, you

consider the costs to the people in need of help if you should decide not to offer your assistance. Will they die or suffer serious injury if you fail to help (high cost for them)? Or will they simply be inconvenienced, until someone else gives them directions or they figure out how to read the map (low cost to them)? In other words, how much will they benefit if you help?

Suppose, as you are walking home, you see someone being beaten in a parking lot. You think that if you get involved, you stand a good chance of being injured yourself. This means that the costs of helping would be very high for you. On the other hand, if you do nothing, the chances are that the person who is being beaten may be seriously hurt or even killed. This is a high cost for the victim.

When faced with this combination of costs you might do one of two things. You might convince yourself that the person really doesn't need your help and escape the situation, or you might try to help in an indirect and safe way. If you choose the first option, you will avoid the situation and walk away. If you choose the second, you will run to the nearest telephone and call for help.

Other Factors Determining Helping Behaviour

Below are some other factors that affect a person's willingness to help:

The Number of People Watching an Emergency

Generally, the greater the number of people watching an incident, the less likely that the person will be helped. What seems to happen is that the spectators *share* the responsibility for helping. As the size of the crowd grows, the amount of responsibility that each person feels apears to shrink or become weaker. "Oh well, someone else will help" is the thought that occurs to individuals in the crowd. This is called the **diffusion of responsibility.**

The "Just World" Theory

We tend to believe that in a just and fair world, the good should be rewarded and the bad should be punished. As a result, people who have problems through no fault of their own are helped more often than people who seem to have caused their own troubles. For example, whom would you most likely help: someone lying drunk beside the road, or an elderly person struggling with some packages?

Guilt

If people feel guilty about something, they are more likely to offer help. This may be because guilt is an unpleasant feeling and people want to do something to get rid of it. Helping someone usually makes people feel good about themselves.

Similarity

People are more likely to help someone they think resembles them than someone with whom they seem to have little in common. They may *identify* with that person, and imagine themselves in the problematic situation.

Mood

People are more likely to help a person if they are in a good mood rather than a bad one.

Time

People are more likely to help others when they are not faced with things that need to be done immediately. If they don't have to worry about missing an appointment or a deadline, they can devote the time required to help.

From Ideas to Action

1. Explain how the cost of helping would influence the behaviour of each person in the following situations:

   a) Harvey was on his way to a date when he saw a man chasing a woman with what looked like a knife. He pulled over at the next gas station and called the police.

   b) Corinne found an unmailed envelope on the floor of a phone booth. As she passed a mail box on her way to work, she mailed it.

   c) John was walking home after a long day at school. In the parking lot of the grocery store, he saw two groups of young boys fighting. He noticed that one of the boys had a piece of pipe and was swinging it wildly. John quietly moved off in the other direction.

2. Read the following description of an experiment. Then predict how you think the various participants will respond to an apparent emergency.

   Students were recruited to do an experiment. Each participant was placed in a booth where he or she could not see anyone else . The participants were told that they were either *alone* or working with two, four or six other students participating at the same time in other booths. Actually the people in the other booths were hired actors.

   Through a microphone, the experimenter said she was interested in hearing about the sorts of problems that students faced and that each participant would have two minutes to discuss this topic. The participants were told they would be able to hear the comments of other participants through a speaker in each booth. The first "participant" to respond was one of the actors. He said that he was feeling very worried these days and that the stress he was under sometimes caused seizures. After a few minutes, this actor pretended to have a violent seizure and called desperately for help. Each participant knew that the experimenter was seated at a desk just down the hall.

   How do you think the participants who thought they were alone behaved? Those who thought they were in a group of two? Of four? Of six? Why?

   Answer: Eighty-five per cent of participants who thought they were alone reported the emergency immediately to the experimenter seated down the hall. One hundred per cent of the people who thought they were in a two-person group reported the emergency. Thirty-one per cent of those in four-person groups contacted the experimenter. Sixty-one per cent of those in six-person groups reported the emergency. Did you predict similar responses? If not, how would you explain the difference between your prediction and what actually happened?

Who Helped the Jews in Nazi Europe?

In 1939, the Germans invaded Poland and carried out the Nazi's policy of annihilation of the Jews. In the capital of Warsaw, Jews were isolated in a special area of the city called the ghetto, where they suffered starvation and disease. Eventually they were sent to concentration camps, where they were either killed or forced to do hard labour.

Very few people were prepared to risk arrest or death to help the Jews. However, in the midst of all this, a young Christian girl named Fusia began smuggling food, medicines and clothing into the ghetto. By the end of the war, she had hidden and saved 13 Jews in a secret room in her attic. It is estimated that there were probably less than a few thousand people involved in this sort of dangerous rescue work. Who were these brave few and why were they willing to risk their lives when so many people would not?

A number of studies based on actual interviews with surviving rescuers have uncovered some interesting facts about these people. They tended to share at least one of three characteristics, and often a combination of all three:

1. **Deeply held moral values**

Rescuers had a strong sense of what was right and wrong and felt a real moral responsibility to help others. Rescuers frequently spoke of a parent who had had a great influence upon their lives. Almost without exception, these parents had also held high moral values.

2. **Emotional attachment to the Jews**

People with this characteristic felt close to the people they rescued. The people they helped were often friends or acquaintances. If they did not know the person, rescuers often helped because, in their own lives they too had been bullied or persecuted for being different. They therefore felt an emotional closeness with oppressed Jews.

3. **A sense of adventure**

Many rescuers had a history of adventurous activity. Some claimed that rescuing others seemed like pretty tame stuff. For the most part, it seemed that a sense of adventure led many people into rescue work in the first place. But either strong moral values or an emotional attachment to the Jews enabled rescuers to sustain their risky efforts throughout the six years of World War II.

How do People React to Being Helped?

You assume that the people you help want your help and are grateful to you. Or are they? Shaun McCormack, a parapleigic, comments "I consider people's attitudes toward disabled people as the most difficult obstacle that I face. It expresses itself as 'We'll take care of you' or 'Don't try so hard. We'll always be here to take care of you.' If only people would stop trying to do everything for us."

Research has shown that people have either positive or negative feelings about being helped, depending on certain conditions. The chart below summarizes the most important conditions that affect a person's feelings about being helped. For each condition, try to guess whether most people would react positively (+) or negatively (-) to being helped. Record your guesses in your notebook. When you have finished, check your answers with the answers on page 293.

Conditions

	Reaction +	Reaction -
1. If the recipients of your help interpret that they need help: a) due to personal inadequacy (lack of ability) b) due to external force(s)		
2. If the helper's motivations are perceived by the recipients to be: a) selfish b) altruistic		
3. If the help is offered freely, assuming there is a need, and help can be freely accepted or rejected		
4. If the recipients must ask for help		
5. If the recipients have an opportunity to pay back the helper in some way, at some time		
6. If the recipients have *no* opportunity to pay back the helper in some way, at some time		

A person with a handicap has the same emotional needs as anyone else. He or she needs to feel independent, accepted and worthwhile as a person. But always being on the receiving end of assistance is hard on self-esteem. Therefore, if you help others, it is important to understand how it feels to be helped. You can't always assume that just because you see an opportunity to help, the person really wants help or will thank you for it. Why do you think people react negatively in the situations outlined in the chart?

How Can We Produce a More Prosocial Society?

The general belief among social scientists is that it would be possible to have a society in which people were more helpful. They also tend to agree that it doesn't really matter why people help.

Whether motives are selfish or unselfish doesn't matter, as long as the result is more people reaching out to help others in need. How we can achieve this goal is a difficult question.

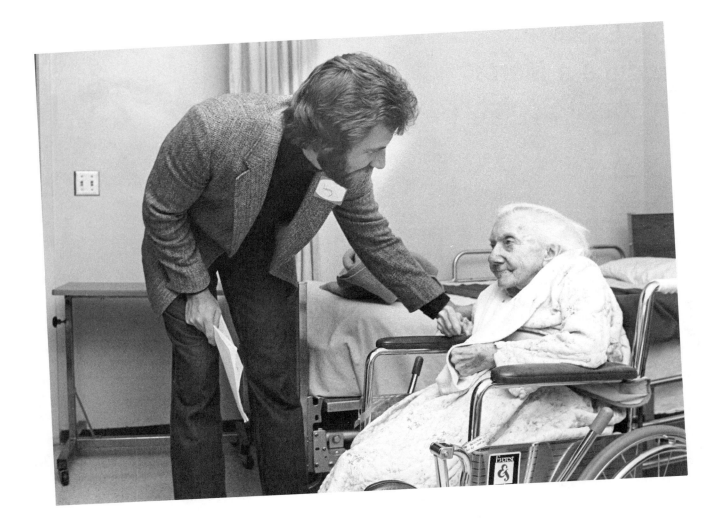

Teaching Children to Be Prosocial

Assuming that only a small amount of our helping behaviour is due to instinct (and even this is not certain), learning must account for most of our willingness to help each other. The research is encouraging here. It is clear that children, if they are rewarded for prosocial behaviour, or if they see someone else being rewarded for helping, will repeat or imitate the helping behaviour.

A problem may arise if parents tell their children to help others, and then five minutes later refuse to put a dollar into a collection pot for the needy. Faced with this contradiction, most children will usually do as the parent does, not as the parent says.

Television, movies and other media to which children are exposed could be used to encourage more prosocial behaviour. Some current TV programs attempt to teach children to be less competitive. Such programs stress helping and co-operation. The question is: Does portraying a prosocial event produce prosocial behaviour in the audience? Research in the United States has shown that children do tend to imitate prosocial behaviour portrayed on television, just as they tend also to imitate aggressive or antisocial behaviour. Since prosocial behaviour is considered desirable, one would hope that more prosocial programs and fewer antisocial programs will be broadcast in the future.

Teaching Adults to Be Prosocial

Teaching adults to be prosocial is a more difficult task. Most people have matured in a society in which competition — not prosocial behaviour — is the norm. As you have seen from examples given in this chapter, adults are not automatically helpful. Special conditions must exist before someone will offer aid to another person.

For this reason, several states in the United States have been experimenting with "good Samaritan" laws. These laws impose penalties on people who do not help in situations in which help is obviously needed.

This represents a legal attempt to raise the costs of not helping for the potential helper. Legislators reason that if it is less costly to help than not to help, a person who sees an emergency will be more likely to offer aid. This is only an experiment, however, and many people doubt that such laws can succeed in promoting prosocial behaviour.

From Ideas to Action

1. Watch a children's program such as "Sesame Street" or "Polka Dot Door," that promotes prosocial behaviour. What behaviours or values do you think are being promoted? How much competition is portrayed among the characters?

2. Outline your suggestions for increasing helping behaviour in your high school in the form of a report to the student council, stating your goals, the kinds of helping behaviour you wish to encourage and the ways you would go about encouraging the behaviour.

Projects, Activities and Explorations

1. You will need to get permission from your teacher and possibly from the principal to do the following simple experiment. During a class, pretend to faint in the classroom. Before you begin, decide what you expect will happen. Predict how long it will take for someone to help. How many people will help. Who will these people be? What sort of help will be given? Position yourself where you can see the total scene. Compare the results with your predictions.

2. Assume that you are a parent. List three things that you would do to encourage your children to be more prosocial. For each idea, explain how and why it would work.

3. With the guidance of your teacher or a teacher/librarian, choose a famous "helper" to research. Find out as much as you can about the person — their parents, upbringing, interests, abilities, etc.

   Now, pretend you are the person that you have researched. Have someone interview you with a videotape machine and camera, or a tape recorder. The goal of the interview is to find out how and why you became extremely prosocial. Several students could work on this project and present it to the class. After the class has seen or heard all the interviews, discuss whether these famous helpers had any characteristiscs in common.

4. Investigate the activities of a group or organization that operates largely with volunteer labour. Interview one or two volunteers about the kind of work they do, why they do it and the rewards they receive. Present your research as an essay or report to the class, or re-enact the interview with a fellow student.

5. Visit an agency that helps people in need. Phone well in advance and arrange a meeting with someone who works for the agency. Find out how and why they chose to work for the agency, as well as the rewards and the frustrations involved in their work. Tape record or write up the interview and present it to the class.

What Have You Learned?

If you have covered everything in this chapter, you should be familiar with the following topics:

1. Characteristics of prosocial behaviour

2. Characteristics of altruistic behaviour

3. Theories that explain the origins of prosocial behaviour (Instinctive Theory, Social Learning Theory and Developmental Theory)

4. Kohlberg's Six Stages of moral reasoning

5. Factors which determine helping behaviour

6. How the cost of helping may influence prosocial behaviour

7. How people react to being helped

To Help You Study

The following chart will help you
to review the words, facts and
ideas introduced in this chapter.
Copy the chart into your notebook
and fill in the missing information.

Word, Fact, Idea	Example in a Sentence	Page	Definition
prosocial	She acted in a prosocial way when she helped the blind man across the street.	275	action that helps or benefits others
altruism			
heroic behaviour			
moral reasoning			
Instinctive Theory			
Social Learning Theory			
Developmental Theory			
the cost of helping			

Answers to chart on page 288:
1. a) - b) +, 2. a) - b) +, 3. +,
4. -, 5. +, 6. -

Aggression

15

Look at the pictures on these pages and answer the following questions. Compare answers with one or two other students.

1. Which of these pictures do you feel good about and which ones upset you? Why?
2. Have you ever been involved in situations similar to the ones in the pictures? How did these experiences make you feel?
3. What do your answers suggest to you about the effects of aggressive and non-aggressive behaviour in our society?

These pictures show us some of the worst and the best in human beings. Are we hurtful creatures or are we helpful creatures? Or are we both? Chapter 14 dealt with the helpful nature of human beings. This chapter will discuss our aggressive and non-aggressive behaviour.

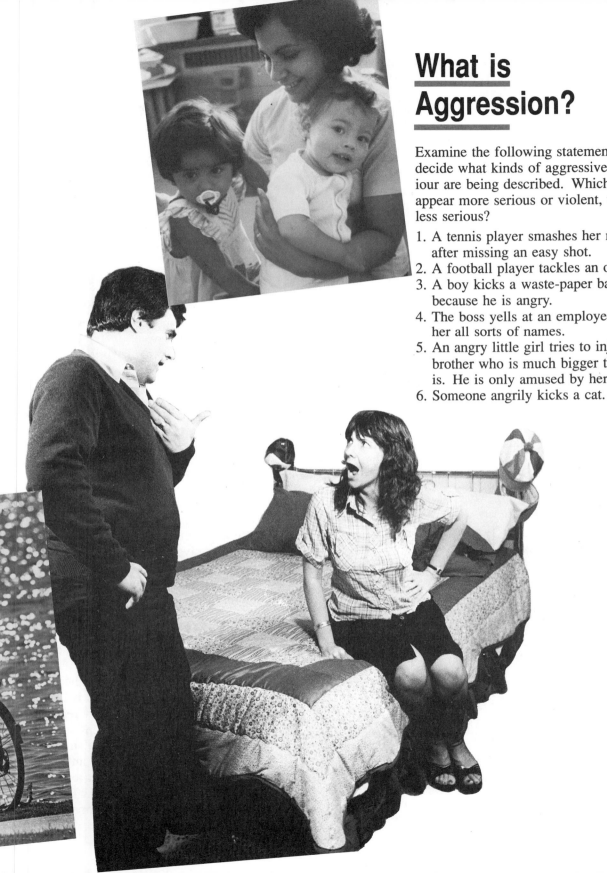

What is Aggression?

Examine the following statements and decide what kinds of aggressive behaviour are being described. Which ones appear more serious or violent, which less serious?

1. A tennis player smashes her racket after missing an easy shot.
2. A football player tackles an opponent.
3. A boy kicks a waste-paper basket because he is angry.
4. The boss yells at an employee, calling her all sorts of names.
5. An angry little girl tries to injure her brother who is much bigger than she is. He is only amused by her efforts.
6. Someone angrily kicks a cat.

295

We use the term aggression to refer to many kinds of behaviour. You can be "aggressive" in supporting your right to privacy and not be physically or verbally violent about it. This aggressive behaviour is sometimes called *assertiveness*. You are being assertive when you pursue something of value to you as a person. An "aggressive" sales person is also pursing something of value, the sale of a stereo or a car perhaps. You may not like the aggressive style but it will do you no harm. "Aggressive" hockey is another example of a goal being pursued strongly. Aggressive hockey allows physical aggression that car sales do not, but it is not violent if played within the rules of the game.

The **aggression** we are concerned with in this chapter is behaviour that is intended to harm others either physically or emotionally. Other kinds of aggressive behaviour may be beneficial to society, in helping us reach goals and maintain our values. Harmful aggression is a social problem that effects all of society.

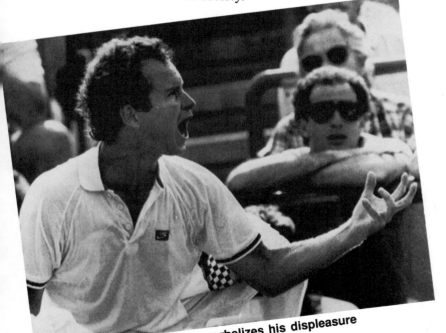

Tennis player John McEnroe verbalizes his displeasure at calls by officials during a match.

Origins of Aggression

Human beings have an amazing ability to be aggressive. This fact has concerned psychologists, police, politicians and ordinary citizens for many years. They all ask the same question: Why do we do so much harm to our own kind? This is a very difficult question to answer. At least part of this difficulty stems from the different theories explaining aggression. This chapter will present two important theories about the origins of aggression: Instinctive Theory and Social Learning Theory.

Aggression: An Instinctive Behaviour?

According to Instinctive Theory, all animals, including human beings, have to fight members of their own kind. They do this for survival as they struggle for food and mates.

There is, however, one major difference between human aggression and the aggressive behaviour of most animals. Animals are capable of killing with their own teeth and claws. If they fought to the death in every fight, an animal species would soon kill itself off. To prevent this, animals have a set of instinctive behaviours that limits the extent of the aggression.

For example, when dogs fight they rarely injure each other. This is because one of the contestants quickly recognizes the superiority of its opponent and instinctively does something to show this. This can take such forms as putting the tail between the legs, or lying on the back with the throat exposed. The victor instinctively understands the meaning of these gestures and backs off. This prevents fatal wounds from being inflicted.

Human beings, on the other hand, are instinctively aggressive, but have no way of naturally limiting this aggression. This is what makes our forms of aggression much more dangerous than those of animals.

According to this viewpoint, we will never be able to remove aggression from our society completely, because it is our nature to be aggressive. All we can do is find ways of controlling the urge to be aggressive. Some psychologists argue that since aggressive energy must somehow be released, we can create relatively safe ways for this to happen. Contact sports may be one outlet in which people can work out their aggression. At least in sports, rules can keep aggression from becoming violent.

- -

From Ideas to Action

1. For each of the following situations, decide whether harmful aggression is involved. In each case, be prepared to explain your answer.

   a) Sam became so angry he rammed his head against a wall.

   b) Indra was so anxious to get a promotion that she spread unpleasant rumours about her rival co-workers behind their backs.

   c) Sandy and Hans are members of the same local boxing club. They love to fight each other in practice sessions because they are so evenly matched.

   d) A nurse gives a patient a polio shot. The patient hates needles because they are painful.

   e) The male lion attacked the intruder that had strayed into his territory.

   f) A fight broke out. Apparently one person had insulted the other.

   g) A young teenager dreams of beating up a rival for his girlfriend.

   h) Someone accidentally trips the person whom he is helping across the street.

2. Arrange to watch a prime-time television drama with at least one other student. List every aggressive action that you see, keeping in mind the definition of harmful aggression. Keep your list private. After the program, compare the aggressive behaviours that you saw with those seen by your partner(s). If you have approximately the same actions on your lists, then you all probably understand the definition of aggression. If your lists are different, discuss why they are different and review the characteristics of aggression.

3. Interview as many members of your school's hockey or football team as you can. Record their views on aggression in their sport. Try to find out what kinds of behaviour they consider aggressive. When do they feel that another player is acting aggressively (with an intent to harm) rather than just playing the game? What causes players to be aggressive? Do they consider aggression to be an important part of their sport? After you have completed your investigation, draw some conclusions about aggression in sport.

How Aggressive Are Human Beings?

Here are a few statistics that may shock you:

- In the last 150 years, 70 million people have died in wars.
- Since 1965, the number of murders in North America has increased 120 per cent, and beatings have climbed 150 per cent.
- Approximately one in ten adolescents in Canada live in a home where physical violence is a regular occurrence.
- One in two females and one in three males are the victims of unwanted sexual acts, including threats, exposures, touchings, and attempted and actual assaults.
- Four in 100 females in Canada have been raped.

Aggression: A Learned Behaviour?

Some psychologists believe that human beings are not born to be aggressive. Instead, we have learned our aggressive behaviour from our parents, friends and other influences such as television. As we grow up, we are exposed to people who behave aggressively. We observe their behaviour and imitate it. If the behaviour we imitate is acceptable to the group, it is rewarded. If not, we are punished.

Too often in our society, aggressive behaviour is acceptable for boys and is rewarded. Think of some of our movie idols. "Rambo" (Sylvester Stallone) and "Dirty Harry" Callahan (Clint Eastwood) are heroes who are admired. In hockey, team mates congratulate a "goon" for knocking someone unconscious during a game. In war and crime movies and sports, aggressive "heroes" are likely to be men. Boys may assume that this is appropriate behaviour and may try to imitate it to get rewards.

In contrast, passive and co-operative behaviour is often valued and rewarded as characteristically female. Girls are encouraged to play quietly with dolls, and are praised for being neat and tidy. They are usually given toys that encourage peaceful play, whereas boys are often given toys that encourage aggressive play. Today, many teachers and parents are trying to encourage children to accept less aggressive heroes.

People who favour the social learning theory of aggression see some hope of reducing aggression in our society. We can decide what non-aggressive behaviours we want to reinforce and then teach them to our children. Parents can reward co-operation and helping, rather

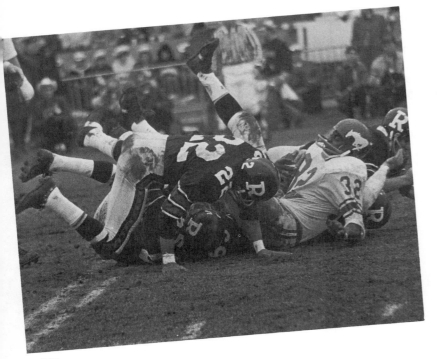

than competition and aggression. Particularly among boys, parents can stop rewarding and encouraging "macho" behaviour and provide them with non-aggressive toys.

Some people also feel that aggression in our society can also be controlled by censoring violence in the media. Violent heroes such as "Rambo" give aggression a good image. They teach that the key to popularity and acceptance is tough, aggressive behaviour. If you favoured this position, you might also call for a ban on pornographic media. Some movies, literature and rock music often link aggression and sex and may, therefore, teach that it is socially acceptable to be violent towards women.

People who support the social learning theory of aggression believe that we can have a much less aggressive society. We must be prepared to remove the sources that teach aggressive behaviour. We are not aggressive by nature; we have simply learned to be.

From Ideas to Action

1. Develop an organizer to compare your thoughts about the instinctive and social learning theories of aggression. The following structure might be helpful. If you need to refresh your memory on developing organizers, consult the skills exercise in Chapter 1 on Developing an Organizer.

Categories	Instinctive Theory of Aggression	Social Learning Theory of Aggression
Origins of Aggression		
Control of Aggression		

2. Explain the behaviour of the people in the following situations according

Some societies, such as the Amish, discourage all forms of aggressive or violent behaviour.

299

to the instinctive theory of aggression. Do the same using the learning theory of aggression.

a) Lisa wanted a promotion at work, but promotions were difficult to come by. She saw her opportunity when her section head started arriving late a few days a week. Lisa went to the store manager and mentioned that she would have liked to have had a project done on time, but she was unable to find her section head to get approval for her plan.

b) Bill desperately wanted to get on the football team. The competition was very tough. During one practice, he took advantage of a play to deliver a crushing blow to one of his major competitors. The player suffered injuries serious enough to miss the rest of training camp.

c) Sheila was furious at her teacher. She had failed her final exam by one mark. At home, her unsuspecting brother made the mistake of asking her how her day had gone. She screamed that his loud music had made it impossible for her to study and that he was responsible for her failing the exam.

3. If you were a parent, what position would you take on violence in television and in the movies, and why? Base your decision on the following factors:

   i) the age of the children
   ii) your own views on the origins of aggressive behaviour
   iii) the time that you would be prepared to spend
   iv) the chances of enforcing or carrying out your actions
   v) any other factor(s) that you consider important in making a decision.

Now choose one of the following. Would you:

a) Let your children watch all the violent media they want to?
b) Let them watch what they want, but make it clear that you disapprove of violence?
c) Let them watch violent media, but watch it with them, stopping during the commercials to discuss the differences between fantasy and reality?
d) Ban excessively violent shows but allow your children to watch programs that have moderate amounts of violence?
e) Pull the plug on the television altogether?
f) Write the television station, asking them not to air violent programs?
g) Some combination of the above, or a different course of action?

To complete this task, you could:

1) Write your response to this problem as a report.
2) Discuss the problem with a group of students.
3) Discuss the problem with your parents.
4) Design a survey to get the opinions of a large number of students regarding the problem.
5) Develop a video presentation that shows the pros and cons of each course of action. Show this to the class and ask them to choose among the alternatives.

The "Dirty Harry" Killing

Examine the following case study and explain how it supports the **social learning theory** of aggression.

The story behind the "Dirty Harry Killing"

Social psychologists have primarily studied the long-term effects of violent television. But sometimes a violent television program can have an immediate effect. In the early fall of 1977, NBC presented the movie "Dirty Harry". Newspaper columnist Bob Greene tells what happened.

Saturday night, Dolphus and Micros had watched "Dirty Harry". The movie, originally released in 1971, is a violence-soaked police drama in which [Clint] Eastwood portrays Harry Callahan, a San Francisco cop who doesn't mind taking the law into his own hands. Thus his nickname — Dirty Harry. The movie was such a box office success that it spawned several sequels.

Near the beginning of the movie, Dirty Harry approaches a criminal sprawled on the street. The criminal's gun has fallen out of his hand, but is within reaching distance. Dirty Harry pulls out his own gun and aims it at the criminal. There has been a shootout: it is not known whether Dirty Harry has any more bullets left in his gun. The question is, should the criminal reach for his gun?

Dirty Harry says approximately the following:

"Listen, punk, this here is a .44 caliber magnum revolver, the most powerful handgun ever made. Now you're probably thinking, 'Did he fire six shots or just five?' Well, to tell you the truth, in all the excitement I kinda lost count myself. It just depends. Do you feel lucky today?"

The criminal's hand trembles.

"Well, do you, punk?" Dirty Harry says.

The criminal looks up the barrel of Dirty Harry's magnum. He trembles and decides to give up and be arrested by uniformed officers. Dirty Harry walks away.

"Hey mister," the criminal calls.

Dirty Harry turns around.

The criminal gestures towards Dirty Harry's gun.

"I gots to know," the criminal says.

Dirty Harry carefully takes aim at the criminal's head and squints his eyes. The man shrinks back in fear. Dirty Harry pulls the trigger. The gun clicks on an empty shell. Dirty Harry laughs.

Later in the movie the same scene is repeated, this time featuring a different criminal. This time the criminal feels lucky. He reaches for his own gun. This time dirty Harry fires again. This time Dirty Harry's gun has a bullet in it. And this time the criminal is shot to death.

That is what Dolphus and Micros Thompson saw on television Saturday night.

According to Columbus Police Dept. homicide Sgt. Tom Aurentz, this is what happened Sunday morning:

Dolphus and Micros decided to play "Dirty Harry".

Dolphus got a .22 caliber two-shot derringer from his father's nightstand.

The two boys went to Dolphus' bedroom, where a toy "Star Trek" ray gun was lying on a table near Micros.

Dolphus said:

"In all the confusion, I bet you don't know if this gun is loaded." He then ordered his younger brother to reach for the toy gun. Micros Thompson did.

Dolphus Thompson shot him once in the chest. Micros took a few steps into the hallway, collapsed and died.

When Columbus police arrived at the scene, Dolphus told them, "We were just playing "Dirty Harry".

Factors That Influence Aggression

Psychologists have done a great deal of research on the various factors that influence peoples' willingness to be aggressive. One of the key factors is a person's general tendency to be aggressive. Clearly, this varies from person to person. Surely, you have known people who are aggressive "at the drop of a hat," and others who calmly put up with anything. Because social scientists are looking for general laws of behaviour that can be applied to all people, this factor will not be discussed further. But remember, a person's tendency to be aggressive or non-aggressive is an important factor in any aggressive situation.

The following theories deal with the factors that generally lead to aggression. These theories are important because they may help you understand why you or others become aggressive. They may also help you to predict when people are likely to become violently aggressive: an important social skill if you need to avoid getting hurt!

Frustration-Aggression Theory

At one time, psychologists thought that frustration would always lead to aggression and that all aggression was caused by frustration. Since then, however, opinions have changed somewhat. Repeated studies have failed to support such a sweeping theory. Now it is generally accepted that frustration is only one of several factors leading to aggression. It is also recognized that, depending on the situation, a frustrated person may not become aggressive at all. For example, if you repeatedly fail to win the love of a certain person it is unlikely that your frustration would cause you to walk up to and scream at that person. You are more likely to become depressed, rather than aggressive.

What seems most important in determining whether frustration will lead to aggression is the way you interpret the cause of your frustration. Let's say that you are in a hurry to get to class. The stairwells are crowded and moving anywhere is difficult. Suddenly the person in front of you stops and has a long chat with someone going in the opposite direction.

Let's look at another case. This time, as you are heading down the stairwell, someone just ahead of you accidentally drops her books. Everyone on the stairs comes to a halt.

In which case are you more likely to be aggressive towards the person who is preventing you from achieving your goal of getting to class on time? Obviously, you are going to be frustrated in both cases, but it is unlikely you will be hostile to the person who dropped her books. The talker, however, may get a cutting comment from you. In the first case, the person was deliberately preventing you from achieving your goal. When the cause of the frustration is deliberate, you are more likely to be aggressive. However, if you know that the person who has caused your frustration did so accidentally, you will probably withhold your aggression.

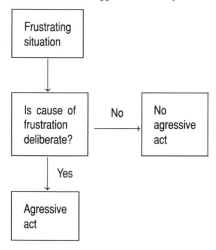

Flow Chart Summary of
Frustration-Aggression Theory

Arousal and Labelling Theory

This theory is sometimes called the two-stage theory of aggression. This means that you go through two stages before you become aggressive. First, you become aroused and, second, you label the situation. Arousal, discussed in Chapter 8, refers to the physical changes that occur when a person becomes emotionally excited.

Psychologists have discovered that people who are aroused, no matter what the cause, are more likely to be aggressive than people who are not aroused. In one experiment, some students first listened to loud and unpleasant noises. This resulted in physical arousal. They were then insulted by someone. These students became more aggressive towards their attackers than did other students who were insulted but had not heard unpleasant noises.

Will you always become aggressive when you are aroused? The answer is "no." Whether or not you respond aggressively depends on how you **label** the situation. Just as companies put a label on a can to identify the kind of product inside, you put a label on a situation to identify what kind of situation it is.

If you decide that in a particular situation aggression is desirable or even expected, you will probably become aggressive. For example, in the case of the student who accidentally dropped the books, you were aroused but you labelled the situation as one that did not call for an aggressive reaction. The diagram below shows how arousal and labelling work to determine if people will become aggressive.

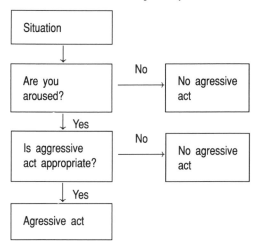

Flow-Chart Summary of Arousal
and Labelling Theory

Knowledge of arousal and labelling can help you to decide how to act in a given situation. To illustrate this, imagine that you want to discuss with your parents their curfew rules, which you think are unreasonable. As your mother comes in from work, you hear her say that she has had a terrible day. She got into a fight with one of her co-workers and the car broke down on the way home. There can be no doubt that she is already aroused!

Your questioning of the household rules at this point will only arouse her further. She may also label your questioning the curfew as a threat to her authority as your parent. In this situation, she may feel that it is necessary to act aggressively in defense of her position. The chances are very good that even if you are reasonable, you will end up in a heated argument. You would be wise to approach your parents later concerning the curfew.

From Ideas to Action

1. In which of the following situations would you expect aggression to occur? Why?

    a) Two strangers meet. Unexpectedly, one calls the other an "airhead" and other unflattering names.

    b) Your brother barges into your room to tell you about his successful job interview. In the process, he knocks the contents of a soft drink bottle all over your new cassette tape.

    c) You and five friends sneak to the front of a long line for a movie.

    d) A person repeatedly applies for jobs, only to find that each time another person with a better education has already been promised the position.

    e) A teenager discovers that the reason she did not get the job for which she was qualified was because the employer distrusts teenagers.

2. Role-play with a classmate a situation in which arousal and labelling act together to cause aggression. Try to re-create a situation you have experienced.

3. Taking into account all that you have learned about aggression, what would you do and/or say in each of the following circumstances?

    a) In a conversation with two friends, you hear about someone they know who has just been given a long prison term for badly beating someone. This person has had a long history of violent behaviour. Your friends ask you if you think the punishment was too harsh.

    b) Someone walks up to you in school and asks you to sign your name to a petition calling for an end to hockey in schools because of violence during the games.

    c) You plan to buy a Christmas present for your ten-year-old cousin. You know that he wants a toy rifle.

After the Violence: What About the Victims?

Until recently, social scientists, the police and the courts have been interested primarily in those people who act aggressively in our society, rather than in their victims. Recently, it has become clear that the victims of such violent acts as rape, robbery or physical assault suffer serious mental distress.

Some of the problems that victims face arise from something called the "Just World" theory, as discussed in Chapter 12. This theory states that most people believe that the world is a just and fair place, and that the good people are rewarded and bad people are punished. This creates difficulties for the victims of violent crimes. People may believe that the victim must have done something wrong to deserve the terrible thing that happened to them. Often, even the victims themselves assume that they must have done something to cause the violence. They feel guilty and sense that they cannot get help without being judged negatively by others. This is one reason why some violent crimes go unreported.

Other problems arise from the experience of being a helpless victim of crime. Most people are used to having some control over the events in their lives. During a crime, however, victims do not have any control. They are powerless and helpless when facing the aggressive person. Their lives may be at risk. If victims of a crime can act in some way, perhaps by shouting for help, they can regain some sense of control over their lives. However, most victims of crime suffer the frightening experience of loss of control and helplessness. These experiences can cause the victims to feel humiliated and worthless. Even if the aggressive act was a burglary, many victims of burglary report feeling personally violated by the intruder.

Stages Experienced by the Victim

Victims of violent crime often go through three different stages as they try to come to terms with their experiences.

Stage 1: The Impact Phase
This occurs hours or perhaps days after the crime. During this phase, the victims may lose their ability to function altogether. They experience both shock and confusion. They may be physically unable to report to the police or hospital staff what has happened to them.

Stage 2: The Outward Adjustment Phase
During this phase, victims try to regain control of their lives. Outwardly, they are functioning normally, going to work or to school and seem to be putting their lives back together. But often they replay the event over and over again in their minds, looking for an explanation for what has happened to them. They may arrive at the conclusion that it was all their fault. This self-blame can shatter the positive image that they had of themselves, and they may lose their trust in other people. Many victims of crime seek professional help at this point to discuss their feelings about being helpless to defend themselves against aggression.

Stage 3: The Resolution Phase
Eventually, victims try to see their violent experience in a realistic way. At best, they will see the event as an unfortunate occurrence, that should not be allowed to take over their lives. They will

try to move on to new experiences. Regardless of how successful victims are at this stage in coping with their feelings, they tend to carry within themselves an emotional scar.

What Can You Do for a Victim?

First of all, you should recognize that you are going to feel uncomfortable around someone who has been the victim of a violent crime. Society does not usually teach us how to react to other people's suffering due to a violent experience. Avoid trying to downplay the importance of the event. Saying that "things could be worse" will only cut off communication with the victim. From the victim's point of view, nothing could be worse.

Most of all, try to be supportive by listening rather than offering specific advice. Above all, avoid judging the victim. If he or she seems unable to cope, you may wish to suggest professional help.

Interpreting a Table — Level 2

The purpose of this exercise is to give you practice interpreting a table. Your objective is to learn how the main parts of a table provide information. If you have forgotten the main parts of a table, you may wish to review the first skills exercise on using tables (Chapter 13, p. 267).

Examine the table below and then answer the follow-up questions.

Effects of Crime on Women

	Had Nervous Breakdown	Thought Seriously of Suicide	Attempted Suicide
Non-victims	3.3%	6.8%	2.2%
Victims of:			
Attempted Rape	8.9%	29.1%	8.9%
Completed Rape	16.0%	44.0%	19.0%
Attempted Sexual Molestation	5.4%	32.4%	8.1%
Completed Sexual Molestation	1.8%	21.8%	3.6%
Attempted Robbery	0.0%	9.1%	12.1%
Completed Robbery	7.7%	10.8%	3.1%
Aggravated Assault	2.1%	14.9%	4.3%

1. Where can you find the purpose of this table? What is it?
2. In a sentence, explain what the first row in the table tells you.
3. In a sentence, explain what the third column of figures in the table tells you.
4. By comparing the information in row one with the information in rows two to eight, what general comparison between women victims and non-victims can you make?
5. Which type of crime had the greatest effect on women? Which had the least effect?
6. Use what you have learned about the stages experienced by victims to explain why crime might have these effects on women.

Adaptation of chart "The Effects of Crime on Women" from *Psychology Today*, Feb. 1986 p.48.

Problem: Focus on Child Abuse

• •

The articles on the following page should help you begin to ask some questions about the tragic problem of child abuse. As you finish reading each source, take a few moments to compile a list of questions on points that you are curious about, based on what you have read.

After you have read the material and compiled your list, compare your questions with those of other students. See if you can group your questions into different categories. Then narrow your list by selecting the two or three questions that you think are the most important. Make these the focus of your exploration of the problem.

Edmonton city police Det. Marion Smith holds up the rag dolls used to help children describe their experiences of sexual abuse.

What Is Child Abuse?

A common definition of an abused child is the one used by the Ontario Government. It states that an abused child (someone under the age of sixteen) is one who has been:

- **physically harmed** (external or internal bruises, burns, fractures, wounds, brain damage or poisoning)
- **sexually molested**
- **physically neglected** (failure to feed, house and clothe a child sufficiently to ensure healthy growth and development)
- **emotionally abused** (consistently telling a child that he or she is "no good," withholding the warmth and affection necessary for the normal growth and development of a child)

Causes of Child Abuse

Examine the following sources of information on the causes of child abuse. Which do you think provides the best explanation for this social problem? How do these sources relate to each other? Do they support or contradict each other?

307

Emotional abuse lacks recognition

By Suzanne Morrison, *The Spectator* (Hamilton)

Emotional abuse of children is a little-known and elusive issue but one of the most important problems social workers deal with, a child abuse expert said yesterday.

Heather Sproule, training co-ordinator at the Ontario Centre for the Prevention of Child Abuse, said the issue lacks research, a definition, and strategies for intervention.

She showed a film, entitled "Assault on the Psyche", which was designed to show how a middle class couple emotionally abuses their son and daughter.

In a living room scene, the father blows up at the son and calls him a dummy when the boy accidentally drops a bowl of peanuts the father is handing him.

At one point he tells him he wishes he'd never been born.

Later, the daughter talks about her nightmares and the confusion she feels when her parents say they both love and hate her.

Social workers said they were upset by the film because it was so true to life in many families today.

Ms. Sproule outlines five forms of emotional abuse, a term which professionals call psychological maltreatment:

- Rejection by refusing to recognize accomplishments, actively pushing a child away, expecting a child to accomplish things he/she can't, degradation (a child stands second in his/her class and parents ask why they weren't first), refusing to listen;
- terrorizing a child by intentionally suggesting the world is hostile and unsafe;
- ignoring a child by not showing him/her emotions;
- isolation (preventing children from participating in activities appropriate for their age);
- corruption around the areas of sexuality, aggression and substance abuse.

Ms. Sproule said emotional abuse results from a number of pressures on the family which can vary as widely as an intense preoccupation with upward mobility to poverty, social isolation and poor or crowded housing.

In these families she said there is a dominant/submissive pattern in the parents' relationship, marital discord, assault, and value conflicts.

As well, between the parent and child there are attachment problems, perinatal stress (unwanted or unplanned children, difficult delivery, separations during the perinatal period), scapegoating, role reversals, and generally poor parenting abilities.

The consequences of emotional abuse are very much the same as those for other forms of abuse, Ms. Sproule said.

Behaviour management and parent education isn't necessarily the right way to treat families where children are being emotionally abused, Ms. Sproule said.

More often parental depression is the problem and that's the issue that should be tackled, she said.

"We don't look at parental depression in these situations as often as we could."

(Reprinted with permission from the *Hamilton Spectator*.)

The Tragedy of Child Abuse

By Margo Roston *The Citizen* (Ottawa) (Saturday, February 2, 1985)

Laura is a bright, attractive 22-year-old woman, working in Ottawa as a nanny and leading an active social life.

Her cheerful smile makes it hard to believe she's spent the last year undergoing therapy for depression caused by sexual and emotional abuse.

The offender: Her stepfather.

Laura didn't want to use her real name. "My mother would know right away that it was me," she says, "and she has no idea my stepfather ever touched me."

But Laura will never forget it: The tickling, touching and fondling she grew to despise and fear. And the guilt that grew with the experiences.

"I don't remember too much before I was 11," she says, "but it took until I was 14 and bigger and stronger before I could make him stop."

Laura knows other people have suffered more aggressive sexual assault from trusted family members. But even what she went through led to bouts of depression, guilt and sexual problems.

"There are terrible scars," she says. "I went for counselling because I hadn't dealt with the guilt and I was easily intimidated by sexual situations. I had a tendency to flash back."

A surprising number of children in our community go through the type of abuse Laura suffered — and worse.

There was a 50 per cent increase last year over 1983 in the number of confirmed child abuse cases examined at the Children's Hospital of Eastern Ontario. A quarter of them involved sexual abuse, a 26 per cent increase over 1983.

In some cases children are tortured.

One can only imagine the horrible memories that will stay with three young children in the Cornwall area who were abused by their mother's 41-year-old boyfriend.

The man and his girlfriend were charged November 17. Before his sentencing November 18, the man pleaded guilty to two charges of aggravated assault and one count of assault causing bodily harm.

He was sentenced to six years in prison. The children are now under the care of the Children's Aid Society.

The Badgley report, *Sexual Offences Against Children,* released in August 1984 said half of all Canadian females and a third of all males are at some time victims of unwanted sexual acts, 80 per cent of which occur when the victims are children or youths.

The Children's Hospital of Eastern Ontario's year-end report showed 59 per cent of the reported sexual abuse cases involved children seven years of age or under.

In almost 93 per cent of the sexual abuse cases the abuser was known to the children and almost 94 per cent of the offenders were men. . .

"Within society today there's a tolerance for violence and there have been many changes in the family structure. Perhaps that's why we're seeing an increase

in sexual abuse," says Beth Allan, senior social worker of the Children's Protection Program at CHEO. "They are even using younger and younger kids in suggestive advertising."

She points to stress, new social values, isolation, multiple moves and the fact that there are few extended families in large communities as possible reasons for the consistent increase in reported child abuse cases in the past ten years.

However, Allan feels most of the increase in cases is due to more awareness of the problem. Officials don't seem to know just how much of the reported increase in cases represents an actual increase in child abuse.

CHEO's 50 per cent increase in child abuse cases in 1984 follows a 40 per cent increase in sexual and physical abuse cases the previous year.

Last year hospital officials saw 73 confirmed cases of sexual abuse and 122 cases of physical abuse. . .

Reports about child abuse originate [come] from teachers, neighbors, health practitioners, relatives, parents and others.

"The only source of evidence for sexual abuse is the child," says Pat Russell, senior social worker with the CAS.

"The emotional damage of sexual abuse is much more serious than for physical abuse. Someone in a position of trust has betrayed them. People will more readily admit to physical abuse than sexual abuse."

Ontario law requires everyone to report cases of suspected child abuse to the Children's Aid Society. The legislation imposes a $1000 fine on professionals, including teachers, doctors, social workers, dentists, clergymen and

child care workers who fail to report information relating to child abuse.

There was almost a 50 per cent increase in the number of abuse cases reported to the provincial register in 1984. The 1584 reports included 508 reports of physical abuse, 1064 of sexual abuse and 12 of emotional abuse. Eight of the children died from physical abuse. . .

Officials at the register say many cases of abuse are never discovered by authorities. They remain a family secret.

Allan of CHEO says most people who abuse their children report the abuse themselves.

"Most abusive parents are not ill," says Allan, "but suffering a reaction to stress and difficulties in their own personal relationships.

"Everyone can relate to those feelings. It's the low self-esteem most abusive parents have that leads to a state of crisis."

Many victims of abuse become abusers themselves.

Elizabeth Camden, who was herself beaten as a child, has a history of beating her son. When he was eight, she burned his hands with scalding water to teach him not to light fires. Then she called an ambulance and the Children's Aid Society.

Jean Francis from the Sexual Assault Support Centre, a volunteer self-help group in Ottawa, finds most incestuous relationships begin when girls are five to nine years of age. Some incest situations have continued for seven to 12 years.

Solutions to Child Abuse

Read the following article and make a chart that summarizes your findings. Use these headings in your chart: "Solutions," "Advantages" and "Disadvantages."

Therapy urged for child abusers

By Wendy Warburton, *Citizen*
staff writer

TORONTO — Parents who abuse their children often receive no help because there is no system to keep track of them, a Royal Ottawa Hospital child abuse expert said Wednesday.

Dr. John Dimock, director of the hospital's family court clinic, said abusive parents tend to be transient and frequently move from city to city.

Dimock told a legislative committee studying family violence a probationary system should be set up to make sure known or suspected abusers receive therapy.

He also called on police to lay more charges in child-abuse cases.

And he said the responsibility of Children's Aid Society (C.A.S.) Workers for removing children from their homes be turned over to a different group, and doctors be required to reveal confidential information about patients who abuse their children.

Dimock told the committee one of the biggest problems facing families and therapists is making sure abusive parents receive help.

In studying 167 child welfare cases, Dimock said his biggest problem has been keeping track of the families, especially if they move out of Ontario and away from the province's child-abuse registry (official record of child abusers).

Increasing the number of charges laid would help keep tabs on some abusers and ensure they are helped, Dimock said.

He called on the attorney-general's ministry to instruct Crown attorneys to lay more charges in child-abuse cases, similar to a directive [order] issued last year in wife-battering cases.

However, he said, laying more charges would not help in cases where abuse is not proved. Dimock said family court judges should be given the power to place high-risk parents on probation, requiring them to report for help.

Panels of objective professionals would assess each case, and determine what sort of help was required, he said.

Power to make sure the orders are obeyed should be given to specialized CAS workers, he said.

However, social workers who work with the family should not be expected to also act as policemen by removing the child from a dangerous situation, Dimock said.

He said that job should be done by other workers.

Dimock said social workers also lose time because family physicians are reluctant to give out information about abusive parents who are their patients, forcing the workers to find the information themselves.

He suggested laws protecting physician-patient confidentiality could be changed to require doctors to appear before the CAS to discuss such cases.

"I don't think family doctors would objeect if they felt the rights of the patient and child were being protected."

Questions Frequently Asked about Child Abuse

Q. What is child abuse?
A. Child abuse is any form of physical harm, emotional deprivation, neglect, or sexual maltreatment which can result in injury or psychological damage to a child. A child, according to Ontario law, is someone under 16 years of age or up to 18 years of age if the subject of an order under the *Child and Family Services Act*.

Q. How widespread is the problem?
A. It's impossible to say because we have statistics only for cases that are reported to the Ontario Child Abuse Register. The Register recorded over 2,200 cases of child abuse in 1986, including approximately 500 cases of physical abuse, 1,600 cases of sexual abuse and 25 cases of emotional abuse. These statistics do not reflect the true incidence of child abuse which is certainly much higher.

Q. Is child abuse increasing?
A. Although more cases are being reported to the Child Abuse Register, this may be the result of more people reporting suspected abuse rather than an actual increase in cases.

Q. Is child abuse usually a one-time happening?
A. Physical child abuse may be, if a normally patient caregiver is pushed beyond self-control by special circumstance or crisis. Unfortunately, most child abuse reflects a pattern of behaviour,

and is usually repeated until it is detected and stopped.

Q. Are sexual offenders usually strangers?

A. Up to 80 per cent of sexual abuse victims know their abuser, who is often a member of the family or a trusted friend.

Q. Are boys more likely than girls to be abused?

A. In physical abuse, boys and girls are equally likely to be abused until age 13. After 13, more girls are victims. In sexual abuse, more than twice as many girls as boys are abused.

Q. Do children lie about sexual abuse?

A. Rarely. False denials of sexual abuse are much more common than false reports.

Q. What should I do if I suspect a child is being abused?

A. Report your suspicions to your nearest children's aid society, which may also be called family and children's services. Under the provisions of the *Child and Family Services Act*, you are legally required to report if you believe that a child is or may be in need of protection.

Q. Will I have to give my name?

A. Not necessarily. You may report suspected child abuse and remain anonymous. However, your information is much more valuable if you *can* co-operate fully with police and/or chldren's aid workers and help them determine if abuse has occurred.

From *Child Abuse Prevention*, Ontario Ministry of Community and Social Services, 1987. Reprinted by permission of the Institute for the Prevention of Child Abuse.

Interpreting a Table — Level 3

To be able to use statistical tables effectively, we have to be able to identify different kinds of trends and think about what these trends might mean. A **trend** is a pattern that occurs in a series of statistics, for example, a series of numbers that increases, decreases, or remains relatively unchanged or constant.

Age Group of Abused Child and Relationship of Offender, 1970–77

| Relationship to Child | Age Group of the Abused Children | | | | | |
	0–2	3–5	6–12	13+	Total	%
Both Parents	185	90	63	44	382	7.6
Mother	478	433	658	204	1683	33.5
Father	269	246	597	576	1688	33.5
Substitute Father	113	142	219	143	617	12.3
% of total	24	21	33	22	100	

You can see a trend in a table by examining all or most of the information at one time, by looking at only one row or column at a time or by comparing the information in rows or columns. You can also make **inferences** (that is, draw conclusions) from these facts.

Find the trends and make inferences from the table above by answering the following questions:

1. What general trend do you see with regard to whether children are usually abused by both parents or just one parent?

2. Look at the bottom row. Which age group is abused the most?

3. Look at column two. Which parent is more likely to abuse a child aged 0–2 years?

4. What other trends can you see in this table?

Projects, Activities and Explorations

1. Make a "Family Violence Self-Help Kit." Explore all the agencies that provide help in cases of family violence. The telephone book or your school guidance office are good places to begin your search. Collect telephone numbers and addresses for the agencies that you find. Call each, explain what you are doing, and ask if you can come to their office to pick up pamphlets or other printed material. If possible, try to arrange to speak to someone at the agency about the services they offer. Once you have collected all your infomation, arrange it neatly in a folder. You might offer to leave your kit in the guidance office so that students who are in family-violence situations can benefit from your work. Here is a list of some places you might contact:

   a) ambulance services b) Children's Aid Society c) second-hand clothing and furniture stores d) counselling services e) employment services f) welfare agencies g) hospitals h) income-assisted housing agencies i) Parents Anonymous Groups j) Legal Aid offices k) police l) employment retraining agencies m) singles groups n) special treatment centres o) transition homes (shelters for battered women) p) Y.M./Y.W.C.A.

2. Cut and paste pictures, newspaper headlines and articles onto a large piece of bristol board to create a collage. Some possible themes for your collage might be:

   a) Why I think violence happens b) A world without aggression c) Human and animal aggression: Is there a difference? d) Preventing wife battering/child abuse e) Things I would teach my children about aggressive behaviour f) Dealing with wife battering/child abuse g) Sports violence and a violent society

3. With the help of your teacher, organize a panel discussion. Invite a member of the police, the Children's Aid Society, a school board social worker, and someone who works at a battered women's shelter to discuss the issue of family violence and how society ought to deal with it.

   Before the panel discussion, it is important to prepare some questions to ask your guests. These can be presented until the audience (your class or the school) feels comfortable enough to ask questions of their own.

   An alternative would be to visit each of these people separately, and to record their responses to your prepared questions. The most important parts of your taped interview could then be played to the class and discussed.

4. Some cultures such as the Amish and the Hutterites have very little incidence of aggression and violence. Read about their lifestyles and try to explain why they have less aggression compared to our society.

5. Design and administer a survey that looks at the practices and attitudes of high school students towards the disciplining of children. Or, do a survey on attitudes towards child abuse or wife battering. Remember to pre-test your survey before you hand it to a large group of people.

6. Start clipping articles, pictures and program descriptions from TV guides that involve aggression. Examine your "media log" to see if there are any patterns or trends in the way the media deals with aggressive topics.

7. Scan the inventories of some local toy stores. Classify the toys in the store as aggressive, prosocial or neutral. After you have done your inventory, talk to the store owner about the most popular toys for boys and girls, and how the store decides what toys to put on the shelves. You might ask the owners for their views on aggressive toys.

8. Review a wide sample of fairy tales, nursery rhymes, and other children's literature. Determine the degree to which these sources are aggressive in their content.

What Have You Learned?

If you have covered everything in this chapter, you should be familiar with the following topics:

1. The different meanings of aggression
2. The theories that try to explain why human beings are aggressive (Instinctive Theory of Aggression, Social Learning Theory of Aggression)
3. How each theory views the possibility of controlling aggression
4. The factors influencing whether people behave aggressively (frustration, arousal and labelling)

5. The effects of violence on victims
7. Child abuse
8. More information on how to determine facts, opinions and arguments
9. More information on how to interpret the information contained in tables

To Help You Study

The following chart will help you to review the words, facts and ideas introduced in this chapter. Copy the chart into your notebook and fill in the missing information.

Word, Fact, Idea	Example in a Sentence	Page	Definition
aggression	I don't like to watch aggression on TV because people are shown being hurt and killed.	296	behaviour intended to harm others physically or emotionally
Instinctive Theory of Aggression			
Social Learning Theory of Aggression			
Frustration Theory of Aggression			
Arousal and Labelling Theory of Aggresion			
impact phase			
outward adjustment phase			
resolution phase			

Issues in Culture — Prejudice

Choose a Tenant For Your House

Suppose one of your parents has been assigned a job in a foreign country for a year. This raises the problem of what to do with your house. Your parents decide to rent it to a tenant for the year. They place an advertisement in the local newspaper and receive six applications. They ask you to read the applications and to give your opinion as to who should rent the house.

Carefully read the following summaries of the six applications. Decide to whom you would rent the house, and why. Also, consider the reasons why you would reject the other applicants.

HOUSE FOR RENT
IDEAL TENANTS WANTED
APPLY WITHIN

Application #1
This application was submitted by a native Indian, his wife and two school-aged children. He wishes to move into your area, where he has recently taken up employment with an electrical firm as an electrician. He previously worked in Hobbema, Alberta, and had worked as an electrician in Wetaskiwin for eight years. His wife has also found employment as a checkout clerk in your neighbourhood food store.

Application #2
This application was submitted by four young women. They are all new Canadians. Two of them arrived recently from the Philippines and are employed as nurses in a nearby hospital. One is a lab technician, having arrived in Canada several years ago from Taiwan. The fourth member of the group is from Jamaica and is a daycare supervisor.

Application #3
This application came from a woman in her mid-thirties who is divorced and has three children ranging in age from four to sixteen. She is also expecting a fourth child. She is a welfare recipient; however, the agency has approved the amount of rent involved.

Application #4
This application comes from three single men in their mid-twenties. Their occupations were listed as bartender, waiter and taxi-driver.

Application #5
This application comes from another new Canadian who originally came from India. He is a well-known surgeon. His family consists of his parents, a wife and one small child.

Application #6
This application was submitted by a third generation Canadian of English ancestry. He was recently promoted to the position of manager of a neighbourhood branch bank. His family includes his wife and seven children, ranging in age from two to thirteen years. They also have two large dogs.

Consider individually your answers to the following questions, and what they reveal about your own prejudices:

1. Which applicant(s) did you choose? Why?
2. Which applicant(s) did you reject? Why?
3. What factors influenced your decisions?

What Is Prejudice?

The activity on the previous page was designed to make you think about how we tend to judge people in advance, often without any direct contact with these people. Forming pre-judgments in this way is called **prejudice**. Prejudice has been defined as a feeling, favourable or unfavourable, toward a person or thing, prior to, or not based on, actual experience.

For instance, let's assume that you are about to start school in September. You have to repeat mathematics because you failed it last year. You and the math teacher did not get along very well. You look at your timetable and notice the name of a new math teacher. You think, "Mr. Smith... he's new this year... Oh well, he's a math teacher. They're all alike: boring, and picky." You have lumped Mr. Smith into your preconceived category of "math teachers." You are assuming that all math teachers, including Mr. Smith, have certain negative qualities. You have already formed a negative opinion of Mr. Smith, even though you have never met him. In other words, you are prejudiced against him.

In prejudiced thinking, a person refuses to revise opinions, even when new experience or facts disprove those opinions. For example, suppose that when you arrive at Mr. Smith's class, he greets you warmly. In class, he has the students play a mathematics game instead of doing exercises from the textbook. You leave the classroom thinking that Mr. Smith is quite different from your previous teacher, and that you might enjoy the course after all. You are

no longer prejudiced towards this man. However, suppose you think, "He's just conning us into liking him and his dumb math course. He's really no different from the rest!" You are refusing to alter your pre-judgment, despite new and contradictory information. You are clinging to a prejudice.

We can be either negatively or positively prejudiced towards people or things. In the case above, you are obviously negatively prejudiced towards Mr. Smith. If your pre-judgment favours someone or something, you are positively prejudiced. Buying your favourite singer's new album without listening to it first shows a positive prejudice towards the singer.

Whether a prejudice is positive or negative, it is always a way of looking at the world that limits or distorts reality. Instead of judging each case on its own merits, we are led by prejudice to hasty conclusions. When prejudice leads to slotting people into pre-defined categories, it can be harmful. This chapter will explore the origins and the effects of prejudice.

From Ideas to Action

1. Decide whether each of the following situations involves prejudice. Be prepared to defend your decisions in a class discussion.

   a) A restaurant owner interviewed several high school students for a waiter's position. Finally, the owner chose a tall, striking, blond-haired boy who had good references and good marks in school. Two of the five applicants were black. They complained to their guidance counsellor that they had been victims of the owner's prejudice against blacks.

   b) Hakam: Women are terrible drivers.
      Bill: But statistics show that women drivers have far fewer accidents than men do.
      Hakam: That's because they *cause* accidents, but they actually avoid accidents themselves.
      Bill: How do you know that?
      Hakam: Well, yesterday a woman cut me off. I slammed on my brakes and it nearly caused a "box car" collision. The woman just drove away as though nothing had happened.

   c) A landlord was having a dispute with one of his tenants, a recent immigrant to Canada from Lebanon. The landlord was threatening to evict the tenant. The tenant insisted that the landlord simply wanted to get rid of the building's Lebanese tenants for no good reason. The landlord replied, "That's not true. You had a party last week and ruined the rugs in the apartment. And I've collected three bad cheques from you since you moved in."

   d) A manager was about to interview applicants for a sales position with the assistant manager's help. Before they began, they both read over all the application forms. Suddenly the manager said, "Oh, I see this one went to Grier High School. That's my old school, you know. Turns out fine young people. Let's hire him."

2. In those cases above that you believe involve prejudice, how would a non-prejudiced person have behaved?

3. a) Describe a group in your school or neighbourhood that you do not associate with. Did you choose not to associate with this group? Did the group exclude you?

   b) Describe any characteristics that make you different from the group that you identified.

   c) Do you have positive, negative or neutral feelings towards this group?

   d) To what extent might prejudice play a role in your non-involvement with this particular group?

317

Stereotypes

A stereotype is an exaggerated belief associated with a category.

Prejudice and Stereotyping

Prejudice often has its roots in stereotyped thinking. When you hear someone begin a sentence with "All women want..." or "All teenagers are...", you are probably about to hear a stereotype. As you learned in Chapter 5, a stereotype exists when an individual is judged on the basis of exaggerated and distorted characteristics assumed to be common to his or her group. In other words, the individual's unique characteristics are ignored when stereotyping occurs. All members of a group are falsely assumed to be alike, and exceptions are ignored or their existence denied.

The common responses in the previous matching activity resulted from stereotyped thinking. We all seem prone to summon a ready-made description for almost any ethnic or professional group. This makes it difficult for members of these groups to be seen as individuals. They are sometimes rejected as friends or co-workers without being given a chance to demonstrate their individual, personal qualities.

The Origins of Stereotypes

Why do we create stereotypes? One explanation involves the way the mind works to help you cope with a complex world. The mind is always looking for ways to organize incoming information into categories of similar experience. This makes decision-making easier. When new people are encountered, the mind finds it simpler to fit these people into an already existing mental category. It does this rather than open a new "file" for every new person. In short, we are often misled by our need to make a very complicated world a little simpler to deal with.

Sometimes stereotypes arise from a single unpleasant experience. Suppose a person is cheated by someone who happens to belong to a certain ethnic group. The wronged person may angrily assume that all people in that ethnic group are cheats and cannot be trusted.

Once a stereotype has been created, it is often difficult to eliminate it from one's thinking. This happens because we tend to see what we *expect* to see. For example, if one stereotypes all students as noisy and irresponsible, one is more likely to notice only those students who are loud or obviously irresponsible. This tends to reinforce a stereotype.

There might be no awareness of some students who are behaving calmly and responsibly. Or, there might be an assumption that these people who contra- dict the stereotype are not students, or that they are simply an exception to the rule.

From Ideas to Action

1. Decide whether stereotypes are involved in each of the following situations:

   a) Mr. Lester sighed. It was the first day of school. Seated in front of him were the students in his new history class. Almost all of them were wearing black leather jackets. He thought, "What a crew! And I was hoping to have a pleasant year!"

   b) The store owner moved quietly towards Michelle, one of the sales clerks. He whispered, "Get over to the record department. There's a teenager who's been browsing just a little too long. You've got to watch them. They'll rob you blind".

   c) Late one Saturday night, a police constable saw a car he thought had been reported as stolen. He gave chase and pulled the car over. The three boys in the car were furious. The driver complained, "The only reason you're hassling us is because we're teenagers."

   d) A high school principal and a department head were discussing an applicant for a teaching position.

   "From his resumé," commented the principal, "I see he's from the East End. You have to be wary of these people. They're loud and pushy and often don't respect authority. I don't think we want to take a chance on him."

2. Write down a list of characteristics, such as active, calm, hardworking, adventurous, aggressive, considerate, assertive, well-mannered, energetic, etc. Show this list to a sample of students in your school. Ask them to label each of the characteristics as either male, female or both. Do the responses reflect any sexual stereotyping? You might compare the students' responses with those of a group of adults.

3. a) Suppose you are about to be married, and are drawing up a marriage contract with your partner. Design a contract that assigns specific household duties and responsibilities to each partner.

   b) Compare your contract with those designed by some of your classmates. Do the contracts show any evidence of male and female stereotypes common in our society?

Ethnocentrism

Each of the following maps is used to represent the world to students in three different countries. Look at the maps closely and compare them.

The World Viewed from North America

The World Viewed from the Soviet Union

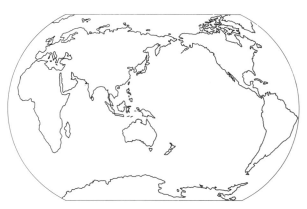

The World Viewed from China

As a class or in groups, discuss the following questions:
1. How do the three maps compare?
2. How do you account for your observations in question 1?
3. What would students learn from these maps?
4. Why do we tend to measure other human beings in terms of our own culture and experience? Is this a desirable tendency? What effects can this have?

Another reason that prejudice exists is related to the way we view our culture in relation to other cultures. We tend to judge how other people think and behave in terms of what we consider normal in our way of life. We also tend to consider anything that differs from our culture to be somehow inferior.

The attitude that one's culture is superior and that other cultures are inferior by comparison is called **ethnocentrism**. The term "ethno" comes from the same Greek root as the word "ethnic." "Centrism" is related to the word "centre." Therefore, ethnocentric thinking involves thinking that one's culture is at the centre of things. One particular culture becomes a standard against which all other cultures are compared.

Often people think in ethnocentric ways because they have had little or no experience with people of other cultures. This prevents them from appreciating that there are other, equally valid ways of dressing, eating, worshipping one's god, etc. However, contact with or knowledge of other groups might alter an ethnocentric person's sense of superiority. He or she might learn through direct experience that different beliefs, foods, clothing styles, etc., are not necessarily inferior.

However, some people are unwilling or unable to recognize that ways of life that differ from their own are just as valid and worthy of respect. This prevents them from seeing the common conditions and problems facing humanity. This blindness can be harmful for both the person who insists on feeling superior, as well as for the people who have been classed as inferior.

. . . .

From Ideas to Action

1. This team activity highlights the concept of ethnocentrism. On slips of paper, write down some common activities in our culture, such as playing football, dating, going to the dentist, etc. Place the slips of paper in a hat. The class is divided into two teams. Members of each team take turns drawing slips of paper out of the hat, and describing the activity selected. The challenge is to describe the activity *from the perspective of someone from an entirely different culture*. Each team must try to guess the activity being described by their opponents.

 ## An Experiment in "Boxed-in Thinking"

In a study of prejudice, a psychologist persuaded a teacher to let a substitute take over his class for awhile. Just before the substitute arrived, the psychologist handed all the students written descriptions of the new teacher.

The descriptions the students received were not all the same. For half the students, the substitute was described as "a rather warm person, hardworking, critical, practical, determined."

For the other half of the students, the substitute was described as "a rather cold person, hardworking, critical, practical, determined."

As expected, the two groups of students reacted differently when the substitute arrived and began to teach. During the lesson, the group that had received the description of a "warm" person were very active in discussions. The students who had been told the teacher was "cold" did not participate actively in the lesson.

Later, all the students were asked to write a profile of the substitute. The students who had been active during the class described the substitute in terms of characteristics often seen in "warm" people. The students who had not actively participated described the teacher in terms of characteristics often associated with "cold" personalities.

What accounts for the difference in how the students viewed the substitute? How does this experiment illustrate the process of prejudiced thinking?

Discrimination

In small groups, carefully examine each picture below. Rank the pictures in terms of increasing degree of harm to the victim (most harm = 1, least harm = 5).

As a class or in groups, compare your rankings and explain your choices. Then discuss the following questions:

1. Can you suggest examples of actions similar to the ones shown in the pictures?

2. What kinds of actions shown in the pictures are most common in our society? Why?

3. What might cause people to act upon their prejudices, instead of simply keeping their opinions to themselves?

4. Suppose you actually witness each of the events shown in the pictures. What, if anything, *could* you do? What *would* you do?

Acting Out Our Prejudices

One person assumes that all people who wear black leather jackets belong to motorcycle gangs. Another person believes that only heavy metal music is worth listening to. These are prejudices: harmless, misinformed ideas. However, there is a great difference between misinformed thinking and *doing* something based on misinformed thinking.

For example, suppose you are an employer with a negative prejudice towards people who wear black leather jackets. You might refuse to hire an applicant wearing a black leather jacket, regardless of the person's ability to do the job. If you were prejudiced in favour of heavy metal music, you would probably turn down an invitation to a classical music concert. In both cases, you would have acted upon your prejudices. Action based on prejudice is called **discrimination**. Some forms of discrimination can cause a great deal of damage. For instance, in the first case mentioned above, someone would be denied a job because of a senseless prejudice involving an article of clothing.

Levels of Discrimination

There is a hierarchy of discrimination. These levels of discrimination are marked by increasing intensity, as well as by increasing potential harm to victims. In *The Nature of Prejudice*, Gordon Allport analyses the behaviours associated with each level of discrimination:

1. **Antilocution** (talking about the victim in unflattering terms). At this least intense level of discrimination, people freely discuss their negative feelings towards a certain group of people.

2. **Avoidance**. At this level of discrimination, the negative feelings are more intense and the prejudiced person may choose to avoid the target of the prejudice. This does not directly harm the victim.

E

323

3. **Political, Social and Economic Discrimination**. At this level the bearer of the prejudice acts out openly against the victim. Victims may be refused employment or membership in certain organizations. They may lose their right to vote or to own property. They may be forced to live in certain areas or to send their children to separate (segregated) schools.

4. **Physical Attack**. When prejudice becomes highly intense and emotional, direct or indirect violence can result. Victims may be threatened or assaulted. They may have their homes or businesses vandalized.

5. **Extermination**. At this most harmful level of discrimination, prejudice is so intense that the victims are seen as less than human. They become the targets of murder, and perhaps even mass extermination.

Allport points out that most people never go beyond the level of talking about the targets of their prejudices. They may not necessarily avoid the group they don't like. Other prejudiced people might refuse a job to a member of a certain group, but they would be shocked at the suggestion that members of that group should be attacked or killed.

However, Allport also states that discrimination at one level seems to make it easier to progress to the next level. For example, Adolf Hitler's outspoken hatred for the Jews in Germany led some Germans to avoid their Jewish neighbours and friends. This increased the likelihood that people would support laws restricting the freedom of Jews. The introduction of these laws seemed to justify physical attacks against Jews and their places of worship. Finally, these attacks escalated into the establishment of death camps and a plan to exterminate the Jews altogether.

From Ideas to Action

1. Which of the following situations involve discrimination and which do not? In each case, briefly explain your answer.
   a) Ted had always disliked immigrants. He thought that they took away jobs needed by Canadians.
   b) Ms. Franklin's father was killed in Hong Kong when the Japanese invaded the city during World War II. Now that she has her own business, she has never hired a person who looked in the least Oriental.
   c) Sam owned a small barber shop in town. One day a black teenager asked for a haircut. The other customers glared at Sam. The barber nervously and quietly told the boy that while he would be happy to cut his hair, he would lose a lot of customers if he did. He suggested that if the boy returned near closing time, he would cut his hair.
   d) Two East Indian families had their garbage thrown all over the street almost every week. They had called the police, who said there was little that could be done.

2. What level of discrimination is involved in each of the following situations:
   a) "I'd never live beside one of those people!" said Mr. Johnson to a few close friends at a party.
   b) The tiny country of Spotsvania experienced a political revolution.

Within weeks, the members of a small religious group were arrested. No one ever saw them again.
   c) As she walked down the street, a woman was approached by a group of people singing religious songs and passing out pamphlets. The woman quickly crossed to the other side of the street.
   d) A sign in the window of the restaurant read "Help Wanted." In small print were the words: "No Blacks Need Apply."
   e) A rabbi discovered that during the night someone had painted swastikas all over the walls of the synagogue.
   f) A gang of students cornered Rajid and started pushing him against a locker while calling him names.

3. a) In your view, what role could each of the following play in reducing discrimination in Canada?
   i) police ii) schools iii) churches iv) minority organizations v) government vi) courts vii) employers viii) the media (television, radio, magazines, etc.) ix) you

   b) Order the items listed in a) above according to how effective they could be in reducing discrimination (1 = most effective, 2 = next most effective, etc.). Be prepared to justify how you rank each item.

Causes of Prejudice

Why Are These People Prejudiced?

Read the following fictional cases and see if you can figure out why the "subjects" quoted might be prejudiced.

Case A: "I've always wanted to start my own restaurant business. But what chance do I have with all these Emwatta* restaurants everywhere? I can never seem to get enough money or friends together to help me open my business. Meanwhile the Emwattas are opening their lousy food joints every place you look. It just isn't fair!"

Case B: "We're a lot better than those Emwattas. They are low-class dirt, right guys? Maybe if they had some harsh discipline like I had at home they might learn something. My dad says they are lazy, stupid and untrustworthy. Boy, am I ever glad that we're not Emwattas."

Case C: "Sure, I only pay these Emwattas the minimum wage. Why shouldn't I? That's the reason I have the most profitable business in town. It's a dog-eat-dog world. Besides, Emwattas are too lazy and slow to have really good-paying jobs."

* Note: Emwattas are a fictional group of people.

Now as a class or in small groups, share your answers and discuss the following questions.

1. What factors might influence a person to be prejudiced?
2. Can you think of real situations in Canada, or elsewhere, that involve prejudice arising from causes similar to those in the cases above?
3. What could be done to ensure that certain personal goals, problems or desires do not lead to prejudice?

Why Does Prejudice Exist?

The Learned Prejudice Theory
According to this theory, prejudice and the willingness to discriminate are attitudes that are learned. The learning of prejudice begins in early childhood. Prejudiced parents may prevent their children from associating with groups that are viewed as inferior. The children aren't allowed to have positive experiences with these groups and they hear only one (negative) opinion, that of their parents. Other environmental influences such as television, books, friends, etc. can also contribute to teaching children prejudice.

The Frustration-Aggression Theory
Life can be frustrating. We all experience times when we are prevented from accomplishing our goals. If frustration continues for years, people search for explanations for their difficulties. Some people begin to blame others for their personal frustration and become aggressive towards them. They often target a particular group as the source of their frustration. This leads to the formation of prejudices and to discrimination.

Suppose a student wants very much to attend a certain college, but again and again fails to make the minimum grade

These fishing boats were confiscated from Japanese-Canadians by the Canadian government during 1942. Over 40 years later, the Canadian government agreed to compensate Japanese-Canadians for the property it had confiscated during the war.

required for acceptance into the school. Discouraged and frustrated, the student becomes resentful of the many Chinese students who are scoring high marks and being admitted into the college. He decides that he will never get into the college because the Chinese students are filling all the places.

The Chinese students become a convenient target. The unsuccessful student can relieve his feelings of frustration and inadequacy by blaming them. The Chinese are completely innocent of robbing any Canadian of a place in the college. However, they are a visible minority and therefore, they make easy victims of discrimination for people frustrated in their goals.

The Competition Theory

People in our society openly compete for jobs and other scarce resources. To give themselves a competitive edge, a dominant group may try to exploit (take advantage of) another, less powerful group in order to control these resources. To justify this desire to exploit another group, the dominant group may choose to see the group they are exploiting as inferior. This opens the door to prejudice and discrimination.

The treatment of blacks in countries such as South Africa illustrates the competition theory of discrimination. The great majority of South Africa's inhabitants are black. Yet the government and large businesses are all controlled by a white minority. The blacks are used

327

as cheap labour in mines and factories, and have few rights. If blacks had equal rights, they could compete for better jobs and for positions in government. This would threaten the power of South African whites, who are greatly outnumbered by the blacks.

To keep their advantageous position, many South African whites have developed prejudices towards black Africans. They argue that blacks are incapable of running a country responsibly and efficiently. The minority rulers insist that whites, better educated and more experienced, must therefore do the job for the blacks. The education system discriminates against black Africans, so that it is very difficult for blacks to receive a good education.

This attitude on the part of whites seemed to justify the passage of laws that prevented blacks from voting, denied them access to certain kinds of education and barred them from all-white neighbourhoods. These laws have, of course, increased the distance between blacks and whites. Like a vicious circle, this has, in turn led to deeper feelings of prejudice and harsher forms of discrimination.

• •

From Ideas to Action

1. Which theory of prejudice would you associate with each statement below? (Each statement may be matched with more than one theory.)
   a) "Spare the rod and spoil the child."
   b) "Senior students get to date the best-looking people in the school."
   c) "If you give immigrants jobs, they take all the good ones that we unemployed Canadians need. There should be laws prohibiting immigration."
   d) "I've warned you to stay away from those children. They're from another country. Who knows what diseases you might pick up?"

2. Which theory or theories do you think best explain(s) the following historical events?
   a) Between 1882 and 1930, the number of lynchings (hangings without a trial) of southern American blacks in any one year could be predicted on the basis of the price of cotton during that year. Cotton was the biggest money-making crop in the southern United States during that era.
   b) Low-paid Chinese workers were imported to help build the Canadian Pacific Railway. When the railway was finished in 1885, the Chinese had to search hard for work. They often took back-breaking jobs for little pay. An "anti-Asiatic" feeling developed in Canada, particularly in British Columbia. Unions across the country demanded laws to prevent employers from hiring cheap Chinese labour.

3. Research the victimization of the Jews in Germany during the rise of Adolf Hitler and the Nazis. Find out whether the theories of prejudice that you have learned about can be applied to the treatment of the Jews. Read especially about economic and political conditions in Germany between 1914 and 1932. Also, research the early life of Adolf Hitler, to try to find some explanation for his personal hatred of the Jews.

Prejudice in Sports

Many sports are dominated by black athletes: however, there are few blacks in positions of leadership or management. There are only a handful of black quarterbacks in the National Football League, and major league baseball has almost exclusively white managers and team executives. In 1987, Ted Koppel of ABC TV's "Nightline" (and millions of viewers) were shocked to hear Al Campanis, an executive with the Los Angeles Dodgers, state that blacks do not have "the necessary qualities" to become executives in major league sports. When Mr. Koppel asked Mr. Campanis to elaborate further on his views, Mr. Campanis went on to say that whereas black people have many physical attributes, they do not have the ability to lead or manage. Two days later, the Los Angeles Dodgers fired Mr. Campanis from his position.

The Effects of Prejudice

How Do the Victims of Prejudice Feel?

Carefully examine the fictitious statements below. These people are victims of prejudice and discrimination. For each one, try to figure out what they might be feeling and why.

- "My name is Dan Monroe. Our name use to be Mirvolcheski, but I would rather not think of the past. Today I am just a Canadian."
- "They are all out to get us. There isn't a good one among them."
- "We keep to ourselves. We live in our own area, and go to our own clubs. That's the best way. Then there is no chance for problems to start."
- "Why did I have to be born an Emwatta? Everyone knows we are no good."
- "We just have to work twice as hard to prove ourselves. As our success in society shows, we are worthwhile people."
- We need to help the Emwattas. They don't deserve to be mistreated. My family suffered from prejudice too. I know what it is like to feel alone."

Now as a class or in small groups, discuss your views and answer the following questions.

1. How does each person above seem to be dealing with the fact that they are the victims of prejudice?
2. Have you ever seen victims of prejudice reacting in these ways? Explain.
3. Do any problems arise from these reactions to prejudice? If so, what are they?

How Victims React to Prejudice

Suppose you were always told by others that you were stupid, lazy, dirty or untrustworthy. In time, this would have some effect on your personality. For the sake of self-protection, you would alter the way that you saw yourself and the way you dealt with the world. Here are some ways in which victims react to prejudice and discrimination.

Obsessive Concern

When someone is "obsessive," he or she is constantly preoccupied by certain thoughts. The constant victim of prejudice and discrimination may become obsessed with the idea that he or she is being discriminated against, and begin to see discrimination and hatred in any actions of people outside his or her group. In other words, victims sometimes develop a "chip on their shoulder" and, because of past experiences, come to expect that everyone will treat them badly. This tends to make them hostile even towards people who are not prejudiced.

Denial of Membership

For people who have no obvious traits that would associate them with a particular group, this is a common form of self-protection. A person from Poland may start to tell "Polish jokes" in an effort to seem like a member of the majority group, and to avoid being discriminated against. Blacks who straighten their hair may also be denying membership in their racial group. This tactic requires a person to betray his or her own group, which can be very uncomfortable.

Withdrawal

Instead of reacting aggressively to insults or harsh treatment, many victims decide that it is easier to appear unaffected by the attacks. They seem to passively accept their lot in life. This may give the attackers the impression that the victims are satisfied with the way things are, when the opposite is true.

Strengthening Ties with Other Victims

Often, victims of prejudice react by shutting out the groups that oppress them and associating only with members of their own group. They may live together in the same neighbourhood, thereby reducing contact with other groups. This may lessen the number of times that they are treated as victims. However, it may also increase their persecution, since attackers often fear or mistrust obviously separate groups.

Self-Hate

In a withdrawal response, the victim only appears to agree with the negative image that an attacker has formed of the victim's group. In a self-hate response, the victim actually believes that the group they belong to is inferior. They may come to despise and be ashamed of the accident of birth that has made them a member of a particular group.

Prejudice (or Sympathy) Towards Other Groups Who Are Victims

One key point is that victims of prejudice often display high degrees of prejudice towards other minority groups. This is the result of the frustration and anger they feel as victims. Unable to strike out at the attacker, victims may choose to attack other, less powerful groups.

The reverse may also occur, however, because they see other minorities in much the same way as they see themselves. They therefore sympathize with other victims. In this case, the victim of prejudice is more likely to try to help other victims, and to have fewer personal prejudices towards them than does the general population.

Enhanced Striving

"If you can't join 'em, beat 'em at their own game." Striving hard to achieve something is a common competitive reaction seen in victims of prejudice and discrimination. Instead of withdrawing, some victims double their efforts to do well in the society that oppresses them. They study or work harder.

As a result, they are more likely to enter professions or to make their businesses profitable. Their success may win them the grudging respect of their attackers. It may also increase their own self-respect, by proving to themselves that they are not the failures their attackers say they are.

However, attackers may feel threatened by the victims' success. They may decide that these supposedly inferior people "try too hard" or that they must cheat to be so successful. So, enhanced striving can have a "backlash" effect on the victim.

Costs to the Attacker

Prejudice and discrimination do not benefit the attacker either. As you have learned, attackers often experience high levels of personal frustration and insecurity. Prejudice and discrimination become ways of shifting the angry or bad feelings they have towards themselves onto safer target(s): "inferior" victims. It is always easier and less painful to blame someone other than themselves.

However, this is a self-defeating strategy. The attackers never come to grips with the real sources of their negative feelings about themselves. Some psychologists believe that, to some degree, the attacker suffers guilt about hating and/or harming an innocent group. This tends to make an already insecure person feel even more insecure. In any event, the failure to look for the real cause of their personal problems can rob attackers of the chance to develop healthier self-images.

From Ideas to Action

1. You have studied seven different ways in which victims react to prejudice and discrimination. Consider the following situations. In each case, identify the victim's reaction.

   a) On average, Risha son spent five hours a night on her high school studies in order to get into the best university possible. Once enrolled, she worked even harder to achieve the marks necessary to get into dental school.

   b) Ravinder, a Sikh, was required to wear a turban to cover his hair, which he was not supposed to cut. This was a tradition in his religion. He was constantly made fun of by the other boys in school. One day, to his parents' horror, he came home without his turban and with a short haircut. He announced that he had had enough jokes and slurs. He said he just wanted to look like other Canadians.

   c) Yuri was a recent immigrant from Russia. He did not find it easy to get or to keep a job, since he did not speak English well. He heard that a group of Central American immigrants were going to march in Ottawa in protest against the tightening of immigration laws. He phoned and offered to help organize the rally.

   d) While visiting a town in the United States, Tina was shocked to see whites calling blacks names in public. What she found even more surprising was that the blacks showed no apparent reaction to the verbal attacks. They just ignored the whites and kept walking.

e) Fearing discrimination, many ethnic groups in Canada and the United States in the early 1900s founded cultural organizations. These groups organized festivities to keep traditional dancing, food and other customs alive. These organizations also served as social clubs for lonely immigrants.

f) Tony's parents were Italian immigrants. At school he was constantly called names and some students half-believed that his father was a member of the Mafia. One day Tony was stopped by a sales clerk in a store and asked if he needed any help. Tony replied angrily, "I suppose that just because I'm Italian, you think I'm going to rob you!" The clerk was stunned.

2. In small groups, try to role-play the following situations. Afterwards, discuss with the class how the characters must have felt, and why.

a) While attending a community college, Parminder Singh, a recent immigrant from India, met a Canadian named Anne Morton. They fell in love. Anne's parents have quietly let her know that they disapprove of her dating boys from other racial or religious groups. The couple have nevertheless decided to get married. Role-play a conversation in which Parminder and Anne inform her parents of their intention to marry.

b) William Cardinal is a ten-year-old native Canadian raised on a reservation. He has enrolled in a new school in southern Manitoba because his father has found construction work in Winnipeg. Most of the students in William's new school are white. For weeks they make fun of him. When he can stand it no longer, William summons his courage and tells his father and mother about the name-calling. Role-play this conversation.

3. Invite a member of a minority group organization to your classroom. Discuss the impact of prejudice and discrimination on members of the community represented by the organization.

Can the cycle of prejudice and discrimination be stopped?

● ●

I'd often see Indian people in the town. Sometimes they'd come into the restaurant where I worked, but I never tried to be friendly. Most of the time they were drunk, and sometimes they would get into fights. They would leave their children in their cars, or on the street, and sit in the bar for hours. I saw white people do the same thing too, but I didn't give a damn about them. Many of the young girls came to the restaurant, and the white men would make crude jokes and try to pick them up. Many times I burned with rage and hatred, but I tried to suppress these emotions. But it was hard, and once I hit a man with a pop bottle and cut his head because he was pawing a young girl.

There was another time when two little Indian boys came in. They were about four and eight years old. The place was nearly full, and in order to reach the bathroom they had to walk the length of the restaurant. About halfway down the room sat a group of white men who had just come out of the bar, drunk and noisy. The little boys caught my eye as soon as they walked in. The mother had come in with them, but when she saw all the people she stayed outside. The children stood there, tiny, ragged, and big-eyed. They looked so much like my little brothers a lump came to my throat. As they started down the aisle one of the men yelled, "Watch it! The bow and arrows are coming." The older child stopped for a second when everyone started to laugh, put his arm around his little brother and, with his head up, continued walking. The men laughed at them and the younger boy started to cry and they ran

the rest of the way. I shouted at the men to stop. I was so angry I could scarcely speak. The place became very quiet. No one looked at me when I ran to the washroom and brought those little boys out. The little one was crying and I carried him out to the car. I didn't say anything to their parents — I just wanted to go away and forget the whole incident. Every so often the memory would come back of that little boy with his arm around his brother, and each time it filled me with frustration, hopelessness and despair. I might have blamed the parents for being too gutless, but how could I? Deep down inside I understood why they were afraid, because I was afraid too, only I showed my fear in a different way.

From *Halfbreed* by Maria Campbell. Used by permission of The Canadian Publishers, McClelland and Stewart.

1. What examples of prejudice and discrimination do you find in this excerpt?
2. From what you have learned in this chapter, how would you explain the behaviour of the whites and the person telling this story?
3. Consider the impact the person's yell has on the rest of the people in the bar. What does that suggest about how to stop prejudicial behaviour?
4. What can individuals do to oppose stereotyping, prejudice, and discrimination?

• •

Senior citizens rally in Toronto to protest Prime Minister Brian Mulroney's plan to de-index pensions.

Maurice Walsh, *Canada and the World*, September 1981

The following stereotypes don't fit the majority of old people.

When they get old they don't need as much as we do. They are more indifferent . . . and don't feel things the way we do.

Old people don't need company the way younger people do. They like to live with their memories. They talk a lot, always about the way things used to be.

Old people are happy not to have the responsibilitiy of a job or looking after a family. All they want to do is sit in the sun and talk about the past.

When they get old, they become sick and feeble. They are no longer able to work and should be "put on the shelf" to let younger people have jobs.

Old people dislike change. They don't try to adjust to new conditions or ideas.

If we try to get old people to help with activities or projects, they will only mix things up and get in the way.

When they get old their minds go to pieces. They become forgetful and shaky. They can't take care of themselves. They should be put in nursing homes.

Old people get along best when they live with other old people in senior citizens' apartments.

We shouldn't use terms like "aged" or "old" when we speak of old people. They don't like to be reminded they are different, or that they are dying. It is kindest to call them senior citizens even though that is just a name and doesn't really mean anything. It sounds important.

There is nothing we can learn from old people that will be of any use in today's world.

There are some clear answers to those stereotypes.

Does the whole pattern of human needs, emotions, and abilities change between 64 and 65?

No. The aged still feel the same emotions and require the same chances to express them. As human beings they are individuals and their needs remain the same as those of any younger person.

They do, however, face a whole battery of changed circumstances . . . loss of status, possible illness or poverty, exclusion from the activities of society, rejection, loneliness, and depression. Our production geared society sees them as unproductive. Many of the old accept this rejection and withdraw more and more into themselves.

Many vigorous old people have

found second careers, starting their own new businesses. Many are active as teachers, artists, needle-workers, writers, or craftsmen. Some drift with circumstances, enjoying freedom from responsibility, travel and the good things that economic well-being makes possible.

Too many, because of poverty, poor education, ill health, or insufficient motivation or skills have been (to quote Margaret Mead) "set aside to rot and die on the rubbish heap of a throwaway society."

Does human health and mental ability disintegrate overnight between 64 and 65?

Mental faculties, scientists say, do show a gradual very slow decay after 30. Brain cells die and are not replaced, but normally this causes no great change in mental sharpness.

Genuine brain damage may come from hardening of the arteries of the brain, injury, or brain disease, particularly Alzheimer's. Researchers say it will probably affect 70 of every 1000 people over 65 who suffer brain damage.

As the fifth greatest killer, Alzheimer's disease has been a subject of intensive research in Canada since the 1960s. It causes gradual loss of memory, beginning with one's most recent memories and working back to one's earliest memories. It ends in death when the personality disintegrates, producing total helplessness. No cure is known.

Most individuals will be more fortunate. The loss of memory that produces our stereotype of the absent-minded old is usually not caused by brain damage. It may be due to any of a number of causes, among them loss of interest caused by exclusion from active life. A psychology professor once said, "there is no such thing as a good memory or a bad memory . . . We remember what we want to remember." Perhaps, the rejected elder prefers to recall happier times.

As for constant reference to the past and to past ways of living. . . .

Don't we all tell other people how we think they should do things? Don't we, then, refer to our own way as the standard? From the aged, this may become irritating because of differences in moral standards, values, childrearing and attitudes to duty, discipline, responsibility, and economy. But they, as the rest of us, speak from what they have experienced.

And, inflexible thinking is not the sole preserve of the old.

Few of us willingly change our ways or ideas except under very great pressure. Consider the inflexibility of youth who have left home rather than change their ideas or habits to agree with those of their parents. And how about those parents?

The aged have lived more years than the young or middle-aged. Those years have followed a pattern that has become second nature. Are younger folk perhaps being just as rigid in their expectations of the aged?

1. Make a two-column chart. In the column on the left, list stereotypes of the elderly mentioned in the article above. In the column on the right, list the facts related to these stereotypes.

2. Reread the last four paragraphs of the article. Then answer the following questions:

   a) "Don't we all tell other people how we think they should do things? Don't we, then, refer to our own way as the standard?" Do you agree with this statement? Why or why not?

   b) "Few of us willingly change our ways or ideas except under very great pressure." Do you agree with this statement? Explain how it relates to the idea of stereotyping.

3. Examine some television advertising portraying senior citizens. Do these ads reinforce or disprove stereotypes about this age group?

Projects, Activities and Explorations

1. Most provinces in Canada have a Human Rights Commission. Find out what the Commission in your province does and how it operates. With the help of a librarian, locate the Commission's annual report. This report usually lists the most important cases that the Commission has had to investigate during the past year.

   Your teacher will divide your class into three groups. One group should consist of only three or four students. This group will select a case for the other two groups to decide on. The larger groups should have no idea what the Commission's final ruling was. When both groups have decided on a fair ruling for the case, they can announce their decision and compare it to the Commission's actual ruling.

2. Watch some films that show the effects of ethnocentrism on interpersonal relationships, such as *Crocodile Dundee, The Gods Must Be Crazy* or *Witness*. Present a brief report to the class on the impact of ethnocentrism on the characters in the film.

3. Research how the Canadian government treated Canadian residents of Japanese descent during World War II. Then discuss whether the government should now formally apologize to the Japanese community and repay them for the losses they suffered during the war.

4. Bring some comic books to class and analyse any stereotypes you see in them. You might compare comic strips such as *Blondie* and *Archie* with *For Better or Worse* and *Cathy*. Study how these comic strips portray men and women. How would you account for these portrayals?

5. Research the contributions of some major world leaders who were over the age of 65 when they assumed power.

6. Do a survey of greeting cards aimed at older people (for example, birthday cards, retirement cards, etc.). Do these cards stereotype the elderly? If so, in what ways?

7. Research how some other cultures treat elderly people. How does the treatment compare with our society's? How might you explain any similarities or differences?

What Have You Learned?

If you have covered everything in this chapter, you should be familiar with each of the following topics:

1. The nature, causes and effects of prejudice
2. The interrelationship between prejudice and stereotypes
3. The meaning and implications of ethnocentrism
4. The nature, causes and effects of discrimination
5. How increasing levels of discrimination involve increasing degrees of harm to victims
6. Some theories that attempt to explain prejudice and discrimination
7. The possible effects of prejudice and discrimination on both the victim and the attacker

To Help You Study

The following chart will help you
to review the words, facts, and
ideas introduced in this chapter.
Copy the chart into your notebook
and fill in the missing information.

Word, Fact, Idea	Example in a Sentence	Page	Definition
ethnocentrism	Assuming that ethnic foods you've never tasted are disgusting demonstrates ethnocentrism.	320	the viewpoint that your culture is superior and other cultures are inferior
prejudice			
discrimination			
antilocution			
avoidance			
extermination			
The Learned Prejudice Theory			
The Frustration-Aggression Theory of Prejudice			
The Competition Theory of Prejudice			
obsessive concern			
enhanced striving			
denial of membership			
withdrawal			
self-hate			

Social Change

17

How Has High School Changed Since the 1950s?

Carefully examine the pictures below. How does the life of a teenager in school in the 1950s compare to your life today?

As a class or in a group, discuss the following questions:

1. Do you think that the life of a teenager has changed from the 1950s for the better or for the worse, or are things basically the same as today? Why?

2. If you had the power, what changes would you make to your school? Do you think you would be successful in making these changes? Why or why not?

3. In your view, how much power should individuals have to change society?

Defining Social Change

Nothing stays the same, whether you like it or not. Your life has probably

changed a great deal since you entered high school. At the same time, high schools have changed considerably over the years to keep up with a rapidly changing society.

This chapter is about **social change**. When we talk about social change, we are referring to a special kind of change that has three characteristics:

1. the changing ways in which an entire society is organized
2. the new ways in which people relate to each other in groups such as the family, the school, the workplace
3. those changes that affect a large number of people who report the same or similar reactions to the change.

For instance, imagine what would happen if someone invented a machine that could teach you everything you needed to know in less than five years. This would change the way that society is organized. Thousands of young people would suddenly be prepared to take their place in the work force at the same time. Human interaction would also change. Rather than having a human relationship with a teacher, you would learn from a machine. The impact of such changes would be staggering. They would affect a large number of people in much the same way. In fact, these changes would affect our entire society.

Social change also leads to changes in individual lives. As major social changes occur, people react and adjust to these changes. These adjustments are somewhat different from person to person. Rapid social change can be very disturbing for individuals in society.

In this chapter we will look at the most common causes of social change and the problems the changes can create. You will see how people cope with change, by either participating or trying to resist it.

Causes of Social Change

The following items are some of the possible causes of change in our society. Copy the list into your notebook and add any other items that you think should be on the list. Then rank the list from the most important cause of change to the least important cause. Be prepared to explain your choices.

television
computers in the workplace
special interest groups (e.g. Greenpeace)
trade with other nations
telephones
lasers
political parties
our new Charter of Rights
women entering the workplace
immigration
communication satellites
labour unions
nuclear weapons

As a class or in a group, discuss the following questions:

1. In what ways can your list of causes of social change be grouped or classified so that you can see different kinds of change?

2. What kinds of change have had the most impact on our society? Why?

3. Why do you think it is important for social scientists to identify and to study the causes of major social change?

Technology

Technology is the application of human discoveries and inventions. When an individual or a group suddenly realizes

Ideas and Social Change

Ideas exist only in our minds. The idea of "equality" is a good example of a notion that has led to great social change. At one time, it was generally accepted that only wealthy landowners had the right to take part in government. This group also tended to enjoy special social privileges, such as greater protection under the law. During the seventeenth and eighteenth centuries, some philosophers began to write about the idea of equality. They argued that individuals were born equal and that the class system was, therefore, unfair.

Over time, the idea of equality caused drastic social changes. Democratic forms of government arose that gave power to greater numbers of people, regardless of social class. Laws were passed that protected the rights of all individuals. The idea of equality continues to give rise to social change, as groups in our society that feel unfairly treated organize to voice their needs and demands. Clearly, ideas have the power to move people to action, and action brings about social change.

Cultural Diffusion

Cultural diffusion refers to the spreading of new ideas, values, customs, products and behaviours from one culture to another. A good example of cultural diffusion is the habit of smoking cigarettes. Smoking became popular in the seventeenth century after it was discovered that a smooth-tasting tobacco could be grown in America. The habit spread from the New World to Britain. From there, it was exported to Holland. Soon the habit of smoking caught on in Europe and Russia. Eventually, it made its way eastwards all the way to Alaska. In less than 100 years the "nicotine habit" had spread around the world.

something new about the way the world works, a new way of doing something or a machine that never existed before may arise from the discovery.

Often, these bright new ideas or inventions can greatly change a society. Let's look at something fairly obvious — your calculator. The calculator is a technological invention. It was made possible by the early discovery of a number system that included zero. It was also made possible by the invention of the "microchip." This invention enabled shrinking a powerful calculating device from the size of a giant computer to something that would fit into your pocket.

Some people argue that as these tiny computers become more powerful, they will make it unnecessary for people to know much more about mathemetics than how to punch numbers on a calculator.

There are a variety of ways in which cultural diffusion can take place, such as through trade, or invasion during war. Perhaps the most common way is through immigration. New immigrants from one culture come to live in the midst of another culture. When these different cultures come into contact, they learn from each other. New foods, ways of dress or attitudes may be shared among the cultures. This is a particularly important source of social change in Canada. Our multicultural heritage has created a rich and diverse culture in this country.

Group Action

Most social change takes place by **evolution**. This means that change is a

slow and gradual process. Sometimes change happens as a result of **revolution**. This involves rapid change, and it usually occurs as a result of the efforts of an organized group dedicated to a change of some kind. This kind of action can come from government when a new party comes to power and brings about the changes it wants.

More often, revolutionary change is brought about by groups outside of government who are interested in specific social problems or issues. For example, in the 1960s, a number of women's groups were formed in Canada. They wanted to bring about social equality for women. They fought hard for womens' rights through protest marches and media campaigns.

Through the efforts of organized women's groups, social attitudes towards women changed dramatically in 20 years. Vast numbers of women entered the work force. They forced government to take notice of women's needs and to pass laws to reduce the mistreatment of women in such areas as wages, work benefits, daycare, spouse abuse and pornography. Clearly, the women's movement has and will continue to cause social change.

Geography and Climate

When people move from one place to another, they frequently encounter a different geography and climate. Often, their previous way of life or culture does not suit the new environment. The choice is straightforward: change or suffer.

This situation occurred when Europeans began to settle in North America. They originally came looking for gold. They had not really planned to stay for long and certainly did not expect to have to change the way they lived.

Gradually, Europeans adapted their ways of life to their new environment. They sought help from the native Indians, who showed them how to make medicines from various plants. The Indians also taught them how to grow food crops such as corn. Thus, new behaviours were added to the culture of the settlers.

The new environment changed European attitudes and values as well. Life was usually harsh for every settler in the New World. The difficulties of survival tended to break down the strict divisions between classes. A more equal society was created, in which more and more people gradually acquired the right to play a role in running society. This was something new in terms of social organization.

From Ideas to Action

1. Identify the cause or causes of change in the following cases:

   a) In the 1830s, the idea that a greater number of people should play a role in decision-making in society became more and more popular. In both Canada and the United States, this idea led to more people being allowed to vote. In Canada, some people argue, it led to a series of elections and to a rebellion in 1837 that eventually gave the lower classes more power in the government, and Canadians greater control over their affairs.

   b) Sam journeyed to South America to study the natives of the Amazon region. In order to survive in the jungle and to win the natives' trust, he had to live just like them. They would laugh at his pants and shirt which seemed ridiculous things to wear in temperatures over 30°C. Eventually, Sam replaced his clothing with a simple loin cloth, which was much more comfortable.

   c) From the earliest days of Canada's settlement, native Indians have been put on reservations. This was supposed to give the Indians areas of land that whites could not settle in or take away from them. However, many natives were nomadic. This meant that they lived by following game animals wherever they roamed. The reservations hemmed in the nomadic tribes. They had to turn to other means of survival. This changed their culture, which, in turn, has led to further problems for these natives.

   d) The Greenpeace organization has done dangerous things to stress the point that wildlife and the environment must be saved from human beings. For example, they deliberately ran their small boats between some large whaling vessels and the whales these ships were hunting. Eventually, Greenpeace and its dramatic forms of protest drew public attention to the killing of whales. The resulting public outcry caused the International Whaling Organization to move towards a ban on whaling.

   e) Punk styles of dress and behaviour began in England. Gradually these styles made their way to North America, through rock music, television and other media.

2. Interview your teacher and/or the principal of your school. Ask them to describe how education has changed since they began their teaching careers. Ask them to identify the causes of these changes, and how each cause has led to specific change. To conclude your interview, you might ask them to rank the list of causes that they mentioned, from most important to least important.

3. Develop a chart to compare the pros and cons of the following statement: "Violence is never justified as a method of bringing about change in society."

4. Do you agree with the saying that, when it comes to getting things done in our society, "the squeaky wheel always gets the grease"?

Cherished Teenage Values

There are more than 2.5 million people in Canada between the ages of 15 and 19. In 1985, two researchers gave out questionnaires to 3600 teenagers in a program called "Project Teen Canada." The results were published in 1985 in a book entitled *The Emerging Generation*.

The following chart shows the percentages of teenagers who said that certain given values were "very important" as goals or positions they would like to attain.

Friendship	91%
Being Loved	87%
Freedom	84%
Success	78%
Comfortable Life	75%
Privacy	68%
Family Life	65%
Excitement	58%
Acceptance by God	41%
Recognition	41%
Being popular	21%

[Adapted from *Canada and the World*, Vol. 51 No. 4, December 1985, p. 17.]

1. What does the chart tell you about the most cherished values of teenagers? Why do teenagers desire these things?
2. Can you suggest any changes taking place in your life or in society that might threaten your achieving the goals in the list. What could you do about these changes?

Why Do People Resist Change?

Slowing Down Change

Imagine that the school board has announced it must close at least one high school in your area to cut costs. Your school is named as one of the possible closures. If this happens, you would be bused ten miles to another high school that has always been your school's rival.

Decide which, if any, of the following you would be prepared to do to stop the closure of your school. Add your own ideas to the list, if any come to mind.

a) Do nothing. Maybe the Board of Education will close another school.

b) Join a community group that has been formed to fight the closure.

c) Write letters to the local newspaper protesting the closure.

d) Write letters and call your local school trustee. State that you will work to make sure he or she is not re-elected if your school if closed.

e) Write letters to your member of your provincial parliament. Ask her or him to put pressure on the Minister of Education to stop the closures.

f) Write letters of protest to the Minister of Education.

g) Participate in a protest rally in front of the Board of Education offices.

h) Boycott classes to protest the school closure, and invite the local media to cover this example of mass disobedience.

i) Help to put up "Save Our School" posters all over the community.

As a class, discuss the following questions:

1. Take a vote to find out how many students in your class would choose each of the options listed above (or any others that have been suggested). Record the results of the vote on the board. What patterns do you see? How would you account for the students' choices?

2. Suppose you were asked by a newspaper reporter why you opposed the school board's intended changes. What would you say?

3. Why do you think people try to stop change?

4. Are there any circumstances in which people should always try to stop change? Are there any circumstances in which people should not be allowed to stop change?

Cherished Values

As a general rule, people resist change when it threatens something they value highly. For example, if you believe that human life is sacred, you would probably feel uncomfortable about any new law that threatened the rights of individuals to live.

For example, you might protest an attempt to bring back the death penalty. Your regard for human life might cause you to act to prevent a social change that you saw as a threat to your cherished value.

Vested Interests

People resist change for other reasons besides cherished values. Sometimes they have a **vested interest** in keeping things the way they are. This means that, in the present circumstances, they have some privilege or advantage they want to maintain for themselves. As you might predict, these people will resist

What vested interests do these people have?

any change that threatens this desirable situation.

For example, suppose that someone suggests that robots be used to build cars in the auto plant where you work. This would make car production more efficient and profitable. You know that this is true, but it would also threaten the wages and other benefits that you enjoy under the present arrangement. You might be laid off in the long run. Therefore, you and your union have a vested interest in keeping the robots out of the plant.

Habit and Fear of the Unknown

Habit also plays a role in slowing the pace of change. You do some things without even thinking. These habits may be part of your personality and, therefore, may be hard for you to change.

Recall how hard it was for many people to adjust to new seat belt laws. Out of habit, people simply started their cars and drove away. For awhile, people grumbled as they received fines for forgetting to "buckle up." Some groups even argued that seat belts were danger-ous in some situations. However, most people have now developed the habit of doing up their seatbelts, and the change has been generally accepted.

Many people feel fairly secure in their day-to-day lives. They see their world as ordered and predictable. Change can upset this comfortable feel-ing. People may not be able to imag-ine how their lives will be better after a change has occurred. They may be-come nervous because they do not know the consequences of a change, and how they will be affected. This is commonly

---

Five Faulty Predictions

Many intelligent people have failed to see the long-term effects of some discoveries. Here are some of the worst predictions:

- **The Automobile**
  "The ordinary horseless car-riage (automobile) is at present a luxury for the wealthy; and although its price will probably fall in the future, it will never, of course, come into common use."
  — *The Literary Digest*, Octo-ber 14, 1889

- **The Atomic Bomb**
  "That is the biggest fool thing we have ever done...the bomb will never go off, and I speak as an expert in explosives."
  — Admiral William Leahy, U.S. Navy Officer speak-ing to the President of the United States in 1945.
  Two atomic bombs were dropped on Japan a few months later, killing over 200 000 people.

- **Highways**
  "The actual building of roads devoted to motor cars is not for the near future, in spite of ru-mours to that effect."
  — *Harper's Weekly*, August 2, 1902

- **The Commercial Television**
  "While theoretically and techni-cally, television may be possible, commercially and financially I consider it an impossibility, a development of which we need waste little time dreaming."
  — Lee De Forest, inventor and early pioneer of radio

- **The Electric Lightbulb**
  "The idea for this invention may be good enough for our Ameri-can friends... but it is not worth the attention of practical or sci-entific men."
  — A committee of the British Parliament, 1878

(Adapted from *The Book of Predictions*. Copyright © 1981 by David Wallechinsky, Amy Wallace & Irving Wallace. Reprinted by permission of William Morrow & Co.)

called "fear of the unknown."

For example, imagine that your school board proposes to pass a rule that all students in your school must wear uniforms. You begin to wonder: "How will this change affect me? I really value personal freedom. Won't this rule reduce my freedom? I spend my money to look good, and I like looking good. Besides, I've always worn jeans. Are they doing this so that somewhere down the road they can really tighten up the discipline in school? What are they *really* trying to do? As you can see, fear of the unknown can develop easily.

Society is naturally cautious about change, and social change is a relatively slow process. As changes begin to develop, individuals weigh the impact of these changes. In the end, they decide to participate willingly in the changes, or to grudgingly accept the new ways, or to resist the changes. In a sense, the fate of some changes depends to a certain extent upon the decision of each individual.

From Ideas to Action

1. Why do you think the people in each of the following cases resisted change?

   a) Ted had a successful store along a busy street. He found out that the city planned to make the street into a bus mall. This would mean that traffic would be eliminated from the street. Ted and other merchants felt that this would seriously harm their businesses, and so they formed an association to fight the proposed bus mall.

   b) As the rock music of Elvis Presley and other entertainers became popular in the 1950s, many parents and church leaders reacted to the new music by organizing burnings in which thousands of rock records were melted.

   c) During World War II, people in Europe saw negative changes in the way that Jews were treated. As time went on, this mistreatment became persecution. Some people bravely resisted the anti-Jewish policy of the Nazis and secretly hid Jews in their homes.

   d) In the 1960s and early 1970s, long hair was popular among men. However, in the late 1970s, hairstyles gradually became shorter. Some men kept their hair long despite the changing style. To this day, there are a few men, now in their 30s, who still wear their hair very long.

2. Survey some students in your school to determine if the results of "Project Teen Canada" were accurate. Ask each student to state whether they think each value is "unimportant," "slightly important," "somewhat important" or "very important" as a personal goal. As an interesting comparison, you might also survey some adults to see how they feel about the same values.

3. Listen to local TV or radio news reports. Identify examples of resistance to change. In each case, find out what change is being resisted, why and what methods of resistance are being used. Report your findings to the class.

4. Do you generally accept or resist change? Why?

Problems Caused By Change

Read the following list of changes. You are probably coping with some of these changes or may have to cope with them sometime in the near future.

- achieving new and more mature relations with peers of both sexes
- achieving emotional independence from your parents
- preparing for the world of work and long-term economic independence
- preparing for marriage and family life
- becoming more socially responsible
- acquiring your own personally acceptable set of values with which to guide your behaviour

a) As a group, brainstorm a list of problems, tensions or conflicts that some or all of these changes have created for you.

b) For each change listed, score how well you are coping. Use the following scale for each change.

	Score
Coping very well	1
Coping well	2
Coping adequately	3
Having some difficulty coping	4
Not coping	5

(Adapted from: *Canada And The World*, Vol. 51, No. 4 Dec. 1985, p. 16–17, 30.)

Total the scores that you gave yourself. You may wish to compare and discuss your total score with others in your group.

When you have completed these activities, discuss the following questions as a class or in a group:

The "irreplaceable" horse and carriage.

1. Identify those changes that seem to create the most problems or which seem to be the most difficult to cope with. What ways might exist to cope with these changes?

2. What are some possible signs that someone is, or is not, coping very well with these changes?

3. What might happen to people who cannot cope with these changes?

The Impact of Change Upon Individuals

Look at some recent social changes. The nature of work has changed. In future, people will probably have several different careers in their lifetimes. What are you training for now? The family appears to be a very unstable unit, with almost half of all marriages ending in divorce. Are you wondering if a long-term relationship is worth it? Changes in technology have raised our standard of living and the pace of life. Can you keep up? Will our great inventions eventually bring about our downfall?

Clearly, the world is often a very confusing place. This can take its toll on individuals. The rules of society seem to change so often that few things are as predictable as they once were. This can lead people to feel powerless. It can also cause them to question whether it is worthwhile striving for anything. After all, the goal you hold dear today may no longer exist after the next major social change.

It is perhaps not surprising that some researchers have noticed that the rates of suicide, alcoholism and drug abuse increase during times of rapid social change. This was particularly true during the 1960s and early 1970s. During this time, many people were alerted to the changes caused by science and technology. Pollution, war, crime and poverty in the midst of great wealth seemed to indicate that society was out of control.

Faced with rapid change, some people began to experiment and to search for new meaning in their lives. Unfortunately, some found no meaning and, in one way or another, dropped out of life. To what extent are things different today? Are people in the 1980s still overwhelmed by the pace of the changes around them?

The Impact of Change Upon Society: Culture Lag

Do you know what is going on inside a computer? Do you care? Can you operate one? Do you feel ready to take your place in a world where the computer will be as important and common as a television set or a telephone?

If you answered "no" or "I don't know" to some of the questions above, you may be experiencing **culture lag**. This means that some parts of a culture (for example, beliefs, ways of acting or material things) can be "out of step" or behind other parts. This creates tension and conflict potentially damaging to society.

Consider the computer — it has made possible the quick storage and retrieval of vast amounts of information. While this has modernized business and industry, it has caused problems in other areas of society. Many traditional jobs have disappeared. Personal information about you that was once hard for people to get at is now available by tapping into a computer memory bank.

Unions have generally fought hard to soften the impact of computer technology and to give their members time to adjust to it. People worried about the right to privacy have had to find new ways of controlling and protecting information. This has led to conflict and social stress in the form of strikes and legal battles.

It is worth noting that some social scientists believe that our culture is in a permanent state of culture lag. In other words, some aspects of our lives may never catch up with the rapid changes that are taking place. If this is true, then various groups in society will always be in conflict.

Coping With Change

> This week has been a disaster! Why does my family have to pick *now* to move to another area? I've just got one more year in school to go.
>
> My guidance counsellor has been bugging me to select courses for next year. I've got to pick the courses that I'll do best in — but I just don't know which ones!
>
> To top it all off, I didn't get my old summer job back. Now I have to start looking all over again! Why all these changes now? It's just one crisis after another.

Now in a group or as a class, discuss the following questions:

1. Which of the changes facing Ted did he know about in advance? Which changes are a surprise to him?
2. Which of these changes would be easiest to deal with? Why?
3. What factors determine how easily you can handle changes such as these?

Ted obviously feels overwhelmed by the changes he is facing. He is having trouble coping and adjusting to them. But let's step back and look at things from a different angle. Everyone goes through transitions in life. Regardless of age, a person's roles, relationships, daily routines and assumptions about life are always changing. This is a normal part of life.

Types of Changes

Ted faces a full range of types of changes. Some changes are expected. These are called **anticipated transitions**. Examples of this kind of change are Ted's selection of courses for the next year and his graduation from high school. He knew both of these changes would be occurring.

Other changes are not expected. These are called **unanticipated transitions**. In Ted's case, he did not expect to have to change high schools.

Finally, there are **non-event transitions**. These are changes that were expected and planned for, but which failed to happen. For example, Ted had expected to get his old summer job back, but this did not happen.

Coping With Transitions

Ted's first task is to determine how much each of these changes will affect his life. How much will they actually change the roles he plays, his relationships with others, his daily routine or his assumptions about life? Some changes may actually have less effect than he previously thought.

Suppose that Ted decides that these changes are going to seriously affect his life. Studies of change have shown that people bring both strengths and weaknesses to every situation involving

351

change. These strengths and weaknesses will determine how well a person copes with change. There are four categories of strengths and weaknesses involved when changes begin to affect your life.

- **Situation**: Do you see the situation itself as good, bad or neutral? Is it happening at a good time or at the worst possible moment? Do you have some control over the change, or are you stuck with things the way they are?

  In Ted's case, the situation has generally weakened his ability to cope. The move to a new school, in particular, couldn't have come at a worse time. This change complicates everything else and is beyond his control.

- **Self**: Do you have some inner strengths or resources for coping with the situation? Is there something about your personality that would be particularly useful in coping with a change?

  Ted's family has moved frequently in his lifetime: usually every five years. He has coped with moves before. He also has a strong personality. He is independent and has a good

sense of humour. He is bright and can usually find solutions to problems. In terms of "self," Ted has considerable strengths.

- **Supports**: For some changes, this can mean, "Do you have the financial resources to cope with the change?" However, most often this refers to how much emotional support you can get from others to help you deal with the stress.

  Ted has close ties with his family. Their frequent moves have made it important for family members to be sensitive to each other. He is especialy close to his twin brother. His parents care about his feelings and will willingly offer their help.

- **Strategies**: This final category involves what you actually do to deal with the situation. Do you sit paralysed, or do you actively pursue other options? Do you seek out the advice of others — friends, parents, counsellors, clergy or social agencies? Can you change the way that you see the situation — and perhaps see hidden possibilities rather than disaster?

Ted finally decides to see this move differently: as an opportunity to grow and to meet new people. After all, he has always made good friends no matter where he was. He also decides to visit the guidance counsellor at his old school, at his new school and at a nearby community college. He hopes to get some useful advice to give him a clearer picture of what courses to take next year. Finally, he concludes that he was getting limited job experience in his old summer job anyway. A new job may give him valuable new experience that will look good on a resume. Ted is well on his way to coping with the changes in his life!

Change can be less terrifying than it seems. This is particularly so if you first take stock of how much the change will really affect your life. Once you have this firmly in mind, the next step is to consider the four "S's" (situation, self, supports and strategies) to determine your strengths and weaknesses for coping with the changes. Clearly, you will do better if you have strengths to draw on or if you can somehow turn weaknesses into strengths.

From Ideas to Action

1. What problems might be caused by each of the following changes?

   a) Joe had lived all his life on a farm. His nearest neighbour was three miles away. Suddenly his father sold the farm and moved to the city to take a new job.

   b) In the nineteenth century, there was a fairly rapid movement of large numbers of people into cities from the countryside, and from other countries, to take jobs in factories.

   c) The divorce rate was relatively low in Canada until the government suddenly changed the divorce laws in the late 1960s. The new laws made it easier for couples to get a divorce. As a result, the divorce rate increased rapidly.

   d) For thousands of years, families in China were very large. The more children there were in a family, the more potential labourers and wage earners there were to guarantee the family's survival. Also, in the days before pensions, children were necessary to support elderly parents. The size of a family became a sign of a family's wealth and prestige. Recently, the Chinese government has banned large families. The government is worried that China's population is growing too large. Fines are imposed on those who have more than one child. Also, those who have only one child are given better housing and other privileges.

2. Explain how the following cases demonstrate culture lag.

   a) In the early 1900s, cars were regulated by many of the same laws that were designed to control the use of horses. For example, speed limits in some areas of Canada were 20 km/h, although cars could go faster. In some places, people wishing to cross an intersection in their car were expected to first sound a horn and to fire a gun into the air.

b) In World War I, generals insisted on ordering their troops to attack by running in a straight line at enemy positions. They used this strategy despite the wide use of barbed wire, which slowed the attackers' advance, and the machine guns which simply mowed the attackers down. Thousands of soldiers were killed before they ever reached the enemy.

3. Make a four-column chart like the one below to organize the information on page 353 about Ted's strengths and weaknesses in coping with the changes that he faced.

	Situation	Self	Supports	Strategies
Strengths				
Weaknesses				

4. Identify some change that you have faced or are facing today. Using the chart above, analyse your strengths and weaknesses for coping with the change. Is there anything that you can do in terms of the 4 S's that would increase the strengths that you bring to the situation?

5. Role-play someone who is facing a major change in life. Divide the class into groups of three to act as expert advisers for this person. After the person has described the "situation" and answered questions about "self" and "supports," each group should develop "strategies" to help the person cope with the change. Have the groups compare their strategies and discuss their effectiveness.

6. Discuss the pros and cons of the sayings, "Variety is the spice of life" and "A change is as good as a rest."

How to Debate Effectively

This exercise outlines the main features of a debate. It will help you debate effectively.

The Debate Structure

Introduction: State clearly and forcefully what you intend to prove. In longer debates you may also want to indicate the major areas you will discuss.

Arguments and Illustrations: Speak clearly and slowly. Take the time to explain your ideas fully and to support them with facts. A few carefully developed arguments are better than many unclear or unsupported ones.

Rebuttal: Make point form notes on your opponents' arguments as they are speaking. Use these plus counter arguments you prepare in advance to disprove what they are saying.

Conclusion: The final speaker for your side should sum up your position on the debate. About one sentence should be used for each major argument. Be clear and authoritative. You might also end with a provocative question that will help swing the audience to your side of the debate.

Example: Are Women Equal Today?

Introduction: We will prove convincingly that women today are still not treated equally in our society. To do this we will look at women's roles in the economy, politics and cultural affairs.

Arguments: The first reason we feel women are not treated equally in our economy is that their earnings are not equal to men's. For example, in 1985, only 16% of working women earned more than $25 000 whereas 48% of men did.

Rebuttal Notes:
Arg. Women are paid equally in education.
Reb. Yes, but they have not had an equal opportunity for promotion as is shown by how few schools have female principals.

Conclusion: We have shown that in Canada today women are not treated equally. In our economy, women earn less than men on average and have less opportunities for promotions or access to higher paying jobs, in politics... etc. A question all of you should ask yourselves is, would you want your daughter to have an equal chance in our society?

Pre-debate Preparation

1. Research your topic using a wide variety of sources, to get a broad perspective and enough current and up to date arguments and facts for your side of the debate.

2. Prepare short illustrations that will clarify and support your arguments. These might be statistics, quotes or case studies. Very simple charts, pictures or overheads might be used briefly.

3. Organize your debate so that there is a logical pattern to it. Know who is doing and saying what in your debate team.

4. Learn your arguments so that you can say them convincingly. Do not read them, as this suggests that you do not really know what you are talking about. Refer to your notes only for cues or for exact quotes.

5. Prepare counter arguments for the rebuttal. You must try to anticipate your opponents' arguments and devise ways to disprove or weaken them.

6. Use understandable words and carefully explain any unusual terms or ideas.

7. Make your debate relevant to the feelings and concerns of your audience. They have to feel that your arguments affect them if they are to be convinced.

8. Show enthusiasm and confidence for your side of the debate. You can't convince others if you do not sound convinced yourself.

Example: Women Face Inequality

1. *Research your topic*
For this topic, search the vertical file in the library and weekly news magazines such as *Chatelaine* or *Maclean's.* For statistical data check *The Canadian Year Book.* Also books such as *Perspectives on Women in the 1980's* by J. Turner (ed.) are useful.

2. *Prepare illustrations*
Quotes from leading feminists on the inequalities facing women today, a chart showing the unequal housework duties of the sexes, or statistics that compare women's average earnings with men's, would be very useful.

3. *Organize your debate*
In a short, two person per team debate, the first person might introduce your view and give 3 arguments on the first sub-topic. Then the second person would challenge the opponents' arguments, plus give 1–2 arguments on the second topic and conclude with a summary.

4. *Learn your arguments*
Arg.#1: women are paid unequally...
Fact: In 1985, the average earnings of women were $11 613 less than men.

Quote: Ontario women earn less than men because they are stuck in segregated job categories. *Toronto Star* 06/09/86

5. *Prepare counter arguments*
If they argue that women's pay is not equal because they are not as educated as men, you might counter with the fact that Statistics Canada shows a woman university grad earns an average of $1000 less per year than a male high school graduate.

6. *Use understandable words*
For example: prepare an explanation for such terms as "Pay Equity Legislation".

7. *Make your debate relevant*
You might point out that if women gain real economic equality many females in the class will earn more as adults than they might now. Also future husbands could expect more family income when their wives are paid more fairly.

8. *Show confidence*
Say: "We will prove without any doubt that women are still not equal in our society today."
Not: "We are supposed to argue..." or "I think, maybe, that..."

Debate Topics to Try

1. Resolved that pay equity legislation should cover all women in the labour force immediately.
2. Resolved that women will never gain true equality until they have an equal role in politics.
3. Resolved that women are at least as responsible as men for the current inequalities that face women in Canadian society today.
4. Resolved that the immigration of large numbers of people from many different cultures is a very positive cause of social change in Canada.
5. Resolved that television is not a positive force for social change in our society today.

The fight for women's rights is closely tied to the changing role of women in our society. The two have interacted with one another to produce a Canadian society far different from the one women faced at the turn of the century.

World War I was a major event leading to the growth of the women's rights movement and a new role for women. Before the twentieth century, women had been forced into the workplace for one reason: survival of the family. Wages were so low that mothers and daughters were pressed into service to help keep the family alive. During the First World War, working women were needed to replace the men who had gone to the front. This meant that women were working at jobs previously defined as "men's work." Their wages were better than their nineteenth-century counterparts. As well, women took on more hazardous duties serving as nurses on the battlefront. They too played their part in defending Canada.

The first step in gaining voting rights for women took place when the Canadian government decided to give the right to vote to the wives of soldiers serving overseas. This was the beginning of all women getting the right to vote.

Women's groups continued to push for greater rights during and after the war. There was great resistance to the belief that females were "equal" to males and should be treated as such.

From this single example, you can see the way in which changing roles for women and a push for women's rights worked together to produce social change.

Most of us today recognize the changes that have occurred in our society. Today women play an important role in the workplace. Their role in the home too has changed. Many women have chosen to delay childbirth until later in their lives or have chosen not to have children. The demand for daycare facilities reflects the number of mothers who continue to work out of necessity or choice after their children are born.

Accompanying these changes has been an altered perception of the role of the male in the Canadian family. He is no longer perceived as a lesser or passive partner in the raising of children.

Change brings more change. The women's rights activists of the 1960s and 1970s were different from those of the early twentieth century and are different from the "new activists" of the 1980s. Read the accompanying article to discover the nature of these new activists.

The New Feminists

July 26, 1985 *Toronto Star* By Cathy Dunphy

Feminism isn't what it used to be. Neither are feminists.

There's a new generation of them coming on the scene. They are not nearly as numerous as feminists were in the early '70s when women everywhere were raising consciousnesses and dedicating themselves to stamping out male chauvinism.

New-age feminism is all wrapped up with things like peace activism, racism, environmental concerns, health in the workplace and the role of high-tech information systems. Feminism is no longer the whole; it is but one of the parts.

"The standards have changed, it's a whole new spirit," says Anne Rochon Ford, Women's College Hospital's first co-ordinator of women's health-care programs. "They have to have the best, which was never part of my reality. They take for granted they will move up in their professions." At 32, Rochon Ford says she is part of the old guard of feminists, the ones in their 30s, 40s and 50s who are still leading the movement.

"More of us had to fight for what we have now," she says. "Women in their 20s were too young to have been a part of it. They didn't go through the consciousness-raising groups we went through and I think this has made a fundamental difference in how they approach the issues."

That is *if* they approach the issues. Many younger women seem to care more about lifestyles and getting ahead than getting equality, she says.

"I can be guaranteed if I approach a women of my own age or older that we are of the same mind," says Rochon Ford. "Younger feminists can't. They have to have a very strong commitment."

They do. These three young feminists are women to watch. They very well may make a difference to the future.

Maria Wallis

"There has to be a change and the only way to get it is for me to do it along with other people."

Maria Wallis, 26, pulls a face as she makes a mock confession. "Yes, I am a feminist, one of the small minority working away at it," she says.

In Wallis' case, "working away at it" means working hard, working day and night and weekends, and working for free. Her paying job is part-time. She takes home $119 a week for two days' work a week at *Our Times*, a union magazine. Then she works for Women Working With Immigrant Women, (she chairs their employment equality committee), the brand-new Coalition of Immigrant and Visible Minority Women, the Cross-Cultural Communications Centre and the International Women's Day Committee.

She works for them because, she says, she has to.

"There has to be a change and the only way to get it is for me to do it along with other people," she says. "With your own life you set an example."

"She's done that. Her parents point to her five sisters, working toward their careers in fields like social work or hospital administration, and wonder why their eldest daughter also can't aim for the middle-class life.

But it's because of her parents — and what they experienced 10 years ago when they came to Brantford from Pakistan — that she can't.

"My father had a good job in Pakistan but when he came here he had to take a job in a factory," she says. "The first day they made him sweep the floor and he was humiliated. My mother has a hard job sewing garments in a textile factory."

"My youngest sister — she was so small, she must have been in Grade 3 — someone in a passing car took the rind of an orange and threw it at her. She cried and couldn't understand why. How do you explain to her they hate her because of the color of her skin?"

She must fight racism, she says, even before she fights sexism. But Wallis fervently believes she can battle both by encouraging immigrant women to work together for a better life.

That's why she is going back to school this fall to study sociology. "I want to learn how to put together quantifiable data to prove a lot of the shortcomings that immigrant women and women of visible minorities face," she says. "So many of the problems are not written and if they're not written you can't lobby and you can't change things."

Nikita Crook

"I suppose I have a motherly quality and want to share what I have."

So far in her career, Nikita Crook has worked under the assumption that "women can be connected to issues that affect their lives."

That's why she was a researcher for the Badgley Report on sexual offences against youths and children, worked on the Fraser Committee on pornography and prostitution, and was fundraiser and research co-ordinator for Education Wife Assault last year.

"My focus has always been the underdog role of all women," Crook says, "I feel affiliated with the victim mentality. I suppose I have a motherly quality and want to share what I have."

She's never been a victim; she's always been a leader. And she's pretty well always got what she wanted. Junior tennis champion, high school leader and scholar in middle-class Oakville, she never had to apply any brakes until she got so involved in a fundamental religion, she decided she would become a minister. Then she found out women weren't allowed to become ministers with her religion.

"Intellectually I developed my feminism before I knew what to label it," says Crook, a 26-year-old freelance researcher.

She went to university to take a law degree to change some things in society, she says, but got "hooked" on her women's studies courses instead. "I am a feminist," she says. "I can say that without gulping because I know what the word feminism means. I'm a humanist first but women have gotten a lot of bad breaks."

She has some big dreams herself — starting some sort of national communications system that would help grass-roots organizations promote their causes, having children, travelling when and where she wants.

She may get it all. When she decided she simply had to attend the international women's conference last year in Nairobi, she dropped in to meetings of women's groups all over town and asked them to sponsor her. In return she promised to bring them back material relevant to their cause.

She pulled it off, too. All together she raised $3200.

Kate Sutherland

"I see the need to recognize the specific problems of women but I don't see this as a woman's cause."

Kate Sutherland knows Metro's first feminists, the high-powered, well-respected women who are out on the frontlines of the movement — and in the headlines of the newspapers. National Action Committee for the Status of Women former president Chaviva Hosek is a friend and mentor; lawyer, activist and Berger Commissioner May Eberts is her stepmother. But Sutherland is not a feminist like them, she says.

"I feel more comfortable with the title humanist and I see feminism as a really important part of that. I see the need to recognize the specific problems of women but I don't see this as a woman's cause. I see it as humanity's cause," she says.

Energy Probe's urban transport researcher, Sutherland, 28, says she's a feminist, humanist, peace activist, environmentalist. I'm a lot of "ists." True feminism is consistent with all these things."

Sutherland sees herself as a facilitator, the person who connects the people and the ideas who then make things happen. She's sure of this because although she is only 28 she knows herself and what she wants.

She was very young when her father, a Supreme Court judge taught her that she was good at buying second-hand clothes simply because she didn't have to, she says.

Educated in alternative schools and encouraged by a mother who is now a bio-energetics therapist and a good friend, Sutherland is now applying her high intelligence and independent streak to promoting bicycle paths and biking in Metro. As a "simple solution to complicated problem," biking, she says, is indicative of what's needed in our city.

Reprinted with permission — *The Toronto Star Syndicate*

1. According to Anne Rochon Ford, how are the new women's activists of the 1980s different from those of the 1960s and 1970s?
2. Why do you think these changes have taken place?
3. Create an organizer which will help you to compare the three women interviewed in this article.
4. How do you define "feminism"? Does your definition differ greatly from the two women interviewed in this article?

Resistance to changing roles in the workplace goes beyond the issue of promotion. Read the following article and answer the questions.

Closing the wage gap

Halyna Koba, *Canada and the World*, March 1987

The problem is easy to state: men are paid more than women. In Ontario, as an example, the 2.1 million working women earned 63 cents for every dollar earned by male workers. What is far from simple is finding a solution to this wage gap.

The principal of equal pay for equal work is not difficult to grasp. It means that men and women, working for the same employer, should be paid the same for doing the same job, or a job that is basically the same. Equal pay for work of equal value, however, compares different kinds of jobs done for the same employer; this is where the questions come in.

Labour Canada statistics from 1984 list the average weekly wages of data entry operators as $373 and maintenance workers as $521 — a difference of $148. The operators, mainly female, enter data into computers. The maintenance workers, largely male, make sure the machinery works. Are the tasks performed by data entry operators less significant than those of the maintenance workers?

Although there are laws covering equality of pay for men and women in the public sector, plans for the private sector aren't common in North America.

In 1976, Quebec passed a law which gave women in the public and private sectors, who felt they were being paid less because of their sex, the chance to present their cases to a provincial human rights body. In 1977, the federal government passed a pay equity law, but it was limited to federal employees. In 1986, Manitoba established the Pay Equity Act, which uses formulas to set the value of jobs. This is aimed at finding out if there is pay discrimination in public sector jobs.

A major concern is just how an efficient, fair system can be set up to evaluate jobs. In Ontario, a proposed law says that, in both the private and public sectors, women should be paid the same as men for different jobs that are of comparable value. The comparison would be made on the basis of skills, effort, responsibility and working conditions. The province would call for adjustments to be phased in over six years, and for a pay equity board to be the overseer.

The chief complaint raised by business is the cost of applying the law. One estimate, only for the public sector, is that the cost of adjusting wages would be about $100 million for every 240 000 women.

People in the private sector argue that small companies will be badly affected by heavy costs, some to the point of being put out of business. There are concerns, too, about government intrusions into the business world.

Whatever the effect of the passage of laws, one thing is clear, governments are no longer waiting for business and market forces to establish equal pay for work of equal value.

1. What is the difference between "equal pay for equal work" and "equal pay for work of equal value"? Which is the easier to achieve? Why?

2. What criticisms have been made about legislation to end pay inequity?

3. Do you believe new laws will provide greater equality for women? Give reasons for your answer.

Projects, Activities and Explorations

1. Collect photographs of yourself from infancy until the present. Organize these as a mobile to show the various stages of change you have experienced throughout your life. Set up a class display of mobiles.

2. Research some societies such as the Hutterites and the Amish that have successfully resisted many of the changes of modern society. Try to find out why and how they have succeeded.

3. Write letters expressing your feelings for or against a change that is going on in your local area. With your teacher, you can decide to whom the letter should be sent. Research the issue you are writing about. You might even try to interview people who are affected by the change. If you receive any replies, share them with the class.

4. Make a collage that summarizes the major social changes going on today. Compare it with the collages of other students in your class. Do you share the same views as to which are the most important changes facing society?

5. Research the efforts of a major group that has been organized either to achieve change or to prevent it. If possible, interview members of this group about their goals and methods. If time permits, and if you can get permission from your teacher, ask a representative from the organization to speak to your class or to hear your report on their activities.

6. Invite a psychologist or another helping professional to your class to discuss methods of coping with the stresses caused by change.

7. Conduct an interview with a mother or grandmother to determine their perceptions of how women's roles have changed over the years. Determine their views on the advantages and disadvantages of these new roles.

8. Create a collage of ads related to women. How do these ads support the expanded role of women in today's society?

What Have You Learned?

If you have covered everything in this chapter, you should be familiar with the following topics:

1. The difference between change in society and change in individuals
2. Various causes of social change
3. The reasons why people resist change
4. Some problems caused by rapid social change
5. Methods used by individuals to cope with various kinds of change

To Help You Study

The following chart will help you
to review the words, facts and
ideas introduced in this chapter.
Copy the chart into your notebook
and fill in the missing information.

Word, Fact, Idea	Example in a Sentence	Page	Definition
social change		339	
technology			
cultural diffusion			
revolution			
vested interests			
culture lag			
anticipated transitions			
unanticipated transitions			
non-event transitions			

The Future 18

Thinking About the Future

The date is February 11, 2013. You have decided to view the main headlines in the *Canadian Investigator*. Like all newspapers of the time it appears on a computer monitor. Readers select the topics they are interested in which are then displayed on their monitor.

Either individually or in groups, read the following items and consider the following questions:

1. What is the main idea in each article?
2. Are the events described in each article likely to occur in the next 25 to 30 years? Explain.
3. What are the advantages and disadvantages of each of these future situations? Explain.

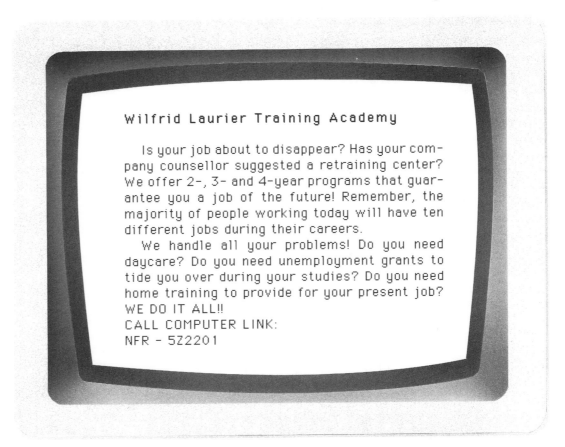

Wilfrid Laurier Training Academy

Is your job about to disappear? Has your company counsellor suggested a retraining center? We offer 2-, 3- and 4-year programs that guarantee you a job of the future! Remember, the majority of people working today will have ten different jobs during their careers.

We handle all your problems! Do you need daycare? Do you need unemployment grants to tide you over during your studies? Do you need home training to provide for your present job? WE DO IT ALL!!
CALL COMPUTER LINK:
NFR - 5Z2201

Third Smoker Jailed

Today Justice John Vincento sentenced Marilla Adams to 500 hours of community service for a smoking violation. Justice Vincento argued that this stiff sentence was necessary. This was Adams' third conviction for tobacco smoking. He noted that there had been an increase in such offences in the last six months and that her sentence would serve as a deterrent to others. Most smokers are buying their tobacco from sellers who grow the plants illegally in underground gardens.

The Attorney General agrees with these harsh decisions. She said that, "Too many people were not being helped by the anti-smoking clinics, therefore more severe actions were needed to curb this disgusting and dangerous practice."

Editorial

We think it outrageous that the member of Parliament for Scarborough East has aired publicly his criticisms of parent-arranged marriages. Not only is the member attempting to cause unrest among young men and women, he is also questioning the values of our Charter of Rights.

Since the Charter was amended in 2005 to read "only parents may arrange marriages for sons and daughters under the age of 25", our divorce rate has been reduced from a high of 48% in the 1980s to a current low of only 10%.

In addition, a survey conducted last fall showed that young adults appreciate and support the care and concern parents are showing in selecting mates for them.

A respected member of Parliament, such as the representative from Scarborough East, should consult his constituents before making erroneous and potentially damaging statements.

Last Plant Worker In Canada Retires

Today marked an historical event in Canadian history. Steven Woodman, the last human being to work in the production area of a manufacturing plant, retired.During the interview, Mr. Woodman said he was glad to retire. Working among all the robots in the assembly area had left him lonely and feeling like an intruder. He had spent his last two years repairing robots. This work is no longer necessary since the introduction of "repair" robots.

Canada has now completed the process of change that began back in the 1980s. Most futurists had predicted the change to robots would be faster but conflict with workers' rights organizations has slowed the process.Statistics Canada now reports 2 385 000 robots working in the manufacturing sector of the economy.

Woman's Right to Die Appeal Case To Be Heard Today

"My right to die has been denied!" This is the sign Suzanne Richard wears as she moves her robot-controlled wheelchair in front of the robot camera.

Only twice in the last ten years has the Death Tribunal refused to allow a person the right to end his or her own life. In both of those cases, the Appeal Court overruled the Death Tribunal.

Many feel this case should have been allowed automatically. But the Tribunal, made up of Dr. Morris Smith (representing the hospital), Mrs. Anita Singh (the appointed government lawyer) and Ms. Sophie Ho (the citizens' delegate) had voted against Ms. Richard's appeal.

This case is unusual because normally the type of paralysis involved is cured by installing replacement limbs. In Ms. Richard's case, she had limited success with the replacements but doctors testified that she could walk if she underwent further replacement surgery.

The Tribunal ruled that the first requirement for death was present, namely that Ms. Richard was "of sound mind." But they felt that the second requirement, that "a person be unable to live life in reasonable comfort" did not apply to her. They ruled that further surgery would help her situation. Ms. Richard, aged 53, argues that after four years of institutional care she has endured enough anguish.

The Appeal Court's decision will be handed down today.

The Individual Vision of the Future

The simplest and oldest way of predicting the future uses nothing more than one's own imagination and personal feelings. This kind of personal vision is very creative and appeals to us now as it did centuries ago, for it has a long history of use.

In Ancient Rome, the inhabitants regularly consulted people whose specialty was predicting future events. Everyone believed in astrology, prediction of the future from the position of the stars, and augury, prediction of the future from omens, such as the flight of birds or the entrails of slaughtered chickens. Even public officials would not declare war or pass a law without first consulting an astrologer or an augur. Ancient Greeks also used oracles, people who foretold the future while in a trance. Greek statesmen would ask the oracle for guidance on matters of state and receive answers that could be interpreted in many ways. In this way, the oracle's prediction was never "wrong", only the interpretation of the hearer was wrong.

Often, people who make predictions are very intuitive. They can sense in what direction society is moving. Some of these people have been great philosophers, such as Plato and Francis Bacon. Others have become famous science fiction writers such as Jules Verne, H.G. Wells and George Orwell. Their descriptions of the future have frequently been very accurate.

Despite a few notable successes, however, visions of the future based on magic or brilliant hunches have usually turned out to be wrong. At best, these personal visions of the future have served to prod us into becoming interested in the future. Their warnings have often forced us to re-examine our present and to look at new alternatives. In this sense, while personal visions of the future are not very accurate, they can be very influential and useful.

Jules Verne

Francis Bacon

H.G. Wells

George Orwell

The Science of Predicting the Future

We want to create more accurate predictions of the future than those we can make from reading our horoscope. If we had *reliable* predictions, we might be able to avoid political turmoil, economic hardship or environmental disaster. We might be able to give the next generation a desirable future. The people who apply *scientific* methods to their study of likely futures are called **futurists**.

Projecting Trends

One of the most common methods used by futurists involves looking for trends. A **trend** is a pattern that develops over time. A futurist will examine past and present events to see if there are any patterns to the events. This examination requires collecting statistics over many years about particular aspects of life, such as the number of hours worked per week or the number of children in families. Any strong or obvious pattern would be considered a trend. Trends are then projected into the future. Since this method focuses on the use of numbers, futurists often called it **statistical trending**.

For instance, the divorce rate in Canada has increased over the last twenty years. Graphs illustrating the number of divorces per 100 000 population between 1968 and 1988 produce a curve that moves steadily upwards until 1982 and then begins to decline. You could extend the graph into the future and continue to draw the curve using the same slowly declining angle. This

Alvin Toffler (left) and Isaac Asimov (below) have written books describing their view of the future.

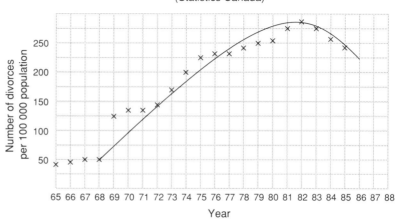

Divorce rates per 100 000 population
(Statistics Canada)

366

would allow you to predict the divorce rate in the year 2000.

The predicted divorce rate for the year 2000 might be quite low. This would probably lead you to assume that such a change would affect other areas of society as well. For instance, would a low divorce rate affect school populations or the need for apartments? As you can see, the trend begins to shape a likely vision of the future based on solid research.

John Naisbitt, the author of the 1982 book *Megatrends*, uses another method of identifying trends called **newspaper trending**. Naisbitt's assistants gathered some 2 000 000 newspaper and magazine articles to give them an idea of what was going on in the United States. They grouped the articles that they collected under broad categories and then analysed what they found in each category to see if any trends were apparent.

Here is how his method worked. Let's say he was researching the future of manufacturing in the United States. By the time all articles were collected from various sources he had learned the following:

Manufacturing

Closings or Shutdowns

- eighty-five slowdowns in heavy industry — eg. manufacture of machinery
- ten midsize companies closed producing large equipment
- increase in imports of less expensive, heavy machinery
- decrease in steel production

New Industries

- forty-three start ups of small industry manufacturing computer components and other communications equipment
- two large corporations sell off all their involvement in manufacturing farm equipment and move into design and production of satellite components

---

This information might indicate a trend toward smaller companies and growth of the high technology industry. As well, by identifying the town or city where the newspapers were published, Naisbett felt he could also locate in which part of the country these changes would take place.

Some critics of this method argue that newspaper articles don't carry enough hard data or statistics to identify trends. Those who favour the approach suggest that a single newspaper will not help predict the future, but a large collection can certainly give us an indication of where the events in the present will lead.

Limits to Using Trends

The central problem with both the statistical and the newspaper method of identifying trends is that no attempt is made to discover the causes of the patterns or trends. The assumption is that whatever forces caused the trend to develop in the past will continue to work in the future. Clearly, this is a risky assumption. A sudden invention or an accidental event could seriously alter the direction in which events are moving.

However, provided that two conditions are met, projecting trends can be an accurate method of predicting the future. First, we must have correctly identified the trend using a large amount of valid information. Second, the forces that shaped the trend in the past and in the present must remain constant at least for the forseeable future.

From Ideas to Action

1. In your notebooks, create a chart to compare the individual vision and trend projection methods of predicting the future. The format of your chart might look like this:

	Method of Prediction	
	Individual Vision	Trend Projection
How the Method Works		
Advantages of Using Method		
Disadvantages of Using Method		

2. a) List in your notebooks ten events that you predict will most likely happen to you within the next month. Rate them from most likely to least likely to occur.
   b) Choose any three of the above and for each explain:
   - the reason for the event happening
   - any actions that must be taken to ensure the event taking place
   - situations that could occur which would prevent you from experiencing that event

   c) What factors make events more likely or less likely to occur?
   d) Did this exercise cause you to think differently about your future?

3. a) What are the disadvantages of using the visionary approach to predict the future?
   b) Despite these disadvantages, this method gets a great deal of public attention. Why?

4. Assume that you are a futurist using the statistical trending method. What kinds of statistics might you look for to identify trends for each of the following:
   a) diet in North America
   b) the use of prisons to deal with criminals
   c) leisure time

5. Assume that you are a futurist who uses Naisbitt's newspaper trending method. Brainstorm all the possible types of articles and other items in newspapers that you might collect to identify trends for each of the following:
   a) dating practices
   b) international violence (war, terrorism)
   c) music

Consensus Methods of Predicting the Future

Consensus Decisions

A **consensus** is a group agreement on a problem or an issue. It is usually hammered out after a great deal of discussion about the alternatives available. Finally, the whole group adopts a point of view that everyone in the group can accept and support.

Can we apply this idea to the study of the future? Consider the problem of re-

ducing violent crime in the future. You could bring together a group of experts in the field of criminology and ask them their opinions. What will crime look like 20 years from now? What should we do about it now? Presumably, after a period of discussion, the experts would arrive at a consensus. We would then act on that expert group opinion.

In fact, face-to-face discussions between experts rarely produce a consensus on a given question. Perhaps a few members of the group have good ideas but are not good speakers. Perhaps more powerful individuals dominate the meeting and take the discussion in the wrong direction. The result may look like a consensus because everybody seems to agree, but really some may have just given up the fight. In the end, the group may make a poor or even a wrong prediction.

The Delphi Technique

To solve the consensus problem futurists use something called the **Delphi technique**, named after a famous Greek oracle. Experts receive a questionnaire in the mail asking them to respond on a given issue. Their answers are then collected. Researchers look at the wide range of opinion and use this to develop a second questionnaire on the same issue. It is then sent to the same experts along with the results of the first survey.

This forces the experts to compare their original point of view with the views of the other experts. Perhaps they will see something interesting in what others are suggesting and revise their original point of view. The experts then respond to the second survey.

These results are collected again and analysed to see if a consensus has been reached. If not, the process is repeated over and over again until the researchers find that the experts agree, at least in general, on the issue.

Shortcomings of the Delphi Technique

The shortcoming of this method is that the result is the agreed opinion of a group of experts. The consensus may leave out individuals who have serious reasons for disagreeing with the group decision. Also, experts have been known to be wrong. As is the case with trend projection, no one can foresee when the forces that shape our lives may suddenly change. However, assuming that the expert consensus is accurate, we may be forced to take notice of the prediction. Thus, acting on a prediction based on expert consensus may save human civilization from future misfortune.

From Ideas to Action

1. Add consensus methods to the chart you used to compare the individual vision and trend projection as methods of predicting the future. The format of your new chart might look like this:

	Method of Prediction		
	Individual Vision	Trend Projection	Consensus
How the Method Works			
Advantages of Using Method			
Disadvantages of Using Method			

2. a) With the help of your teacher or the teacher-librarian in your school locate articles or books of two futurists who have written on the *same topic*. Develop a chart to compare their views on the future of this topic. Your chart might look like this:

Topic to be compared: _____

Sources: 1. _____

2. _____

	Author #1	Author #2
Main Point or Belief of the Author		
Positive Aspects of the Future Seen by the Author		
Negative Aspects of the Future Seen by the Author		

b) What consensus, if any, is there about this topic?

c) Upon what do they disagree?

d) Which author do you agree with most? Why?

e) Write a report on your findings to share with other students or your teacher.

Scenarios and Simulations — Making the Future Seem Real

Take a minute to imagine what life in Canada will be like 200 years from now *assuming each of the following present trends continues.* Then answer the questions that follow.

a) The superpowers are spending millions of dollars on research into travel and defence in space.

b) We are using billions of litres of oil per year. Oil is a non-renewable resource.

c) The birth rate in Canada has been steadily declining since 1960. More couples than ever before are deciding to have only one child or to remain childless.

1) Choose one of the trends above that interests you. Make some quick point-form notes to describe your vision of the future in Canada 200 years from now as it has been influenced by that change.

2) Compare your vision of the future with some other students. Do they agree with your vision? Why or why not?

3) Are your visions of the future generally negative or positive? How would you account for this?

4) What could be done to change the present trend so that the future will be better?

Scenarios As a Method of Predicting the Future

A scenario is an author's description of a likely future world. Usually the writer bases the scenario on trends already identified by futurists or on the predictions of experts in the subject that the scenario deals with. The activity you have just completed asked you to experiment with writing scenarios.

Scenario writing is different from science fiction writing. Science fiction authors usually create their vision of the future from their imagination or from personal hunches, though they may have a good grasp of scientific information as well. Scenario writers rely on scientific research as the basis for their work. They do not invent trends. They suggest that if certain conditions are allowed to continue, the inevitable result will be the situation described in the scenario.

The following selection is a good example of a scenario. It was written in 1969 by Paul Ehrlich, a famous environmentalist. At that time scientists realized that a chemical insecticide, called DDT, was dangerous to plant and animal life. Many experts worried that the long term use of this chemical could cause an environmental disaster.

The end of the ocean came late in the summer of 1979, and it came even more rapidly than the biologists had expected. There had been signs for more than a decade, commencing with the discovery that DDT slows down photosynthesis in marine plant life. It was announced in a short paper in the technical journal, *Science*, but to ecologists [scientists who study the environment] it smacked of doomsday. They knew that all life in the sea depends on photosynthesis, the chemical process by which green plants bind the sun's energy and make it available to living things. And they knew that DDT . . . had polluted the entire surface of the earth, including the sea.

(from "Eco-catastrophe" Ramparts, Sept. 1969, p.13).

In this scenario, Ehrlich used scentific knowledge to creatively describe a possible future. Like other scenario writers, he was not saying that this would be the future, only that it might be if nothing were done to solve the problem. Ehrlich's scenario was intended to persuade people to look at what he thought was a serious problem and to act on their new awareness. Ehrlich and others were succesful. The use of DDT was eventually banned.

Disadvantages of Scenarios

There are critics of the scenario method of looking into the future. They argue that each scenario is merely one person's personal view of what is a serious problem. The author may be biased and see only one issue. In fact, there may be many more serious world trends that need attention. However, because the scenario author's writing is so powerful and so widely read, the problem may get a great deal of attention, while other problems are neglected.

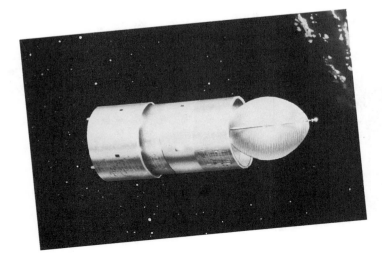

Simulations as a Method of Predicting the Future

No doubt you have seen film footage of car manufacturers purposely crashing their new cars into concrete barriers at high speeds. You have also seen what happens to the dummies in these doomed cars. This is an example of a simulation.

The people who stage simulations try to create a situation or event that is identical to the real world situation. In this case, the simulated situation is a head-on collision. The dummies are constructed so that they show the impact that a real human body would suffer in such a crash.

As in a laboratory experiment, researchers can control all the forces that affect what happens in the situation. Then, by changing one factor in the simulation, researchers can see how the change will affect the entire situation. In this way, many factors can be safely tested without having to wait for a real situation to occur.

Because of these characteristics, simulation is a powerful tool in the hands of futurists. Some futurists have designed computer programs to simulate such complex events as the world's weather system. These simulations have been used to predict what would happen to our weather in the future if we continue to dump poisonous chemicals into the air, soil and water.

Problems With Simulations

Despite their usefulness, simulations have much the same problem as other forecasting methods. Their design often depends on the use of trends. As you have already learned, the forces that cause a specific trend may not always remain the same. If they change, the simulation will no longer imitate the real world. For instance, people who plan superhighways use simulations. Their simulations are based on the the idea that people will continue to drive automobiles. What if the price of of gasoline suddenly jumps to $20.00 a litre because of an unexpected interruption in the supply of oil? What if some genius invents transporters like the ones you see in *Star Trek* movies? These forces would affect the simulation drastically.

From Ideas to Action

1. a) Add scenarios and simulations to the chart you have been building throughout this chapter to compare various methods of thinking about and predicting the future.

   b) Rank a list of methods of thinking about and predicting the future from poorest to best method.

   c) Share your ranking with other students or with the class as a whole. Why did you choose this order? Why is it difficult to reach a consensus of opinion?

2. Remember that a scenario is a creative piece of writing based on observable trends. This makes it a cross between science fiction and real science. Write your own future scenarios for the following trends in our present society. You will have read background information to give you a factual basis for your scenario.

   a) Scientists can take the genetic code for one living thing and put it into another cell from the same or a related species. This is called genetic engineering. The new cell will grow and multiply to develop into an exact duplicate of the original. This is called cloning. The duplicate is called a clone.

   b) Since the late 1970s doctors have been succesfully transplanting a variety of organs from one person into another. The list of organs that this can be done with continues to expand.

3. Examine a trend in your own life. Select something that has been developing for some time (an interest, an attitude towards life, a life goal). Write a scenario describing your life ten years from now, assuming that the trend that you have selected continues.

4. There are many kinds of simulations in use in education, business and industry. Investigate one of these simulations by talking to someone who uses simulations at work. During your interview, try to find out answers to the following questions:

   a) What was the simulation designed to discover?

   b) How does the simulation work?

   c) How is the simulation used?

   d) What are the limits to the usefulness of the simulation?

   Write a report on the results of your interview and share it with the class.

Deciding About the Future

Congratulations! You have just won $100 000 in a lottery! Individually, decide what you would *really* do with this money in the next five years. Be prepared to explain your choice of action(s) to other students. Do not read any further until you have finished this exercise.

Now compare your choice of action(s) with other students. Make a list of all the possible courses of action that were created by this situation. Once you have completed your list, discuss the following questions:

1. Did people choose alternatives that you did not even think of? How would you account for this?
2. In hindsight, were some of the alternatives suggested by others wiser than the one that you chose? Why?
3. How would you know when you have made the best decision?
4. Why worry about how to make future decisions?

Deciding on the best action to take for the future takes time and thought. Most of all, it requires new skills in thinking. One of the skills you may have acquired in using this book can help you decide among alternative actions.

Using Organizers to Make a Decision

An organizer is really a chart that displays information so that it can be easily seen at once. We can also use an organizer to compare possible actions that we are considering in the future. The

chart can then become a "workbench" for us to make a final decision.

Let's take the example of a common problem faced by teenage students: "How do I get enough money to afford the things I want?" To reach a decision you would go through five steps.

Step One: Brainstorm Possible Solutions

Brainstorm a list of possible solutions. It may be helpful to try this first on your own and then again with other people, such as your parents and your friends. Here are some reminders to help you brainstorm effectively.

- Think of wild ideas.
- Think of as many ideas as you can.
- Don't criticize the ideas.
- Look for ways that ideas can be combined; let other people's suggestions lead your imagination to new options.

Step Two: Select Interesting Solutions

Select between five and ten of the most interesting solutions. Give yourself as many solutions to choose from as possible. Let's suppose that you selected four solutions:

1. Get a part-time job at a local restaurant or retail store.
2. Quit school and get full-time job.
3. Ask for a raise in my allowance in return for doing more work around the house.
4. Change my lifestyle to fit my present budget.

Take a few moments, either on your own or with others, to see if you can add to this list of options.

Step Three: Determine Criteria

Decide what factors or criteria are important when you evaluate each possible solution. The criteria may be practical, such as the financial cost. For example, taking a part-time job at the shopping centre may be appealing until you consider the added cost of transportation or clothes for work. Other criteria may be related to your values. If you value getting an education to improve your future chances of success, you may find the option of quitting school impossible to accept.

Some criteria for this problem might be:
- Financial Rewards
- Impact on school work
- Impact on social life
- Time required
- Financial cost

Decide which of these criteria you think are important. Add to the list if you wish.

Step Four: Evaluate the Solutions

Copy the chart below into your notebook. Transfer your list of the possible options and the criteria you have chosen in the correct blanks in the chart. You may need to expand the option column and the criteria rows to hold more choices.

Now consider each option from the viewpoint of your first criterion, in this example, financial rewards. Rank each option from 1 (poorest option) to 6 (best option) if you were ranking six options. If you were considering only four options, you would rank them on a scale of 1 to 4.

In the chart, there are four possible options that may solve the problem. Some may think that quitting school is the most risky option and therefore the poorest. For this reason, quitting school would receive a risk score of 1. Others may feel that "asking for a raise in my allowance" is the least risky and therefore the best. The "raise" option would be given a risk score of 4.

Now finish the rankings on the chart. When you have completed this, move to Step Five.

Criteria

Possible Options	$ Rewards	School Work	Social Life	Time	$ Cost	Risk	TOTAL
1. Part-Time Jobs							
2. Quit School							
3. Ask For Raise							
4. Change Life Style							

Step Five : Total and Plan

On your chart, add the scores for each possible option and enter the score under Total. The option with the highest score at right is probably the best decision for your future. Now you are ready to develop a plan of action and carry out the decision you have made. Your plan of action might look like this:

1) List in detail all the things that have to be done to carry out your decision. This should include the people to contact, forms to fill out, etc.

2) Arrange the list of things to be done in the order in which they have to happen. For example, if you are job-hunting, you will probably want to check the classified ads before actually going to businesses to pick up application forms.

3) Set dates for starting and finishing each item on your list. Try hard to stick to these dates. If you don't meet your own deadlines, you may be underestimating the difficulty of the option you chose.

This five step method can be applied to the future questions in your own life. It can also be used to decide between solutions to serious social problems of the present and future such as ending poverty, reducing crime, and avoiding war. In the end, however, it is not our willingness or ability to use the method itself that really counts but our will to act on the decisions we reach by this kind of systematic method. A good decision is worthless unless we carry it out.

From Ideas to Action

1. Brainstorm a list of five possible solutions for each of the following problems. Once you have finished, you may wish to share your list with other students.
   a) We are able to travel to the moon. What should we do in the future with the moon?
   b) Schools are rapidly emptying. School closures will continue and probably increase. Where will we find the students of the future?
   c) The world's population continues to expand beyond the ability of many countries to feed all their people adequately.
   d) How do we reduce the number of teenage suicides?

2. Choose two of the problems in the previous question that you are interested in. For each, list the criteria that you feel you should use to measure the possible solutions that you have created.

3. Create an organizer for one of the problems that you worked with in the previous question. Use the criteria to evaluate each of the possible solutions. Total the scores to arrive at the best solution.

4. Choose a problem or an issue that is presently important to you. Use the five step method for using an organizer to decide what to do.

Robotics: Helpful or Harmful?

• •

Not all people agree on the direction that the future should or will take, as the following two articles illustrate. Read both articles and answer the questions that follow the readings.

The Robot Age — It's About Time

Filmgoers were delighted when the science fiction Star Wars films introduced robots R2D2 and C3PO with their specialized abilities and distinct personalities. The robots at work in the 1980s lack the personalities of the robot film stars, but they announce the beginning of a greater robot revolution. Robots will soon be in our homes, our factories and our institutions. But will they serve just as a toy or will they benefit all aspects of our society? Without question our evaluation is positive.

Robots will be a tremendous help in factories. Japanese and American automobile manufacturers already make use of production robots. They are consistently more precise than humans and are less likely to make mistakes. The high initial costs will be offset by the fact that robots do not need wages, go on strike, or need special compensations such as dental care and pensions. They will work 24 hours a day without charging overtime. Production costs will be lowered. More goods will be available to more people, thus lowering the retail price. The consumer will benefit from this.

Those who argue that robots will cause major unemployment in industry are forgetting that a whole new area of robotics will open up new jobs in the design, installation, programming and repair of robots. In turn, these jobs create new fields in the advertis-

ing, marketing, sales and service of robot products to new markets. Also, people will be free to perform more interesting jobs. Robots will give them the time needed to train for the new jobs of the future.

In the home the robot will become a servant. The robot will relieve family members of household chores such as cooking and cleaning. This will allow more time for the members of the family to pursue leisure interests.

Consider the role of robots in the homes of the elderly. Robots could perform basic patient care

such as monitoring vital signs, maintaining charts and transporting the elderly from one area to another. With the increased intelligence of these robots they may well become indispensible companions for the elderly, isolated or lonely people in our society. Studies have already shown that some people find it easier to 'talk' to a computer because it does not judge or criticize behaviour.

In almost all areas of human effort, robots will assist in making life more rewarding and interesting. It seems clear that robots are the way of the future.

Should We Reconsider The Robot?

The potential use of robots in many areas of life should cause us to reconsider seriously the direction of this misguided policy.

The greatest threat to society from robots is unemployment. In industry, the modern assembly-line robot can outwork its human counterpart in accuracy and hours worked. This means that one robot will replace *many* workers, not just one. Where will these people find work? Will they have the skills and the desire to be retrained for more demanding jobs? The results could be massive unemployment.

Developed countries and large corporations will benefit most from this technology. Although the lower costs of production may put tremendous pressure on less developed countries to robotize their industries, initial costs of start-up are too high. Eventually, robots may force these non-robot companies out of business. The failure of companies in less developed countries will damage the balance of international trade and contribute to internal unrest in other countries.

Robots are designed to increase production and lower the cost of production. This assumes that natural resources will be available to match the quickened pace of production. Can we be guaranteed a steady supply of raw material to fuel this new rapid production of manufactured goods? The effects of this demand on the resource

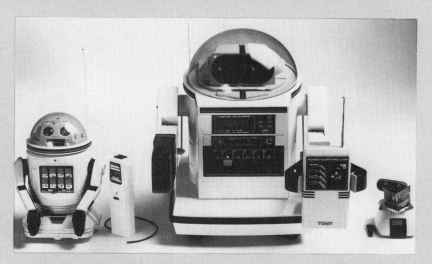

and transportation industries is staggering.

How will robots help families in the long term? One of the values that families teach their children is responsibility. Parents can encourage a sense of responsibility by having the children assume tasks around the house. The family then has a chance to work together and develop a sense of cohesiveness. A family robot will not only put an end to responsibility and togetherness, it will create a child who cannot care for itself or the home. As the children leave home, can we guarantee that their new environment will include a robot?

The family robot will be the 21st century status symbol, just as a pool, family cottage or a three car garage is today. It will be available only to the wealthy of our society. The gulf between the rich and poor will be widened by this new slave.

Robots will continue to develop at a rapid pace. Thanks to research in AI (Artificial Intelligence), it is likely that robots of the future will be capable of making their own decisions, in other words, of thinking for themselves. If they possess such intelligence, won't we think of them as human in other respects? Could we 'pull the plug' on an aging but loyal family robot?

Though these questions appear fantastic, they are the natural result of developments in robot engineering. Based on these arguments I think we must carefully reconsider the role of robots in the future of our industries, our homes and our lives.

1) What is the main idea expressed in each article?
2) Summarize the main argument used to support each side.
3) Which side makes better use of facts to support their arguments?

· ·

Schools of the Future

The Futurist, August 1985

Schools will be responsible for preparing students who are adaptable and able to respond quickly to the changing requirements of new technologies. In the near future, workers' jobs will change dramatically every five to ten years. Schools will train both youths and adults; adult workers will need re-education and retraining whenever business and industry update their operations. In the future, workers will be displaced frequently and will be moving constantly from one occupation to another. They will need periodic retraining because each new job will be different from the previous one....

Schools of the Future

By 1990, most adults will be working a 32-hour week. During the time that they are not at work, many will be preparing for their next job. While the adult working week is getting shorter, the student schoolweek will be getting longer.

Not only will the normal academic day be longer for children, but the buildings themselves will be open a minimum of 12 hours a day. Schools will be providing services to the community, to business, and to young students who will use the recreation facilities, computer labs, and job simulation stations — modules that combine computers, videodiscs, and instrumentation to duplicate job-work environments.

**No More Pencils,
No More Books?**

As software improves, computers will begin to replace some kinds of textbooks; they already can replace drillbooks. Software can be tailored to meet individual student needs and can be updated more quickly and inexpensively than textbooks....

Computers themselves could even provide income for the school: Parents might come to school to learn how to use computers in their businesses, and companies could use school computer facilities to run their data at night. And computers can be linked with videodiscs or with equipment that simulates the job environment.

Computers linked with videodiscs will provide sight, sound, and movement. Some lessons in history, language, politics, psychology, math, word problems, and music, art, or dance could be taught or reinforced from one videodisc. Software, written by a member of a teaching team, will program sequences of visual images from a disc. The computer program will stop and start the disc every so often to ask the student questions.

Many schools may be open 24 hours a day. They will be training centers for adults from 4 p.m. to midnight; some will also serve business through their computer and communication facilities from midnight until the next morning when young students arrive again...

Individual communities may conduct classes that include both adults and high-school students. But if for some reason this combination is unsuccessful, the groups can separate and work independently. In some communities, adults might take over portions of school buildings that have been closed because of declining school enrollments...

Widespread use of computer-linked equipment will not be a major feature of schools until the twenty-first century, but certain schools will use computers in this way long before 1995...

As schools provide more resources for teaching adults, they will be able to offer job training based on jobs that are actually available, not those that are becoming obsolete.

From the eighth grade on, many students may actually be placed in different businesses that use the skills they are learning. If businesses that might provide a wide range of experience are not immediately available to the school, students will be able to travel to a learning center staffed with instructors and containing the latest equipment suited to students' career fields.

In either location, students will have their work supervised and graded by employers' standards. A trainer will watch them at the work site or via television hookup. The trainer will be able to talk with the student. After this experience at the work site, students will return to the school to have their performance reviewed. The school will then judge whether the students need additional attention, practice at a simulator, or study....

Reproduced from *The Futurist*, August 1985. Original excerpts from *Schools of the Future: How American Business and Education Can Cooperate to Save Our Schools* by Marvin Cetron with Barbara Soriano & Margaret Gayle, © 1985 by Marvin Cetron. Reprinted by permission of the publisher, McGraw-Hill Book Company, N.Y.

1. What are three major changes mentioned in this article that will occur in education in the next 20 years?

2. In your opinion, will these changes improve the quality of education? Will they help all students equally? Give reasons for your answer.

Projects, Activities and Explorations

1. Collect pictures of aspects of daily life or present world events. For example, you might find pictures of a nuclear explosion, poverty, terrorists, farming, soldiers in combat, striking workers, space technology, people helping people, church worship, school classroom, typical family, etc. Try to imagine what the future will be like based on these images from the present and the past. Select any five of these pictures and from your point of view, write a description of what each will be like in the future.

2. Create a mobile or collage to depict your future as you see it. On one side of your mobile illustrate how you would see your life ten years from now. Try answering these questions to get you started.
   - Where will you be living?
   - With what company will you be working?
   - Will you be married?
   - In what city will you be living?
   - What activities will interest you?

   Now, use the other side of your project to answer the same questions for your life 25 years from now.

3. a) In groups, prepare a list of films and books about the future which group members have seen or read.
   b) In your group, create an organizer to help you categorize these films and books.
   c) Now discuss as a class how the groups organized the films and books.
   d) What are the general views of the future presented in these films and books?

4. Create a collage of newspaper articles that tell us something about the present but indicate future change. This should cover several topics.

5. Begin a futures file. Choose one or more categories to research that interest you (art, government, space, religion, health, etc.). Either individually or as a group, begin to collect articles that you think relate to your chosen categories. Stretch your collection as far back into the past as you can using such sources as the periodical index in your library and microfilm or microfiche collections. Put whatever you find into a manilla filefolder that you keep in the classroom. Once you have collected a large number of items, do the following:
   - Look at all the items and decide whether it is necessary to divide the items into sub-categories.
   - Review all the items in your categories. Do any trends seem clear?
   - How would you account for these trends?
   - What other groups of people or aspects of society might be affected by the changes that you have noted? Why would they be affected?
   - Based on the trends that you have noted, what would you expect the future to be like? Why?

6. Invite older people to your class to discuss what life was like when they were young. How has life changed in their opinion? Is it better or worse?

7. Research one of the futurists mentioned in this chapter and read one of their books. Prepare a report on that book.

8. Investigate jobs of the future and prepare a presentation which can be given to the class.

9. Establish your own "Futures Studies Group". Invent a name and a logo for the group. As a group, select projects to do for the year. These might include:
   a) Research on key issues or trends that are developing in the world. Use the methods for thinking and deciding about the future that have been covered in this chapter.
   b) Invitations to guest speakers who are experts in the field that you are studying

   At the end of the year, write up the results of your projects or create displays to demonstrate what you have been studying. Ask to have your work displayed somewhere in the school.

   You might also invite an outside expert on one or many of your projects to hear a report of your activities and then to comment.

10. Make up a crossword puzzle or some other game that will help other students review the methods of thinking and deciding about the future. Have them try and evalute your work.

What Have You Learned?

If you have covered everything in this chapter, you should be familiar with the following topics:

1. Individual vision as a method of predicting the future
2. Trend projection as a method of predicting the future
3. Consensus methods of predicting the future
4. Scenarios as a means of predicting the future
5. Simulations as a means of predicting the future
6. Using organizers to make decisions about the future

To Help You Study

The following chart will help you to review the words, ideas, and facts that were introduced in this chapter.

Word, Fact, Idea	Example in a Sentence	Page	Definition
Trend	In North America there has been a trend towards longer life over the last 100 years.	366	a trend is an obvious pattern that has developed over time
newspaper trending			
consensus			
delphi technique			
scenario			
simulation			
organizer			
criteria			

Skills Index

Index

Photo Credits

The publishers wish to thank the following sources for photographs used in this book. We will gladly receive information enabling us to rectify any errors in references or credits.

Addison-Wesley Photo Files 58 (no.1), 61 (right), 72, 100 (left), 200 (right), 201, 369; Alliance Productions 93; Animals, Animals 12; Bell Canada Telephone Historical Collection 84 (no. 2); Bettman Archive 5 (top), 160, 365 (top left, top right, bottom left, bottom right), 366 (top); Canadian Jewish Congress National Archives 331; Canapress 2 (nos. 3, 4), 3 (nos. 5, 6, 8), 27 (top left, bottom left, top right), 38, 42 (no. 3), 51 (bottom), 53 (top right), 59 (no. 7), 71 (top), 76, 77, 87 (bottom), 88, 94, 100 (right), 102, 106 (top), 129 (bottom), 152 (nos. 2, 6), 155 (left, right), 161 (top, bottom), 163, 194 (top), 203 (left, right), 221 (top), 225 (top), 237 (bottom), 239, 241 (top), 242, 274 (nos. 1, 3), 275, 281 (top, bottom), 284, 287, 294 (left), 295, 296, 307, 308, 334, 346 (top, bottom), 356, 366 (middle), 379; Chatelaine 85 (no. 4); P. Clarke 75 (top), 84 (no. 1); Coca-Cola Ltd. 94 (no. 2); Ian R. Crysler 34, 35, 159 (bottom left), 175 (right); Fraser Day 32, 37, 79, 90, 97, 106 (bottom), 147, 165, 167, 199 (bottom), 236 (bottom), 380; Employment and Immigration Canada 60; Financial Post/Peter Redman 204 (left); Four By Five 3 (no. 7), 25 (no. 3), 64, 65, 70, 187 (bottom left); Harvard University News Office/Jane Reed 135; Health and Welfare Canada 94 (no. 3); Grant Heilman 46 (bottom), 53 (left, bottom, right), 55 (bottom); Hydro-Québec 10 (bottom); Image Bank 14, 21 (top, bottom), 50 (left), 61 (left), 67 (top), 209, 254 (bottom), 258, 263, 274 (no. 2), 323, 371; Rob Johnston 46 (top); Labatt's Ontario Brewery 94 (no. 1); Mike Luther 146; Masterfile 10 (top), 11, 47, 50 (right), 59 (no. 6), 75 (bottom), 84 (no. 3), 87 (top), 89 (top, bottom), 92 (right), 96 (top), 109 (left), 126 (top, bottom), 128 (left, right), 142, 152 (no. 4), 153 (no. 5), 154, 157, 159 (top), 174 (bottom), 186 (top, bottom), 187 (top right, bottom right), 194 (bottom left, bottom right), 197 (top), 198 (top), 220 (middle right), 225 (second from top), 236 (top), 295 (top); McMichael Canadian Art Collection 197; Miller 2 (nos. 1, 2), 3, 11 (top, middle, bottom), 13, 20, 24 (no. 1), 27 (bottom right), 42 (nos. 2, 4), 43 (nos. 5, 6, 8), 44, 45, 54, 55 (top), 58 (no. 2), 71 (bottom), 75, 88 (top, bottom), 96 (bottom), 108, 109 (right), 127 (top, bottom), 129 (top), 134, 152 (no. 3), 158 (bottom), 159 (bottom right), 164, 175 (left), 187 (top left), 195 (left, right), 197 (bottom), 198 (bottom), 199 (top), 200 (left), 212, 220 (top left, bottom right), 227 (top, bottom), 230, 237 (top), 241 (bottom), 252, 253 (top, bottom), 254, 260 (top, bottom), 264, 276, 277, 278, 285, 290, 295 (bottom), 298, 299, 338 (bottom left), 340, 341 (top, bottom), 343 (bottom), 378; Jennifer Mix 92 (left), 156; National Museums of Canada 5 (bottom); Olivetti of Canada 95; John Phillips 24 (no. 2), 42 (no. 1), 43 (no. 7), 51, 59 (no. 5), 86 (left, right), 121, 138, 204 (right), 247, 248, 279, 289, 294 (left), 318, 324, 327, 342; Public Archives of Canada 91 (C-13225), 244 (PA-30212), 343 (PA-11479) (top); Royal Botanical Gardens 343; Jim Russell/Mosaic Press 25 (no. 4), 58 (no. 3), 59 (no. 4), 66 (left, right), 67 (bottom), 174 (top), 220 (top right), 254 (top); Toronto Star 102, 114; United Press Canada 90; University of Wisconsin Primate Laboratory 158 (top left, top right); UPI/Bettman Newsphotos 6, 161 (right), 338 (top left, bottom right), 365; Vintage Radio and Gramophone Co. 84, 85 (no. 5)